Immersive Environments, Augmented Realities, and Virtual Worlds:

Assessing Future Trends in Education

Steven D'Agustino
Fordham University, New York

Information Science
REFERENCE

Managing Director:	Lindsay Johnston
Editorial Director:	Joel Gamon
Book Production Manager:	Jennifer Yoder
Publishing Systems Analyst:	Adrienne Freeland
Development Editor:	Myla Merkel
Assistant Acquisitions Editor:	Kayla Wolfe
Typesetter:	Erin O'Dea
Cover Design:	Jason Mull

Published in the United States of America by
Information Science Reference (an imprint of IGI Global)
701 E. Chocolate Avenue
Hershey PA 17033
Tel: 717-533-8845
Fax: 717-533-8661
E-mail: cust@igi-global.com
Web site: http://www.igi-global.com

Library of Congress Cataloging-in-Publication Data

Immersive environments, augmented realities, and virtual worlds: assessing future trends in education / Steven D'Agustino, editor.
    p. cm.
  Includes bibliographical references and index.
  Summary: "This book presents current research and performance of trends in education, examining cyber behavior and the use of virtual worlds, immersive technologies and augmented realities to improve teaching and enhancing learning"--Provided by publisher.
  ISBN 978-1-4666-2670-6 (hardcover) -- ISBN 978-1-4666-2701-7 (ebook) -- ISBN 978-1-4666-2732-1 (print & perpetual access) 1. Virtual reality in education. 2. Educational technology. I. D'Agustino, Steven, 1965-
  LB1044.87.I33 2013
  371.33--dc23
                        2012031913

British Cataloguing in Publication Data
A Cataloguing in Publication record for this book is available from the British Library.

All work contributed to this book is new, previously-unpublished material. The views expressed in this book are those of the authors, but not necessarily of the publisher.

List of Reviewers

Eleanora Bilotta, *University of Calabria, Italy*
Karen Kaun, *Columbia University, USA*
Christopher Luchs, *Front Range Community College, USA*
Randall McClure, *Georgia Southern University, USA*
Linda Pincham, *Roosevelt University, USA*
Alan Reid, *Brunswick Community College, USA*
Assunta Tavernise, *University of Calabria, Italy*

Table of Contents

Section 2
Social Learning

Section 3
Future Trends

Detailed Table of Contents

Section 1
Teaching and Learning

Chapter 1

Brian G. Burton, Abilene Christian University, USA
Barbara Martin, University of Central Missouri, USA

This chapter's goal is to examine the student engagement and the creation of student knowledge in undergraduate students using a 3D Virtual Learning Environment.

Chapter 2

Shannon Kennedy-Clark, University of Sydney, Australia
Kate Thompson, University of Sydney, Australia

The chapter explains the role of scenario-based MUVEs and educational games in science education and presents both the benefits for students and the challenges of using these forms of technology in a classroom setting.

Chapter 3

Jason A. Chen, The College of William and Mary, USA
Nick Zap, Simon Fraser University, Canada
Chris Dede, Harvard University, USA

The purpose of this chapter is to bring a rigorous and well-studied theoretical framework of motivation to the study and design of virtual learning environments.

This chapter researches current math practices, math in virtual worlds, number sense, and subitizing to fortify the direction of the efforts. The authors' journey progresses from the physical (paper and cubes) to the virtual (online flash-based programming) to the immersive (3D in Second Life).

This chapter describes a teacher's journey of integrating Virtual Worlds or MUVEs in her teaching and learning, both for adult learners and a Malaysian secondary school.

Humans rely heavily on their sense of vision and learn from didactic images within their environments. For this reason, in traditional educational environments, educators care about visual representation. However, as today's technology brings images to wider audiences with diverse cultural backgrounds in the virtual world global community, the process of automatic cognition helps people build new knowledge based on prior regional experience.

Section 2
Social Learning

This chapter reports the findings of two surveys taken by players of the video game Rock Band. The purpose of the surveys was to determine what differences, if any, exist between the ways that males and females learn to play the game, are motivated to improve, interact with other players both online and in real life, and interact with other players in online communities for the game.

This chapter is organized in five parts. The authors provide (1) background information about relevant constructs and ideas that impinge on their work; (2) a brief description of the two projects, the CSCL and the journalism projects, informing this chapter; (3) some instructional implications for designing and holding learning activities in virtual worlds; (4) a description of the discourse issues associated with politeness and face work in learning activities held in virtual worlds; and (5) a discussion of what needs further investigation and development in educational uses of virtual worlds and in research on such worlds.

This chapter chronicles co-curricular activities held in the virtual world, Second Life. The event activities included standard content delivery vehicles and those involving movement and presence.

A survey of 100 undergraduates and 30 post-secondary faculty members was conducted in order to examine the current attitudes and perceptions of both groups toward the integration of social media sites such as Facebook and Twitter in education.

In this chapter, the authors propose that some inherently immersive virtual worlds can be used as educational sandboxes that allow business students to practice their business tools. The authors provide a set of examples as to the specific kinds of knowledge they can attain and practice in the virtual environment and conclude with sample lesson plans for enterprising professors.

Section 3
Future Trends

The chapter aims to discuss the challenges behind VW implementation in educational process from three main perspectives. The authors analyze how virtual worlds can enhance knowledge acquisition and development of key competences, increasingly needed by new generations.

Social networking has been a global consumer phenomenon during the last few years, and online communities are changing the way people behave, share, and interact within their daily lives. Most communities are mainly focused on sharing contents and communication using a traditional Web interface. However, virtual worlds are computer-simulated environments that the users can "inhabit" and in which they can interact and create objects.

This chapter examines state-of-the-art approaches of learning in and with virtual worlds in relation to the features of such environments and then proposes a research agenda tailored at making the learning experience truly interactive, collaborative, multi modal, and situation- and context-aware.

This chapter discusses findings from a study that looked at organizational leadership in the massively multiplayer online game World of Warcraft® in an attempt to inform the future of leadership in schools and other online and blended learning organizations.

Preface

This publication is an attempt to capture the current trends in the use of virtual realities in teaching and learning. *Immersive Environments, Augmented Realities, and Virtual Worlds: Assessing Future Trends in Education* is divided into three sections: "Teaching and Learning," "Social Learning," and "Future Trends." Each section focuses on the various constituent groups in education and the effects of technologically generated and supported realities in education.

Section one, "Teaching and Learning," considers various strategies for developing learning environments in virtual worlds. Chapter one explores the creation of knowledge and student engagement and the positive effects of interactions in virtual worlds on learning outcomes. Chapter two examines multi-user virtual environments in the science classroom and the challenges of implementing these innovations. Chapter three describes the effects of using virtual environments to stimulate students' interests in pursuing STEM careers. Chapter four provides some promising practices for mathematics instruction using visualization. Chapter five presents a practitioner's perspective on the use of virtual reality in a classroom setting. The final chapter in this section, chapter six, examines how virtual worlds impact students through visual learning.

Section two, "Social Learning," focuses on how virtual realities can impact social learning and the effects of social structures on virtual worlds and how these processes manifest themselves in technologically-generated environments. Chapter seven examines the differences in gaming skills acquisition between male and female students. Chapter eight examines new discourse patterns that emerge in virtual environments and considers the effects of these emerging modes of discourse on learners. Chapter nine examines the impacts virtual environments have on learner engagement and the changing roles that these virtual worlds can create among teachers and learners. Chapter ten provides insights into the differences between digital identities created through social media and face-to-face behaviors. Chapter eleven examines how immersive worlds can function as sandboxes to improve learners' business competencies.

Section three, "Future Trends," focuses on what comes next in the use of virtual worlds and simulations in teaching and learning. Chapter twelve considers the decline in popularity of virtual worlds and the implications for the future of virtual environments as educational tools. Chapter thirteen presents an argument for how virtual worlds can bring together intellectual resources globally with great immediacy for synchronous collaboration. Chapter fourteen reviews current instructional practices in virtual environments and proposes a research agenda to enhance learning in these spaces. Chapter fifteen, the final chapter, is an innovative and exciting examination of how leadership in virtual environments can provide insights into instructional leadership.

This book is intended to provide a way forward for current and future educators. It is impossible to predict what the future of technologically generated realities will be, but the work of the contributing authors presents ways forward that are exciting and creative. It is my hope that educators will find this book a valuable resource to guide their own development as teachers and learners.

Steven D'Agustino
Fordam University, USA

Section 1
Teaching and Learning

Chapter 1
Student Engagement and the Creation of Knowledge Within a 3D Virtual Learning Environment

Brian G. Burton
Abilene Christian University, USA

Barbara Martin
University of Central Missouri, USA

ABSTRACT

This chapter's goal is to examine the student engagement and the creation of student knowledge of undergraduate students using a 3D Virtual Learning Environment. After creating a 3D didactic constructivist virtual environment, student conversations were recorded for engagement dimensions using Hara, Bonk, and Angeli (2000) framework and Nonaka and Takeuchi (1995) knowledge creation theory. Findings revealed that five forms of student engagement amplified the learning process and that a complete knowledge spiral occurred emphasizing the four modes of knowledge conversion. Although limited in time and scope, results further suggest that a highly engaged community of learners was created.

INTRODUCTION

Tsiatsos, Andreas, and Pomportsis (2010) noted, "Elearning systems have gone through a radical change from the initial text-based environments to more stimulating multimedia systems" (p. 65). Additionally, Dalgarno (2002) argued, "Three Dimensional (3D) environments have the potential to

harness technological developments and facilitate new levels of learner-learner and learner-computer interaction" (p. 1). Due to improvements in technology and the utilization of 3D environments on a successful commercial basis (Blizzard, 2010), there has been renewed interest in the utilization of 3D environments as learning tools. 3D immersive VLEs utilize additional technology to provide an

DOI: 10.4018/978-1-4666-2670-6.ch001

immersive environment for the learner to participate. This environment allows the participant to 'touch' and manipulate items in a virtual universe. Three-Dimensional (3D) VEs come with a myriad of features; though, normally most provide three main elements: the illusion of 3D space, avatars that serve as the visual representation of users, and an interactive chat environment for users to communicate with one another (Dickey, 2005). Salzman, Dede, Loftin, and Chen (1999) made a case for the use of immersive Virtual Reality (VR) for the teaching of complex or abstract concepts: Consequently, these "three-dimensional thematic environment [was] created with the objective of providing a space where the users can interact" (Kirner, et al., 2001). Created as cyber Cafés, University classrooms, chat rooms, and the likes, these virtual places often become a place where students are afforded opportunities to post suggestions, useful resources, and technical advice (Grubb & Hines, 2000). These postings and interactions' serve as knowledge capital that may contribute to a knowledge spiral within the learning environment (Nonaka & Takeuchi, 1995; Nonaka, 1991). Many researchers have undertaken various projects to investigate aspects of virtual learning environments. Some research has focused on the technical aspects of collaboration such as providing voice with lip-sync (DiPaola & Collins, 2003), others have focused on a specific discipline such as mathematics (Elliott & Bruckman, 2002) or science (Dede, Nelson, Ketelhut, Clarke, & Bowman, 2004), and others have examined collaboration within a virtual environment (Burton & Martin, 2010). With this increased interest in 3D environments and a desire to utilize the popularity of such environment for the education of the millennial generation (Dede, 2005), the evaluation of such environments for pedagogical purposes is appropriate. This case study was conducted to add to the body of research where a dialectic constructivist 3D VLE is used to create a learning environment that encourages student creation of knowledge. The following research questions guided this inquiry:

1. Does student engagement within a 3D VLE construct an environment for the four elements necessary for the creation of knowledge?
2. What are the perceptions of the students regarding the effectiveness of the creation of the knowledge spiral within the 3D VLE?

CONCEPTUAL FRAMEWORK

Two conceptual frameworks guided the study: student engagement and knowledge creation theory. Student engagement (Hara, Bonk, & Angeli, 2000) was used to explore how students are interacting using reasoning in a 3D virtual environment. Knowledge creation theory (Nonaka & Takeuchi, 1995; Nonaka, 1991) was employed by the researchers to identify which of the four modes of knowledge conversion were used in a virtual learning environment.

Student Engagement

Bonk, Kim, and Zeng (2006) when surveying higher education faculty who had taught online found, "Most respondents saw the potential of the Web in the coming years as a tool for virtual teaming or collaboration, critical thinking, and enhanced student engagement (p. 556). Primarily these "three-dimensional thematic environment [was] created with the objective of providing a space where the users can interact" (Kirner, et al., 2001). During Dede et al.'s (2004) River City 3D VLE project, students were placed in an environment where they must discover why the people of River City are becoming ill. During the first implementation, students made many suggestions for the improvement of the project as a result of various outcomes, one of which was for the MUVE interface's option of having two communication modes—a chat and a whisper function—was confusing to students. As a result, most of them relied on the whisper function, which interfered with group collaborative work. To correct these problems, Dede et al. (2004) created a new version of River City. In the new version, the redesigned chat system allowed for scaffolding and a more collaborative environment. Such projects as River City (Dede, et al., 2004) or Quest Atlantis (Barab, et al., 2005) show some of the potential of dialectical constructivist 3D VLE that encourage a collaborative engagement between the students.

According to Koopman (2011), "They [students] need opportunities for sharing. Online communication tools are one answer to an ancient problem, getting them all to think deeply" (p. 27). In addition, Koopman further noted, "Students reported that they thought about the questions posed online more frequently than when they engaged in face to face discussions in the classroom" (p. 26).

Identified by Henri (1992) were five dimensions that could facilitate assessment of discourse on line. These five dimensions were participative, social, interactive, cognitive, and metacognitive. Reasoning, critical thought and self-awareness are indicators of the cognitive and metacognitive dimensions. However, since the indicators for each of these five dimensions were not clearly delineated by Henri (1992) in her work, the coding system used by Hara, Bonk, and Angeli (2000) informed the indicators for analysis of student engagement in this inquiry. Five reasoning skills form the basis of the framework used by Hara, Bonk, and Angeli (2000). The first reasoning skill is elementary clarification with indicators such as the ability to identify relevant elements and to reformulate the problem by asking pertinent questions. In-depth clarification occurs when the participant cam define terms, identify assumptions and establish referential criteria while seeking specialized information and ultimately summarizing that information. Inferencing evolves when the participant draws conclusions, makes generalization, and formulates a proposition. Next judgment occurs when the individual judges the relevance of the solutions and makes a value judgment as to agreement or not. Observation of application of strategies happens when the participant makes a decision that reflects appreciation, evaluation,

and even criticism of the solutions. Since a Hara, Bonk, and Angeli (2002) classification system lends itself to easier coding, it was used in this inquiry.

However not all researchers are finding that students are engaged in the 3d virtual environment appropriately. Lim, Nonis, and Hedberg (2006) found in their study of virtual environments on student science tasks that "engagement in the 3D MUVE space might not necessarily lead to engagement in the learning task. A student could be engaged in the 3D MUVE by exploring the different worlds, avatars, and quests but fail to engage in the learning" (p. 229). As Lim and Chai (2004) have earlier argued, when too much exertion is put into navigating and engaging with the avartar presented in hypermedia, mental resources accessible for the task itself diminishes. Consequently, as Lim, Nonis, and Hedberg (2006) postulated, "The whole move is towards a more complete virtual world without the discontinuities that break up the patterns of engagement" (p. 230).

Knowledge Creation

Baumard (1999) called the knowledge creation process "visible and invisible, tangible and intangible, stable and unstable" (p. 2). Much of the research on organizational knowledge creation has revolved around Nonaka and Takeuchi's (1995) *The Knowledge Creating Company* and Peter Senge's (1990) work *The Fifth Discipline*. Nonaka and Takeuchi (1995) stated in a simplified overview, "When organizations innovate, they actually create new knowledge and information from the inside out, in order to redefine both problems and solutions and, in the process, to re-create their environment" (p. 56). Nonaka (1991) postulated that "creating new knowledge is not simply a matter of 'processing' objective information. Rather it depends on tapping the tacit and often highly subjective insights and intuitions" (p. 97). In order to have an environment that creates new knowledge, individuals must be given time and processes by which to share tacit knowledge.

Nonaka and Takeuchi (1995) have identified this process as the four modes of knowledge conversion. This knowledge conversion is essentially the "interaction between tacit and explicit knowledge" (p. 61) and consist of socialization, externalization, internalization, and combination. In effect, the modes signify a process that begins with shared mental models (Senge, 1990) and spirals through different conversions to become knowledge that is explicitly stated and used in everyday practices. Socialization essentially occurs when tacit is shared with tacit or when an individual learns something new through observation, imitation, and practice (Nonaka, 1991, p. 99). However, socialization is limiting because no new insights to the learning has occurred because the learning has not become explicit. Conversely, an individual in a learning environment can collect information from everyone (explicit) and from that collective information create new information (explicit) resulting in externalization (p. 99).

The person has in essence synthesized the information but has not created new knowledge. However, when tacit and explicit knowledge interacts then powerful learning can occur. This occurs when a learner goes beyond just developing an answer for a problem but creates an innovative way to solve the challenge by taking in the tacit knowledge and interacts that tacit learning with the explicit knowledge of others (p. 99). This results in the knowledge conversion mode labeled internalization. After this explicit learning has occurred it will then be shared throughout the learning environment, explicit to tacit, and other learners will begin to utilized these new and innovative learning through the conversion mode of combination (p. 99). In fact, the other learners use the new learning in such a fashion that it becomes a part of themselves and ultimately of the total learning environment. Thus, as argued by Nonaka and Takeuchi (1995), new knowledge must first begin with the individual. An individual's knowledge can then be transformed into group

knowledge when certain knowledge creation modes exist (Nonaka, 1991).

Baumard (1999) and Choo (1998) supported Nonaka and Takeuchi's (1995) conceptualization that shared tacit knowledge must be converted into useable information for the learning environment through the conversion of knowledge. Moreover, Choo (1998) went on to note that during knowledge conversion "members share their personal knowledge through dialogue and discourse, and articulate what they intuitively know through analogies, metaphors, as well as more formal channels" (p. 3). Kerfoot (2003) added that this type of knowledge is invaluable and will become embedded throughout the learning environment. Likewise, Stacey (2001) and Von Krogh et al. (2000) referred to knowledge conversion as an active process, but Stacey (2001) and Nonaka and Takeuchi (1995) disagreed on the beginning point of the process. Stacey (2001) more closely examined the foundation of tacit knowledge, whereas Nonaka and Takeuchi (1995) began their explanation with tacit knowledge already existing in the minds of individuals. During the combination process Nonaka and Takeuchi (1995) identified, "Individuals exchange and combine knowledge through such media as documents, meetings, telephone conversations, or computerized communication networks" (p. 67). "Our dynamic model of knowledge creation is anchored to a critical assumption that human knowledge is created and expanded through social interaction between tacit and explicit knowledge" (Nonaka & Takeuchi, p. 61). This process can be extremely complex and iterative. As Hisnanick (2003) stated, "Knowledge creation is an extension of the social process in that it involves relationships among individuals, teams, and organizations. Knowledge creation plays in all aspects of our everyday existence and cannot be denied" (p. 3). Becerra-Fernandez and Stevenson (2001) acknowledged this point by noting, "Knowledge capital integrates the structural, staff, and student contributions to the learning organization" (p. 2) and probably the most important aspect of knowledge creation is the "how." Nonaka (1991), after studying Japanese companies, identified that redundancy is essential for knowledge creations to occur. In other words, information in the learning environment must overlap in not only content but also context. This redundancy allows for the learner to retain the information. This redundancy allows for frequent conversation and dialogue among the learners in a virtual environment.

Since the research within 3D VLEs is limited in scope, and while some promising research has been conducted within 3D VLEs, significant research is still lacking. In this case study, a 3D virtual learning environment utilizing a dialectic constructivist approach was constructed. Next, learners were given a project, which provided the organized scaffolding for learning and the opportunity for the learner to create knowledge with other learners to further develop their opportunities for learning.

METHODOLOGY

Rationale for Case Study

According to Bogdan and Biklen (2007), direction in qualitative research is determined by open-ended questions. During the course of the conducting the research, the questions will evolve, providing greater insight into the topic of research (Bogdan & Biklen, 2007; Yin, 1989). Due to the nature of the qualitative study, questions and assumptions may change during the iterative process of data collection and review. Merriam (1998) recommended a case study design when the researcher is interested in a greater insight and discovery of a phenomena rather than testing a hypothesis.

Patton (1997) noted that quantitative research provides us with the opportunity to measure "things that can be counted" (p. 273), while qualitative data seeks to capture an experience and what it meant to the participants. As Patton

stated, "Numbers are parsimonious and precise; words provide detail and nuance" (p. 273). Bogdan and Biklen (2007) noted that researchers can never obtain a perfect connection between what they wish to study and what they actually study. Since a perfect connection is not possible, findings from this study may lack generalizability. Bogdan and Biklen further noted that the reliability of the interview questions is not subject to the same scrutiny as in quantitative research. When considering whether to conduct qualitative or quantitative research, these researchers decided to utilize a case study with a mixed-design so as to capture the best of both worlds of data. By using such a design, it is hoped that such research will assist in providing insight into current assumptions and a point from which one can perform future research in the field of 3D VLEs.

Population and Sample

In qualitative data collection, the researcher is the primary instrument (Merriam, 1998) in all facets, including the identification of the sample. When selecting a population and sample for a case study, the researcher must select participants that will contribute to the study and provide further information to the research (Yin, 1989). Merriam (1998) noted that "purposeful sampling is based on the assumption that the investigator wants to discover, understand, and gain insight, and therefore must select a sample from which the most can be learned" (p. 61). To this end, the sampling design selected was purposeful sampling (Bogdan & Biklen, 2007); specific subjects were selected to "best help the researcher understand the problem and the research question" (Merriam, 1998, p. 185), subjects who "are believed to facilitate the expansion of the developing theory" (Bogdan & Biklen, 2007, p. 73). To bolster the effectiveness of the study, the researchers sought multiple participants from two sites so as to maximize variation (Merriam & Associates, 2002); the logic being that, "if there is some diversity in the nature of the sites selected (a public vs. a private university, for example) or in participants interviewed... results can be applied to a greater range of situations by readers or consumers of the research" (Merriam & Associates, 2002, p. 29).

The sample of this case study consisted of 28 college students at a small, public college in the Midwest and a small private college in the South-central areas of the United States enrolled in computer game programming courses. Both sets of students were enrolled in courses designed to teach the fundamentals of game design and development. Seventy-five percent of the students were male and ten percent were minority. The sample was drawn from a population of 1600 students attending an open-admissions two-year campus and 4800 students attending a private, religiously oriented campus. Within the population of the public campus comprising 1660 students, 47 percent are full-time, 65 percent are female, 35 percent are male, and 55 percent are traditional college students. The population of the private campus comprised 4800 students, 86 percent are full-time, 55 percent are female, 45 percent are male, and 89 percent are traditional college students. While students at the public college typically considered minority are few in number (4%), the students attending this university are economically and educationally disadvantaged (89% receive financial aid, 74% require one or more developmental education course). The private college had a higher diverse enrollment with 21% being classified as minority.

Data Collection and Instrumentation

Used during the course of this research were two methods of data collection. First, as a part of this research it was necessary to create a dialectic constructivist 3D Virtual Learning Environment to see if student engagement and knowledge creation occur within such an environment. The 3D VLE utilized the Torque Game Engine produced by Garage Games (2006) and was developed by one of the researchers. Specifically, the Torque Game Engine was modified to create an environment that enabled learners to interact in a dialectical constructivist environment that facilitates student engagement and knowledge creation (Dalgarno, 2002) (see Figure 1).

The 3D VLE was modified first to incorporate the ability of the avatar to interface with a database and to enable the tracking of the learner through the project. The 3D VLE was further adapted by the researchers to allow the development of the dialectic constructivist system, and the logging of engagement evidence. Beyond these engine modifications, the virtual environment had to be built using the 3D modeling software 3DS Max by Autodesk, painted using Photoshop, and incorporated into the virtual environment. A great deal of time was spent creating an environment that would encourage a collaborative mindset among the participants.

A complete record of all electronic conversations was created while the learners participated in the learning project. Data captured included the individual user, the date and time of the text and the conversation itself. Also collected during this phase of the research was the second set of data, which comprised the engagement of the student in the identifying and resolving the programming challenge.

Data Analysis

According to Thomas and Brubaker (2000), the first step in organizing data is classifying the data. Bogdan and Biklen (2007) noted that data analysis must involve working with, organizing, and breaking data into manageable units. The process of coding, or identifying categories, classifications, and themes derived from the participants of the study was useful in the organizing of the data. Utilizing the framework proposed by Hara, Bonk, and Angeli (2000), student interaction was categorized into five classifications:

1. **Elementary clarification:** Observation and identification of a problem and its elements.

Figure 1. Collaboration and interaction within 3D VLE

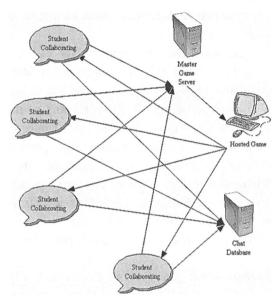

This includes identification of linkages to gain a basic understanding of the problem.

2. **In-depth clarification:** Gaining an understanding of the problem so that it "sheds light on the values, beliefs, and assumptions which underlie the statement of the problem" (p. 125).
3. **Inferencing:** Use of induction and deduction in the analysis of the problem.
4. **Judgment:** Making a decision.
5. **Application of strategies:** "Proposing coordinated actions for the application of a solution" (p. 125).

Next, the dialogue between the students was analyzed using the four modes of knowledge conversion of socialization, externalization, internalization, and combination. Socialization essentially occurs when tacit is shared with tacit or when an individual learns some new through observation, imitation, and practice (Nonaka, 1991, p. 99). Externalization occurs when an individual collects information from everyone (explicit) and from that collective information create new information (explicit) (p. 99). Internalization occurs

when a learner creates an innovative way to solve the challenge (p. 99). After this explicit learning has occurred it will then be shared throughout the learning environment, explicit to tacit, and other learners will begin to utilized these new and innovative learning through the conversion mode of combination (p. 99).

The second step is axial coding to aid in making comparisons and connections between and among the identified themes. The final step is summarizing (Thomas & Brubaker, 2000). The summarizing process is designed to promote synthesis of the data, identification of patterns, and aid in the discovery of what was important, could be learned, and what could be shared.

The quantitative data was analyzed using SPSS 16.0 using descriptive statistics such as Mean, frequencies, and standard deviation. This data were used to gain a better understanding and insight of the engagement rate of the participants and their conversations during the study.

In summation, the qualitative data were analyzed in a multi-step process to ensure triangulation of data. First, the quantitative data of frequencies of interactions that measured engagements were computed to aid in the analysis of qualitative data. Second, qualitative data from the actual conversations recorded in the research was coded and classified.

DISCUSSION OF FINDINGS

The researchers examined the student engagement by utilizing qualitative data gathered from the chat records of the 3D VLE. The chats captured from the 3D VLE provided a rich texture of collaborative data. Of the 682 conversations that occurred during the two weeks of data gathering, a vast majority (62.6%) were found to be collaborative in nature (see Table 1).

Initially, the majority of conversations were off-topic or focused on learning the environment. However, participants were able to easily move and communicate within the 3D VLE (see Figure

Table 1. Number of chat conversations by classification (N=682)

Classification	Conversations
Elementary Clarification	201
In-Depth Clarification	92
Inferencing	35
Judgment	37
Applicatin	62
Off-topic	174
Salutations	67
Flaming	14

2). After approximately two and a half (2.5) hours of working inside the 3D VLE, there was a dramatic drop in off-topic conversation. At this same point, there was a noticeable change toward student engagements through conversations that were seeking in-depth clarification and application. From the surveys, several comments were made concerning the initial general engagement. As one student said, "Most of it was us helping each other understand the mechanisms of the environment, figuring out what was tied to what." Another student found that the student engagement through dialogue allowed for the "clarification of goals, discussion of problems, fun banter, answered questions that others raised, and some arguments when misunderstandings arose."

Additionally, one participant that was interviewed stated, "Online, there were many different types of discussions, from productive collaboration to general silliness. Outside of the VLE, more productive communication occurred via text messaging and e-mail chat programs."

While the amount of flaming (a hostile or demeaning statement directed at another student) was relatively low (14 total occurrences, or 2% of the total conversations), it was mentioned by some respondents on the survey. Some considered it "fun banter," while other students mentioned the flaming stating that "I was flamed and was

given advise on the hot keys and how to crash the game," and another noted, "Well when I was on with other people there was a lot of joking, some flaming...."

Again using the data from the 3D VLE the researchers analyzed the conversation data through the framework of Nonaka and Takeuchi's (1995) knowledge spiral. The beginning of the knowledge spiral must show the transference of tacit knowledge to explicit knowledge, passing through the four modes of knowledge conversion: socialization, externalization, combination, and internalization. This process became evident from the chat records recorded in the 3D VLE. One example of the Knowledge Spiral is presented:

RedShirt_Rich: The Prof says he switched to code on the CLIENT side only for switching between characters

Furry: Yeah but it is set up differently than the tank code

Furry: He is calling to two different cs files instead of one

RedShirt_Rich: Whatever he switched turned off the animations, and I'm not sure the server would EVER see the Ava model...

RedShirt_Rich: ...if the server side code doesn't have the new selection methods

Furry: Let s throw in blue man to see if the code is defaulting to the player.css

Imber: Hey is the problem of not showing the animations and not loading AV in the aiplay.cs?

Imber: OMG i got the animations to work...

Imber: All problems are in the aiPlayer.cs

Furry: That s why the[y] have to be in the same file

RedShirt_Rich: No[w] what?

Imber: w[ait] ill change to adam

Imber: ok thats weird

Furry: See you broke it:)

Imber: Whatever the server host chooses gets cast to all other players

RedShirt_Rich: *Ava s animations worked for servers AND clients. Adams s animation ONLY works on the Server.*

Imber: *The call backs need to be uncommented and the male needs to be taken out of the aiplayer.cs file*

In this sample of conversations, the students completed all four (4) of the modes of knowledge conversion: socialization, externalization, combination, and internalization. During the socialization process, tacit knowledge is shared with other students. From the data, one can see the students start out by collaboratively sharing what they have learned by experimentation and from others. In Statement 1 and 2 of the conversation, RedShirt_Rich and Furry discuss what they have learned thus far from others and observation inside the 3D VLE. This socialization process ensures that they are both at the same starting point as they prepare to address the avatar and animation problems in the learning environment.

In the externalization conversion of tacit to explicit, a hypothesis is proposed as to where the problem is located. Statements 3 through 7 represent this move from tacit to explicit. Furry notes to RedShirt_Rich that two data files are being accessed in the computer program instead of just one data, which they had seen in another example. RedShirt_Rich makes a hypothesis that this might be the cause of the animation problems. Furry (in statement 6) proposes a method of checking to see if this might solve the problem. At this point, Imber, in statement 7 notes that the problem being discussed seems to be originating from one data file, beginning the transfer to the combination mode.

As the students move into the combination mode, students create a structure for the problem and attach it to one location with the program files. Statements 8 through 14 show the development of the structure and application of the hypothesis developed in the externalization process. Imber initially believes he has solved the problem by making a change to the data files. As he further applies the hypothesis, it creates other visual problems within the 3D VLE, causing Furry to, in good natured fun, tell him that he just broke the system.

During the final internalization phase of the Knowledge Spiral, the students take what they have learned thus far and apply it. In statements 15 through 17, the three students discuss what was done to create the differences in the virtual environment and what files were edited. This creates new observations about the problems that they are addressing, which starts a new cycle of the Knowledge Spiral. Thus the data reveals that

Figure 2. Conversations within the 3D VLE

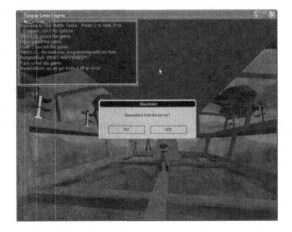

the 3D VLE provides and supports opportunities for the students to practice Nonaka and Takeuchi (1995) Knowledge Spiral, which they refer to as "learning by doing" (p. 69) (see Figure 3). While the students do not completely resolve the problem in this conversation, it does form the bases of future conversations of tacit to explicit knowledge creation that eventually leads to a solution being proposed.

CONCLUSION

In this inquiry, one key finding was, individually, students assumed a myriad of roles to solve the problems. Some began as the leader, then switched to the encourager then perhaps back to the leader, etc. Furthermore, the majority of the students appeared to engage in the content and the context of the learning using the entire dimensions of reasoning skills as postulated by Hara, Bonk, and Angelis's (2000) framework. Also according to Hara, Bonk, and Angeli (2000), the frequency of the social cues might be an indicator of the level of learner engagement on the learning task. As one can see from the data set, the frequency of the social cues were high throughout these graduate courses as the students continued to solve the problems, even as the student messages because less formal perhaps due to students feeling suc-

cess collectively in solving the learning tasks or perhaps they were just more comfortable with each other (Kang, 1998).

Consequently, in studies comparing face-to-face to computer-mediated communication (Walther, 1996), it has been reported that students do develop social relationships similar to those in a face-to-face class but generally it takes longer. However, the data from this inquiry found that students after just a short time frame settled into an engagement that was focused on solving the problem(s) yet went outside the arena of the virtual environment to have phone conversations and hold discussions via emails. Thus, it can be concluded that a 3VD learning environment can enhance the reasoning skills of the participant, if designed in such a fashion that a significant amount of engagement between the participants is provided to resolve the issue. The design of the pedagogy of the virtual learning environment is essential to this myriad application of reason skills.

To assess the extent of knowledge creation the learners with other learners, we utilized Nonaka and Takeuchi (1995) knowledge creation theory. Those researchers theorized that the active creation of knowledge progresses through four phases, and that while not every instance of socially constructed knowledge may move spirally through each successive phase equally, they are nonetheless consistent with much of the literature related to constructivist knowledge creation. As Wulff, Hanor, and Bulik (2000) noted, the instructor can aid the development of collaboration within a constructivist approach by "redistribut[ing] learning control and power by supporting and/or developing interaction-exchange formats, such as synchronous and asynchronous chat sites and display rooms to cultivate social and individual presence" (p. 150). This non-foundational view of learning allows students to learn in a collaborative fashion, rather than with the traditional foundational view in which knowledge is dispensed from the teacher (Bruffee, 1999) was the focus within the creation of this 3VD learning environment.

Figure 3. Nonaka and Takeuchi's knowledge spiral

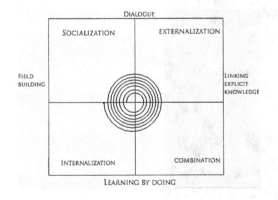

This effective constructivism allowed for the creation of knowledge for the learner (Fosnot, 1996).

Consequently, a second key finding from this inquiry is that a well-constructed 3D virtual learning environment should be designed around a knowledge creation focus to be effective. Within this knowledge creation focus, then new knowledge can be categorized and contextualized in an effort to make it accessible and of value to the widest range of students. Thus it can be concluded some the of design will incorporate the "soft" knowledge of how to engage the students throughout the course in a meaningful and a critical thinking process, while allowing for students to reflect and discussion in such a way that the knowledge creation spiral is established that reflects the four dimensions. Of course just as valuable is the new "hard" knowledge that incorporates the actual educational tool one uses to create the virtual learning environment.

Implications for Practice

The implications for practice focus almost entirely on how the teacher designs the 3D virtual learning environment, first understanding that dialogue and collective reflection must exist. The virtual learning environment must be designed to allowing the learner's thinking to be observable, learners must be allowed to engage in reflection in different phases of problem completion. Designers should include a model of the process of reflection, by providing examples of experts' thinking. Moreover, multiple perspectives can become apparent by providing ample opportunities for collaboration through dialogue and reflection.

Secondly, time and space for student engagement must be in the forefront of design. Designers must create group problem based projects that give students extra motivation to work with others in the class and share ideas. In online contexts, instructors must strive to optimize interaction between learner-instructor, learner-learner, and learner-content through effective modes of communication (Chen & Willits, 1999; Jung, 2001). The facilitation of dialogue must involve an evaluation of the opportunities for dialogue as well as an analysis of the quality of the dialogue that occurs (McBrien, Jones, & Cheng, 2009).

Next, the designer of the virtual environment must provide networking opportunities and the linkage of explicit knowledge. To encourage knowledge sharing and creation in an online or 3D VLE course, the instructor must develop trust by allowing students to participate in activities that build on personal social contact. Within the virtual learning environment, there must be collective conversation and sufficient time for exchanging ideas. The instructor can establish incentives for those who share their knowledge, allowing capacity building leading to enhanced creative thinking. Having a zero tolerance of "flaming" is a requirement so that there is an appreciation of any scheme irrespective of the avatar that provided it. Finally, the instructor must encourage students to admit knowledge gaps and problem failures, which will lead to more risk taking within the environment.

Lastly, the instructor must understand that learning occurs by doing and using experimentation. As Jukes, Mc Cain and Crockett (2011) argued, "To ensure that the task produces the engagement and relevance necessary for effective learning, the problem should have a link to the world outside" (p. 20). Therefore, the designer of such 3D virtual learning environments will need training not only in content but also in problem- based instruction. This shift from content driven instruction to problem based also will emphasize the need for instructors to have a firm understanding of brain research. Because as Pink (2006) articulated, "In a world tossed by Abundance, Asia, and Automation, in which the left brain-directed thinking remains necessary but no longer sufficient…We must perform work work…that satisfies the aesthetic, emotional, and spiritual demands of a prosperous time" (p. 61). As emphasized by Jukes et al. (2011), "If we want to see the kinds of changes necessary to bring schools in line with the new reality, then we have no option but to radically reprioritize and restructure professional development for teachers" (p. 21).

FUTURE DIRECTIONS FOR RESEARCH

Since beginning this study, other educational tools such as Alice (2007) have become available. While Alice does not incorporate collaborative components that the 3D VLE has, it can have a powerful impact upon on teaching and learning computer programming. According to Burton and Chin (2007), participants spend a great deal more time on programming projects when they consider the project fun. Does this improve learning? What impact would the addition of collaboration have upon these tools?

With collaboration now being established within 3D virtual environments, many areas remain to be researched and their impact upon student learning outcomes. What impact does being able to select and design the avatar have upon learning outcomes? If a student is given an avatar and told that the avatar is very good in a subject that the student struggles with, is learning impacted? Is cheating more or less prevalent in a virtual learning environment? An additional field of research deals with the development of virtual real estate. With online environments such as Second Life (Linden Research Inc., 2007) available, how will this impact traditional learning?

Of course, more research into the area of collaboration and its utilization within 3D VLE is needed. As this was a case study, the application of this research is limited. Further large-scale research is called for to ensure the validity and application to a broader range of research.

SUMMARY

This chapter's focus was to present the discussion and findings from a case study that examined the engagement and the creation of student knowledge of undergraduate students using a 3D virtual learning environment. Using two frameworks (Hara, Bonk, & Angeli, 2000; Nonaka & Takeuchi, 1995) to analyze the student conversations, as they solved problems in this 3D virtual environment, several relevant conclusions were drawn. Findings revealed that five forms of student engagement amplified the learning process and that a complete knowledge spiral occurred emphasizing the four modes of knowledge conversion. Implications for practice were discussed and presented as well were recommendations for future research.

REFERENCES

Alice. (2007). *Website.* Retrieved August 15, 2007, from http://www.alice.org

Barab, S., Thomas, M., Dodge, T., Carteaux, R., & Tuzun, H. (2005). Making learning fun: Quest Atlantis, a game without guns. [from http://inkido.indiana.edu/research/onlinemanu/papers/QA_ETRD.pdf.pdf]. *Educational Technology Research and Development*, *53*(1), 86–107. Retrieved July 3, 2010 doi:10.1007/BF02504859

Baumard, P. (1999). *Tacit knowledge in organizations*. London, UK: Sage.

Becerra-Fernandez, I., & Stevenson, J. M. (2001). Knowledge management systems & solutions for the school principal as chief learning officer. *Education*, *121*, 508–519.

Blizzard. (2010). *World of Warcraft*. Retrieved from http://us.blizzard.com/en-us/company/

Bogdan, R. C., & Biklen, S. K. (2007). *Qualitative research for education: An introduction to theory and methods* (5th ed.). Boston, MA: Pearson/Allyn and Bacon.

Bonk, C. J., Kim, K. J., & Zeng, T. (2006). Future directions of blended learning in higher education and workplace learning settings. In Bonk, C. J., & Graham, C. R. (Eds.), *Handbook of Blended Learning: Global Perspectives, Local Designs* (pp. 550–567). San Francisco, CA: Pfeiffer Publishing.

Bruffee, K. A. (1999). *Collaborative learning: Higher education, interdependence, and the authority of knowledge* (2nd ed.). Baltimore, MD: Johns Hopkins University Press. doi:10.2307/358879

Burton, B., & Chin, J. (2007). *Inclusion of game concepts in introductory programming courses.* Paper presented at Illinois Online Conference. Chicago, IL.

Burton, B., & Martin, B. N. (2010). Learning in virtual environments: Collaboration and knowledge spirals. *Journal of Educational Computing Research, 43*(2), 259–273. doi:10.2190/EC.43.2.f

Choo, C. W. (1998). *Information management for the intelligent organization: The art of scanning the environment.* Medford, NJ: Information Today.

Dalgarno, B. (2002). The potential of 3D virtual learning environments: a constructivist analysis. *E-Journal of Instructional Science and Technology, 5*(2). Retrieved November 24, 2010, from http://www.usq.edu.au/electpub/e-jist/docs/Vol5_No2/dalgarno_frame.html

Dede, C. (2005). Planning for neomillinnial learning styles. *EDUCAUSE Quarterly, 1*, 7–12.

Dede, C., Nelson, B., Ketelhut, D. J., Clarke, J., & Bowman, C. (2004). Design-based research strategies for studying situated learning in a multi-user virtual environment. In *Proceedings of the Sixth International Conference on the Learning Sciences,* (pp. 158-165). Mahwah, NJ: Lawrence Erlbaum. Retrieved May 20, 2010, from http://muve.gse.harvard.edu/muvees2003/documents/dedeICLS04.pdf

Dickey, M. (2005). Brave new (interactive) worlds: A review of the design affordances and constraints of two 3D virtual worlds as interactive learning environments. *Interactive Learning Environments, 13*(1), 121–137. doi:10.1080/10494820500173714

DiPaola, S., & Collins, D. (2003). A social metaphor-based 3D virtual environment. In *Proceedings of the Educators Program from the 30th Annual Conference on Computer Graphics and Interactive Techniques, Quicktakes,* (pp. 1-2). Quicktakes.

Elliott, J., & Bruckman, A. (2002). Design of a 3D interactive math learning environment. In *Proceedings of the Conference on Designing Interactive Systems: Processes, Practices, Methods, and Techniques,* (vol. 1, pp. 64-74). IEEE.

Fosnot, C. T. (1996). Constructivism: A psychological theory of learning. In Fosnot, C. T. (Ed.), *Constructivism: Theory, Perspectives, and Practice* (pp. 8–33). New York, NY: Teachers College Press.

Garage Games. (2012). *Website.* Retrieved January 5, 2006, from http://www.garagegames.com

Grubb, A., & Hines, M. (2000). Tearing down barriers and building communities: pedagogical strategies for web-based environment. In Cole, R. (Ed.), *Issues in Web-Based Pedagogy* (pp. 365–380). Westport, CT: Greenwood Press.

Hara, N., Bonk, C. J., & Angeli, C. (2002). Content analysis of online discussion in an applied educational psychology course. *Instructional Science, 28*, 115–152. doi:10.1023/A:1003764722829

Haynes, S. N., Richard, D. C., & Kubany, E. S. (1995). Content validity in psychological assessment: A functional approach to concepts and methods. *Psychological Assessment, 7*(3), 238-247. Retrieved May 7, 2006, from http://www.personal.kent.edu/~dfresco/CRM_Readings/Haynes_1995.pdf

Henri, F. (1992). Computer conferencing and content analysis. In Kaye, A. R. (Ed.), *Collaborative Learning Through Computer Conferencing: The Najaden Papers* (pp. 116–136). Berlin, Germany: Springer-Verlag. doi:10.1007/978-3-642-77684-7_8

Hisnanick, J. J. (2002). Knowledge emergence: Social, technical, and evolutionary dimensions of knowledge creation. *Journal of Economic Issues, 36*, 819–821.

Jukes, I., McCain, T., & Crockett, L. (2011). Education and the role of the educator in the future. *Phi Delta Kappan, 92*(4), 15–21.

Kang, I. (1998). The use of computer-mediated communication: Electronic collaboration and interactivity. In Bonk, C. J., & King, K. S. (Eds.), *Electronic Collaborators: Learner-Centered Technologies for Literacy, Apprenticeship, and Discourse* (pp. 315–337). Mahwah, NJ: Erlbaum.

Kerfoot, K. (2003). Learning organizations need teachers: The leader's challenge. *Nursing Economics, 21*, 148–151.

Kirner, T. G., Kirner, C., Kawamoto, A. L., Cantao, J., Pinto, A., & Wazlawick, R. S. (2001). Development of a collaborative virtual environment for educational applications. In *Proceedings of the Sixth International Conference on 3D Web Technology,* (pp. 61-68). IEEE.

Koopman, B. L. (2011). From Socrates to wikis using online forums to deepen discussions. *Phi Delta Kappan, 92*(4), 24–27.

Lim, C. P., & Chai, C. S. (2004). An activity-theoretical approach to research of IIT integration in Singapore schools: Orienting activities and learner autonomy. *Computers & Education, 43*(3), 215–236. doi:10.1016/j.compedu.2003.10.005

Lim, C. P., Nonis, D., & Hedberg, J. (2006). Gaming in a 3D multiuser virtual environment: Engaging students in science lessons. *British Journal of Educational Technology, 37*(2), 211–231. doi:10.1111/j.1467-8535.2006.00531.x

Linden Research, Inc. (2007). *Second life.* Retrieved October 5, 2007, from www.secondlife.com

McBrien, J. L., Jones, P., & Cheng, R. (2009). Virtual spaces: Employing a synchronous online classroom to facilitate student engagement in online learning. *International Review of Research in Open and Distance Learning, 10*(3), 5–10.

Merriam, S. B. (1998). *Qualitative research and case study applications in education.* San Francisco, CA: Jossey-Bass.

Merriam, S. B. (2002). *Qualitative research in practice: Examples for discussion and analysis.* San Francisco, CA: Jossey-Bass.

Nonaka, I. (1991, November/December). The knowledge-creating company. *Harvard Business Review*, 96–104.

Nonaka, I., & Takeuchi, H. (1995). *The knowledge-creating company: How Japanese companies create the dynamics of innovation.* Oxford, UK: The Oxford University Press. doi:10.1016/0024-6301(96)81509-3

Patton, M. Q. (1997). *Utilization-focused evaluation.* Thousand Oaks, CA: Sage Publications, Inc.

Pink, D. (2006). *A whole new world.* New York, NY: Berkley.

Rubin, H. J., & Rubin, I. S. (2005). *Qualitative interviewing: The art of hearing data* (2nd ed.). Thousand Oaks, CA: SAGE Publications.

Salzman, M. C., Dede, C., Loftin, R. B., & Chen, J. (1999). The design and evaluation of virtual reality-based learning environments. *Presence.* Retrieved August 12, 2009, from http://www.virtual.gmu.edu/ss_pdf/presence.pdf

Senge, P. M. (1990). *The fifth discipline: The art and practice of the learning organization.* New York, NY: Doubleday/Currency. doi:10.1002/pfi.4170300510

Stacey, R. D. (2001). *Complex responsive processes in organizations: Learning and knowledge creation.* New York, NY: Routledge.

Thomas, R. M., & Brubaker, D. L. (2000). *Theses and dissertations: A guide to planning, research, and writing.* Westport, CT: Bergin & Garvey.

Tsiatsos, T., Andreas, K., & Pomportsis, A. (2010). Evaluation framework for collaborative educational virtual environments. *Journal of Educational Technology & Society, 13*(2), 65–77.

Von Krogh, G., Ichijo, K., & Nonaka, I. (2000). *Enabling knowledge creation: How to unlock the mystery of tacit knowledge and release the power of innovation.* Oxford, UK: Oxford University Press.

Walther, J. (1996). Computer-mediated communication: Impersonal, interpersonal, and hyperpersonal interaction. *Communication Research, 23*(1), 3–43. doi:10.1177/009365096023001001

Wulff, S., Hanor, J., & Bulik, R. J. (2000). The roles and interrelationships of presence, reflection, and self-directed learning in effective world wide web-based pedagogy. In Cole, R. (Ed.), *Issues in Web-Based Pedagogy* (pp. 143–160). Westport, CT: Greenwood Press.

Yin, R. K. (1989). *Case study research: Design and methods.* Newbury Park, CA: Sage Publications.

Chapter 2
A MUVEing Success:
Design Strategies for Professional Development in the Use of Multi–User Virtual Environments and Educational Games in Science Education

Shannon Kennedy-Clark
University of Sydney, Australia

Kate Thompson
University of Sydney, Australia

ABSTRACT

The chapter will explain the role of scenario-based MUVES and educational games in science education and will present both the benefits for students and the challenges of using these forms of technology in a classroom setting. This chapter presents the findings of two case studies on the use of a scenario-based Multi-User Virtual Environments (MUVE) in science education. The chapter will consider strategies for designing professional development programs for teachers and pre-service teachers to enhance both the teachers' skills and their confidence in using and designing classroom activities suitable for MUVEs and educational games in science inquiry learning.

INTRODUCTION

Virtual worlds, serious games, and Multi-User Virtual Environments (MUVEs) have garnered much attention recently in educational circles for their ability to engage and motivate students. Thus far, only a small number of research studies have been undertaken on the roles of teachers and pre-service teachers in using these environments successfully in a classroom. Successful, in this context, does not only mean noticeable learning gains for students, but also but also means that students and teachers effectively use the virtual world or computer game in a classroom setting in a way that is meaningful and worthwhile. The purpose of this chapter is to present two case studies on the

DOI: 10.4018/978-1-4666-2670-6.ch002

use of *Virtual Singapura*, a scenario-based MUVE, to develop scientific inquiry skills. The chapter will provide a background of the technology and will discuss both the benefits and challenges of using this form of digital media in an educational setting. The chapter will conclude by providing an overview of strategies and design considerations for professional development and the use of scenario-based virtual worlds and educational games in educational contexts. Where relevant, reference will be made to *Virtual Singapura* and to other educational games or virtual worlds that educators can readily access.

BACKGROUND TO GAME-BASED LEARNING

Recent research that has been identified as containing aspects of game-based learning has broadened the concept of a definition of game-based learning and has resulted in the articulation of dimensions or common factors identified by practitioners and researchers. The term game-based learning is often used simultaneously with terms such as 'serious' games, educational games, and virtual learning environments. However, before moving ahead this chapter it is worthwhile to clarify exactly what these terms means so as to distinguish what a scenario-based MUVE is and what it is not.

Game-based learning is the use of a computer-based game, also called a video game, in an educational context (Gee & Shaffer, 2010; Watson, Mong, & Harris, 2011). Game-based learning can incorporate the use of Commercial Off-The-Shelf (COTS) games, such as *Civilization III*® (Squire, 2004). The use of the term 'game' or 'serious game' is often used in this context as the technology used in virtual environments is often drawn from gaming technology, and 'game' is also a user friendly term in that a member of the general public can identify with the concepts of online gaming. This research will avoid the use of the term game to describe

Virtual Singapura as this environment does not engage the use of features such as scores, which are identifying markers of 'game.' Moreover, as Squire (2007) explains, the term 'serious' is also part of a branding schemes for commercial purposes. McKerlich and Anderson (2007) in their research into *Second Life* in educational settings clarify that the terms 'game' and MUVE should not be used interpedently indicating that MUVEs are not games but are neutral, changeable environments, whose purpose may not be to entertain but may be for education or business. Therefore, this chapter will differentiate between a MUVE and a game where necessary. However, for the purpose of the introduction the term game will be used as much of the current literature does not distinguish between the different forms.

There are several factors that underpin the move towards the use of game and virtual technology in educational contexts. The use of game technology to engage learners is one of the main motivators for educators. The problem of engagement and motivation of learners has been recognised as a factor faced by many institutions (Gee, 2005) and the use of games is viewed as a way to access the 'Nintendo age' or 'video game generation' (Barab, Thomas, Dodge, Carteaux, & Tuzun, 2005) which are the generation of learners that have grown up alongside the rapid developments in the game industry. In fact, the use of computer games is so ubiquitous that Ferdig (2007) indicates that 70% of college students in the United States play some form of game, whether it be online, video or computer, single player or multi-player. This is supported by Squire (2006) who indicates that children spend more time playing games than watching television. Dodge et al. (2008) explain that games may offer a way to empower students as classrooms are often passive, and because the learners are not able to control their learning experience, games may afford learners this control. The widespread use of games provides educators with opportunities to harness the motivating factors, such as fantasy, challenge, immersion, communication to enrich the learning experience of students.

The notion of games as a play space provides opportunities to use games both as an educational tool and to engage learners. There is a general consensus that learning through games is possible and affords learners a safe place to play (Gee, 2003; Gros, 2003; Squire, 2005). Play, for both adults and children, can occur on several levels, individuals can play for progress, power, fantasy and for self empowerment and can provide a powerful way to learn (Rieber, 1996; Squire, 2005). Games are viewed as tools that not only engage learners, but also provide context which can be developed into a field of expertise that can be supported through experiences both outside and inside the classroom such as trips to a museum and classroom material that build connections between the game and real environment (Shaffer & Gee, 2007). The gaming environment creates an 'affinity space,' a place that renders the usual distinctions of age, gender, race, socio-economic background obsolete, and participants can develop and control their identity, and games are also viewed as 'third places,' a place outside of family and formal environments, such as school and work, which allows participants to build connections on the basis of a shared experience (Shaffer, 2008). Hence, the use of play in an educational context can present learners with an opportunity to control their learning experience and to build a sense of a shared learning experience or a community of learners within a classroom environment.

VIRTUAL WORLDS AND SCENARIO-BASED MULTI-USER VIRTUAL ENVIRONMENTS

As they are proving to be an effective means of attracting and gaining students' attention, virtual worlds and virtual realities have been touted to be one of the technologies to watch over the next five years (Johnson, Levine, Smith, Smythe, & Stone, 2009). This factor combined with teachers' interest in ICT and increased access to ICT as a result of the Digital Education Revolution[1] in Australia were motivating factors in this study into the use of virtual worlds in science education. A virtual world can be defined as 'an electronic environment that visually mimics complex physical spaces, where people interact with each other and with virtual objects, and where people are represented by a virtual character' (Bainbridge, 2007).

These virtual worlds can be single player or multi-player. In the online environment, the evolution of multi-player virtual worlds began in the 1970s with text-based Multiple-User Dungeons (MUDs) which evolved into Multiple-User Dungeons Object Oriented (MOOs) which are based on fantasy role-playing games such as *Dungeons and Dragons*. These were superseded by Massively Multi-Player Online Role-Playing Games (MMORPGs), which include spaces such as *EverQuest®* and *World of Warcraft®*. The development of educational virtual worlds, such as *River City, Whyville,* and *Quest Atlantis* (Barab, et al., 2005; Kafai & Ching, 2001; Ketelhut, Dede, Clarke, & Nelson, 2006) can be viewed as a response to the potential learning benefits, such as visualising complex data, of game-based learning. The main distinction between a virtual world and a scenario-based virtual world is that a virtual world often mimics 'real' life in that lectures, meetings, classrooms are all held within the virtual space—virtual worlds are popular in distance education and are often hosted in *Second Life* (Gregory, et al., 2010). A scenario or narrative-based virtual world is founded on a story or narrative and information is built into the environment (Barab, et al., 2009).

A scenario-based MUVE is a virtual environment derived from game technology that includes features such as an avatar that represents the participant, a 3D virtual environment, the ability to interact or manipulate objects within the virtual environment and the ability to communicate with other participants and, in some instances, communicate with in-world characters. Educational MUVEs are usually based on a 'real world' context that is created to provide an authentic experience that a student may not be able to encounter in a classroom environment (Barab, et al., 2005; Dalgarno & Lee, 2010; Jacobson, Lee, Hong Lim, & Hua Low, 2008).

As with most computer games, a scenario-based MUVE is underpinned by a narrative that forms the basis of the learning experience. A further benefit of using a scenario-based MUVE in an educational space is that learners can interact with an environment that they may not be able to access in real life. There is a growing body of research that supports the use of scenario-based MUVEs in inquiry learning in secondary school science education due to their potential to enable high quality learning. That is, they may provide opportunities for learning of high intellectual quality as students are actively involved in constructing knowledge rather than reproducing another's conception of knowledge, which results in authentic learning (Newmann & Associates, 1996). As Herrington et al. (2004) state:

A complex and sustained activity can motivate students to learn. It can provide meaning and relevance to complex content, enable collaborative problem solving, justify the creation of polished products, and provide integrated assessment of achievement (p. 5).

Scenario-based MUVEs such as *Quest Atlantis, River City,* and *Virtual Singapura* have all shown that the environments are both highly motivating and challenging to students and can be used for collaborative problem solving. Research to date has shown that the value of these tools in maintaining student motivation is substantial (Barab, et al.,

2005; Edelson, Gordin, & Pea, 1999; Ketelhut, Nelson, Clarke, & Dede, 2010, 2004).

The use of scenario-based virtual worlds in education indicates a shift in people's perceptions about how people can connect and relate to each other socially. *Quest Atlantis*[2] and *Whyville*[3] are two popular multiplayer virtual worlds designed for use in educational contexts. Both of these worlds show how virtual worlds can be used for scenario-based learning activities. Using virtual worlds can allow learners to interact with the material bridging the gap between information representation and experimental learning. The 'real world' context and rich immersive environment are cited as being motivating factors for learners—the intense visual, aural and textual stimulation support the learning of material in context (Rieber, 1996; Shaffer & Gee, 2007). In a scenario-based MUVE environment, students are encouraged to control their own learning experience and it is through this proactive engagement with the environment that learning can occur.

This enriched learning space allows learners to become the authors of their own experiences which in turn allows for exploration without the repercussions of the real world (Rieber, 1996). As Goldsworthy et al. (2000) note, for learners the synergy of content, knowledge, and learning combined with increased agency contributes to a better relationship with the material. Gee (2003) supports this in stating that learning with virtual worlds allows for the 'sand box' principle wherein a participant can explore the world while still feeling safe. Overall, the implications of the use of virtual worlds in an educational context can contribute to greater engagement and motivation, which can encourage life-long learning. These environments can also build a community of practice 'affinity space' and can be used to develop technical literacy and a sense of community in learning environments such as seen in *Quest Atlantis* and *Whyville*.

VIRTUAL SINGAPURA

This chapter will provide two case studies on the use of *Virtual Singapura*[4], and will also make reference to several readily available virtual worlds that pre-service teachers and teachers can access for use in the classroom. The story or scenario for the virtual world lends itself to collaborative scientific inquiry learning. *Virtual Singapura* is set in 19th century Singapore and is based on historical information about several disease epidemics (malaria, cholera, and tuberculosis) during that period. The students are transported back in time to help the Governor of Singapore, Sir Andrew Clarke, and the citizens of the city try to solve the problem of what is causing the illnesses. The supporting activities are designed to develop appropriate inquiry skills such as defining the scope of the problem, identifying of research variables, establishing and testing hypotheses and presenting findings. In order to create an authentic learning experience, 19th century artefacts from Singapore have been included in the environment. These artefacts include historical 3D buildings and characters that represent different ethnic groups in Singapore at the time such as Chinese, Malay, Indian, westerners, and authentic historical items such as paintings, medical records, and period photographs.

STAKEHOLDERS EXPECTATIONS OF VIRTUAL WORLDS IN EDUCATION

The strategies proposed for using virtual worlds in the classroom are derived from the results of the two case studies and findings from relevant literature on the use of technology in the classroom including, but not limited to, de Winter (2010), La Velle et al. (2007), Hennessy et al. (2005), Davis et al (2009), and Webb and Cox (2004). This will consider factors such as the impact of school and classroom ecology, technological barriers and materials design on the use of virtual worlds in schools. The section will also discuss strategies to enhance a teacher's skills and confidence in using technology such as mentoring, on-going professional development, domain specific training, and communities of learning.

Students

The use of scenario-based virtual worlds and educational games in education naturally supports student-centred and collaborative learning. Feedback from students in using these environments has been overwhelmingly positive (Barab, et al., 2005; Gee, 2005; Jacobson, Kim, Miao, Shen, & Chavez, 2009; Squire, et al., 2004). Students involved in a recent study we conducted using an online game all supported working in teams and using online games[5]. Their main reason for preferring collaboration was because they could discuss their opinions and gain new perspectives, especially when faced by challenging materials. Collaborative learning requires a plan for the work process, critical thinking, and scaffolded learning. Learners need to engage in these steps to effectively use the collaborative learning environment. Determining priorities, therefore, is also an important part of the collaborative learning process. The learner's perception of the technology is also an important component of the collaborative learning process, as learners must be scaffolded within their learning environments (Beatty & Nunan, 2004).

A collaborative learning environment in science also provides students with an authentic learning experience because scientists work in a social work environment (Kozma, 2003). In a review of 26 studies covering almost all grades, and subjects that included social studies, science, and physical science, Johnson and Johnson (1985) found that 21 studies showed that cooperative learning promoted higher achievement, two studies had mixed results, and three had no differences between treatments. Most of the current research agrees that students need to be scaffolded in their collaborative activities (Gilllies, 2003; Maloney & Simon, 2006; Manlove, Lazonder, & de Jong, 2005). In this study, collaborative learning was not scaffolded, nor was there a group goal. However, in the case of group projects without a correct answer, or solving complex problems, it may be that hearing others' thinking processes is beneficial, even if teaching does not take place (Slavin, 1996). In fact, from the results of our classroom study discussed later in this chapter it was clear that of the 41 students that responded to the questions on collaboration in a posttest, all but two found the experience to be positive. The two that did not find the experience to be positive cited people stealing their ideas and missing relevant classes to be the negative factors. The positives of collaboration were in being able to listen to other's ideas, to discuss problems, and to divide tasks.

Our study found that because all of the students had the same government issue laptop and were working in class together, technical problems were minimised as students would help each other. Although there was a range of abilities within the group in terms of academic, linguistic, and technical competence, the online games were presented in a manner that students could access. Consequently, teachers need to start with manageable activities. While worlds such as *Virtual Singapura* are rich and dynamic, they are also more complicated to use in a classroom setting.

Parents

Educational games are not always viewed positively in sectors of the community, which can result in a resistance to adopt the technology within a learning space, such as a school. Parents and educators are often hostile to the use of games in the classroom as they are poorly integrated. Since, parents see the games as time wasting—playing games is not learning—the value of games in terms of a triad of education, entertainment, and social commitment is often undervalued or ignored as the

emphasis is placed on achieving national standards (Bagley & Shaffer, 2012). The view of games solely as entertainment for adolescents needs to be reviewed before mainstream society will value the use of the technology as a learning tool.

Games are often portrayed negatively by the media, which influences parental and educational views of the products. Games are often demonised by the media as causing deviant social behaviour, and as the main demographic using the products, adolescents are often viewed as the source of the problem (Steinkuehler, 2006). However, Barab et al. (2005) argue that research to date has shown no link between video games and deviant social behaviour and given the number of people playing games around the world the likelihood that the game industry is spawning millions of mass-murders is unlikely. Goldstein (2001) adds that much of the research on violence in video forces participants into an unnatural settings that focuses on violence and does not replicate the natural or voluntary aspects of game play. Goldstein (2001) also draws on children's inability to discern violent actions, such as blowing up or torturing characters, in cartoons such as *Bugs Bunny* or *Road Runner*, indicating that children do not view the violence as a reality. The negative view of games in an education context comes largely from a lack of thorough understanding and knowledge of the field; however, as society is changing, education institutions will need to consider this shift in popular culture.

The commercial agenda of a COTS game also needs to be considered before institutions adopts games as part of the curriculum as many products that are marketed as being educational, 'edutainment,' are driven by a commercial agenda, and are simple not educational as there is no value in terms of social process (Shaffer, 2008). Rather it is the marketing of the educational value of games that appeals to institutions and parents. As Gros (2003) explains, it is adults that select the educational software and players that select games. Hence, adults select games that they view as appropriate in terms of learning, while gamers play for the entertainment and challenge. This divide is indicative of the potential barriers that the wide-scale adoption of games may face.

Pre-Service Teachers

There is a limited body of research on pre-service teacher training and pre-service teachers' attitudes towards ICT—especially in regards to using MUVEs in education. A pre-service teacher in this instance refers to an undergraduate or post-graduate student that is majoring in education that has not yet commenced classroom teaching. The limited and inadequate amount of training that pre-service teachers often receive before entering a classroom means that pre-service teachers, in many cases, do not feel that they have the technical support, the skills, or a pedagogical rationale for implementing ICT in the classroom (Angeli, 2004; Lee, 1997).

Henriques (2002) suggests that to overcome the negative attitudes to using ICT in the classroom, pre-service teachers need to see the use of technology in the context of science education, and to see the relationships that exist between the two. Moreover, ICT should be presented as both accessible and worthwhile to pre-service teachers, rather than just as a box ticking activity. Pre-service teachers entering the school system that are interested in using technology in the classroom should be encouraged to explore this domain (de Winter, et al., 2010). In this context, virtual worlds such as *Virtual Singapura* can bridge the gap between science education and technology by presenting teachers with a rich medium to present case studies and science based problems that are free (in the case of *Quest Atlantis* and *Virtual Singapura*), easy to use, and provide students with an opportunity to interact with a motivating and engaging learning experience.

However, as Dede (1997) notes, in order for ICT to be seen as worthwhile and to address the negativity surrounding ICT implementation in schools, factors such as pedagogy, curriculum, assessment, and school organizations need to be addressed simultaneously rather than in a piecemeal fashion. Another factor that needs to be considered is pre-service teacher views on teaching. Many pre-service teachers tend to maintain an ideological underpinning for their teaching, such as facilitating a student-centered classroom, before they gain hands on teaching experience. Yet when they enter the classroom they tend to use teacher-centered approaches, so at this early stage in their teaching career their attitudes and values towards teaching have not yet solidified and tend to be more malleable as a result of their early experiences (Simmons, et al., 1999). Changing the attitude of pre-service teachers needs to be supported in school and access to training and technologies such as virtual worlds needs to be maintained both in higher education settings and in the classroom.

Pre-service teachers need to be exposed to and have time to explore online games and virtual worlds. As previously mentioned, some of these spaces are complicated and a pre-service teacher may avoid using such activities with good reason. However, introducing context-based games and worlds that can be completed in one lesson is not only achievable, but is also relatively easy as sites such as *The Jason Project*[6]; *NASA* online games[7] for primary school students and for older students[8]; and the *BBC UK*[9] provide easy to use, free, online educational games and virtual worlds and are accessible to both teachers and pre-service teachers to use in a classroom. Students need to be presented with these activities within a particular context so that they can perceive the pedagogical value.

Teachers

The role of teachers in implementing any form of ICT into a classroom is a critical factor that can contribute to the success or failure of the activity. Teachers are often presented as being resistant to using such technologies as MUVES, for reasons that include the additional time pressure to learn new skills, teacher self-efficacy, lack of technological support within the school, and concern over the pedagogical value of the technology (Barab, Hay, & Duffy, 1998; Dede, 1997; Henriques, 2002). However, a teacher's views on science and science education, their epistemological and philosophical stance, is perhaps the most influential aspect of how teachers view and use technology (Siorenta & Jimoyiannis, 2008). Using ICT in a classroom requires an addition to a teacher's knowledge and may results in changes to their teaching practice and personal beliefs about science education, and their ability to change depends on their values, beliefs and to what extent they perceive ICT to be a threat (Webb & Cox, 2004; Webb, 2005). Consequently, there is a need for clear planning of the use and desired outcome of using ICT, but as Webb and Cox (2004) explain, to date, there has not been much research undertaken on the role of the teacher in planning ICT. In our research, we use a design-based research approach (Barab, 2006), which allows the needs of all stakeholders including teachers, in the design of the world, the materials and the research. This research approach is suited to this type of project, as Ketelhut, Clarke, and Nelson (2010) have reported in their research on *River City*. They describe design-based research as "an iterative process where investigators engage in design, implement in classroom settings, research the learning in context, refine theories of learning, engage in redesign and continue the cycle of implementation" (p. 94). The role of the teacher in an ICT experience is a principal factor determining the success of the experience; however, there are a number of barriers that need to be considered and addressed before the value of ICT can be realized.

There is considerable depth in the research that has been undertaken on the barriers to the use of ICT in the classroom, and there is a consistency in the reported findings. The barriers to the use of ICT in the classroom are divided by Urhahne et al. (2010) as first and second level barriers and these barriers incorporate the temporal, spatial, technical and personal factors that influence a teacher's implementation of an ICT activity. First order barriers are extrinsic or external factors such as lack of access to resources; a lack of software; insufficient time to plan activities and units of work; and insufficient technical and administrative support. Second order barriers are described by Urhane et al. (2010) as intrinsic factors and these include a teacher's beliefs about teaching and computers; a teachers establishes instructional practices; and a teacher's willingness to change. While it may be difficult to address all of the first order barriers, it is no doubt equally, if not more difficult, to remedy the second order barriers. Overall, there is no single factor that may cause a teacher to avoid using ICT but an interlinked network of extrinsic and intrinsic factors.

Changing teachers' beliefs and attitudes towards ICT is not a rapid or swift change, it is a progressive transition that is a result of positive and fulfilling experience gained from using ICT in a manner that it brings meaning to the subject and the benefit of using the technology in that it provides an enhanced experience for the learners (Flores, Lopez, Gallegos, & Barojas, 2000). Caution in using ICT is understandable, teacher commitment is important, teachers need to recognise the value of the technology, and they need to see using ICT as an addition that builds and extends and not something that replaces current practice (Hennessy, et al., 2005; Webb, 2005). Research studies, such as those by Zacharia (2003) have shown that teachers' attitudes towards ICT have changed for the better as a result of using ICT. Hence, through thoughtful and well-planned professional development, shifts in beliefs and attitudes towards technology can be realised.

Schools

While teachers may be motivated to use virtual technologies in a school environments there are a number of factors that need to be considered before this can be achieved. The school will need to have sufficient bandwidth to run the program, this may sound relatively simple, but environments such as *Virtual Singapura* are troublesome to run as the download is often slow and only a few computers can be used at one time, so a teacher will need to be prepared to either have students share computers or to download single player versions if the school's system cannot support a multi-player version. The Internet Provider (IP) address may also cause obstacles as school firewalls may block access to the world—worlds such as *Second Life* are routinely blocked in schools. The issue of cost also needs to be considered. There are a number of free worlds, such as *Quest Atlantis* and *Whyville*. Therefore, the cost of software is not the prohibitive factor in introducing ICT into a school. The main costs occur in ongoing training and developing infrastructure to support these technologies.

One aspect of concern for many schools is that of duty of care. Virtual worlds such as *Second Life,* which are popular with tertiary institutions, are not suitable for school students and have an over-18 age restriction. Schools need to ensure the safety of students when in world to prevent not only possible harm from external sources but cyber bullying from peers. Worlds such as *Whyville* allow students to create an avatar so that a student's identity is protected and they constantly monitored to make sure that students are safe and that there is no bullying. Other worlds, such as *Virtual Singapura,* are closed worlds meaning that access is restricted so that the only people in the world are the class that are using it at that time.

The school ecology is also important, a school with a collective high self-efficacy (Bandura, 1997) is more likely to see the benefit of using technology. In terms of classroom ecology, teachers are central, chief figures in creating the classroom environment and incorporating ICT may affect the dynamic and disrupt the ecology (Davis, et al., 2009). However, as Eisner (2000) notes, most schools have a resilient ecology in that external and internal pressures may shift the

ecology, but tends to re-establish itself naturally. Therefore, in this context a one of a kind positive or a negative ICT experience will not do long term harm to a school.

Researchers

Researchers have been important stakeholders in the projects described in the case studies below. Researchers have led the development of materials and provided professional development for teachers and training and in-class support for the students. We used a design-based research approach in this study as it suited the fluid and naturalistic design of the research. Design-based research is a research methodology or approach that is used in the field of education in naturalistic settings and is distinct from action research. Design-based research is aimed at exploring educational problems and refining theory and practice by defining a pedagogical outcome and then focusing on how to create a learning environment that supports the outcome (Reeves, Herrington, & Oliver, 2005; Wang & Hannafin, 2005). The needs of this group are important because they often plan virtual learning projects, and because the research performed and reported on will inform further projects. In particular, the issues to consider for researchers are data collection and storage, and support for users.

Data Capturing

The use of virtual worlds and game technology for education is still nascent and research-based practice in encouraged. Indeed, in a design-based research approach, the collection and storage of data on which to base decisions about further iterations of the design is necessary. If the technology itself can be designed in such a way as to seamlessly capture the experiences that students have, the activities that they perform, and the learning outcomes, then this will only further help practice. Minimally, this would involve a server to store data (video and audio files as well as log files and text files containing answers to activities in order to track learning outcomes).

One example of a relatively seamless way to collect interaction data (both between collaborating students and their interaction with the virtual world) is through the use of screen capture software such as *Camtasia*. *Camtasia* records the participants' actions in the world (e.g. moving the mouse, changing screens, clicking on objects), a headshot video of the pair and their audio communication. In a recent study in which the authors were involved *Camtasia* was used to capture data with university students (Kennedy-Clark, Thompson, & Richards, 2012). This provided a detailed picture of how students were actually using *Virtual Singapura* and led to the conclusion that without proper scaffolding and instruction students often do not engage in the problem-activity. While transcribing data may be time consuming, the combination of video, audio, and screen capture provides a multi-faceted analysis of student processes.

User Support

A rapid response, or just in time support, is crucial to avoid disillusionment leading to a stalling of momentum. Proactive support for those just starting to use a virtual world plus ongoing access to advice is also helpful. This is related to the professional development of teachers and instruction for students. In addition to the provision of any initial training, ongoing support both for the use of the virtual world and regarding the pedagogy and classroom logistics are necessary.

Some of the issues identified in the field of mobile learning can be applied to virtual worlds—due to the similarities of using innovative technologies in a classroom environment. Some issues identified are to do with failures with the equipment (although less so in a virtual world, unless the server on which it is kept fails in some way), and some with the software or the network (Stewart, Thompson, Hedberg, & Wong, 2009). Those concerned with the software and network are worth mentioning here. In order to have soft-

ware installed on a school's computers, and any further access to the network (for transfer of the data captured mentioned in the previous section) also usually requires a set up, in other words, a staff member who can give researchers access to the system for setup, and who is available to help with troubleshooting on an ongoing basis.

The issues discussed in this section must be considered by stakeholders (teachers, schools, and researchers), who want to use virtual worlds in a classroom environment. The following section will describe two of the projects that the authors have been involved with as case studies in order to demonstrate some of these features, and identify other issues and further areas of research.

CASE STUDIES

The two case studies presented below both used *Virtual Singapura*. The aim of presenting the case studies is to highlight the differing needs of both groups.

High School Teachers

This case study will focus on the role of the teacher in use of *Virtual Singapura* in a secondary school science unit of work in an Australian High School. This case study will present the views of nine science teachers on the role of virtual worlds in science education including the factors that affect a teacher's likelihood to use virtual technology, the teachers' perceived constraints to ICT integration within the school and possible solutions to overcome the barriers. The teachers all held tertiary qualifications in science education and their teaching experience ranged from five years to 30 years. None of the teachers were frequent computer game players.

The views of the teachers were obtained during two professional development sessions and an in-school trial of *Virtual Singapura*. The teachers involved in this case study have had a major impact on the design and developments of the materials and the integration of *Virtual Singapura* into the classroom. The teachers accepted the invitation to participate in the study with alacrity. The feedback from the teachers was obtained from a sixteen-question open-ended survey, emails, and verbal feedback during the training sessions and in school trial.

User Support

We maintained regular contact with the school during the five months of the study. Although teachers were provided with email contacts, we found that most communication was through the Head of School prior to the study. We also liaised with the school's IT department to ensure that we could run the world and to test the equipment. During the school-based trial, teachers were provided with folders containing all of the materials, lesson plans, and FAQs sheets. They were also briefed on the lessons and learning outcomes. Teachers participated in all of the classes, but preferred for this initial study that one of the research team led the class.

Curriculum Context

We engaged the teachers in all aspects of the materials development and teachers provided detailed feedback on what area the though needed clarification. The study was aligned with the NSW Board of Studies stage 4 and 5 syllabus on scientific inquiry learning.

Professional Development

We provided two in-school training sessions. The first session provided a walk-through of the world and an overview of the problem. In the second session, the teachers used the student materials and completed the activities. The main reasons for this were to gauge the level of difficulty, as we were not sure if the materials were appropriate for year 10 students and to see if the approach to inquiry learning we designed would be relevant and in-line with the current curriculum.

Expectations of Technology

The main concern of the teachers was in relation to how the technology would work during the school-based study. Download time was slow and teachers became frustrated that they could not move as quickly through the virtual environment as they had hoped. The teachers indicated that they were concerned that it was taking 10 to 15 minutes just to get started and in a classroom setting, this was wasting valuable teaching time. This was a concern for the teachers as they were not sure whether or not we would be able to run the world with an entire year group simultaneously. The teachers were also concerned that the students would be distracted by their avatars and getting the avatars to move around. Being off-task was not seen as that much of a concern and was on par with poor graphic quality and no online data collection facility.

The teachers' expectations of the technology in terms of the learning gains were diverse. Motivation, enjoyment, and engaging with the activities were all perceived as being benefits of using virtual worlds. However, the teachers also indicated that the experience would be beneficial as students could learn science skills and could actually participate in an experience that they would not be able to encounter in a normal classroom based science lesson. This suggests that teachers do perceive the pedagogical value of the technology as well as the novelty value. The other benefits that were raised were that students could work at their own pace and could work in an area of their own interest (see Table 1).

The main issue identified regarding the use of such technology was that it was time consuming to install and download the software. The program had to be installed manually and the first time *Virtual Singapura* runs, it takes a considerable amount of time to download all of the objects. On

Table 1. Teachers views on the potential advantages, benefits, problems, and issues of using virtual worlds in a classroom setting

Perceived Benefits		Perceived Problems	
Characteristic	**%**	**Characteristic**	**%**
Enjoyment	15.38%	Distracted by avatars	14.28%
Motivating	15.38%	Off-task	7.14%
Work at own pace	7.70%	Technical problems	28.57%
Engaging	15.38%	Time consuming	28.57%
Learn science skills	15.38%	Too expensive	7.14%
Focus on area of interest	7.70%	No online data collection	7.14%
Access to experience not possible in real world	23.08%	Poor graphic quality	7.14%
n	13	*n*	14

second and subsequent visits to the world, the time required for download is usually less. For the school-based trials, we planned to download *Virtual Singapura* ahead of time and test runs will be completed so that this problem is not encountered in future activities.

School-Based Study

We ran a school-based study of *Virtual Singapura* in November 2010. The study was run over nine classroom lessons and 60 students participated in the unit of work. Unfortunately, due to problems with bandwidth we could not run the online version of the virtual environment. Despite months of planning, we could not get more than 10 computers to run the world simultaneously without crashing. It should be noted here that this was the second school involved in this trial that did not have the technical requirements to run the program. While this may seem like a total failure, we used a paper-based version of the world supplemented by a video *The Painted Veil* that was based on a cholera epidemic in rural China in the 1920s and the students completed *Death in Rome*, an online inquiry game. The students were disappointed that the virtual world did not work and made comments in their posttests expressing this disappointment. However, the teachers were very supportive and were very pleased with the

outcome as the students still used online activities and were engaged (see Figure 1).

Outcomes and Reflections

The main outcome of this study is that schools are still lacking many of the technical requirements to run programs such as *Virtual Singapura*. The school that we worked with was an independent school with excellent facilities and IT support and we still encountered problems. Issues such as dealing with private IP addresses were also time consuming. The teachers, IT support staff, and the students were all positive and supportive. The teachers indicated that while they liked the virtual world, the paper-based version worked very well and they would be happy to use a similar blended learning approach again in following years. Therefore, despite the technical failings, the teachers were still open to using and exploring the technology.

Pre-Service Teachers

The second case study will describe the use of *Virtual Singapura* as part of a pre-service teacher unit of work on problem-based learning in science. The virtual world was presented to the 28 students as a means of incorporating technology into the class to provide students with authentic cases.

The participants had all completed at least one in-school practicum and were from either Bachelor of Education (18 participants) or Master of Teaching (10 participants) degree programs. This case study will present the pre-service teachers views on the perceived benefits of the technology along with the problems and challenges they believe that they will encounter if the use this technology in a classroom setting. Several of the pre-service teachers were frequent computer game players.

Curriculum Context

The session was run in a science education course. As all of the participants were majoring in science education it made it easier to develop a session that they could all find relevant. We ran the session as part of a unit on teaching case-based learning. We discussed how the world could be used to investigate infectious diseases and public health. After the students used the world, we discussed in greater detail the possible uses of this form of technology in the classroom. One of the main benefits of a world such as *Virtual Singapura* is that students can return to the environment and focus on different features, for instance they can explore water borne disease (cholera), air-borne disease (tuberculosis) and vector-borne disease (malaria). Students can also explore public health and historical cases. The benefit of this is that students become familiar working within the environment and develop technical literacy and confidence. The problem is that the complexity of the environment may be challenging to students on the first encounter.

Professional Development

During the study, the pre-service teachers were able to interact within the environment in the role of a student. The pre-service teachers were given the student materials and were asked to think about how they as teachers may use this technology in a classroom setting.

The pre-service teachers worked in small groups of three students and controlled one avatar per group. The participants noticed that they could manually change their avatars in the tool bar, and both groups of participants spent a considerable amount of time changing into frogs, dogs, ducks, and different characters. They all noted that this ability to change avatars would also be amusing to students, and this issue was raised in data; the fact that students being off task was seen as a negative consequence of using a virtual world as being off task meant that students were not learning. The pre-service teachers were also concerned that they could not monitor all of the teams using the virtual world, and, thus, would need a master computer to make sure that students were not distracted by the interface.

The chat function was also seen as a distraction, and the participants were concerned that their students would spend more time chatting with other teams rather than completing their in-worlds activities. This issue was also seen as a technical limitation, as not all of the teams worked out how to use the chat function.

In terms of professional development, the pre-service teachers found the idea of using virtual worlds to be appealing; however, as the session was brief there was not sufficient time to

Figure 1. Students using BBC UK online game Death in Rome during the school based trial

develop a level of proficiency in using the world (see Figure 2).

Expectations of Technology

The results of this study suggest that pre-service teachers perceive the issues relating to behavior as more influential on their chosen method of delivery than the technical or potential learning benefits of the virtual world. This shows that while pre-service teachers may be willing to use a tool such as *Virtual Singapura*, they would weigh this up against factors such as class size, class temperament, access to technology and skill requirements. This focus on behavior management is perhaps a result of their inexperience as classroom teachers. This raises the question of whether experienced classroom teachers would present a different set of attitudes to ICT.

When asked whether they would use a virtual world in the classroom over seventy-percent of the pre-service teachers indicated that they would use the technology, but many provided further details to clarify their views on the technology:

Yes. If it can fill my class time whilst teaching and engaging then I'll definitely use it! Provided that it has good feedback from others

Yes, because students will be engaged as it'll be a game also to provide them with problem based learning experience about real-world situations which cannot be done through reading a text

Not really - as I have no experience with such games I would have trouble finding time to weight up academic benefit... I also have little personal interest i.e. I would have difficulty being the teacher of such an activity

Maybe: if I thought that students would benefit from the experience by gaining knowledge or skills in order for this to happen students must be engage in the activity

The benefits of using the virtual world raised by the pre-service teachers:

Students can see the impacts of their decisions on a larger scale in virtual worlds this would be virtually impossible in science labs.

It creates an engaging environment or situation and motivates students to want to learn more by integrating science concepts and ideas into the learning allows different areas of science to be included as well as exploring different skills/ methods that can be used.

They can conduct experiments not possible or too expensive to conduct in real life.

Can see the effects of things rather than just reading about them interactivity can also enhance relevancy.

These statements indicate that pre-service teachers see the value of using a MUVE in the classroom in terms of the ability of this mode of ICT to present learners with an opportunity to engage in scientific practices that would not be possible in a normal science classroom setting.

When asked about the issues associated with the use of virtual worlds in a classroom setting. Over half of the pre-service teachers indicated that students being off-task was a major concern for the pre-service teachers. This indicates that, unlike the classroom teachers, the technology was not the main concern. Off-task in this case meant that the students were not focusing on the prescribed activities. Responses included:

May be distracting and children may be caught up with exploring the world and their avatar without completing the activity. May also be complicated for those not familiar with virtual games.

Keeping all students on task – need a master computer if guidelines or strict assessments to keep them focused

Kids not saving work using the game as a chat room instead of a learning environment if working in groups some students may hog the computer

Student disengagement – not liking games, inappropriate use of chat feature. Time wasting - not on task

Can't control activities – so students cab waste time chatting/ chasing each other through the environment

The responses indicated that the tools available in the virtual world, such as the chat function and the complexity of the environment may contribute to students being off-task.

In Table 2, several terms need clarification. While terms such as visualization, motivation and engaging may be easy to decipher in this context, the benefit 'risk free' meant that students could perform and experiment without the associated risk of exposure to diseases, such as cholera. In the perceived problems, a lack of resources meant a lack of computers, too complicated meant that navigation in the world was too difficult to master, too expensive meant having enough computers and sufficient bandwidth to run the program, and repetitive meant that as there are six worlds that students can visit, by the time they have completed a few experiments they may become bored with the structure of the virtual world.

The pre-service teachers had clear expectations and perceived advantages and disadvantages in using a virtual world in a classroom setting. The advantages may be interpreted as being the ability to visualize information that would not be possible from a text or normal classroom setting. While the disadvantages may be that students would be off-task and that it would be difficult to make sure that they were completing the activities when the teacher could not monitor student progress.

Outcomes and Reflections

Overall, the study with the pre-service teachers indicated that the one-off training session while providing students with background information, would not result in sufficient knowledge on how to access virtual worlds or to design learning activities that may be incorporated confidently into the classroom. The level of skill required to use *Virtual Singapura* confidently and the complexity of the problem-space are in a sense prohibitive. That is not to say that the pre-service teachers were lacking in aptitude, but rather that more time would be needed to master this technology. Consequently, when running this session again we would expose pre-service teachers to more 'user-friendly' science- based worlds and games.

ISSUES AND FUTURE DIRECTIONS

This section of the chapter will summarize the main issues in using virtual worlds in education and will provide an overview of future research directions.

Figure 2. University students using Virtual Singapura

Table 2. Pre-service teachers views on the potential advantages, benefits, problems, and issues of using virtual worlds in a classroom setting

Perceived Benefits		Perceived Problems	
Characteristic	%	Characteristic	%
Visualization	41.7%	Off-task	53.3%
Motivating	20.8%	Lack of resources	20%
Interactive,	16.7%	Not liking computers	10%
learner centered	8.3%	Too complicated	6.7%
Engaging	8.3%	Too expensive	6.7%
Risk free	4.2%	Repetitive	3.3%
Team work			
n	24	*n*	30

Issues

There are a number of issues that arose during the course of the two studies.

Technical Issues

In both of the studies, we experienced ongoing technical problems using the virtual world. The download time was slow and in a number of instances; the computers froze when trying to teleport between worlds. However, websites such as *The Jason Project* have better technical capabilities and offer teachers a more stable means of accessing virtual worlds.

Social Issues

It was apparent in both of the studies that the term 'game' did raise concern for the pre-service teachers and teachers as the associations of the word game tend to counter the need to make students learn. Once the groups understood that the environments are designed for education, both the pre-service teachers and classroom teachers became more accepting, especially when the term 'game' in this context was explained.

The greater familiarity that pre-service teachers have with computer games and virtual worlds, the more likely they are to consider using this tech-

nology in their classrooms. Correspondingly, as a greater proportion of male pre-service teachers in this study use computer games more frequently than females, more male pre-service teachers would be likely to use virtual worlds in their science classes. The results of this study indicate that there is potential for a disparity in the use of ICT in science education, which depends on both gender and technical literacy. This suggests that when developing teacher training programs on the use of ICT in classrooms requires consideration on the fact that different levels of technological understanding and usage will impact upon the perceived benefits of a technology. As none of the teachers were frequent game players we cannot explore the issue of gender and ICT.

Pedagogical Issues

The use of collaboration in virtual worlds is worth raising here as many of the studies using collaborative computer supported learning have discussed the value of collaboration. Working in small teams and pairs can result in better learning outcomes. Studies have found that students in learning groups out-performed individual learners in a biology subject (Singhanayok & Hooper, 1998). Cooperative learning, or working with another person or team, encourages interaction with the tool (Singhanayok & Hooper, 1998); supports a range of learning styles (Wang, Hinn, & Kanfer, 2001); and allows group members to explain concepts to each other (Kramarski, 2004), which is a metacognitive strategy. Suthers and Hundhausen (2003) showed that a shared graphical representation made central characteristics of the learning object salient, which provided representational guidance to the learning discourse.

A number of authors have investigated collaboration in science education (Jeong & Chi, 2007; Suthers & Hundhausen, 2003). These authors identify *convergence* as the main advantage of a collaborative learning environment. Convergence occurs when students engage in collaborative inquiry learning and mutually construct understanding of the phenomenon (Roschelle, 1992). Jeong and Chi (2007) analysed conversations and determined that the convergence in their study could be attributed to collaborative interaction. They also found that a modest amount of convergence is typical in an unstructured, naturalistic collaborative learning situation. That suggests that in this study, which is unstructured, but in which students were randomly allocated to dyads, less convergence is expected. These authors say that convergence is due to interaction and shared input of ideas by the students.

The use of structure is also another pedagogical area that is relevant to virtual worlds. Structure can be both in world in the form of prompts and guidance or it can be external, such as teacher led or paper-based activities. The use of structure in problem solving activities has been addressed by a large body of research, which explores how learners can solve problems when supplied with the right structure, tools, and structures to do so. Structure in this context does not mean leading a student to the right answer, but rather supporting students in their approach to problem solving (Li & Lim, 2007). Structuring is often achieved through instructions such as written and verbal prompts, argumentation templates, questioning, supported collaboration activities, and modelling

(Ge & Land, 2004; Li & Lim, 2007). Structuring may be faded out or on-going and there is much debate about what is the most effective form of structure in complex problem solving activities.

Future Directions

The research team is going to be working with a cohort of pre-service science teachers to further develop the work started last year. This year we will focus on providing pre-service teaches with access to several online games and virtual worlds that are tied specifically to problem-based learning. We will be following the pre-service teachers when they go into the schools for their practicum and will be on hand to provide support and materials that they can use in their lessons. Our aim is to make it easy for the pre-service teachers to use the technology so that develop the confidence and skills to sustain their motivation to use these forms of technology when they move into the classroom.

Purpose

Before commencing any use of ICT, a teacher will need to decide on the purpose of the professional development. For example, will the training session be an introduction to online tools followed by games and immersive environments aimed at a specific area, such as inquiry learning for pre-service teachers or will it be a targeted training session in using *Whyville* and materials development. Many professional development courses in using ICT are not aimed at developing usable skills and materials for the classroom, so having a clear purpose is essential. It may also take several months to ensure that the technology that training session is aimed at is also useful in the classroom.

Medium

Decide on the medium. Will the professional development be aimed at single player or multiplayer virtual worlds, online games, or COTS. Decide whether to go for a virtual experience or to access an online game or activity. This will impact upon how the session is run.

Context

Any training needs to be context bound and subject specific. For example, if pre-service teachers are majoring in science or history they should be introduced to sites that are relevant to the subject.

Materials

It has been shown that the high cognitive load of virtual environments can results in frustration and confusions. So when designing materials, it is important to prime or provide sufficient background so that participants have a full understanding of the domain knowledge. This may sound relatively straight forward, but often these environments are marketed as being beneficial for open-ended problem exploration.

Sufficient Guided Practice

Educators and students need sufficient time to develop confidence in using virtual and game technologies, and it should not be assumed that technical literacy in one medium is applicable to another. Students are often presented as having high levels of technical literacy; however, this literacy is often domain specific, for example, being confident in using word processing software or social networking sites does not result in an understanding of game environments. Moreover, as one pre-service teacher, who was a self-confessed 'gamer' noted that different games require different skills and that it would take him a while to work out how to use *Virtual Singapura*. We found that using *Death in Rome* was manageable in a classroom lesson, and after a single run through, teachers were familiar with the game. On the other hand, after two training sessions in *Virtual Singapura*, teachers were still not confident with the technology. The differing levels of complexity of both the environment and the problem need to be weighted against time constraints.

Feedback and Materials Development

The development of materials that support learning in virtual worlds and deciding how best to support students in world through are still in their early stages. This research study has gone through numerous iterations of the materials development, and feedback from stakeholders involved in the study provided valuable insights into how to design the materials. One of the benefits of using a design-based research approach is that the relative expertise of members of the group, whether they are subject specific, technical or school-based, can result in modifications to both big picture and micro-elements of the materials. For example, the teachers provided big-picture feedback on including background historical information and microelements such as where to place different items in the instructions, such as moving an explanation several pages forward. Overall, we found that the feedback from teachers and students provided detailed insights into what worked and what was frustrating or lacking in pedagogical soundness.

Design Considerations

As with all forms of ICT, using virtual worlds and game technology in a classroom requires careful consideration of the design and implementation of the technology in order to present students with a valuable learning experience. Scenario-based virtual worlds are fun and motivational, and may present learners with opportunities to engage and visualize complex events and authentic environments. However, the investment in time for both the learners to learn how to use the world, and for development of the world itself is high, and they require ongoing technical assistance and upgrades. Schools need to have the appropriate bandwidth and facilities in order to run a virtual world. Teachers require extensive hands-on training in order to master the technology at a level where they can manage a classroom implementation of the world. So given these obvious and considerable constraints what elements of learning design do virtual worlds afford that may not otherwise be attainable in a normal classroom. Table 3 identifies the design affordances, issues, and considerations of scenario-based virtual worlds.

CONCLUSION

As with many emerging technologies used in education, we run the risk when using virtual worlds of throwing the technology at the students and expecting them to just learn because it is interesting. What has continued to come out of our research is that these experiences need to be carefully designed in order for the potential of these authentic, powerful, and complex learning environments to be met. We see this as the future trend in multi-user virtual worlds in science education: that the lessons we have learned from other

Table 3. Scenario-based virtual worlds: design affordances, issues, and considerations

Scenario-Based MUVEs		
Design Affordances	**Design Issues**	**Considerations**
• Thoughtfulness – students engage with scenario	• Memorization – lack of transfer from MUVE to 'real world'	• In class or 'in world' activities to ascertain what students are learning
• Whole task – see the complete picture	• Skills – students may have difficulty completing skill components	• Scaffolding and trucutre – identify initial weaknesses and pre-existing gaps in knowledge
• Diverse learning experience – student in control of learning experience	• Assessment – difficult to assess individual student use of MUVE	• Teachers can access data capture technology but time consuming. In class discussions and activities may complement different learning routes
• Breadth and depth of knowledge – students can focus on whole picture and small details	• Exposure – in order for students to notice all elements of MUVE will need time 'in world'	• Difficult for students to spend a lot of time 'in world' in a classroom environment
• Indirect learning – students learn through doing	• Assessment – difficult to ascertain if all students learn the necessary skills	• Classrooms and teaching still governed by expected outcomes
• Fun learning – MUVEs are engaging and motivating	• Attitude – student's may not view experience as serious	• Playing games often seen as less serious than teacher led classes
• Learner centred – learner controls experience	• Technical literacy – some students may lack technical literacy and skills to navigate through world	• Difficult for teachers to monitor the whole class – students can get lost or off task
• Natural learning – students learn through participating in virtual activities	• Inefficiency – students may take a considerable amount of time to master the environment	• The organization of supporting activities – guided inquiry or Productive Failure may compensate for time limitations
• Authentic – students can interact with 'real' artefacts and enhanced visual and audio environment	• Artificial – level of engagement 'in world' dependent on students	• MUVEs engage students in experience that they may not otherwise encounter, but still limited by fact that 'authentic' is still bound to a computer screen
• Reflection – students can reflect on actions	• Diversion – students may miss the learning opportunities	• Reflection will need to be guided.
• Teacher as facilitator – teacher can assist students with their own learning	• Teacher as technical support – many issues that arise are technical or linguistic	• Teachers may not be able to address all of the learning needs of students given the diversity of the environment

emerging technologies and from extensive work in the learning sciences, be incorporated into the design of the environment so that students can actually experience the virtual world to the best of their ability.

Given the technical problems that were encountered when using the virtual world it may be questioned as to why this chapter is titled as 'A MUVEing Success,' despite the problems there *have* been many successes. There was success in that the teachers found the experience to be positive and will participate in future studies, success in the pre-service teachers gaining access to a new technology, success in the students participating in the use of online activities, success in the collaborative aspects of the research and materials development, success in that we are finding new ways to use these innovative technologies. Overall, virtual worlds are a relatively new technology in educational contexts and developing a robust understanding of how best to use them will take time; while this happens, however, educators have access to a myriad of spaces and places that can motivate and engage students and have the potential to facilitate authentic and deep learning.

REFERENCES

Angeli, C. (2004). The effects of case-based learning on early childhood pre-service teachers' beliefs about the pedagogical uses of ICT. *Journal of Educational Media*, *29*(2), 139–151. doi:10.1080/1358165042000253302

Bagley, E., & Shaffer, D. W. (2009). When people get in the way: Promoting civic thinking through epistemic game play. *International Journal of Gaming and Computer-Mediated Simulations*, *1*(1). doi:10.4018/jgcms.2009010103

Bainbridge, W. S. (2007). The scientific research potential of virtual worlds. *Science*, *317*(5837), 472–476. doi:10.1126/science.1146930

Bandura, A. (1997). *Self-efficacy: The exercise of control*. New York, NY: W. H. Freeman and Company.

Barab, S. A., Dodge, T., Ingram-Goble, A., Volk, C., Peppler, K., & Pettyjohn, P. (2009). Pedagogical dramas and transformational play: Narratively-rich games for education. In Lurgel, I. A., Zagalo, N., & Petta, P. (Eds.), *Interactive Storytelling* (pp. 332–335). Heidelberg, Germany: Springer. doi:10.1007/978-3-642-10643-9_42

Barab, S. A., Hay, K. E., & Duffy, T. M. (1998). Grounded constructions and how technology can help. *TechTrends*, *43*(2), 15–23. doi:10.1007/BF02818171

Barab, S. A., Thomas, M., Dodge, T., Carteaux, R., & Tuzun, H. (2005). Making learning fun: Quest Atlantis, a game without guns. *Educational Technology Research and Development*, *53*(1), 86–107. doi:10.1007/BF02504859

Beatty, K., & Nunan, D. (2004). Computer-mediated collaborative learning. *System*, *32*, 165–183. doi:10.1016/j.system.2003.11.006

Dalgarno, B., & Lee, M. (2010). What are the learning affordances of 3-D virtual environments? *British Journal of Educational Technology*, *41*(1), 10–32. doi:10.1111/j.1467-8535.2009.01038.x

Davis, N., Preston, C., & Sahin, I. (2009). Training teachers to use new technologies impacts multiple ecologies: Evidence from a national initiative. *British Journal of Educational Technology*, *40*(5), 861–878. doi:10.1111/j.1467-8535.2008.00875.x

de Winter, J., Winterbottom, M., & Wilson, E. (2010). Developing a user guide to integrating new technologies in science teaching and learning: teachers' and pupils' perceptions of their affordances. *Technology, Pedagogy and Education*, *19*(2), 261–267. doi:10.1080/14759 39X.2010.491237

Dede, C. (1997). Rethinking: How to invest in technology. *Educational Leadership*, *55*(3), 12–16.

Dodge, T., Barab, S. A., Stuckey, B., Warren, S., Heiselt, C., & Stein, R. (2008). Children's sense of self: Learning and meaning in the digital age. *Journal of Interactive Learning Research*, *19*(2), 225–249.

Edelson, D. C., Gordin, D. N., & Pea, R. D. (1999). Addressing the challenges of inquiry-based learning through technology and curriculum design. *Journal of the Learning Sciences*, *8*(3/4), 391–450.

Eisner, E. W. (2000). Those who ignore the past...: 12 'easy' lessons for the next millennium. *Journal of Curriculum Studies*, *32*(2), 343–357. doi:10.1080/002202700182808

Ferdig, R. E. (2007). Preface: Learning and teaching with electronic games. *Journal of Educational Multimedia and Hypermedia*, *16*(3), 217–223.

Flores, F., Lopez, A., Gallegos, L., & Barojas, J. (2000). Transforming science and learning concepts of physics teachers. *International Journal of Science Education*, *22*(2), 197–208. doi:10.1080/095006900289958

Ge, X., & Land, S. M. (2004). A conceptual framework for scaffolding ill-structured problem-solving processes using question prompts and peer interactions. *Educational Technology Research and Development*, *52*(2), 5–22. doi:10.1007/BF02504836

Gee, J. P. (2003). Turning games into learning machines. *Game Developer*, *10*(9), 56.

Gee, J. P. (2005). Good video games and good learning. *Phi Kappa Phi Forum*, *85*(2), 33 - 37.

Gee, J. P., & Shaffer, D. W. (2010). Looking where the light is bad: Video games and the future of assessment. *EDge*, *6*(1), 1–19.

Gilllies, R. M. (2003). Structuring cooperative group work in classrooms. *International Journal of Educational Research*, *39*, 35–49. doi:10.1016/S0883-0355(03)00072-7

Goldstein, J. (2001). *Does playing violent video games cause aggressive behaviour.* Retrieved from http://culturalpolicy.uchicago.edu/papers/2001-video-games/goldstein.html

Goldsworthy, R. C., Barab, S. A., & Goldsworthy, E. L. (2000). The STAR project: Enhancing adolescents' social understanding through video-based, multimedia scenarios. *Journal of Special Education Technology*, *15*(2), 13–26.

Gregory, S., Lee, M., Ellis, A., Gregory, B., Wood, D., Hillier, M., et al. (2010). *Australian higher education institutions transforming the future of teaching and learning through virtual worlds.* Paper presented at the Curriculum, Technology & Transformation for an Unknown Future, AS-CILITE 2010. New York, NY.

Gros, B. (2003). The impact of digital games in education. *First Monday*, *8*(7).

Hennessy, S., Ruthven, K., & Brindley, S. (2005). Teacher perspectives on integrating ICT into subject teaching: commitment, constraints, caution, and change. *Journal of Curriculum Studies*, *37*(2), 155–192. doi:10.1080/0022027032000276961

Henriques, L. (2002). Preparing tomorrow's science teachers to use technology: An example from the field. *Contemporary Issues in Technology & Teacher Education*, *2*(1).

Herrington, J., Reeves, T. C., Oliver, R., & Woo, Y. (2004). Designing authentic activities in web-based courses. *Journal of Computing in Higher Education*, *16*(1), 3–29. doi:10.1007/BF02960280

Jacobson, M. J., June Lee, B. K., Hong Lim, S., & Hua Low, S. (2008). *An intelligent agent augmented multi-user virtual environment for learning science inquiry: Preliminary research findings.* Paper presented at the 2008 American Educational Association Conference. New York, NY.

Jacobson, M. J., Kim, B., Miao, C.-H., Shen, Z., & Chavez, M. (2009). Design perspectives for learning in virtual worlds. In Jacobson, M. J., & Reimann, P. (Eds.), *Designs for Learning Environments of the Future: International Perspectives from the Learning Sciences.* New York, NY: Springer. doi:10.1007/978-0-387-88279-6_5

Jeong, H., & Chi, M. T. H. (2007). Knowledge convergence and collaborative learning. *Instructional Science, 35*, 287–315. doi:10.1007/s11251-006-9008-z

Johnson, D. W., & Johnson, R. T. (1985). The internal dynamics of cooperative learning groups. In Slavin, R., Shlomo, S., Spencer, K., Hertz-Lazarowitz, R., Webb, C., & Schmuck, R. (Eds.), *Learning to Cooperate, Cooperating to Learn* (pp. 103–124). New York, NY: Plenum.

Johnson, L., Levine, A., Smith, R., Smythe, T., & Stone, S. (2009). *Horizon report: 2009 Australia - New Zealand edition.* Austin, TX: Horizon Report.

Kafai, Y. B., & Ching, C. C. (2001). Affordances of collaborative software design planning for elementary students' science talk. *Journal of the Learning Sciences, 10*(3), 323–363. doi:10.1207/S15327809JLS1003_4

Ketelhut, D., Nelson, B., Clarke, J., & Dede, C. (2010). A multi-user virtual environment for building and assessing higher order inquiry skills in science. *British Journal of Educational Technology, 41*(1), 56–68. doi:10.1111/j.1467-8535.2009.01036.x

Ketelhut, D. J., Dede, C., Clarke, J., & Nelson, B. (2006). *A multi-user virtual environment for building higher order inquiry skills in science.* Paper presented at the American Educational Research Association. Retrieved 22/07/2008, from http://muve.gse.harvard.edu/rivercityproject/research-publications.htm

Kozma, R. (2003). The material features of multiple representations and their cognitive and social affordances for science understanding. *Learning and Instruction, 13*, 205–226. doi:10.1016/S0959-4752(02)00021-X

Kramarski, B. (2004). Making sense of graphs: Does metacognitive instruction make a difference on students' mathematical conceptions and alternative conceptions? *Learning and Instruction, 14*, 593–619. doi:10.1016/j.learninstruc.2004.09.003

la Velle, L., Wishart, J., McFarlane, A., Brawn, R., & John, P. (2007). Teaching and learning with ICT within the subject culture of secondary school science. *Research in Science & Technological Education, 25*(3), 339–349. doi:10.1080/02635140701535158

Lee, D. (1997). Factors influencing the success of computer skills learning among in-service teachers. *British Journal of Educational Technology, 28*(2), 139–141. doi:10.1111/1467-8535.00018

Li, D., & Lim, C. P. (2007). Scaffolding online historical inquiry tasks: A case study of two secondary school classrooms. *Computers & Education, 50*, 1394–1410. doi:10.1016/j.compedu.2006.12.013

Maloney, J., & Simon, S. (2006). Mapping children's discussions of evidence in science to assess collaboration and argumentation. *International Journal of Science Education, 28*(15), 1817–1841. doi:10.1080/09500690600855419

Manlove, S., Lazonder, A. W., & de Jong, T. (2005). Regulative support for collaborative scientific inquiry learning. *Journal of Computer Assisted Learning, 22*, 87–98. doi:10.1111/j.1365-2729.2006.00162.x

McKerlich, R., & Anderson, T. (2007). Community of inquiry and learning in immersive environments. *Journal of Asynchronous Learning Networks, 11*(4).

Newmann, F. (1996). *Authentic achievement: Restructuring schools for intellectual quality.* San Francisco, CA: Jossey-Bass.

Reeves, T. C., Herrington, J., & Oliver, R. (2005). Design research: A socially responsible approach to instructional technology research in higher education. *Journal of Computing in Higher Education, 16*(2), 97–116. doi:10.1007/BF02961476

Rieber, L. P. (1996). Seriously considering play: Designing interactive learning environments based on the blending of microworlds, simulations, and games. *Educational Technology Research and Development, 44*(2), 43–58. doi:10.1007/BF02300540

Roschelle, J. (1992). Learning by collaborating: Convergent conceptual change. *Journal of the Learning Sciences, 2*(3), 235–276. doi:10.1207/s15327809jls0203_1

Shaffer, D. W. (2008). Education in the digital age. *Digital Kompetanse, 1*(3), 37–50.

Shaffer, D. W., & Gee, J. P. (Eds.). (2007). *Epistemic games as education for innovation.* Leicester, UK: British Journal of Educational Psychology.

Simmons, P. E., Emory, A., Carter, T., Coker, T., Finnegan, B., & Crockett, D. (1999). Beginning teachers: Beliefs and classroom actions. *Journal of Research in Science Teaching, 36*(8), 930–954. doi:10.1002/(SICI)1098-2736(199910)36:8<930::AID-TEA3>3.0.CO;2-N

Singhanayok, C., & Hooper, S. (1998). The effects of cooperative learning and learner control on students' achievement, option selections, and attitudes. *Educational Technology Research and Development, 46*(2), 17–32. doi:10.1007/BF02299787

Siorenta, A., & Jimoyiannis, A. (2008). Physics instruction in secondary schools: An investigation of teachers' beliefs towards physics laboratory and ICT. *Research in Science & Technological Education, 26*(2), 185–202. doi:10.1080/02635140802037328

Slavin, R. E. (1996). Research for the future: Research on cooperative learning and achievement: What we know, what we need to know. *Contemporary Educational Psychology, 21*, 43–69. doi:10.1006/ceps.1996.0004

Squire, K. (2007, September-October). Games, learning, and society: Building a field. *Educational Technology*, 51–54.

Squire, K. D. (2004). *Replaying history: Learning world history through playing "Civilization III".* (Unpublished Ph.D. Thesis). Indiana University. Indianapolis, IN.

Squire, K. D. (2005). Changing the game: What happens when video games enter the classroom?. *Innovate: Journal of Online Education, 1*(6).

Squire, K. D. (2006). From content to context: Videogames as designed experience. *Educational Researcher, 35*(8), 19–29. doi:10.3102/0013189X035008019

Squire, K. D., Barnett, M., Grant, J. M., & Higginbottom, T. (2004). *Electromagentism supercharged! Learning physics with digital simulation games.* Paper presented at the International Conference of the Learning Sciences. Santa Monica, CA.

Steinkuehler, C. A. (2006). Massively multiplayer online video gaming as participation in a discourse. *Mind, Culture, and Activity, 13*(1), 38–52. doi:10.1207/s15327884mca1301_4

Suthers, D. D., & Hundhausen, C., D. (2003). An experimental study of the effects of representational guidance on collaborative learning processes. *Journal of the Learning Sciences, 12*(2), 183–218. doi:10.1207/S15327809JLS1202_2

Urhahne, D., Schanze, S., Bell, T., Mansfield, A., & Holmes, J. (2010). Role of the teacher in computer-supported collaborative inquiry learning. *International Journal of Science Education, 32*(2), 221–243. doi:10.1080/09500690802516967

Wang, F., & Hannafin, M. J. (2005). Design-based research and technology-enhanced learning environments. *Educational Technology Research and Development, 53*(4), 5–23. doi:10.1007/BF02504682

Wang, X. C., Hinn, D. M., & Kanfer, A. G. (2001). Potential of computer-supported collaborative learning for learners with different learning styles. *Journal of Research on Technology in Education, 34*(1), 75–85.

Watson, W. R., Mong, C. J., & Harris, C. A. (2011). A case study of the in-class use of a video game for teaching high school history. *Computers & Education, 56*, 466–474. doi:10.1016/j.compedu.2010.09.007

Webb, M., & Cox, M. (2004). A review of pedagogy related to information and communications technology. *Technology, Pedagogy and Education, 13*(3), 235–286. doi:10.1080/14759390400200183

Webb, M. E. (2005). Affordances of ICT in science learning: implications for an integrated pedagogy. *International Journal of Science Education, 27*(6), 705–735. doi:10.1080/09500690500038520

Zacharia, Z. (2003). Beliefs, attitudes, and intentions of science teachers regarding the educational use of computer simulations and inquiry-based experiments in physics. *Journal of Research in Science Teaching, 40*(8), 792–823. doi:10.1002/tea.10112

ADDITIONAL READING

Azevedo, R., & Jacobson, M. J. (2008). Advances in scaffolding learning with hypertext and hypermedia: A summary and critical analysis. *Educational Technology Research and Development, 56*, 93–100. doi:10.1007/s11423-007-9064-3

Bailenson, J. N., Yee, N., Blascovich, J., Beall, A. C., Lundblad, N., & Jin, M. (2008). The use of immersive virtual reality in the learning sciences: Digital transformations of teachers, students, and social context. *Journal of the Learning Sciences, 17*(1), 102–141. doi:10.1080/10508400701793141

Barnett, M., Yamagata-Lynch, L., Keating, T., Barab, S. A., & Hay, K. E. (2005). Using virtual reality computer models to support student understanding of astronomical concepts. *Journal of Computers in Mathematics and Science Teaching, 24*(4), 333–356.

Kapur, M. (2006). *Productive failure.* Paper presented at the International Conference on Learning Science. Bloomington, IN.

Kapur, M. (2008). Productive failure. *Cognition and Instruction, 26*(3), 379–424. doi:10.1080/07370000802212669

Kapur, M., & Kinzer, C. K. (2009). Productive failure in CSCL groups. *International Journal of Computer-Supported Learning, 4*(1), 21–46. doi:10.1007/s11412-008-9059-z

Kolodner, J. L. (2006). Case-based reasoning. In Sawyer, K. (Ed.), *The Cambridge Handbook of the Learning Sciences* (pp. 225–242). Cambridge, UK: Cambridge University Press.

Mazur, J., & Lio, C. (2004). *Learner articulation in an immersive visualization environment.* Paper presented at the Conference on Human Factors in Computing Systems. Vienna, Austria.

Nelson, B. (2007). Exploring the use of individual, reflective guidance in an educational multi-user environment. *Journal of Science Education and Technology, 16*(1), 83–97. doi:10.1007/s10956-006-9039-x

Pathak, S. A., Jacobson, M. J., Kim, B., Zhang, B., & Feng, D. (2008). *Learning the physics of electricity with agent-based models: The paradox of productive failure.* Paper presented at the ICCE. Taiwan, China.

Rieber, L. P. (1996). Seriously considering play: Designing interactive learning environments based on the blending of microworlds, simulations, and games. *Educational Technology Research and Development, 44*(2), 43–58. doi:10.1007/BF02300540

Shaffer, D. W., & Gee, J. P. (Eds.). (2007). *Epistemic games as education for innovation.* Leicester, UK: British Journal of Educational Psychology.

VanLehn, K., Siler, S., Murray, C., Yamauchi, T., & Baggett, W. B. (2003). Why do only some events cause learning during human tutoring? *Cognition and Instruction, 21*(3), 209–249. doi:10.1207/S1532690XCI2103_01

KEY TERMS AND DEFINITIONS

Collaboration: Collaboration is a strategy that places two or more people together in a group to solve a problem or task. Collaboration requires a joint process.

Commercial Off The Shelf (COTS) Computer Games (COTS): COTS are games such as Civilization III that have been used in educational contexts.

Educational Games: Educational games are computer or video games designed for educational and not commercial purposes.

Inquiry: Inquiry is a process of inquiry that encourages students to critically analyse, interpretinterpret, and evaluate a range of sources;, to construct reasoned explanations, and to form hypothesis; to understand, deconstruct, evaluate, and synthesis synthesize different interpretations;, and to develop an understanding of motivation, causation, consequence, and empathy.

Multi-User Virtual Environment (MUVE): A MUVE is a virtual environment derived from game technology that has the following five criteria: a) an avatar that represents the participant, b) a 3D virtual environment, c) the ability to interact with artefacts and agents, d) participants can communicate with other participants and, in some instances, communicate with intelligent agents, and e) a 'real world' context that is created to provide an authentic experience that a student may not be able to encounter in a classroom environment.

Structure: Structure can include step by stepstep-by-step directives;, questions;, prompts;, written and oral tasks;, discussions and educational strategies aimed at guiding or directing a student through an activity.

Virtual Singapura: Virtual Singapura is a MUVE that is set in 19th Century Singapore. In this MUVE students explore the occurrence of epidemics, and try to identify the causes of the diseases.

ENDNOTES

1. Australian Federal Government Digital Education Revolution http://www.deewr.gov.au/Schooling/DigitalEducationRevolution/Pages/default.aspx

2. Quest Atlantis http://atlantis.crlt.indiana.edu/

3. Whyville http://www.whyville.net/smmk/nice

4. *Virtual Singapura* was developed in Singapore as part of a collaborative project between the Singapore Learning Sciences Laboratory (National Institute of Education) and Nanyang Technological University (http://155.69.101.53/wiki/index.php/Main_Page#Introduction).

5. We accessed *Death in Rome* a free online game developed by the BBC UK http://www.bbc.co.uk/history/ancient/ we used this for a scientific inquiry activity.

6. The Jason Project has a range of virtual worlds and educational games addressing topics such as marine ecosystems (http://www.jason.org/public/whatis/start.aspx).

7. NASA online games for kids has a range of games the are suitable for primary school students (http://www.nasa.gov/audience/forkids/kidsclub/flash/index.html).

8. NASA Jet Propulsion Lab has a range of online games for high school students (http://www.jpl.nasa.gov/kids/index.cfm).

9. BBC UK's website has a series of historical games. Some of the games such as *Death in Rome*, are useful for science as well as history (*UK* http://www.bbc.co.uk/history/interactive/games/).

Chapter 3
Using Virtual Environments to Motivate Students to Pursue STEM Careers:
An Expectancy–Value Model

Jason A. Chen
The College of William and Mary, USA

Nick Zap
Simon Fraser University, Canada

Chris Dede
Harvard University, USA

ABSTRACT

The purpose of this chapter is to bring a rigorous and well-studied theoretical framework of motivation to the study and design of virtual learning environments. The authors outline the key motivation constructs that compose Eccles and Wigfield's Expectancy-Value Theory (e.g., Eccles, et al., 1989; Wigfield & Eccles, 1992, 2000), and how it can be used in the creation of a virtual learning environment designed to promote students' interest in and motivation to pursue Science, Technology, Engineering, and Mathematics (STEM) careers. In addition, using Brophy's (1999) model of the motivated learner, the authors outline how this type of motivational virtual environment can be incorporated in classroom instruction to further bolster adolescents' motivation and competence in mathematics. Finally, they describe a NSF-funded project underway at Harvard's Graduate School of Education that seeks to develop a 4-day mathematics intervention, merging innovative technologies with regular classroom instruction to spark students' interest in STEM careers.

DOI: 10.4018/978-1-4666-2670-6.ch003

INTRODUCTION

There is no learning without engagement, a situation that happens all too often in our typically lecture-based classrooms. At the same time, engagement without learning, which frequently happens in today's digital worlds, is not a healthy alternative. Some claim that online gaming is the answer to engaging and motivating students in their academic work. Yet, students can frequently be engaged in these virtual worlds without actually learning anything or being more academically motivated. In this chapter, we argue that Eccles and Wigfield's Expectancy-Value theory (e.g., Eccles, 1983, 1987, 1993; Eccles, et al., 1989; Wigfield, 1994; Wigfield & Eccles, 1992, 2000) offers researchers, educators, and designers useful and theoretically grounded motivation constructs that can be empirically studied in educational contexts. These constructs potentially provide a powerful way of linking engagement and learning.

In the first part of the chapter, we provide an overview of the theoretical frameworks in which prominent *expectancy* and *value* motivation constructs are based. In the second part of the chapter, we situate motivation within a larger picture—Brophy's (1999) model of the motivated learner, which extends Vygotsky's (1978) cognitive Zone of Proximal Development (ZPD) by incorporating a motivational ZPD. As a case study for the application of Brophy's model of the motivated learner, we describe a NSF-funded project underway at Harvard's Graduate School of Education called *Transforming the Engagement of Students in Learning Algebra* (TESLA). The chapter ends with a description of the design decisions in creating a motivating virtual environment for mathematics students in Grades 5-8, along with implications for educational practice.

EXPECTANCY-VALUE MODELS OF MOTIVATION

Although there has been a wealth of research exploring motivation within technological environments, very few of these studies employ frameworks that are grounded in well-studied theories of motivation (Moos & Marroquin, 2010). Eccles and Wigfield's Expectancy-Value theory of motivation (e.g., Eccles, 1983, 1987, 1993; Eccles, et al., 1989; Wigfield, 1994; Wigfield & Eccles, 1992, 2000) provides a useful framework for understanding students' beliefs about how competent they are and what they value within the context of their academic studies. The motivation constructs we describe below are theoretically grounded and have been extensively studied in educational contexts.

Expectancy Beliefs

Students are motivated toward or away from particular activities by answering the question, "can I do this?" This question lies at the heart of the expectancy component of Eccles and Wigfield's model. In this section of the chapter, we describe the following three expectancy constructs: causal attributions, implicit theories of ability, and self-efficacy. We first situate each construct within its theoretical home, and then describe its correlates and antecedents.

Causal attributions: Imagine you have just failed an important math test. What do you do when you discover this troubling news? According to contemporary attribution theorists, you are likely to search for a cause to your failure. Perhaps you failed because you were in a bad mood that day. It is also possible that you believed the test to be too difficult, or because you did not apply the appropriate study strategies when preparing for the test. You might also believe that you simply do not have the math "smarts" necessary to do well on math tests. According to Bernard Weiner (1979, 1984, 1985), students attempt to find the causes of their academic successes and failures. These *attributions* can be categorized using three dimensions: *locus*, which refers to whether a cause is located internal or external to the student; *stability*, which refers to whether the cause changes over time or is relatively persistent; and *controllability*, which refers to whether the cause can be influenced by the student or not. Table 1 illustrates these dimensions and provides examples of each one.

Research in academic settings on attributions typically show that the types of attributions students make have a significant impact on the effort they put forth and how long they will persist, especially in the face of failures. When students attribute failures or difficulties to internal and controllable causes (e.g., inappropriate strategies or insufficient effort), they tend to put forth more effort and persist in the face of difficulties more so than if they attribute these failures to external or uncontrollable causes (e.g., bad luck or lack of ability). Consider, for example, students who believe that they failed their math test because they did not study for the test the right way. If the cause of failure is an inappropriate strategy, these students have reason to believe that if, in the future, they do study using the appropriate strategies, their efforts will be rewarded. However, if students attribute their failures to the fact that the math tests their teacher gives are too difficult, these students have little reason to believe that anything they do will result in a better test score.

Attributions may also have an effect on students' emotional and affective states. Weiner (1986) has shown that students who believe that they succeeded on a math test due to internal causes such as long-term effort or "math smarts" are more likely to experience an elevated sense of self-esteem, whereas failure attributions based on these internal causes may result in feelings of shame or reduced self-esteem. In contrast, attributing successes or failures to external causes (e.g., teacher help or teacher favoritism) are less likely to affect self-esteem. Instead, students are more likely to experience feelings of gratitude (successes attributed to external causes) or anger (failures attributed to external causes).

Clearly, the attributions that students make when they succeed or fail have important motivational consequences. However, how do they arise? Graham and Williams (2009) list a number of attributional antecedents: Students' previous experiences can bias how they view future endeavors. For example, if students have always done poorly in mathematics, this belief is likely to influence the types of attributions they make. Similarly, students' sensitivity to social comparisons can affect the attributions they make. For example, receiving a low grade when everyone else performed well can make certain attributions (e.g., "I just wasn't feeling very well that day") more likely than others (e.g., "the test was too hard").

Students also tend to see effort and ability as inversely related (Kun & Weiner, 1973; Nicholls, 1978). For example, if two students received high grades on the same test, the student who studied

Table 1. Three dimensions of attribution theory with examples

	Internal		External	
	Controllable	**Uncontrollable**	**Controllable**	**Uncontrollable**
Stable	Long-term effort	Ability	Teacher Bias	Difficulty of Task
Unstable	Knowledge or Strategy use	Health or Mood	Peer or teacher help	Luck

the least is typically seen as the more able student because this student exerted less effort with maximal gain.

One antecedent to attributions that is especially relevant to academic situations concerns teacher feedback, in the form of indirect cues (e.g., emotional responses). Graham (1984) showed that a student might use her teachers' emotional responses to infer why she failed. If teachers communicate sympathy after failure, a student is more likely to attribute her failure to low ability. However, if teachers communicate anger or frustration, a student is likely to attribute her failure to insufficient effort (Graham, 1984). We will we save a more in-depth discussion of teacher feedback in the form of praise for later, when we discuss implicit theories of ability.

Implicit theories of ability: According to Dweck and Leggett (1988), students tend toward one of two different personal theories about the nature of their intellectual ability. Those who adopt an *entity* view of ability are more inclined to believe that abilities are relatively static characteristics that cannot be changed. Those who espouse an *incremental* view of ability are more likely to believe that abilities are changeable and thus within one's control. These implicit theories create a meaning system in which ability and effort are given disproportionate weighting—students with an incremental theory are apt to place more import on effort, whereas those with an entity theory tend to place more weight on ability. Individuals' implicit theories of ability can also be domain specific. For example, some students may believe that their math ability is a relatively stable entity but that their abilities in social studies are increasable (Stipek & Gralinsky, 1996).

Dweck and her colleagues have shown that the two theories of ability lead students down two different motivational paths. A fixed theory engenders within students a desire to either show off how smart they are (performance approach goal orientation) or to hide the fact that they are not smart enough (performance avoid goal orien-

tation). In other words, holding a fixed view of ability encourages students to either flaunt what they have or hide what they do not have. For these students, their primary aim is to achieve the highest grade and to show others how smart they are, whereas learning for the sake of learning plays a less important role.

An incremental theory of ability, in contrast, engenders a mastery goal orientation. In other words, students who believe that their abilities are increasable are more apt to learn for the sake of learning. For these students, learning the material is of primary importance, whereas showing others how smart they are is less important.

As in attribution theory, Dweck and her colleagues contend that these two different self-theories color the ways in which students view the value of effort. Those who believe that their abilities are fixed tend to devalue the importance of effort and consider natural ability to be most important. Those who hold a fixed view of ability are likely to believe that, if they cannot figure out a math problem on the first couple of attempts, then additional effort will be of no value because extra work will not change one's ability to solve the math problem. As a result, during times when these students are doing well, this fixed view of ability may not pose an impediment to their success; but, when they encounter setbacks, these beliefs become maladaptive.

In contrast, students who hold an incremental view of ability are likely to view effort in a positive light. If these students do not at first succeed, they are more likely to seek out alternative strategies or exert more effort to succeed. Instead of attributing their failures to lack of smarts or to an unfair teacher, these students are more likely than their fixed theory peers to say things like, "I didn't study enough," or "I didn't study the right way." In essence, students who hold an incremental theory believe that they are in control of their academic success.

Finally, Dweck and her colleagues contend that these two self-theories ultimately lead to two different achievement outcomes. Fixed theorists who hold performance goal orientations are likely to experience academic success *only if* they perceive themselves to be highly competent (Dweck & Leggett, 1988). If, however, they are not confident with their ability to do well, these students are likely to do poorly. Those who hold an incremental theory, in contrast, are likely to experience academic success regardless of their perceived competence.

The implications of research on implicit theories seem clear: Promote an incremental theory and avoid creating a fixed theory. However, how are these beliefs engendered in academic settings? Dweck argues that the most salient factor that promotes these beliefs is the *praise* that significant others (e.g., parents and teachers) provide to students. Contrary to popular belief, not all praise is equal, according to Dweck and her colleagues. Some praise directs attention to students' "smarts" (or lack thereof), whereas other forms of praise directs attention the effort and strategies students used to achieve success. By praising students for their abilities, teachers may be inadvertently promoting the idea that abilities are an entity that students either do or do not possess. In contrast, by praising students for the effort and care they put into doing their work and the strategies they employed, teachers communicate the idea that the ability to succeed is a skill that can be augmented.

Self-efficacy: The third and final expectancy construct that has received considerable attention is self-efficacy, which Albert Bandura (1997) defined as one's perceived capabilities to learn or accomplish tasks at designated levels of performance. The self-efficacy construct is situated within a larger framework—Bandura's (1986) social cognitive theory, which posits that human behavior is a product of people's own past actions, personal factors such as their thoughts and beliefs, and individuals' environmental conditions. A large body of research has shown that academic self-efficacy is related to key motivation constructs such as causal attributions, achievement goal

orientations, academic help seeking, anxiety, and value. Academic self-efficacy has also been shown to predict college students' choice of academic major and their career choices (Brown & Lent, 2006).

Self-efficacy has also been shown to ultimately be related to students' academic achievement (see Pajares & Urdan, 2006). The importance of these self-beliefs is emphasized by Bandura (1997) himself: "People's level of motivation, affective states, and actions are based more on what they believe that on what is objectively true" (p. 2). Teachers are all too familiar with the highly capable student who, beset by his own self-doubts, underperforms on academic tasks. Likewise, there are many accounts of students with very weak academic preparation who still manage to achieve at high levels.

Given the importance of self-efficacy beliefs, researchers have begun to turn their attention to the antecedents of self-efficacy. According to Bandura (1997), self-efficacy is formed by how people interpret information from four sources. The most powerful source is the interpreted result of one's past performance, or *mastery experience*. As individuals engage in tasks and activities, they interpret the results from these experiences and form conceptions about how capable they are in engaging in subsequent related tasks and activities. Students who view their past accomplishments in a positive light are likely to experience a boost in their self-efficacy. Experiences viewed as unsuccessful are likely to have the opposite effect.

Self-efficacy is also influenced by the observation of others' activities. These *vicarious experiences* are thought to be most influential when individuals are uncertain of the standards by which proficiency in an activity are measured. Social models, particularly those individuals perceived as similar (such as classmates), often act as a point of comparison as students form conceptions of their own academic capability.

A third source of self-efficacy comes from the *verbal and social persuasions* that individuals receive from influential others such as teachers, parents, and peers. Encouraging feedback and judgments bolster students' self-efficacy to perform a task, whereas deflating messages undermine it. Bandura (1986) argued that these deflating messages may actually be more effective in lowering self-efficacy than encouraging messages are at raising it.

The fourth hypothesized source comes from individuals' *physiological and affective states* such as anxiety, stress, and fatigue. Interpretations of these states often serve as indicators of students' competence. Accordingly, students who view a heightened level of anxiety as threatening are generally less confident in their academic capabilities than are those who interpret these feelings as energizing.

Information conveyed through these four sources is not inherently informative. Rather, it must be selected, weighted, and incorporated into individuals' judgments of personal efficacy. For example, an elevated heart rate and shaky hands may be the main focus of one test taker's attention, to the point that they are debilitating, but for another student such physiological states may serve as an invigorating motivator. Therefore, information from each of the four sources exerts its influence on self-efficacy only after being cognitively processed by the individual.

Value Beliefs

Now that we have reviewed various constructs about how expectancy influences learning, we turn our attention to a second important component of expectancy-value theory: value beliefs. To be motivated to do something, students must not only believe that they have the competence to do it, but they also need to see the *value* of doing it. Students can easily decide that they are highly capable at succeeding in math; but, if they do not see the point of becoming proficient, there is no reason for them to exert the necessary effort to succeed.

This is a central premise of the expectancy-value framework of motivation.

Eccles and Wigfield (2002) suggest that there are four major components to this value component: *attainment value*, which is the importance of doing well on a given task; *intrinsic value*, which is the enjoyment one gains from doing a task; *utility value*, which is defined as how a task fits into an individual's future plans or personal agenda; and *cost*, which refers to what the individual has to give up in order to do a task and how much effort must be exerted. Research has shown that students' task values predict both their intention to pursue a task and whether they actually do pursue it (Battle & Wigfield, 2003; Durik, Vida, & Eccles, 2006; Simpkins, Davis-Kean, & Eccles, 2006).

One important note we make is that Brophy (2009) has argued the career choices people make are often more about value than they are about perceived competence or expectancies of success. When young people think of possible careers to pursue, many people close the door on an entire field of possibilities either because they know nothing about what is involved with them, or because they perceive these careers or jobs as unappealing. Once students do select a group of careers to pursue (e.g., STEM careers), it may be true that they begin whittling down those possibilities due to self-efficacy or other expectancy beliefs. However, there can still be a further focusing that involves a sense of wanting to belong or a seeking of rewarding experiences that drives individuals to their ultimate career.

There has been little empirical or theoretical work outlining the antecedents of value beliefs. However, some results suggest that parents' and teachers' feedback concerning the usefulness and importance of certain activities help form students' beliefs about value (Wigfield, Eccles, Schiefele, Roeser, & Davis-Kean, 2006). Eccles (2005) has also suggested that perceived cultural norms may have an influence on the value that students place on particular activities. For example, if students perceive computer science to be a field dominated by men and White and Asian ethnicities, then women and students of color may likely shun this field, seeing it as culturally unsuitable.

Motivation and Instruction: Brophy's Model of the Motivated Learner

One of the tenets of Vygotsky's (1978) Zone of Proximal Development (ZPD) is the notion that students should be continually challenged within a zone where the skills and knowledge required for successful completion of the task are slightly out of reach for where the student is presently functioning. However, through guidance, feedback, and sufficient instruction, students can overcome these challenges in ways that are not overly taxing. Brophy (1999) has suggested that such a concept should also be brought to the study of motivation. His concept of a motivational Zone of Proximal Development postulates that there should be a match between the learner's knowledge and experiences and the ways in which learning tasks are presented. By connecting the learning task to students' personal lives, teachers can arouse students' interests in pursuing the activity.

In essence, a learning environment that helps students operate within their motivational Zone of Proximal Development includes teachers or other mentors who enable their students to appreciate the value of learning opportunities and to connect them to students' personal lives and agendas. These "teachers and other mentors" to whom Brophy referred can be students' classroom teachers or even well designed technological activities, as we discuss below. Indeed, Brophy (2004) posited that game-like features help promote learning and motivation and are typically better at accomplishing these goals than are typical commercial games. That said, whereas many game-like activities can help enhance motivation and learning, some games, especially competitive ones or ones that activate students' anxieties, distract from learning,

and can frustrate learners. To better understand how this motivational theory should guide instructional design, we next present a case study,

INNOVATIVE TECHNOLOGY AS A MOTIVATIONAL TOOL: A CASE STUDY OF TESLA

How can motivation based on expectancy-value constructs and Brophy's (1999) model of the motivated learner be incorporated into innovative instructional technologies? This is a main question we are addressing in a new NSF-funded project at Harvard's Graduate School of Education, titled *Transforming the Engagement of Students in Learning* Algebra (TESLA). For this project, we are creating a 4-day mathematics intervention, two days of which will involve one of three technology-based motivational inductions for students in Grades 5-8. The first induction we describe is a Multi-User Virtual Environment (MUVE) that serves as a game-like activity introducing students to the concepts to be learned later in the 2-day classroom math lesson through their avatars' active involvement in an event. The second induction is also based on the MUVE, but students participating in this activity are not interacting directly with the virtual world from a first-person perspective. Rather, students are vicariously watching computer agents in the MUVE think through and model different ways of solving various mathematical problems, with one of these agents being someone with whom the student can identify. The third induction provides a contrast to the MUVE interface, utilizing a non-immersive, passive video presentation typical of what a math teacher might use to foster student engagement. By comparing these three inductions, we can study how the effects of alternative types of motivation might work for various kinds of students.

Like most video games, our two MUVE activities immerse students in a 3-dimensional virtual environment where students are able to either take on the identity of a STEM professional and solve mathematical puzzles in an engaging manner (the first activity), or can vicariously observe others solving these puzzles (the second activity). Unlike commercial video games, however, our activities are designed to target specific mathematical learning goals and motivation variables. In designing a game-like environment that was both instructionally and motivationally sound, we removed elements of commercial games that either undermine or distract from the learning and motivational goals (e.g., competition, time-sensitive pressures, and overt performance goals). Below, we describe each of the two MUVE-based activities and sketch the third technology-based induction. We also describe the ways we used motivation theory to inform our design decisions.

Alternative Technology-Based Motivational Inductions

What are the goals of our 4-day math intervention? First, the lessons are designed to teach students to identify mathematical patterns (e.g., the Fibonacci sequence) that arise while collecting complex data. We also wanted students to be able to generalize these mathematical patterns in such a way that they could use them to solve novel but similar problems. Within the context of the two MUVE inductions, we created a number of cognitive scaffolds to facilitate students' understanding of the mathematical concepts to be taught, as well as motivational scaffolds to aid students in developing their mathematics motivation.

First Induction: Students as Active Protagonists in a MUVE

During the course of the first day of the intervention, students receiving the first induction solve a total of two puzzles in the MUVE that involve recognizing mathematical patterns in the context of a space rescue mission (see Figure 1 for a screenshot of the interface). The first puzzle allows students to become accustomed to the virtual world and how to function and interact in it. As such, the mathematical puzzle is relatively easy so that students can familiarize themselves with the controls and so that they can experience an early success to build their self-efficacy. This first puzzle is similar to a combination-lock problem in that students must identify all possible ways that three numbers can be combined to produce a unique 3-digit number (see Figure 2 for a simple illustration).

When students finish this first puzzle, they proceed to a more complex and difficult second puzzle. This second puzzle is broken down into many smaller steps to scaffold students' learning and motivation. If students were given the entire puzzle all at once, many would be overwhelmed and could quickly become discouraged. This second puzzle serves as the entry point for the 2-day mathematics lesson on the second and third day of the intervention.

For this puzzle, students encounter a door that is locked. Next to the door is a box with some complex circuitry. Parts of this circuit board are complete, but the great majority of it is broken. Students must "fix" each section of the circuit board by building circuits with 1- and 2-unit length fuses. The circuits that must be constructed differ in size—at first, students build a 1-unit long circuit (only one possible combination if presented with only 1- and 2-unit long fuses). Then they build circuits that are 2-units long (2 possibilities: 1+1, and 2), 3-units long (3 possibilities: 1+1+1; 2+1; and 1+2), and so forth, until they reach a circuit that is 9-units in length (55 possible combinations) (see Figure 3 for a simple illustration).

What emerges from this activity is the fact that a Fibonacci series underlies the pattern (1, 2, 3, 5, 8, 13, 21, 34, 55). Because pupils are not explicitly taught the Fibonacci series in school, most students are likely to enter this activity unaware

Figure 1. Screenshot of interface for the immersive virtual world

Figure 2. Illustration of first puzzle

Figure 3. Screenshot of one section of puzzle 2

of this pattern. However, due to its simplicity, the activity is well within students' cognitive zone of proximal development. We have designed this activity with many cognitive scaffolds in the beginning and progressively remove them as they progress. For example, students start out by building actual circuits that are 1-unit, 2-units, and 3-units in length using only 1-unit and 2-unit long fuses. By building each circuit, students are able to see for themselves how many circuits can be built at each height.

When students reach circuits that are 4- and 5-units long, the number of circuits that can be built at each height increases dramatically. Building each individual circuit becomes not only more difficult, but also more tedious. Therefore, students are shown all the different combinations that can be built at 3-units high (e.g., 1 + 1 + 1; 2 + 1; and 1+2 for a total of 3 circuits) and 4-units high. From this information, they must make an educated guess as to how many circuits can be made, using 1- and 2-unit length fuses, when the circuit is 5-units in length. Students are no longer building this circuit from scratch (removing a scaffold). If they guess incorrectly, feedback is provided to students so that they can begin to build the individual circuits in a systematic and orderly fashion.

As students progress through this step to more complicated circuits (6-, 7-, 8-, and 9- units high), more scaffolds are removed so that students are progressively given more autonomy and responsibility for providing the correct response. Again, however, appropriate feedback is provided every time a student does not generate the correct response. At the end (for the 9-unit long circuit that requires 55 unique combinations), the environment is constructed so that students are not given the opportunity to build the circuits if their initial estimate is incorrect. Rather, students are given a visual cue showing the entire series of circuits that have been constructed and highlighting how many circuits were built at each length (1, 2, 3, 5,

8, etc.); students are then asked if they can identify a pattern from these numbers.

To heighten engagement, for every successful circuit students build, they receive a "key," which is a square piece with a design on it. These keys are used to unlock the door in the end; when they are all interconnected, they form the golden spiral, which is a way to help students see the connection between the Fibonacci series and the golden spiral. This design decision was made in an effort to balance the importance of having minor extrinsic rewards with the need to provide intrinsic motivation in the form of an "ah ha" moment when students see the connection between the numerical series and the aesthetically interesting golden spiral, which can be found in nature as a Nautilus shell.

Recall that, in Brophy's (1999) model of a motivated learner, he suggests providing educational activities that are within both the cognitive and motivational zones of proximal development. This MUVE was designed such that cognitive scaffolds provide the necessary increasing levels of difficulty and the appropriate feedback for students to succeed. We also have designed the MUVE with motivational scaffolds that help students recognize that they have the competence to succeed in mathematics (i.e., building self-efficacy), and we have ensured that the content students are learning is interesting and connected to real life (i.e., connecting the Fibonacci series to nature, in the form of a Nautilus shell).

In addressing some other expectancy constructs in the expectancy-value theoretical framework, we took care that students attributed their successes and failures to factors that were internal and controllable. For example, we debated whether, in the second puzzle, students should be given a time limit within which they should finish the puzzles. However, this idea of including a time limit was discarded because students who fail the task (which could be a substantial proportion of the students) would make the unfortunate attribution about the cause of their failure as something that was external to themselves, but *uncontrollable*. If students failed because they believed they lacked sufficient time to be successful, they are likely to experience frustration at the activity or think of the activity as meaningless and unhelpful. In designing the activity such that time is not a factor, and that appropriate strategies are at the heart of the activity, we helped ensure that students would make adaptive rather than maladaptive attributions for their successes and failures.

Furthermore, to focus students on the fact that strategies are at the heart of successfully solving the mathematics problems, we designed the MUVE such that students receive the implicit message that their ability to successfully solve complex mathematical puzzles is dependent on strategies that are well within their own personal control. Successful completion is not dependent on some innate mathematical intelligence that is completely out of their personal control. This design element serves to bolster students' incremental theory of ability and counteract the idea that ability is fixed.

These engagement scaffolds are designed to help students enter the motivational zone of proximal development. By equipping students with the beliefs that they are competent in solving mathematical puzzles, and that these puzzles are not isolated and completely unrelated to real-life, we are helping students enter the second and third days of the math intervention with the cognitive *and* motivational propensities that help ensure optimal learning.

Second Induction: Students as Vicarious Participants in a MUVE

The second technology-based induction was based on the game-like MUVE. However, this *vicarious* activity was created as a video where students watched a 5-minute video clip of a young, real-life, STEM professional who talked about the nature of the work they do (e.g., designing astronaut

space suits), the difficulties they encountered in their K-12 math and science classes, and how they were able to overcome these difficulties. We are developing a number of these videos using a range of demographic attributes of the STEM professionals, so that most students can experience a video in which they individually identify with the person whom they are viewing.

After this clip finishes, students are able to watch a computer-generated agent that looks like the STEM professional they just watched solve the same series of puzzles that were described above in the first induction. This computer-generated agent leads a team of scientists in attempting to solve these puzzles. The student is a vicarious bystander who has the privilege of hearing the conversations of the team.

By listening to the conversations of the team members solving the puzzles, students are able to learn how to solve the puzzles through modeling. The agents convey ideas and demonstrate strategies for learning about how to recognize mathematical patterns. However, these computerized agents do not *only* model cognitive information. They also model *motivational* and *affective* information to help students understand the importance of learning the material and the importance of persisting and figuring out the correct strategies.

In addition, the 5-minute video interview of the STEM professional is meant to convey the message to students that, not only does persistence pay off affectively, but it also can result in a personally rewarding STEM career. Because the models in the interview are young, are in careers that students are apt to view as attractive (e.g., space suit designer for NASA), and are racially/ethnically diverse. We hope that students can readily identify with the role model to whom they are matched and can reap the motivational benefits more easily than if the models were perceived as completely dissimilar to the students.

This principle is congruent with Bandura's (1997) contention that self-efficacy beliefs are formed through vicarious experiences, but that these vicarious experiences are most powerful only when students see the models as similar to themselves. Although there is not much consistent empirical evidence informing us about the criteria that students use to identify similar models, we plan to initiate several pilots to investigate how students identify appropriate vicarious models. Our hope is that this information will help us refine our technological interventions to more finely target students' vicarious experiences.

Third Induction: Students Passively Assimilating Information

We are still developing the details of our third induction, which will use a video-based intervention to motivate students. The video segment will consist of a mixture of documentary material (e.g., the beauty of patterns in nature) and material from the entertainment industry (e.g., science fiction movie segments that involve pattern recognition, such as *Stargate*). This induction is designed to provide a contrast to the MUVEs typical of what a mathematics teacher might use to motivate students.

Inclusion of Other Theories about Instructional Design

Contrasting Our Approach to the ARCS model: Components of these theoretically rigorous motivational frameworks have been used before in Keller's (1987a, 1987b, 1999) ARCS model for instructional design. The ARCS model is based on applying the four factors of Attention, Relevance, Confidence, and Satisfaction to promote and sustain motivation. An instrument, the Instructional Materials Motivation Survey (IMMS), was developed by Keller to address each of these four factors. However, we believe that, by using constructs housed within sound psychological theory (e.g., self-efficacy or implicit theories of

ability), educators, researchers, and designers can more effectively assess participants' motivation.

For example, the IMMS assessment, though attempting to assess things like "confidence," does not validly assess self-efficacy. Bandura (1997) argued that:

The construct of self-efficacy differs from the colloquial term "confidence." Confidence is a nonspecific term that refers to strength of belief but does not necessarily specify what the certainty is about. I can be supremely confident that I will fail at an endeavor. Perceived self-efficacy refers to belief in one's agentive capabilities that one can produce given levels of attainment. A self-efficacy belief, therefore, includes both an affirmation of a capability level and the strength of that belief. Confidence is a catchword rather than a construct embedded in a theoretical system (p. 383).

Nevertheless, the ARCS model was influential in the way we designed our technology activities that went beyond what expectancy-value constructs offered. For example, Attention (from Keller's ARCS model) can be aroused using: 1) *Perceptual arousal*, which uses uncertainty and environmental context; 2) *Inquiry arousal*, which stimulates motivation through the use of challenge and problems; and 3) *Variability*, which promotes motivation through change. Grabbing and sustaining students' attention is not something that is inherently a part of the expectancy-value framework. Yet, this is highly important when designing technological activities for students.

Our 3-D immersive game-like environment implemented challenging puzzles to meet these attention needs. Active participation in solving the puzzles promotes engagement while providing enough motivational and content scaffolding to keep the player motivated to continue. Furthermore, we designed each puzzle to be more sophisticated and technologically advanced than the previous ones that students have encountered.

By increasing how challenging the puzzles are and by varying the context in which students are immersed, we hope to promote students' ongoing motivation to engage with the environment and therefore to continue learning more sophisticated mathematical patterns.

Wlodkowski's time-continuum model: School-aged children living in today's technology-rich culture are accustomed to using technology to know and understand themselves and the world around them. For this reason, it seems clear that mathematics instruction that is both motivating and intellectually rigorous for today's 21st century learner will require both well-designed technological activities and classroom instruction that is seamlessly tied together. For this reason, we used Wlodkowski's (1985, 1989) Time-Continuum Model to help us inject motivationally relevant material at appropriate times. The Time-Continuum Model specifies three stages for learning that occur before, during, and after instruction to help bolster students' motivation. In a sense, the model aids instructional designers in designing and implementing material that will situate students in their optimal motivational zone of proximal development.

The first stage occurs before instruction begins, and focuses on the attitudes and needs of the students. In TESLA, for example, we designed the 4-day intervention such that students would experience a technology-based motivational activity before classroom instruction began. By doing this, students are given the opportunity to explore the content in a fun and rewarding context before beginning formal mathematics instruction. In the first two inductions, the experience of interacting with the content in a 3-D immersive game-like environment that is relevant to learners provides a context of learning that is different from the classroom. Self-directed exploration of the content provides a safe and fun environment for the introduction of the two-day lesson.

The second phase of Wlodkowski's model occurs during instruction. In this stage, attention is focused on increasing students' stimulation and affect. Wlodkowski provided several ways to address students' stimulation and affect during instruction. For example, teachers should make use of relevant questions, different presentation styles, and modes of instruction to keep students stimulated while learning. As an illustration, during the second and third days of our mathematics intervention, students are exposed to a problem-based and inquiry-oriented math lesson. Teachers ask students interesting questions and allow students to work in small groups to brainstorm strategies for solving mathematical problems that are similar to the ones they were introduced to in the technology activities. Furthermore, because the mathematical patterns are explored in the classroom using physical manipulatives instead of digital ones, students are given the opportunity to understand the mathematical concepts using a different context, thereby further bolstering their mathematical understanding.

The final phase of the model focuses on competence and reinforcement after instruction. Wlodkowski argues that the learning experience should end with a strong message that emphasizes student competence through reinforcement. This is best done using targeted and personalized feedback. With TESLA, for example, on Day 4, students are allowed to return to the 3-D immersive environment to explore and test their understanding of the content of the two day lesson. Students are able to see new puzzles that extend and reinforce what they have learned over the course of the past two days of classroom instruction. Feedback and progress in the immersive environment provide the student with necessary feedback of their understanding of the content. The staggered content and motivational scaffolds that are built into the immersive environment reinforce students' beliefs that they possess the knowledge and skills, as well as the competence necessary to succeed in learning mathematics.

CONCLUSION

Our purpose in the TESLA project is to bring a rigorous and well-studied theoretical framework of academic motivation to the study and design of virtual learning environments. We also hope that, by providing a case study of an NSF-funded project underway at the Harvard Graduate School of Education, we could illustrate heuristics for how motivation theory informed the design of our virtual environments, and how Keller's ARCS model and Wlodkowski's Time-Continuum model aided the design of our overall mathematics intervention. By incorporating innovative technologies into a 4-day mathematics lesson for middle school students, we intend to target a "sweet spot" that resides at the intersection of cognitive and motivational readiness. The technology activities bolster students' motivation; and the classroom lessons, framed in problem-based and inquiry-oriented pedagogical practices, support students' cognitive development in learning mathematics. In so doing, we hope to prepare both competent and confident learners who are excited about pursuing the types of careers that are rapidly growing in a technology-based economy.

REFERENCES

Bandura, A. (1997). *Self-efficacy: The exercise of control*. New York, NY: Freeman.

Brophy, J. (1999). Toward a model of the value aspects of motivation in education: Developing appreciation for particular learning domains and activities. *Educational Psychologist, 34*, 75–85. doi:10.1207/s15326985ep3402_1

Dweck, C. S., & Leggett, E. L. (1988). A social-cognitive approach to motivation and personality. *Psychological Review, 95*, 256–273. doi:10.1037/0033-295X.95.2.256

Eccles, J., Wigfield, A., Flanagan, C., Miller, C., Reuman, D., & Yee, D. (1989). Self-concepts, domain values, and self-esteem: Relations and changes at early adolescence. *Journal of Personality, 57*, 283–310. doi:10.1111/j.1467-6494.1989.tb00484.x

Eccles, J. S. (1987). Gender roles and women's achievement-related decisions. *Psychology of Women Quarterly, 11*, 135–172. doi:10.1111/j.1471-6402.1987.tb00781.x

Eccles, J. S. (1993). School and family effects on the ontogeny of children's interests, self-perceptions, and activity choice. In J. Jacobs (Ed.), *Nebraska Symposium on Motivation, 1992: Developmental Perspectives on Motivation,* (pp. 145-208). Lincoln, NE: University of Nebraska Press.

Eccles (Parsons). J. S., Adler, T. F., Futterman, R., Goff, S. B., Kaczala, C. M., Meece, J. L., & Midgley, C. (1983). Expectancies, values, and academic behaviors. In J. T. Spence (Ed.), *Achievement and Achievement Motivation,* (pp. 75-146). San Francisco, CA: W. H. Freeman.

Falk, J. (2004). The director's cut: Toward an improved understanding of learning from museums. *Science Education, 88*(1), 83–96. doi:10.1002/sce.20014

Keller, J. M. (1983). Motivational design of instruction. In Reigeluth, C. M. (Ed.), *Instructional-Design Theories and Models: An Overview of Their Current Status*. Hillsdale, NJ: Lawrence Erlbaum Associates.

Keller, J. M. (1987a). Development and use of the ARCS model of motivational design. *Journal of Instructional Development, 10*(3), 2–10. doi:10.1007/BF02905780

Keller, J. M. (1987b). Strategies for stimulating the motivation to learn. *Performance & Instruction, 26*(8), 1–7. doi:10.1002/pfi.4160260802

Keller, J. M. (1999). Motivation in cyber learning environments. *Educational Technology International, 1*(1), 7–30.

Kun, A., & Weiner, B. (1973). Necessary versus sufficient causal schemata for success and failure. *Journal of Research in Personality, 7*, 197–207. doi:10.1016/0092-6566(73)90036-6

Moos, D. C., & Marroquin, E. (2010). Multimedia, hypermedia, and hypertext: Motivation considered and reconsidered. *Computers in Human Behavior, 26*, 265–276. doi:10.1016/j.chb.2009.11.004

Nicholls, J. (1978). The development of concepts of effort and ability, perception of own attainment, and the understanding that difficult tasks require more ability. *Child Development, 49*, 800–814. doi:10.2307/1128250

President's Council of Advisors on Science and Technology. (2010). *Report to the president: Prepare and inspire: K-12 education in science, technology, engineering, and math (STEM) for America's future*. Washington, DC: Office of Science and Technology Policy.

Tal, R. T. (2001). Incorporating field trips as science learning environment enrichment: An interpretive study. *Learning Environments Research, 4*, 25–49. doi:10.1023/A:1011454625413

Vygotsky, L. (1978). *Mind in society: The development of higher psychological processes*. Cambridge, MA: Harvard University Press.

Weiner, B. (1986). *An attributional theory of motivation and emotion*. New York, NY: Springer-Verlag. doi:10.1007/978-1-4612-4948-1

Wigfield, A. (1994). Expectancy-value theory of achievement motivation: A developmental perspective. *Educational Psychology Review, 6*, 49–78. doi:10.1007/BF02209024

Wigfield, A., & Eccles, J. (1992). The development of achievement task values: A theoretical analysis. *Developmental Review, 12*, 265–310. doi:10.1016/0273-2297(92)90011-P

Wigfield, A., & Eccles, J. S. (2000). Expectancy-value theory of motivation. *Contemporary Educational Psychology, 25*, 68–81. doi:10.1006/ceps.1999.1015

Wlodkowski, R. J. (1985). *Enhancing adult motivation to learn*. San Francisco, CA: Jossey-Bass.

Wlodkowski, R. J. (1989). Instructional design and learner motivation. In Johnson, K. A., & Foe, L. J. (Eds.), *Instructional Design: New Alternatives for Effective Education and Training* (pp. 47–60). New York, NY: Macmillan.

KEY TERMS AND DEFINITIONS

Attributions: The perceived cause(s) of one's successes and failures.

Engagement: The physical, affective, and/or cognitive aspects of an activity that holds a person's attention.

Implicit Theories Of Ability: The belief that one's abilities are either static or malleable.

Induction: An engaging activity that introduces students to a concept.

Self-Efficacy: How confident people are that they can successfully perform a task at a given level of attainment.

Value: Beliefs about how a task meets an individual's needs.

Chapter 4
Cross–Reality Math Visualization:
The SubQuan System Dream Realizations in Immersive Environments, Augmented Realities, and Virtual Worlds

Daniel Cooper Patterson
Dream Realizations, USA & ItOnlyTakes1.org, USA

Rebecca L. Reiniger
Dream Realizations, USA & George Fox University, USA

Anna-Marie Robertson
Dream Realizations, USA & Boise State University, USA

ABSTRACT

Traditionally, the numeric symbols are introduced along with the alphabet. Dream Realizations believes that the introduction of numeric symbols is premature and prevents children from seeing the patterns that various numbers make. Research on subitizing substantiates the natural ability of the human eye to instantly "see" quantities. The early introduction of symbol and process prevents seeing the beautiful metapatterns of polynomials, which are easily recognized when mixed quantities are represented in different base systems: subQuanned. The authors have researched current math practices, math in virtual worlds, number sense, and subitizing to fortify the direction of their efforts. Their journey progresses from the physical (paper and cubes) to the virtual (online flash-based programming) to the immersive (3D in Second Life). This natural progression and ultimate visualization of quantity and metapattern lie in the immersive world. Individuals at all stages of learning can finally see and understand math from a very different vantage point.

DOI: 10.4018/978-1-4666-2670-6.ch004

INTRODUCTION

Dream Realizations is a non-profit corporation that has been designing far-reaching mathematical remediation content corroborated by recent independent neurological findings and immersive educational research. Traditionally, the numeric symbols are introduced along with the alphabet. We believe that the introduction of numeric symbols is premature and prevents children from seeing the patterns that various numbers make. Furthermore, this early introduction prevents seeing the beautiful metapatterns of polynomials, which are easily recognized when mixed quantities are represented in different base systems: subQuanned. Once you subQuan, the fog of math dissipates and numerical instincts are restored. Our own investigation is showing that 100% of all participants that can subitize are capable of subQuanning (the instantaneous perception of very large quantities). We believe the recognition of the metapatterns of polynomial structures, enhanced by subQuanning, will also occur in 100% of these participants.

We, at Dream Realizations, are currently in the design and programming phase of a novel math curriculum required to facilitate in-depth, rapid learning via 3D visualization in virtual worlds. Our primary world is Second Life, but we continue to examine new worlds for viability, sustainability, and expansion. The intended use of Virtual worlds is for the users to inhabit and interact with the environment. The term today has become largely synonymous with interactive 3D virtual environments, where the users take the form of avatars visible to others graphically. Within this environment, many inhabitants learn how to use some of the most advanced computer applications, which can open new career horizons. Although traditional methods of math instruction are just as viable virtually as they are physically, there is a plethora of innovative methods only possible in a virtual world. They run the gamut from performing

conic cross-sections to tessellations to 3D slope measurements (not the old line graph) to examining very large quantities in the SubQuan System: segs, squares, cubes, segs of cubes, etc. The SubQuan System is a cross-reality visualization system that triggers metapattern recognition enabling rapid comprehension of polynomial structures. We plan to institute physical, virtual, and immersive worlds to cement understanding. Also, the ability to recognize metapatterns instantly in multiple large quantities lays the foundation for polynomials and calculus.

Dream Realizations is on the cutting edge of visualizing patterns within patterns in regards to numbers. Visualizing math has huge ramifications for the way math is taught. Imagine recognizing four digit numbers within seconds without having to count. Recognition is just the tip of the iceberg when moving math from the process part of the brain to the visual part of the brain. Triggering the visual cortex to quickly recognize quantities can be done with relative ease in the virtual environment due to the quickness of manipulating large quantities of objects in short periods of time. Addressing the issue of number sense quickly is imperative to American society today as the gap between those who know and those who do not is widening rapidly. A specific example of numeric ignorance among Americans is the concept of how big our National Debt is. A graphic representation of this huge number can be visualized in a virtual world and would make any person, politically inclined or not, aware of its magnitude! (see http://www.usdebtclock.org/). As we are successful, we will not only teach those students the required math concepts that they can get their virtual "hands" on, but also introduce them to an entirely new way of looking at numbers. Collecting data throughout our grant periods will help us measure the impact of visual thinking versus process learning.

BACKGROUND

Technology is a Fundamental Aspect of Math Education

Technology established its beachhead in the math classroom. The use of graphing calculators, smart boards, and online programs that help visualize mathematical concepts continues to grow annually. Concepts themselves have not changed much, just the tools with which they are being taught.

Websites have become more and more accessible to supplement in-class learning or enhance e-learning. Sites like Wolfram-Alpha (http://www.wolframalpha.com/), Mathaway (http://www.mathway.com/), Geogebra (http://www.geogebra.org), and Math.com (http://www.math.com/), are just a few that exhibit math visualization and activate student interaction in an online environment. Many Personal Learning Networks (PLN) are available for educators or interested persons to join online and collaborate in investigating different methods of math instruction. Math 2.0 (http://mathfuture.wikispaces.com/math+2.0) is an example of such groups.

Franklin and Peng (2009) studied a case in which the iPod Touch was used to facilitate learning algebraic equations in middle school mathematics. The iPod Touch provided interesting and informal mobile learning that continued outside the classroom. The research question was to determine if using this technology for enhancing mathematical understanding through video content would be advantageous to student growth both formally and informally. The educators in the study responded in resounding agreement to the technology implementation in regards to learning in the classroom. Students were also in agreement, although some would have preferred to not work in teams, but rather individually in building and viewing their math movies. Many obstacles showed themselves in the implementation of this study such as weather, power outages,

12 hours of teacher pre-training, state-testing changes, compatibility issues, and technology coordinators' resistance, to name a few (Franklin & Peng, 2009).

Mathematical puzzles have been sporadically used in the classroom to stimulate higher-level thinking in students, to make students think 'outside the box,' and to experiment with different ideas and outlooks. Mostly, though, puzzles have been used to augment curriculum by parents or as enrichment activities for gifted students: tangrams and tessellations, for example. Marshall (2004) investigated an urban elementary school as they looked into exercises of logic in order to problem solve and work toward understanding and application during an after-school enrichment program. Students used the Pattern Blocks and Stick Figure game and Logix puzzle cards, also designing their own cards. Students were in accordance with the Logix cards 80% of the time, but the 20% remaining got to the correct answer using diverse methods. Marshall found that it was very important to pay attention to the personal logic of each student as it could vary greatly and "in the constructivist view of learning, this personal construction of meaning is always required" (Marshall, 2004, p. 182).

Technology Moving towards Virtual, Immersive World

During the past decade, technology has become a greater part of existence in and out of education. The development of various Internet related tools has facilitated an overall feeling of connectedness on a local, national, and global scale through social media such as: MySpace, Facebook, Twitter, Moodle, Wiki, Virtual Worlds, etc. Second Life (SL), a Multi-User Virtual Environment (MUVE) headquartered in San Francisco, is one of many virtual worlds available to anyone with the recommended computer hardware and a high-speed Internet connection. As Internet connections expand, wireless abilities flourish, video and audio technologies advance, and virtual immersive environments grow to be more convenient and functional (Warburton, 2009).

Estimations by Gartner Group in 2007 show that close to 80% of Internet users by the end of 2011 will be using at least one virtual space with an 'avatar' (as cited in Wang & Braman, 2009). An avatar is a digital representation of one's self that a computer user can manipulate through a three-dimensional virtual world; it can be human, animal, or an alter ego. The Gartner Group statistic includes spaces designed for preteens, teens, and adults. Not incorporating these worlds and technological advances into education is tantamount to not preparing students to positively use these resources in real world situations (Wagner, 2008).

Dickey (2003) explains the shift from an objectivist learning theory to a constructivist learning theory as a shift in paradigms of learning. She says that learners must have opportunities to explore and manipulate within their learning environment to aid in the construction of new knowledge. However, more than that, constructivist environments must support conversation and discourse among learners. This pattern of communication will allow learners "to share information, test understandings, and reflect on learning" (p. 106). It appears that a new theory of learning has surfaced with the emergence of new technologies that was not available twenty years ago. There seems to have been a shift from teacher-centered learning theories to a more student-centered theory of learning.

Twining (2009) started The Schome Park Programme (SPP) as an alternative form of education. The program's aim was to bring about "a radical rethinking of current education systems" (p. 498). He believed that the best way to keep teachers from teaching the way they were taught was to put them into a radically different educational setting where current pedagogies would not work. These settings Twining labeled "lived experiences." One of these 'radically different educational settings' is the virtual world. The

Schome Parke Programme was built totally in a virtual world. As the Schome Park Programme progressed, its developers became aware of the shift in paradigms from the constructivist theory of learning to a more socio-cultural atmosphere where knowledge was distributed among the learners (Twining, 2009). This initiative was one of the first to allow us to begin to see and experience the advantages of learning in a virtual environment.

Twining, in the implementation of the Schome program, discovered that teachers find it "almost impossible to break free from established conceptions of education" (p. 497). He believes that Second Life and other similar virtual worlds will offer the ideal opportunity for exploring educational alternatives.

In a study reviewed by Hew and Cheung (2010), student tests scores were compared on two projects completed in a graphics design course. One set of students completed the course through the use of a virtual environment and the other set completed the course in a physical classroom. "A 14% increase of the mean examination mark" from the physical learning to the virtual learning" was found (p. 43).

Schliemann (1998) suggests that, based on the contrast between the difficulty that students have with algebra in the higher grades and successful attempts at teaching algebra at earlier levels, it is time to "seriously consider deep changes in the elementary mathematics curriculum and the possibility of having children discussing, understanding, and dealing with algebraic concepts and relations much earlier than is the norm nowadays" (p. 4). This change in curriculum will involve not only a paradigm shift, but a pedagogical one as well. Virtual environments can be used to help with the paradigm and pedagogical shift between hands-on learning and symbolic representation (Dickey, 2003).

The full potential of virtual environments as an educational tool has yet to be explored and therein exist powerful pedagogical uses that have yet to be fully evolved and utilized (Dreher, Reiners, Dreher, & Dreher, 2009). Teachers are trained to be teachers in the physical world with matching pedagogies. As virtual worlds become more and more prevalent, teachers will be asked more and more often to step away from conventional education, and move outside of their comfort zones to grapple with the emerging learning theories and shifting pedagogies that are inherent in the educational technology of virtual worlds.

Existing Mathematics in Virtual, Immersive World

As a MUVE, Second Life is very different from a Massively Multiplayer Online Role-Playing Game (MMRPG), such as World of Warcraft, in that its inhabitants create it. In the creation, innovation, and building in this virtual space, mathematics plays a vital, although often subtle, role in a majority of constructs inside Second Life: landscaping, buildings, furniture, clothing, hair, etc. All building and moving of objects inworld (within SL) use calculations, perspectives, and graphing capabilities. The more accurate one wishes to be while constructing proportional items, the more one must understand the surroundings, including the physics that correspond. For example, when building a chair, vectors should be aligned, sizing should be proportionate, and physical attributes should be applied. The mathematics involved is intuitive and not outwardly explicit. A builder can experiment on objects without quite knowing the exact outcome of the test and in this way learn the math involved for future use. When in the building process, the creator is given the freedom to manipulate objects based upon their own desires without the constraints of heavy calculations and formulas and without the hindrances of monetary and material issues. The edit menu within the build tab is a playground of x, y, and z coordinates relating to the 3D environment (Weber, Rufer-Bach, & Platel, 2008). The building process is a classic

use of geometry in space with no gravitational hindrances.

Not all participants in Second Life build or create objects. Many active users enjoy the environment as social, entrepreneurial, and educational. In regards to non-builder usage, members can purchase pre-made items in order to facilitate setting up a home, wardrobe, or persona. Those who build can create clothing, furniture, housing, and accessories to be purchased within SL by those who access only for social reasons. Because of the high volume of social residents active within SL, the opportunity for marketing and selling products is vast and is accompanied by the rich mathematics used in business.

Correlation to business education or action learning abounds with its implied mathematics, in the setup, inventory, advertisement, and sales of created virtual products (Wagner, 2008). In 2008, Wagner set up a 4-week cooperative assignment to study action learning in his university class where 5-person groups were to develop a virtual organization for economic gain. He observed the students recognition of the connection between planning, action, experience, and understanding with overall learning benefits. Wagner found that business models performed in a virtual world exhibit great learning with little financial outlay and that failure has inconsequential penalties (Wagner & Rachael, 2009). Mathematically speaking, Second Life can become a teaching tool for statistics and money management.

Learning by doing is an important step in making education a life-long goal for students. Motivating students to want to learn deepens retention and connection for the individual student (Jossey-Bass, 2008). Connecting personal experiences to individual learning can often grab the learner's attention. Cheal (2007) argues that constructivism is a theory of information attainment, which happens when students relate to the world to what they already know. By appealing to a student's own environment, their knowledge set, and their actions within it, deeper learning is facilitated. Bloom's Taxonomy, developed from 1948-1956, fits the model of constructivism and its application in virtual worlds clearly: knowledge, comprehension, application, analysis, synthesis, and evaluation. Cheal (2007) translates Bloom's model into Second Life vocabulary:

All of the higher order knowledge skills from Bloom's taxonomy are possible – applying knowledge (e.g. moving about in Second Life.), analyzing (How can I build something realistic with a low prim count?), evaluating (Is it best to build a cathedral ceiling to show support systems or to leave it off to allow avatars to fly in?), and creating (Use SL building skills to build a complete cathedral). Bloom's learning characteristics correlate well with the exploration and interaction inherent in virtual worlds (p. 208).

The application, analysis, and synthesis levels of this taxonomy incorporate the intrinsic mathematical knowledge that encompasses all builds within Second Life, whether it is through science, art, physics, construction, business, or one of many other subject areas.

Problem solving in a virtual world can encompass many domains. The University of Hamburg implemented an Information Systems project in SL in 2008, which is a good example of curriculum integration. The students were asked to design a supply chain of medical goods from sea containers to pharmacies (Dreher, et al., 2009). The goal of this project was to create a true simulation for later presentation. The benefits found in this study included programming skills, system development, project management, and industry/business experience. Inclusive in the project design were a variety of aspects incorporating mathematics, from the design of the plant and ships, the distribution of goods, the business model, the economics, to the statistics.

Another problem solving aspect of virtual worlds could be found in Meyer's case study (2009) involving Club Penguin by Disney, a virtual world where children create penguin avatars and interact with each other in games, exploration, and chat. Rumors abounded about a contest to "tip an iceberg" within the virtual world. Penguins began gathering to try to overturn the iceberg en masse. The escapade made for a considerable amount of speculation and various experiments by players. Children were testing their hypothesis and collaborating with others to find possible solutions. Most conversations by children and their parents regarding this project happened outside of this virtual world: in Web locations such as Yahoo! Answers, Facebook, and other social media (Meyers, 2009). This event showed the power of virtual worlds and is an example in the use of physics, cooperation, proofs, and problem solving involving math that was completely engaging to those that participated.

Math and science also come together in various locations within Second Life, from following the spread of viruses to scrutinizing the physics of objects on the move (Lamb & Johnson, 2009). National Aeronautics and Space Administration (NASA), National Oceanic and Atmospheric Administration (NOAA), the Weather Channel, medical simulations by universities, math sculpture gardens, and many other locations allow for students to investigate and explore real-life situations in a virtual world.

Teaching mathematics as a completely independent topic has yet to be thoroughly investigated within Second Life. Sweeney (2008) conducted research during his math tutorial sessions in regards to eye movement and engagement of students while in the virtual world. An eye-tracking monitor was set up and recordings were made of individual student's eye passivity versus activity. This was then compared with the same test in another virtual environment called RuneScape, a role-playing game. It was determined by quantitative measurement that Second Life is a viable immersion tool for education. Although Sweeney's ability to use the virtual world to actually teach mathematics as an independent topic was limited at that time, due to the higher education coursework and the lack of technological advances in presentation tools, meeting in the virtual world was effective when distance education is a factor. It gave the students a feeling of being physically present in a classroom even if they were sitting at home (Sweeney, 2008).

Holmes/Beaumont (2010) conducted research in Second Life through a graduate class offered by the EdTech department of Boise State University. The course was entitled "Teaching Mathematics in a Virtual World" where students were creating math manipulatives, research presentations, and lesson plans on the feasibility of using this medium to teach an independent math course. Holmes is in the process of validating that this virtual environment is conducive to teaching mathematics. Since the introduction of the SL Viewer 2.0 in the spring of 2010, which gives greater access to media use within Second Life, outside websites can be utilized inworld (within Second Life) like Google Docs, Etherpad, YouTube, Twiddla, Nota, etc., these Blackboard-type activities now facilitate virtual discussions and visualization. One difficulty remains in the client-based websites, where each individual is seeing the media at their own rate. Group discussions become difficult when the instructor does not know exactly what the student is seeing. New inroads are being made in streaming desktops into Second Life via UStream. Students being able to view the teacher's computer in real-time via the virtual world combined with the 3D learning can be a recipe for a rich e-learning environment.

So What is the Impact of this Technology? What is Our Score?

In 2009 the U.S. ranked 32nd out of 65 countries that participated in the international PISA math testing with Shanghai, Finland, and Korea topping as the high scorers, whereas in 2003, the U.S. was ranked 28th out of 40 countries (http://www.oecd.org/document/55/0,3746, en_322523 51_32236173_33917303_1_1_1_1,00.html). The international TIMSS test from 2007 for 4th and

8th graders showed the U.S. above average, but 11th out of 36 countries in the 4th grade and 9th out of 48 countries in 8th grade. With the TIMSS average score being 500, the U.S. scores 529 in 4th grade and 508 in 8th grade. Top scorers were Hong Kong with a score of 607 in 4th grade and Chinese Taipei with a score of 598 in 8th grade. [In both of these tests, Finland did not participate.] In 1999, the TIMSS scores for 8th grade had the U.S. ranked 19th out of 38 countries with a score of 502. Singapore was on top in 1999 with an average score of 604 (http://nces.ed.gov/timss/results99_1.asp) (see Table 1).

Having investigated various methods of teaching math in the school systems, the availability of math education in the virtual world, pairing that with our own number sense, and understanding subitizing and subQuanning, it is noticeable that even with the new technologies and strategies, we are only reconfiguring the same process of teaching mathematics. Math may have more student interaction, constructivist tendencies, and national focus, but it is clear that there is a greater need of conceptual change from the ground up. Current brain research is demonstrating the need to rethink the human capability (Jossey-Bass, 2008). Even though most students can learn math the way it is currently being taught, the curriculum of today and yesterday has not necessarily been related in its optimal form. More directions need to be explored to bring about foundational and fundamental change in math education.

MAIN FOCUS OF THE CHAPTER

Issues, Controversies, Problems

Number Sense: Culprit or Scapegoat

As stated by the National Council of Teachers of Mathematics (NCTM) for pre-K – 2 expectations, "all students should develop a sense of whole numbers and represent and use them in flexible ways, including relating, composing, and

Table 1. Scores

PISA	U.S.	Total Countries	Percentile	Top Countries
2003	28th	40	30th	
2009	32nd	65	51st	Shanghai, Finland, Korea
TIMMS				(Finland did not participate)
1999				
8th grade	19th 502 score	38	50th	Singapore – 604 score
2007				
4th grade	11th 529 score	36	69th	Hong Kong – 607 score
8th grade	9th 508 score	48	81st	Chinese Taipei – 598 score

decomposing numbers" (NCTM, 2006, p. 23). This number sense is believed to be pre-verbal, before the introduction of symbols (Barth, et al., 2006). While counting has been deemed in the past as a pre-requisite for understanding some mathematical concepts, researchers are now entertaining the idea that learning this process before achievement of conceptual comprehension may be detrimental to future mathematical development (Howell & Kemp, 2005).

Scholars and teachers alike debate the concept of number sense. In 2009, Howell and Kemp, *only four years later*, investigated these opinions with an anonymous survey of thirteen academics who had previously written articles in scholarly journals pertaining to number sense. The purpose of this research was to obtain some form of consensus among researchers. Howell and Kemp found that the majority of skills in early number sense rely on counting except matching numerosity, subitizing to three, and comparison of quantities to ten. Participants in the survey also implied that school focus needs to be on early numerical competence (counting) rather than on number sense, which is in opposition to other researchers' findings (Howell & Kemp, 2009).

Wagner and Davis (2010) explored the idea that developing number sense, from a linguistical standpoint, would be better represented as increasing quantity sense, since number sense is rather ambiguous. The researchers stress a need for students to "feel" numbers (p. 45): their magnitude, enormity, and minuteness. The abacus gave individuals more of a connection with quantities than do our current calculators. The researchers promote the need for students to be exposed to the weight of numbers in the classroom (Wagner & Davis, 2010).

Howell and Kemp (2010) further studied this number sense ability in preschool children, finding that there was no significant difference between those children that attended daycare versus pre-school. The children at this age level, chronologically four and five years old, varied in language, vocabulary, and mathematical skills, ranging from that of two to nine year olds. Although, significant differences were found between genders with boys being more successful with quantitative concepts and girls flourishing in subitizing, no conclusive evidence was found to substantiate the need for pre-school in advancing a child's number sense. All the participants in this study demonstrated some success with the workings of number sense. The children seemed to have the most difficulties with understanding number principles (Howell & Kemp, 2010).

Yang and Li (2008) studied 808 third graders in Taiwan to see if number sense was an applicable difficulty at the elementary level. Results indicated that these students performed poorly (34%) on five components of number sense: understanding meanings of numbers, perceiving number size, composing and decomposing numbers, being cognizant of the effects operations have on numbers, developing effective strategies and judging reasonableness of solutions. Yang and Li developed a twenty-five question, online, multiple-choice test, where the scoring was on a sliding scale depending on which answer the students chose. The reasoning could be correct with the answer false and vice-versa for partial credit. Data found the lowest percentage lay in judging the reasonableness of answers, which lead the researchers to believe that drill and practice exercises need to be reduced and instead stress the need for students to have a strong foundation in number sense (Yang & Li, 2008).

Due to the results of the previous study, Yang (2009) conducted another study in Taiwan to find out if 280 pre-service teachers had number sense themselves in order to teach. Strategies can be difficult to come by if the teachers themselves do not have the training. Only one-fifth of teachers in the study were able to implement number sense strategies, whereas the rest employed rule-based methods for solving problems. Yang found that Taiwanese textbooks rely heavily on rule-oriented written methods and although math curriculum reform is underway, it is not yet reflected in current classroom resources.

The goal of Nickerson and Whitacre's (2010) study was to foster number sense in students using methods that were flexible in nature. Individuals with a good number sense have the ability to use many different methods to solve the same problem, whereas without a reliance on number sense, memorized processes were used. The argument then opens between the desire for educators to teach multiple processes for students to grasp the many ways to solve problems or concentrate on one method of solution and make sure that it is retained. Another mode of thought is to allow students to come up with their own unique strate-

gies. Nickerson and Whitacre's goal was to give ample time for students to incorporate their own number sense in mental math and estimation. Students were shifted away from school-learned procedures. For example, a student was asked to subtract 28 from 296. There was no reliance on the process of borrowing, but a pictorial view of differences by a sort-of number line. Representation of the natural number line inherent in our brains allows number sense to make itself known (Jossey-Bass, 2008). By capitalizing on number sense strategies, Nickerson and Whitacre (2010) determined that local instruction theory is imperative to accomplishing classroom-teaching goals.

Number sense or, as some like to call it, quantity sense or number instinct, is important for mathematical understanding across curriculum. Being able to capitalize on and train this innate ability is the next step in education. Howell and Kemp (2009) determined that matching numerosity, subitizing to three, and comparison of quantities to ten were the only mathematical concepts that did not rely on counting. As counting and memorization are the foundation of most rule-oriented processes in math and the human brain is not built like a computer but is associative in nature (Jossey-Bass, 2008), one wonders if there may be another venue that doesn't rely on ancient counting and tedious memorization.

Solutions and Recommendations

Understanding Subitizing

The term subitizing, the ability to recognize small quantities (4-7 objects) quickly without counting, was coined more than half a century ago (Kaufman, 1949). Researchers have found that birds and mammals, in addition to humans, have the ability to see small quantities of numbers without counting (Dehaene, 1997). Research has also been conducted to understand the visual processes inherent in number recognition (see Figure 1).

Dehaene and Cohen (1999) discovered through Positron Emission Tomography (PET) and functional Magnetic Resonance Imaging (fMRI) that there were three regions in the brain, referred to as the triple-code model of number processing, specifically used for mathematics: (1) a visual Arabic code in the left and right inferior occipital-temporal areas, (2) a magnitude code in the left and right inferior parietal areas, and (3) a verbal code in the left perisylvian areas. The visual Arabic code is utilized in identifying strings of numbers and decision of parity. The magnitude code refers to a number's relationship on a number line: comparisons. The verbal code corresponds to rote verbal memories of math facts. With the brain requiring multiple levels of support for mathematics, difficulties abound for inconsistencies. One can understand why individuals may have problems with mathematics if one of these three brain regions is not as developed as the others.

In a Finnish research model, children aged 4-5 years old were assessed on their performance of number related skills (Hannula, Räsänen, & Lehtinen, 2007). Two relationships became apparent: number sequencing is directly associated with Spontaneous Focus On Numerosity (SFON) and this association is based on subitizing (the rapid recognition of 1-4 objects without counting). It was noted that it takes children a long time to find meaningful counting skills after they learn their first numerical vocabulary. Therefore, concepts must be practiced.

Figure 1. Random cubes

Noted in the Finnish research (Hannula, et al., 2007) is the concept that children do not necessarily notice the numbers of objects in a set and that aligns with the conclusion that there are definite differences in learning depending on the practice of the child in quantitative skills. The research of the past has missed a correlation between verbal object counting and subitizing-based enumeration skills in children. This Finnish study investigated the connection of verbosity and enumeration and then determined that the range of subitizing ability increases with intensive practice in both adults and children.

Results of the collective testing (Hannula, et al., 2007) found that children with a strong ability to focus tended to subitize larger quantities and had better counting skills. In addition, SFON and number sequencing was in direct correlation to counting skills and not affected by subitizing-based enumeration. It was noted that detailed follow-up activities needed to be implemented to understand long-range effects and retention. Hannula's study lacks a control group for comparison but it is the first of its kind to indicate that counting, subitizing-based enumeration, and SFON are related. All of this leads us along the path to understanding mathematical development (Hannula, et al., 2007). SFON and subitizing appear to the authors of this chapter to be different names for the same human capability.

In another research project, eye-movement was tracked to determine if subitizing or counting takes precedence in children with dyscalculia (Moeller, Neuburger, Kaufmann, Landerl, & Nuerk, 2009). Two children previously diagnosed with dyscalculia were tested, in addition to a control group of eight average-tested children all at around ten years of age, using eye-tracking software to determine if subitizing methods or counting methods were used to determine quantities from one dot to eight dots randomly spaced. The goal of this study was to determine if the impairment includes "the very basic ability of discriminating and estimating non-symbolic numerical quantities" (Moeller, et al., p. 380). The results mainly focused on the subitizing quantities (1-3 dots) and whether or not there was counting involved. It was determined that encoding of non-symbolic quantity (naming the number of dots) is somehow impaired in these children with dyscalculia. These specific children relied on counting even for small quantities. It was also noted that there was a discrepancy between the two boys with dyscalculia: one had an encoding dot pattern difficulty, whereas the other had problems in determining larger magnitudes with the corresponding symbol words. This means that the data may be different for various forms of dyscalculia: controls may be obscured. In addition, this sample size was relatively small (two) and would need to be reproduced on a larger scale for validation. Three results were determined from this study: 1) children with dyscalculia do have difficulty subitizing, they rely on counting, 2) this difficulty does not depend on their access to number magnitude or a mental number line, but on the quick and automatic recognition of quantities, 3) different children with dyscalculia may have different levels of disabilities.

The development of automatic numerosity processing in preschoolers led Rouselle and Noël (2008) to another study incorporating three different experiments examining three to five year olds and their ability to quantify and catalogue dots and bars, whether they be congruent or incongruent. The researchers were trying to determine if preschooler's performance in quantification tasks is affected by irrelevant numerical and perceptual properties of collections. In the first experiment, dots were used to determine if four to five year olds could distinguish between amounts: numerical properties. Then using the same dot comparison, the children were asked how much black was covered, as the dots were various sizes: perceptual properties. In the second experiment, bars of the same width but not the same length were used in the trials. The identical information was sought

and interpreted. The final experiment included three yearolds and was set up along the same lines as the second experiment.

In current times, the advantage of Arabic and verbal numerals to stand for quantities augments the abstractness of numerical concepts, since one symbol can represent many different types of objects. Also, number size assessment is said to be automatic, as in fast and easy; it starts and continues without conscious thought (Tzelgov & Ganor-Stern, 2005). In application to being literate versus illiterate, when an individual has the capacity to read, it becomes almost a compulsion. Blakemore and Frith determined that one can't help but read as if it is a type of "brainwashing" (Jossey-Bass, 2008, p. 233). Upon further investigation the researchers were able to uncover five different studies that concluded that infants are born with an innate ability to understand numbers, as in a compulsion, which only increases over time (Rouselle & Noël, 2008).

SubQuan: A Solution that Thrives in Virtual Reality

Unquestionable research has now verified that humans are born with the ability to subitize one to three items. Further research shows that subitizing increases to seven items within a few years after birth. Some commercialized training experiments presents preschoolers subitizing up into the teens and higher (http://www.brillbaby.com/teaching-baby/math/subitizing/subitize-this.php). While impressive, the ability to go past nine is not required to realize tremendous benefits of subitizing.

Building on the ability to subitize an organized group of nine items enables the short step to packaging ten items into a container. These containers of ten can be subitized up to nine (ninety items), and ten of these containers can be packaged into a containers of one hundred items. These containers of one hundred can be subitized up to nine

(nine hundred items) and so on. This packaging of units into containers to enable subitization is called subQuanning. SubQuan is the packaging of items into containers to enable our ability to see large quantities quickly. Subitizing is not the only requirement to subQuan. A two-dimensional layout is required to ensure that all containers are full. The incredible 'error detection' of the human eye is so great that we can detect one pixel out of a million going 'bad' on a computer monitor or television screen; therefore, it is trivial to detect one cube missing in a group of one hundred.

The discovery of subQuan led Daniel Patterson to create paper sheets with printed outlines of containers that held 1 cm cubes. Different sheets were created with containers based on two, three,..., ten cubes. Though not required, grouping the cubes consistently, based on the same quantity, yielded Base Number Sheets (BNS). The place values were subitized independently and the entire subitized string is called the subQuan of a quantity in a particular base. Below is the subQuan two-six-five in base seven (a quantity of 145 cubes) (see Figure 2).

The quantity and subQuan are only identical for base A (ten), as the smaller base sheets yield larger and larger subQuans for the same quantity. A problem with a paper-based approach instantly arises. Investigating three tiers of contained cubes (four places values) requires a sheet too large to place on an 18"x24" school desk. The greatest base that fits is base four. Furthermore, just two tiers of containers (three places) in base A (ten) could hold 999 cubes. A small class sharing only ten sheets could have almost 10,000 cubes in use. Every teacher instantly recognizes the insanity of this type of activity: time and asset management (loss of cubes). However, each teacher also recognizes the strength of hands-on experiences.

The next logical step is to go virtual: to use a computer display to represent the items. Patterson developed his first flash program (see www.itonlytakes1.org) to enable exploration into subitizing and subQuanning. The first lesson, Lesson 0, es-

tablishes the time delay from symbol recognition to keyboard entry. This provides a quick check to determine if someone is counting or subitizing in Lesson 1. Lesson 2 introduces subQuanning with two base A (ten) places. By lesson 4, representing three place values, one recognizes that a similar problem to desk size exists: screen size. The most significant digits of large quantities cannot be subitized at the same time that the smallest digit can due to scale difference (see Figure 3).

Most computer setups are smaller than 18"x24" desks, however, since the 1 cm cube is no longer required, the size of objects become relative to screen resolution. Still recognizing hundreds or thousands of objects and being able to see the ones requires zooming in and out. Though the time to display multiple cubes and collecting them has been overcome by going virtual, the restriction to seeing them has not. Furthermore, the attention span to just subitize little cubes lacks the pizzazz of current video games.

There also exists a need to quickly prototype when exploring viable alternatives in lesson design, the ability to zoom in and out and change visual perspective, and the ability to reorganize objects into different arrangements. These all lead to an investigation of immersive 3D environments and the potential development of a viable solution (see Figure 4).

Optimizing the learning of subQuanning might require all three-spaces: physical manipulatives, a virtual program, and an immersive 3D environment. Starting with the computer program, students can acclimate to the containers of subQuan in rapid fashion, practicing for quickness and accuracy with time trials. Once proficiency in subQuanning is developed, the student can move on to the physical base sheets and centimeter cubes. Manipulating the location of cubes on the sheets solidifies learning, especially for those kinesthetic students, and also allows for interaction and the observation of evolving patterns. Three major limitations exist in this exercise: time, matter, and space. Productive use of time manipulat-

Figure 2. 2, 6, 5, base 7

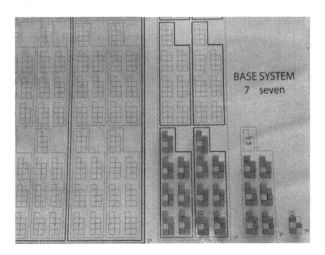

ing physical cubes in containers on base sheets only allows for small quantities. Maintaining an inventory of 1000 cubes requires careful cube management. In addition, subQuanning physically requires large spaces for the sheets. These three limitations can be addressed by subQuanning in a virtual world; time can be minimized by scripting objects to collect in containers on their own, matter is minimized by objects being computer graphics yet still providing the 'feel' of a hands-on experience, and space becomes relative to viewpoint; move close-in for details, move out for panoramic views. The space can appear to be the size of football fields, impossible within a classroom.

Moving from a virtual programming environment, such as Flash, into a virtual world programming environment, such as Linden Scripting Language for Second Life, provided two unexpected benefits. First, the ability to take simple objects and arrange them in different patterns, including simply looking at the arrangements from different perspectives, was extremely quick. This ability to quickly prototype has become the authors' primary reason for advocating immersive 3-D environments for product development. The second unexpected benefit was the ability to call in Subject Matter Experts (SME) on texture, composition, arrange-

ment, look & feel, and other visual and kinesthetic attributes via a simple chat and teleport. Second Life is unique in the quantity of on-line users and the depth of those users. Therefore networking connections with subject matter experts are easy to make. The built-in chat and teleport features allow for a simple, "Can you take a minute and look at my prototype?" and have it literally take 60 seconds: A five-second teleport, a 50 second view and comment, and a five-second teleport back to whence the SME came. Nothing in the real world compares to this efficiency.

The prototyping of subQuan commenced with moving the virtual representations from the Flash program into Second Life. The dashes used in the Flash program really have no physical counterpart but the strong connection of computer graphics already in place naturally directed this path. The initial builds were expanded to quantities greater than 1,000 resulting in containers over 80 meters tall. It was palpable from the SME's expressions that their necks literally were hurting from watching their avatars bend backwards to examining these tall structures. After weeks of adjustments, the connections of the Flash program graphics were abandoned and the real-life plastic cubes were recreated in the virtual world. The daunting task of creating cubes in Second Life brought texture

Figure 3. 5th grader subquanning

experts out of thin air (virtual air). Since clothing and objects that mimic real-life have a history stemming from seven years of development in Second Life, the graphic artists there abound and their skills are unsurpassed. While we could have paid for a graphic artist (and may in the future), most were eager to point the way with tips & tricks in Photoshop and other graphic programs. Even though we were developing a program to help others understand math, the mathematics needed in advanced texturing in Photoshop was unbelievable. Just creating objects in Second Life is a fantastic math lesson!

Now that we were developing subQuan textures to look like real-life plastic cubes, the concept of having students make the transition from reality to immersive-reality became almost transparent visually! Prototyping several alternatives for organizing the containers to reflect the Base Number Sheets (BNS) resulted in a pleasant surprise. We discovered issues within the physical designed BNS and moved the development of the BNS from print-and-test in reality to texture-and-test in virtual reality. Prototyping became not only an asset within Second Life but also for physical life! The project quickly accelerated due to these findings and both realities benefited from the rapid prototyping accomplished within the 3D environment.

Now that the cubes were SL objects, a student lesson we thought would be very challenging to do on the computer became extremely easy. We were able to represent the 2D subQuan values instantly in their 3D form with the 'click' of a virtual button. We even added the pizazz so desperately needed by making the 3D representations look as though they were being projected by the main device (see Figure 5).

The device is easily scaled from hand size to 10 m in length. This enables private viewing by students to shared viewing in an auditorium. The green and magenta buttons along the bottom enable instant combining of base two integer quantities. The three buttons on the side will clear the display, chat the quantity in base two and base ten, and toggle the 3D projections. This tool now behaves as an alien artifact, ripe for exploration and discovery. This device is called The Right Hand. It can be used to teach students how to count up to thirty-one on just their right hand.

FUTURE RESEARCH DIRECTIONS

The ability to subQuan is exciting, but, in itself, does not appear to be very profound. True, there now exists an alternative to counting, but what does this portend? Research is rapidly progressing in many closely related areas. The creation of devices that can facilitate discovery rather than lecture and rote memorization are popping up in very unanticipated areas. The possibility of teaching combining rather than addition and subtraction using colored subQuans for integer arithmetic seems very promising. Examining metapatterns between various Base Number Sheets has already revealed a self-discovery method to Pascal's Triangle. We believe there are many more discoveries to be made mathematically in subQuan.

Technologically speaking, we have discovered an entirely new world. We believe that scientific discoveries of equations can be induced to occur naturally, as they can be modeled virtually and the quantities can be subQuanned instantly

Figure 4. Early base number sheet (BNS) in SL

through new 'ancient artifacts.' The fascination of a virtual world with the innovation of a novel mathematical process based on visual instinct will provide a fertile field for future research for many decades to come.

CONCLUSION

The ability to recognize small quantities without counting, otherwise known as subitizing, has been documented in animals and humans (Dehaene, 1997; Kaufman, 1949). Gregory Bateson coined the term metapattern to refer to a pattern of patterns. By studying patterns and their interconnectedness we can link parts into wholes (Bateson, 1979). Interestingly enough, combining these two concepts with the advancement of technology gives us the ability to tap into natural instincts located in the visual cortex of the brain concerning quantities, regardless of the language attached to mathematical symbols. Children often learn to count orally and when they enter into school, focus is then on the symbolic representations and processes before the full grasp of quantity is understood. A rigid sense of application sans understanding takes precedence (Howell & Kemp, 2005).

To combat the disconnect between number sense and number processes, more connectivity with our natural abilities needs to be attained. Physical manipulatives represent mathematical

Figure 5. The right hand

concepts well, but they are difficult to quickly maneuver. Flash computer programs speed up activities, but are not as interactive as hands-on applications. 3D Immersive Worlds combine the best of both the physical and virtual environments in addition to allowing the students to see very large quantities quickly, manipulate them easily, and recognize patterns and metapatterns within these quantities all without the obstacle of language and process.

The need for children to understand the relationship between numbers and their quantities is great. This allows for the natural number sense of the human to blossom. We are born with a natural ability to recognize small quantities of numbers without counting which is known as subitizing. If those numbers are organized into containers and separated by digits, large quantities of numbers can be recognized quickly which is called subQuanning. The eye is adept at picking out mistakes or absences, so if there is an item missing from a container it will be noticed.

Technology bridges many subject areas, whereas the trend in education is to compartmentalize curriculum: math, science, reading, writing, social studies, art, foreign language, etc. In actuality, these subjects intertwine and overlap. With the incorporation of virtual worlds into education, mathematics will become even more accessible to the students across various domains.

As information becomes ever more quantitative and as society relies increasingly on computers and the data they produce, an innumerate citizen today is as vulnerable as the illiterate peasant of Gutenberg's time (Steen, 1997, p. xv).

REFERENCES

Barth, H., La Mont, K., Lipton, J., Dehaene, S., Kanwisher, N., & Spelke, E. (2006). Non-symbolic arithmetic in adults and young children. *Cognition*, *98*(3), 199–222. doi:10.1016/j.cognition.2004.09.011

Bateson, G. (1979). *Mind and nature: A necessary unity*. New York, NY: Dutton.

Cheal, C. (2007). Second life: Hype or hyperlearning? *Horizon*, *15*(4), 204–210. doi:10.1108/10748120710836228

Dehaene, S. (1997). *The number sense*. Oxford, UK: Oxford University Press.

Dehaene, S., & Cohen, L. (1999). Language and elementary arithmetic: Dissociations between operations. *Mathematical Cognition*, *1*, 83–120.

Dickey, M. D. (2003). Teaching in 3D: Pedagogical affordances and constraints of 3D virtual worlds for synchronous distance learning. *Distance Education*, *24*(1), 105. doi:10.1080/01587910303047

Dreher, C., Reiners, T., Dreher, N., & Dreher, H. (2009). Virtual worlds as a context suited for information systems education: Discussion of pedagogical experience and curriculum design with reference to second life. *Journal of Information Systems Education*, *20*(2), 211–224.

Franklin, T., & Peng, L.-W. (2009). Mobile math: Math educators and students engage in mobile learning. *Journal of Computing in Higher Education*, *20*, 69–80. doi:10.1007/s12528-008-9005-0

Hannula, M. M., Räsänen, P., & Lehtinen, E. (2007). Development of counting skills: Role of spontaneous focusing on numerosity and subitizing-based enumeration. *Mathematical Thinking and Learning*, *9*(1), 51–57.

Hew, K., & Cheung, W. (2010). Use of three-dimensional (3-D) immersive virtual worlds in K-12 and higher education settings: A review of the research. *British Journal of Educational Technology*, *41*(1), 33–55. doi:10.1111/j.1467-8535.2008.00900.x

Holmes, R., & Beaumont, L. (2010). Teaching mathematics in a virtual world. In Frenburg, U., & Reiniger, R. (Eds.), *VWBPE 2010 Presentation*. EdTech Island, NY: Second Life.

Howell, S., & Kemp, C. (2005). Defining early number sense: A participatory Australian study. *Educational Psychology*, *25*(5), 555–571. doi:10.1080/01443410500046838

Howell, S., & Kemp, C. (2009). A participatory approach to the identification of measures of number sense in children prior to school entry. *International Journal of Early Years Education*, *17*(1), 47–65. doi:10.1080/09669760802699902

Howell, S. C., & Kemp, C. R. (2010). Assessing preschool number sense: Skills demonstrated by children prior to school entry. *Educational Psychology*, *30*(4), 411–429. doi:10.1080/01443411003695410

Jossey-Bass, I. (2008). *The Jossey-Bass reader on the brain and learning*. San Francisco, CA: Jossey-Bass.

Kaufman, E. L., Lord, M. W., Reese, T. W., & Volkman, J. (1949). The discrimination of visual number. *The American Journal of Psychology*, *62*(4), 27. doi:10.2307/1418556

Lamb, A., & Johnson, L. (2009). The potential, the pitfalls, and the promise of multi-user virtual environments: Getting a second life. *Teacher Librarian*, *36*(4), 68–78.

Marshall, J. A. (2004). Construction of meaning: Urban elementary students' interpretation of geometric puzzles. *The Journal of Mathematical Behavior*, *23*(2), 169–182. doi:10.1016/j.jmathb.2004.03.002

Meyers, E. (2009). Tip of the iceberg: Meaning, identity, and literacy in preteen virtual worlds. *Journal of Education for Library and Information Science*, *50*(4), 226–236.

Moeller, K., Neuburger, S., Kaufmann, L., Landerl, K., & Nuerk, H. C. (2009). Basic number processing deficits in developmental dyscalculia: Evidence from eye tracking. *Cognitive Development*, *24*(4), 371–386. doi:10.1016/j.cogdev.2009.09.007

NCTM. (2006). *Curriculum focal points for prekindergarten through grade 8 mathematics*. Reston, VA: National Council of Teachers of Mathematics.

Nickerson, S. D., & Whitacre, I. (2010). A local instruction theory for the development of number sense. *Mathematical Thinking and Learning*, *12*(3), 227–252. doi:10.1080/10986061003689618

Rouselle, L., & Noël, M.-P. (2008). The development of automatic numerosity processes in preschoolers: Evidence for numerosity-perceptual interference. *Developmental Psychology*, *44*(2), 544–560. doi:10.1037/0012-1649.44.2.544

Schliemann, A. D., Carraher, D. W., Brizuela, B. M., & Jones, W. (1998). *Solving algebra problems before algebra instruction*. Paper presented at the Second Early Algebra Meeting. New York, NY.

Steen, L. A. (1997). *Why numbers count: Quantitative literacy for tomorrow's America*. New York, NY: College Entrance Examination Board. doi:10.1177/019263659808260020

Sweeney, B. (2008). Mathematics in a virtual world: How the immersive environment of second life can facilitate the learning of mathematics and other subjects. *ReLive 08: Researching learning in virtual environments*. Retrieved November, 2008, from http://www.open.ac.uk/relive08/documents/ReLIVE08_conference_proceedings_Lo.pdf

Twining, P. (2009). Exploring the educational potential of virtual worlds--Some reflections from the SPP. *British Journal of Educational Technology*, *40*(3), 496. doi:10.1111/j.1467-8535.2009.00963.x

Tzelgov, J., & Ganor-Stern, D. (2005). *Automaticity in processing ordinal information*. New York, NY: Psychology Press.

Wagner, C. (2008). Learning experience with virtual worlds. *Journal of Information Systems Education*, *19*(3), 263–266.

Wagner, C., & Rachael, K. F. (2009). Action learning with second life - A pilot study. *Journal of Information Systems Education*, 20(2), 249–258.

Wagner, D., & Davis, B. (2010). Feeling number: Grounding number sense in a sense of quantity. *Educational Studies in Mathematics*, 74(1), 39–51. doi:10.1007/s10649-009-9226-9

Wang, Y., & Braman, J. (2009). Extending the classroom through second life. *Journal of Information Systems Education*, 20(2), 235–247.

Warburton, S. (2009). Second life in higher education: Assessing the potential for and the barriers to deploying virtual worlds in learning and teaching. *British Journal of Educational Technology*, 40(3), 414–426. doi:10.1111/j.1467-8535.2009.00952.x

Weber, A., Rufer-Bach, K., & Platel, R. (2008). *Creating your world: The official guide to advanced content creation for second life*. Indianapolis, IN: Wiley Publishing, Inc.

Yang, D.-C., & Li, M.-N. F. (2008). An investigation of 3rd-grade Taiwanese students' performance in number sense. *Educational Studies*, 34(5), 443–455. doi:10.1080/03055690802288494

Yang, D.-C., Reys, R., & Reys, B. (2009). Number sense strategies used by pre-service teachers in Taiwan. *International Journal of Science and Mathematics Education*, 7(2), 383–403. doi:10.1007/s10763-007-9124-5

ADDITIONAL READING

Attewell, P., Lavin, D., Domina, T., & Levey, T. (2006). New evidence on college remediation. *The Journal of Higher Education*, 77(5), 886–924. doi:10.1353/jhe.2006.0037

Baker, S. C., Wentz, R. K., & Woods, M. M. (2009). Using virtual worlds in education: Second life as an educational tool. *Teaching of Psychology*, 36(1), 59–64. doi:10.1080/00986280802529079

Baroody, A. J., Eiland, M., & Thompson, B. (2009). Fostering at-risk preschoolers' number sense. *Early Education and Development*, 20(1), 80–128. doi:10.1080/10409280802206619

Barth, H., La Mont, K., Lipton, J., Dehaene, S., Kanwisher, N., & Spelke, E. (2006). Nonsymbolic arithmetic in adults and young children. *Cognition*, 98(3), 199–222. doi:10.1016/j.cognition.2004.09.011

Bobis, J. (2000). Dots, dominoes and dice: Developing children's understanding of number. *Primary Educator*, 6(4), 4.

Bull, R., Blatto-Vallee, G., & Fabich, M. (2006). Subitizing, magnitude representation, and magnitude retrieval in deaf and hearing adults. *Journal of Deaf Studies and Deaf Education*, 11(3), 289–302. doi:10.1093/deafed/enj038

Cordes, S., & Brannon, E. M. (2008). The difficulties of representing continuous extent in infancy: Using number is just easier. *Child Development*, 79(2), 476–489. doi:10.1111/j.1467-8624.2007.01137.x

Danesi, M. (2007). A conceptual metaphor framework for the teaching of mathematics. *Studies in Philosophy and Education*, 26(3), 225–236. doi:10.1007/s11217-007-9035-5

Dehaene, S. (2008). Cerebral constraints in reading and arithmetic: Education as a "neuronal recycling" process. In *The Educated Brain* (pp. 232–248). Cambridge, MA: Cambridge University Press. doi:10.1017/CBO9780511489907.016

Esmonde, I. (2009). Ideas and Iientities: Supporting equity in cooperative mathematics learning. *Review of Educational Research*, 79(2), 1008. doi:10.3102/0034654309332562

Faulkner, V. N. (2009). The components of number sense. *Teaching Exceptional Children*, *41*(5), 24–30.

Fleener, M. J., & Matney, G. (2006). Curriculum clearings as being-with-mathematics experiences: Authentic learning through a Heideggerian lens. *Journal of Curriculum & Pedagogy*, *3*(2), 92–106. doi:10.1080/15505170.2006.10411607

Green, C. S., & Bavelier, D. (2006). Enumeration versus multiple object tracking: The case of action video game players. *Cognition*, *101*(1), 217–245. doi:10.1016/j.cognition.2005.10.004

Grugnetti, L., & Jaquet, F. (2005). A mathematical competition as a problem solving and a mathematical education experience. *The Journal of Mathematical Behavior*, *24*(3/4), 373–384. doi:10.1016/j.jmathb.2005.09.012

Heiphetz, A., & Woodill, G. (2010). *Training and collaboration with virtual worlds: How to create cost-saving, efficient, and engaging programs*. New York, NY: McGraw-Hill.

Howell, S., & Kemp, C. (2005). Defining early number sense: A participatory Australian study. *Educational Psychology*, *25*(5), 555–571. doi:10.1080/01443410500046838

Howell, S., & Kemp, C. (2009). A participatory approach to the identification of measures of number sense in children prior to school entry. *International Journal of Early Years Education*, *17*(1), 47–65. doi:10.1080/09669760802699902

Howell, S. C., & Kemp, C. R. (2010). Assessing preschool number sense: Skills demonstrated by children prior to school entry. *Educational Psychology*, *30*(4), 411–429. doi:10.1080/01443411003695410

Jane, M. K., Amanda, K., & Karen, F. (2003). An assessment of students' understanding of angle. *Mathematics Teaching in the Middle School*, *9*(2), 116.

Kapp, K. M., & O'Driscoll, T. (2010). *Learning in 3-D: Adding a new dimension to enterprise learning and collaboration: How the immersive internet will shape the learning and work within the enterprise*. San Francisco, CA: John Wiley and Sons, Inc.

Kaufman, E. L., Lord, M. W., Reese, T. W., & Volkman, J. (1949). The discrimination of visual number. *The American Journal of Psychology*, *62*(4), 27. doi:10.2307/1418556

Kilday, C., & Kinzie, M. (2009). *An analysis of instruments that measure the quality of mathematics teaching in early childhood*. Berlin, Germany: Springer Science & Business Media. doi:10.1007/s10643-008-0286-8

Klibanoff, R. S., Levine, S. C., Huttenlocher, J., Vasilyeva, M., & Hedges, L. V. (2006). Preschool children's mathematical knowledge: The effect of teacher "math talk". *Developmental Psychology*, *42*(1), 59–69. doi:10.1037/0012-1649.42.1.59

Lakoff, G., & Johnson, M. (1980). *Metaphors we live by*. Chicago, IL: Chicago University Press.

Lamb, A., & Johnson, L. (2009). The potential, the pitfalls, and the promise of multi-user virtual environments: Getting a second life. *Teacher Librarian*, *36*(4), 68–78.

Landerl, K., Bevan, A., & Butterworth, B. (2004). Developmental dyscalculia and basic numerical capacities: A study of 8-9-year-old students. *Cognition*, *93*(2), 99–125. doi:10.1016/j.cognition.2003.11.004

Le Corre, M., Van de Walle, G., Brannon, E. M., & Carey, S. (2006). Re-visiting the competence/performance debate in the acquisition of the counting principles. *Cognitive Psychology*, *52*(2), 130–169. doi:10.1016/j.cogpsych.2005.07.002

Lucangeli, D., & Cabrele, S. (2006). Mathematical difficulties and ADHD. *Exceptionality*, *14*(1), 53–62. doi:10.1207/s15327035ex1401_5

Moeller, K., Neuburger, S., Kaufmann, L., Landerl, K., & Nuerk, H. C. (2009). Basic number processing deficits in developmental dyscalulia: Evidence from eye tracking. *Cognitive Development, 24*(4), 371–386. doi:10.1016/j.cogdev.2009.09.007

Murphy, M. M., Mazzocco, M. M. M., Hanich, L. B., & Early, M. C. (2007). Cognitive characteristics of children with mathematics learning disability (MLD) vary as a function of the cutoff criterion used to define MLD. *Journal of Learning Disabilities, 40*(5), 458–478. doi:10.1177/00222194070400050901

Peterson, S. A., & Simon, T. J. (2000). Computational evidence for the subitizing phenomenon as an emergent property of the human cognitive architecture. *Cognitive Science, 24*(1), 93. doi:10.1207/s15516709cog2401_3

Pfeil, U., Ang, C. S., & Zaphiris, P. (2009). Issues and challenges of teaching and learning in 3D virtual worlds: Real life case studies. *Educational Media International, 46*(3), 223–238. doi:10.1080/09523980903135368

Powell, A., & Seed, A. H. (2010). Developing a caring ethic for middle school mathematics classrooms. *Middle School Journal, 41*(4), 44–48.

Qing, L. (2005). Infusing technology into a mathematics methods course: Any impact? *Educational Research, 47*(2), 217–233. doi:10.1080/00131880500104341

Railo, H., Koivisto, M., Revonsuo, A., & Hannula, M. M. (2008). The role of attention in subitizing. *Cognition, 107*(1), 82–104. doi:10.1016/j.cognition.2007.08.004

Rapp, W. H. (2009). Avoiding math taboos: Effective math strategies for visual-spatial learners. *Teaching Exceptional Children Plus, 6*(2), 2–12.

Regina, D.-A., & James, E. R. (2002). The unintended consequences of stigma-free remediation. *Sociology of Education, 75*(3), 249. doi:10.2307/3090268

Salmon, G. (2002). *E-tivities: The key to active online learning*. London, UK: Taylor & Francis.

Shen, J., & Eder, L. B. (2009). Intentions to use virtual worlds for education. *Journal of Information Systems Education, 20*(2), 225–233.

Volk, T., & Bloom, J. W. (2007). The use of metapatterns for research into complex systems of teaching, learning, and schooling. *Complicity: An International Journal of Complexity & Education, 4*(1), 25–43.

Wadlington, E., & Wadlington, P. L. (2008). Helping students with mathematical disabilities to succeed. *Preventing School Failure, 53*(1), 2–7. doi:10.3200/PSFL.53.1.2-7

Wagner, C. G. (2009, July-August). Vizuaizing data. *The Futurist*, 60.

Wagner, T. (2008). *The global achievement gap: Why even our best schools don't teach the new survival skills our children need - And what we can do about it*. New York, NY: Basic Books.

Wankel, C., & Kingsley, J. (2009). *Higher education in virtual worlds: Teaching and learning in second life*. Bingley, UK: Emerald Group Publishing Limited.

Xin, L. (2010). Assessment use, self-efficacy and mathematics achievement: Comparative analysis of PISA 2003 data of Finland, Canada, and the USA. *Evaluation and Research in Education, 23*(3), 213–229. doi:10.1080/09500790.2010.490875

KEY TERMS AND DEFINITIONS

Base Systems: Refer to various counting quantities and how numbers can be grouped. When grouping numbers it is easy to think of them in containers: a dozen eggs, three tennis balls per container, and a six-pack of soda. These containers are all in a base system. We currently teach only in base 10 as that is traditional and yet base two through base x is used in packaging everywhere.

Composing And Decomposing: Numbers relates to operations involving them: addition, subtraction, multiplication, and division. By investigating patterns in various bases, more patterns become visible.

Metapattern: Is a pattern of patterns, relevant here for the patterns recognizable between base numbers when looking at base sheets as they relate to polynomials.

Subitizing: Is the ability to quickly determine the number of small quantities without counting.

SubQuanning: Is the ability to quickly determine the number of large quantities without counting: quantities are placed in containers of various sizes to represent digits (www.itonlytakes1.org): organized subitizing.

Chapter 5

Learn in Your Avatar:
A Teacher's Story on Integrating Virtual Worlds in Teaching and Learning

Mimma Sayuti Mat Khalid
University of Malaya, Malaysia

Raja Maznah Raja Hussain
University of Malaya, Malaysia

ABSTRACT

A Malaysian Smart School document has vividly described components that will make up future classrooms in 2020. Nonetheless, such components can currently be implemented using Virtual Worlds (VW), specifically Multi-User Virtual Environment (MUVE). Integrating virtual worlds effectively in teaching and learning can be very daunting, especially when the tool requires a steep learning curve on the part of the teacher. This chapter aims to describe a teacher's journey of integrating Virtual Worlds or MUVEs in her teaching and learning, both for adult learners and Malaysian secondary school. The technology integration is based on continuous self-reflection of TPACK (Technological, Pedagogical and Content Knowledge) framework. The description will include the strategies used in learning to learn; learning to teach in virtual worlds; and also lessons learned during the learning process of using the technology.

THE IDEAL VISION: MALAYSIAN FUTURE CLASSROOM

By 2020, teaching and learning scenarios could be very much_different from the one we have today... Students would learn in a community-led process (involving parents, teachers, university lecturers, professionals, industry members who actually make up the community) and would have access to the best teachers and the best educational material anywhere in the country...The learning environments would be formed through a programme <u>of</u> interconnected networks that increases communication, connectivity, shared, and experiential learning...Virtual reality teaching and learning experiences would become common through_tele-immersion. Using tele-immersion, three-dimensional virtual images of the teacher

DOI: 10.4018/978-1-4666-2670-6.ch005

could be projected to a student's home. The teacher and student could meet and interact online in real time (Smart School Roadmap, 2005, pp. 52-56).

The concept of future classroom described in the Fourth Wave of Malaysian Smart School implementation can currently be enacted through the use of existing Virtual Worlds (VWs) in teaching and learning. The following illustration in Figure 1 shows how a teaching and learning session takes place in a virtual world.

As illustrated in Figure 1, teaching and learning activities can be carried out in the VW as virtual learning spaces where 3D avatars can be present in 3D replicas of real places (e.g. Activeworld, Second Life, OpenSimulator/OpenSim), or 3D fictional places built by other avatars. In virtual worlds, avatars can walk, run, fly or teleport to different replicas of countries or places in the virtual worlds. Avatars can virtually be present together to complete tasks or outcomes. In this scenario, a session of building virtual objects in the virtual world was taking place among a few avatars—two learners, the teacher, and an invited technology expert.

DEFINING VIRTUAL WORLDS (VW)

Virtual Worlds (VW) refer to "A synchronous, persistent network of people, represented as avatars, facilitated by networked computers" (Bell, 2008). These 3D worlds are continuously gaining popularity as entertainment tools. By September 2010, virtual world users around the world has reached to one billion, with the majority of users comprises of kids and tweens age 10-15 years old (Kzero Report, 2010). Many educational institutions and Special Interest Groups (SIG) choose to use VW, specifically MUVE (Multi User Virtual Environment), or also termed as 'open virtual world' as supplements to existing face-to-face classrooms. In MUVEs like Second Life and OpenSim, individuals enter a virtual space/context

in their avatars; interact with digital objects, communicate with other avatars or intelligent agents; and take part in scenarios that are similar to real world (Dietrtle, 2009). Aldrich (2009) differentiates VW from gaming and simulation 3D virtual environment; thus, social VW depends on the user to create content for its environment.

Virtual worlds, as variants of virtual reality, are claimed to offer many educational affordances. O'Driscoll (2007) listed seven learning possibilities of using VW in teaching and learning: a)The Sense of Self; b) The Death of Distance; c) The Power of Presence; d) The Sense of Space; e)The Capability to Co-Create; f) The Pervasiveness of Practice; and g) The Enrichment of Experience. These possibilities make VW as a powerful tool for teaching and learning as in the specific virtual space regardless of different geographical areas, learners are able to be virtually present, collaborate, and engaged to rich learning content. Educational institutions are also increasingly using virtual worlds for professional developments for teachers and as supplement to classroom practices. Similarly, in the field of distance education, there is an increasing trend of using VW and MUVEs, for both formal and informal learning (Smith & Zane, 2009).

TPACK (TECHNOLOGICAL, PEDAGOGICAL, AND CONTENT KNOWLEDGE) OF TEACHERS

To start using virtual world in my teaching and learning, as a teacher, I need to evaluate my existing knowledge on technology, pedagogy, and content. TPCK (Technology, Pedagogy, and Content Knowledge) is a theory of teachers' knowledge (Mishra & Koehler, 2006) and consists of domains that need to be considered by teachers to effectively integrate technology in classrooms. TPACK can impact the teaching and learning strategies and the approaches in which teachers choose to facilitate learning. A teacher should aim to achieve the triad,

Figure 1. Malaysian future classroom can be enacted using virtual worlds

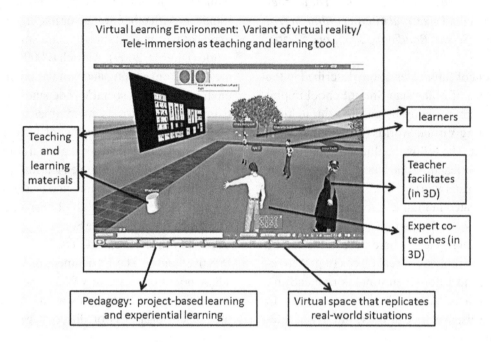

Figure 2. Self-reflection of TPACK strategies applied in integrating virtual worlds into teaching and learning

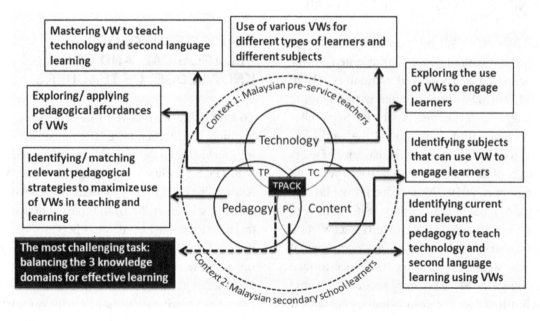

or what Thomson and Mishra (2007-2008) later called as "Total PACKage." It is insufficient for teachers to understand the individual domains on its own. The challenge is to balance the domains as to promote effective learning using technologies.

Reflecting upon my TPACK (refer to Figure 2), in the process of adopting virtual worlds in my teaching and learning, I found that a lot of time is spent on exploring and mastering VW as a learner. The level of learning to use VW depends on the latter's complexity. The technology can be based on text or rich multimedia ranging from 2D multimedia (e.g. Whyville) to 3D multimedia (e.g. World of Kaneva). There are VW that can be embedded in a website (e.g. Smallworlds and the defunct Metaplace), and there are VWs that provide options for high and low broadband capabilities (e.g. Club Cooee). The most popular yet challenging VW to use in education is Second Life (SL). To use SL in teaching and learning, teachers first need to familiarize themselves with the virtual world environment, then only will they be able to maximize the impact of using the tool in classrooms.

Most Virtual Worlds are not meant for education, as such, to create virtual learning environment that uses this technology, considerations of relevant pedagogy strategies are vital. The main focus of a classroom practice is to make learning happen effectively and not simply using VW for the sake of using the tool. In addition to TPACK, it is also important to consider the essential conditions when integrating technology effectively in teaching and learning (Roblyer & Doering, 2010).

For the past two years, I have been testing several VWs, both free and paid, to be used with two types of learners: a group of pre-service teachers of Teaching English as a Second Language (TESL); and a group of 13 years old learners for Information and Communication Technology Literacy (ICTL) programme. Selection of VWs to be used in both groups are based on the age limit, safety considerations, content area to be learned

and most importantly, the facilities available in the institutions the participants are studying.

The result is that different VWs (Figure 3) are used to help the learners in using the tools for their learning. As a teacher and learner, I frequent Second Life since the VW provides spaces for educational organizations to hold workshops, conferences, and meetings. In ReactionGrid, I have been personally coached by the Reaction-Grid Team to learn and develop the tool for my classroom use. Additional VWs were used to train the pre-service teachers. The reason was that there were 80 pre-service teachers learning to use VW but there were only 40 computers available for them to use Second Life. To familiarize the pre-service teachers with VWs, I adopted three other VWs that could be accessed with low bandwidth Internet, and low specification of computers. In this way, the pre-service teachers would be able to use the tool out of classroom time, simultaneously, be critical of the VWs pedagogical affordances. For the young secondary school learners, the priority was to select VWs that are safe for the users. Thus, VWs which were educational and under Parental Guide (PG) categories were used in my classrooms.

Figure 3. Experiencing with various VWs requires considerations of context and learners' needs

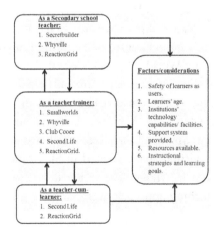

There have been many times when I have to re-consider the matching of my other two knowledge domains to technology knowledge domain. The main reason is because most of these virtual worlds developed are not meant for education purposes. Even though there are more educational virtual worlds created for teaching and learning, I still need to consider the pedagogical and content knowledge domain that can be relevant to the Malaysian context.

LESSONS LEARNED

In the process of establishing the triad of TPACK, there are a few lessons learned. Firstly, utilizing peer-learning in Community of Practice (CoP) in VWs help me to prepare my TPACK; secondly, making changes in adopting VWs in teaching and learning based on technology availability; and finally, exploring different approaches in integrating VW that focus on pedagogy.

Utilizing Peer-Learning in Community of Practice (CoP) of Virtual Worlds

To facilitate learning to use virtual worlds, I participated in several Communities of Practice (CoP) or Special Interest Groups (SIG) since November 2008. There was a lack of local support for me to learn how to use VWs in my teaching and learning, so my first experience was to participate in a six-week online course of Teaching Language in a Virtual World 2009 (TLVW09). The aim of the course was to give exposure and help teachers around the world to use virtual worlds in second language teaching. My first class was an Introduction to Spanish Language, which was carried out in a virtual space created in SL to mirror a real Spanish Village. The avatar instructors use team-teaching approach in training the group of language teachers to communicate in basic Spanish language.

Every week, there would be a virtual class taking place in real time to learn different languages, and there were classes on how to use the SL tools (audio and chat tools) for teaching and learning. In 2010, I participated again in the same online course, together with 30 students who I was teaching. These TESL pre-service teachers became my virtual and face-to-face CoP. Being adventurous, my students experienced more learning than I did, and in return, I learned from them on how to use VW in teaching and learning by reading the reflections in their weekly blogs.

Belonging to a CoP helps me not only to explore the affordances of VW but also allows me to build my own 3D objects in-world. I did not want to pay for private virtual space in SL as the virtual island can be expensive. So, I used to frequent International Society for Technology in Education (ISTE) island to learn more virtual world living skills and was able to 'rez' (create or build) objects temporarily in SL. ISTE has its own private island that is managed by its CoP. Being in the island gave me opportunities to participate in various virtual events there, both formal and informal. There are docents on the island who are on duty round the clock. The docents, comprise of teachers around the world in Real Life (RL), are virtual volunteers to help newcomers to virtual island. From one of my meetings with the avatar trainer, I learned about other virtual worlds that can be used for teenagers. This is due to the reason that the SL has two types of environment or grids. The main grid is meant for adult age 18 years old and above, and the Teen SL is for teenagers. It was from the monthly discussions that I gain knowledge about other SL-like VWs such as the open source platform for operating a virtual world (OpenSim) namely, ReactionGrid. Aside from the CoP available for using Reaction Grid VW, the grid host team provides full support for training the teachers to learn to use the technology.

The Process of Selecting Virtual World: The Changes Made

After a year and half experiencing and learning in virtual worlds, I learned that the more flexible and open a virtual world, the more affordances it can offer for various type of teaching and learning (like SL). However, such flexibility will also mean more effort in learning to use the virtual world. For professional development, there are many virtual spaces that hold formal and informal meetings for teachers who are interested to use the Web as teaching and learning tools. For instance, an island called Edunation in SL is created as meeting space for avatars comprising of language educators and Webheads (teachers and educators using Web 2.0 and Computer-Mediated Communication).

Aside from the age limit problem, SL requires high technology capabilities of hardware. These issues have made me decide to resort to other virtual world. My next selection was to use Metaplace. It was a 2.5D virtual world that can easily be embedded into any website, which means it can run in a browser, unlike SL that needs a viewer, which has to be downloaded onto the desktop. This feature allows me to create a website and arrange the content according to learning outcomes. It is easier to design 2D as compared to 3D virtual learning environment. Unfortunately, after a year of paid virtual space, Metaplace ceased operation. As such, availability and stability of VW are other reasons to consider when selecting a virtual world for learning tool.

The final consideration is to think of my learners. As I want to integrate virtual world which is similar to SL, I explored open source virtual world or OpenSim. The current trend of institutions, schools, and corporate organizations like Microsoft Inc. are to have virtual presence in private islands that are cheaper to buy; free to create content; and form private Communities of Practice. With new technologies, an avatar of these private islands can be 'transported' from one island to another island via hyperlinks or termed as HyperGrid. Being the owner of the virtual world, I can manage the membership of the virtual space. This would ensure the security and safety of my young learners.

The Technology Gain: Different Approaches in Integrating Virtual Worlds into 2D Virtual Learning Environments

To integrate VWs into teaching and learning, I have to consider how it can meet the curriculum requirements; what kind of learning activities that it can promote; and most importantly how to measure learning when using VWs. Since most of VWs are not meant for education, I integrated these tools into my 2D virtual classrooms. I have been using social network application like Ning and Grouply as the main virtual classroom. The purposes were mainly to facilitate the process of learning to use VWs, and to assess learners' performances. After exploring various virtual worlds, I found that most virtual worlds can be integrated to virtual learning environments through 6 approaches (Figure 4). These approaches will depend on the instructional goals and the instructional strategies adopted. Most of the VWs I used functions as additional virtual classrooms for my learners.

The first approach is to link a 2D learning environment to a VW. This can be done by inserting the URL address of the virtual world. Second Life uses SLurl that provides direct teleport links to locations in its world (Figure 4). This approach facilitated my pre-service teachers cum learners in learning how to create virtual learning environment using VW. Besides, similar to my learning experiences with VWs, the website was used for class management purposes, such as making announcements of virtual meetings in SL. Interactions took place in both the website and VW. Learners were assessed from both virtual spaces

Figure 4. Linking VW to existing website/learning management system

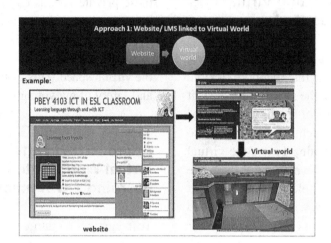

as they blogged about their experiences in learning in SL. In SL, chat logs were saved as part of learners' assessments.

Second, is to link from virtual world to relevant websites (Figure 5). Most virtual worlds are developed not meant for education purposes like Gaia, as such, some VW do not have features that can accommodate classroom activities like reading and writing, or assessing learners' performances. Therefore, a teacher will need to provide the URL address from the VW to the 2D learning environment or resources. Learners will have to leave the VW environment to a 2D environment to be able to read or write. The main reason of making this VW as the main learning platform for the class was for motivation purposes. Gaia, like many other game-like VWs, has its own currency. This currency can serve as reward system for learners as they perform required tasks and achieve goals set for the learning.

Figure 5. Linking virtual world to website

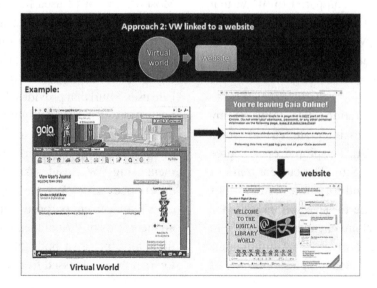

Figure 6. Embedding website in virtual world

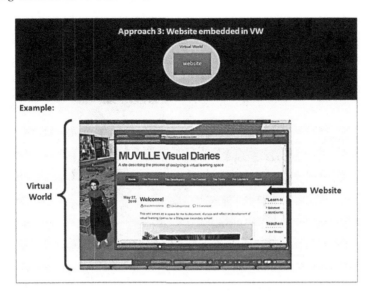

The third approach is to use a virtual world that enables learners to view 2D learning environments or website within the VW environment (Figure 6). VW like Second Life and OpenSim have this capability. Avatar profile can be checked; or a website can be read without having to leave the virtual world environment. However, this type of VW needs higher hardware requirement and sufficient broadband capabilities. I was unable to use this approach throughout the learning process due to these two reasons.

The fourth approach is to embed VW into any 2D learning environment or website (Figure 7). Within the given virtual space where the VW is embedded, avatars will be able to move around the VW, simultaneously, the person can read,

Figure 7. Embedding virtual world in a website

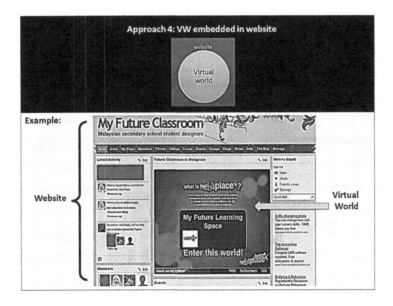

Figure 8. Enriching a website using virtual world

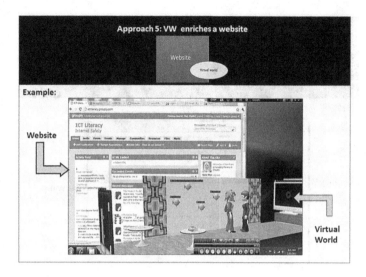

write, and edit on the 2D learning environment or website. Interactions can be in real time in the VW. It will be like reading a textbook while interacting with the content, the teacher, and other learners. Instances of VW for this approach are Small Worlds and the defunct Metaplace. However, not many VWs have this capability.

The fifth approach is to use VW as part of a learning tool for a 2D learning environment (Figure 7). Typical to this is VWs in the form of 3D webchat like Club Cooee and IMVU. These VWs do not require high specification of hardware; as such, they are more accessible. Learners can create content though with limitations. I have been using this approach if I would like to be co-

Figure 9. Transforming a website into a virtual world

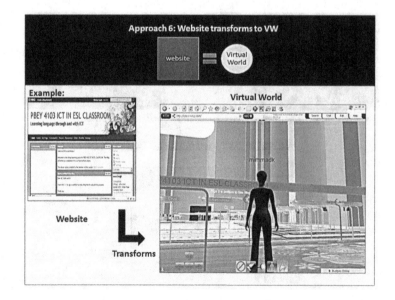

present and carry out online group activities such as virtual discussions with my learners. Chat logs can be saved as part of learners' assessments (see Figure 8).

Finally, is the approach of turning any 2D learning environment or websites to a 3D virtual learning space (Figure 9). In this approach, an avatar will be able to walk around and perform tasks in the transformed 2D website. For now, the known tool is ExitReality. However, I found that navigating in a transformed 2D virtual environment is challenging, because the objects in the 3D learning can be messy.

I have used a few of these six approaches in my classes for the TESL pre-service teachers and secondary school learners. The knowledge of these approaches can facilitate integration of VWs into teaching and learning according to hardware capabilities; and in making instructional design decisions when developing virtual learning spaces. What I learned is that for my adult learners all these approaches can be applicable. However, for my young learners, I used approaches 1 to 3 since I have to be cautious of which VWs to use. I resorted to using a private VW for the young learners to ensure safe learning environments.

CONCLUSION: THE JOURNEY CONTINUES...

Despite having spent more than two years experimenting and experiencing learning events in virtual worlds, I am still in the process of balancing the three domains of teacher's knowledge. A lot of time is focused on understanding and making design decisions on how to integrate VW in teaching and learning effectively.

Virtual Worlds can provide many learning affordances for teachers to use in their classrooms. However, it is important to use VW not for the sake of using the tool, but to think of how the tool can facilitate learning. To achieve a balance of the three knowledge domains is challenging.

However, actively participating in CoPs that discuss best practices of VW integration can help me to continuously improve my teaching and learning practices.

REFERENCES

Aldrich, C. (2009). Virtual worlds,simulaltions, and games for education: A unifying view. *Innovate, 5*(5). Retrieved January 11, 2011 from http://www.innovateonline.info/pdf/vol5_issue5/ Virtual_Worlds,_Simulations,_and_Games_for_ Education-__A_Unifying_View.pdf

Bell, M. (2008). Toward a definition of "virtual worlds". *Journal of Virtual Worlds Research, 1*(1).

Diertle, E., & Clarke, J. (2008). Multi-user environment for teaching and learning. In Pagani, M. (Ed.), *Encylopedia of Multimedia Technology and Networking*. Hershey, PA: IGI Global.

Kzero Worldwide. (2010). *Virtual world registered accounts Q3 2010*. Retrieved from http://www. kzero.co.uk/blog/?p=4448

Mishra, P., & Koehler, M. (2006). Technological pedagogical content knowledge. *Teachers College Record, 108*(6), 1017–1054. doi:10.1111/j.1467-9620.2006.00684.x

Multimedia Development Corporation. (2005). *Smart school roadmap 2005-2020*. New York, NY: Multimedia Development Corporation.

O'Driscoll, T. (2007). *Learning in three dimensions: Experiencing the sensibilities and imagining the possibilities*. Retrieved November 13, 2010, from http://www.youtube.com/watch?v=O2jY4U kPbAc&feature=player_embedded#!

Roblyer, M. D., & Doering, A. H. (2010). *Integrating educational technology into teaching*. Upper Saddle River, NJ: Pearson Educatiion Inc.

Smith, M., & Berge, Z. (2009). Social learning theory in second life. *MERLOT Journal of Online Learning and Teaching, 5*(2).

Thompson, A., & Mishra, P. (2008). Breaking news: TPCK becomes TPACK! *Journal of Computing in Teacher Education, 24*(2). Retrieved October 29, 2010 at http://punya.educ.msu.edu/publications/journal_articles/jcteeditorial-24-2-038.pdf

Chapter 6
Visual Learning in the Virtual World:
The Hidden Curriculum of Imagery in Second Life

Hsiao-Cheng Han
University of British Columbia, Canada

ABSTRACT

Humans rely heavily on their sense of vision and learn from didactic images within their environments. For this reason, in traditional educational environments, educators care about visual representation. However, as today's technology brings images to wider audiences with diverse cultural backgrounds in the virtual world global community, the process of automatic cognition helps people build new knowledge based on prior regional experience. Therefore, when educators employ a technology like Second Life to deliver education, the whole virtual world can be seen as a school. Although most research participants agreed that the imagery in Second Life is fictional, the data shows that users do learn from imagery in the virtual world.

INTRODUCTION

Images have always played a significant role in human lives. Since the early cave drawings, people have used images to "represent, make meaning of, and convey various sentiments about nature, society, and culture as well as to represent imaginary worlds and abstract concepts" (Sturken & Cartwright, 2004, p. 13). The audience for these early images was generally limited to those few who had the same cultural background as the image creators and understood the meaning intended by the image creators. However, due to the advancement of technology, images are now more easily produced and more widely disseminated. From print to movies, images have changed from static to motion. From movies to television, moving images have changed from a localized viewing to national and worldwide broadcasts. From television to computers, moving images have changed from being viewed by audiences to being created by them. From computers to the virtual worlds (like

DOI: 10.4018/978-1-4666-2670-6.ch006

Second Life), moving images have gone from being created by a single source to being collaborative ongoing endeavors. As today's technology brings images to wider audiences with diverse cultural backgrounds, the exchange of these images is "challenging many conventional wisdoms about the seemingly transparent relationships between images and meaning, mind and thought, as well as culture and identity" (Burnett, 2004, p. xv). Williams (2006) adds that "images generated through the physical eye or the mind's eye or by metaphor influence cognitive and behavioral processes before and beyond the process of reason. The integration of intuitive visual knowing with rational cognitive processes generates expressions of whole-mind cognition" (p. 32). As advanced technology and human desire come together, images become even more important today.

Because people may misunderstand others through stereotyped images, stereotyping is another serious issue that should be considered. "A stereotype is a generalization based on inadequate or incomplete information, because one must select among available information about a person, place, or situation, there is no choice but to make judgments on incomplete or inadequate information" (Stern & Robinson, 1994, p. 44). Despite its potential for misinformation, stereotyping is a necessary means of building up people's knowledge and understanding of images. Without stereotypes, when a partly unfamiliar thing is mentioned, people will be unable to create an image, and the communication will fail. For instance, when people are talking about "Asian," a typical Asian face appears in their mind. With this image in mind, people can start a conversation. Without this image, people will not able to start the conversation because they have no idea about what Asian is.

For Dake (1999), "Visual mind is more than a communication system. Visual mind is also a valuable cognitive system" (p. 9). Through human beings' visual sense, people are not only watching, looking, and seeing, but they are also learning from what they see. "Reality is constructed from what we sense based on our experience, emotional condition, beliefs, and so forth" (Miller & Burton, 1994, p. 66). Human perception of the virtual world also follows this theory. The first time people see a new thing, they may not notice it. However, if that new thing is a very noticeable visual image, they may have emotional feelings about it and even be curious about it. If they do notice an image the first time, when they see it a second time, they may not notice it or they may feel excited about it because they have seen this image before. If this image does not have a strong connection with them, after several times, their feelings about this image will substantially decrease. In other words, people's way of seeing is not consistent because different time, place, personal experiences and emotional conditions influence how people look images, people may get used to the images they perceive easily, without really noticing them.

VISUAL COMMUNICATION

The difference between historical communication theory (into the 1990s) and reader response theory depends on active reading or viewing and construction of meaning (Freedman, 2003). Visual communication requires three factors: addresser, content, and addressee (Morgan & Welton, 1992). Successful communication requires the active participation of both addresser and addressee (Morgan & Welton, 1992). The result, or how well addressees understand the message, depends on how the addresser gives the message, through what kind of media, with what content, as well as where, when, and how the addressees receive the message. As Corner and Hawthorn note, "communication studies is about how human meanings are made through the production and reception of various types of sign. It is about visual and verbal sign systems and the technologies used to articulate, record, and convey them" (as cited in Finnegan, 2002, p. 10).

"All communication proceeds from signs" (Jamieson, 2007, p. 34), and signs include linguistic, verbal, graphical, and pictorial representations. The electrical impulses of our brains record visual information billions of times every second (Aukstakalnis, 1991), and the purpose of processing this information is to help us understand our environment. Visual information, in this research, includes all images people can see, such as arts, signs, natural environments, and visual culture, but excludes linguistic words. Images denote and simulate, but images are also opened for connotation (Jamieson, 2007). Images can be perceived more rapidly and readily than texts (Pettersson, 1993; McFee & Degge, 1977). As Finnegan (2002) states:

We are surrounded by sights... We manage and interact with this seen world, and within it, with other living creatures and especially other human beings, selecting and creating the sights for visual communication through our own bodies and our material creations (p. 92).

In visual communication, images carry information not only through shape and form, and through literal and symbolic representation, but also through contextual frames of meaning. "They can be simple or multilayered, and they can be manipulated into reflecting political or philosophical ideologies" (Barry, 1997, p. 139). According to Morgan and Welton (1992), image creators need to convey messages in a way that viewers can "focus on [the message], interpret it, understand it, and possibly act on it" (p. 133). Image creators should make messages as clear as possible because, if the image creator is sending the message without the viewer understanding the message, they are not communicating. However, viewers bring their own preferred interpretations

to images because of their own selective perceptions, mental schemata, past experiences, and personal and cultural backgrounds and values; images have their own preferred interpretations (Barry, 1997; Chandler, 2008; Jamieson, 2007; Pettersson, 1993). That is to say, understanding the meaning of images is an ongoing process, and the meaning of images is grounded between the self and the external world. A shared interpretation requires "a shared or similar background of experience, knowledge, or education" (Jamieson, 2007, p. 47). Moreover, human visual systems have the "ability to perceive depth and to distinguish between even the slimmest differences in color, form, and texture together [and] provide the brain with a tremendous amount of data from which to construct our perception of the world" (Aukstakalnis, 1991, p. 50). These perceptions help people to interact with images and environments. In other words, the visual world is a mental map, not a territory (Barry, 1997).

In postmodern communication theory, the meaning of images is connected to the intention of the image producer. Therefore, viewers can choose to perceive images in the way they desire (Freedman, 2003). Viewers can choose to accept the intention encoded by the image producer, they can choose to ignore the intention, or they can choose to perceive images from their own intention (Darts, 2004; Davenport, 2003; Freedman & Wood, 1999; Tavin, 2003; Marshall, 2004). The intention of image communication in the postmodern era presents opportunities for multiple interpretations.

HIDDEN CURRICULUM OF IMAGES

Vision plays a significant role in people's experience of their culture; McMillin (2007) points out that meaning is created and propagated by symbolic forms. Visual symbols fill spaces and reach people from different points in space as visual perceptions (Dewey, 1934). According to McFee and Degge (1977), ideas and feelings in visual forms are expressed through symbols. That is to say, symbols also are a principal means of communication. When people respond to visual symbols, they not only look at colors, sizes, and shapes of the symbols, they also make connections between the visual symbols and their experiences. In short, they are learning through vision (McFee & Degge, 1977). The context of images and the context of how people view images influence the interpretation of images. As Jamieson (2007) states, "historical and critical perception" is formed by cultural background; people may not consciously be aware of it, but they are influenced and affected by it. Therefore, when people perceive the same visual symbol, they might perceive it in a different way (Berger, 1977). As Berger stated, "We are always looking at the relation between things and ourselves. Our vision is continually active, continually moving, continually holding things in a circle around itself, constituting what is present to us as we are" (p. 9).

According to Myles (2004), images enhance the ability of students with social-cognitive challenges to understand their environment. From the images they see in school, students learn "through osmosis, the ideological underpinnings of schooling, which is often unconscious even to teachers" (Duncum, 1999, p. 297). "The more common [the images] are, the more completely integrated they are with the rest of life, the more powerful they are in both informing and forming minds" (Duncum, 1999, p. 299).

The hidden curriculum is not consciously created by educators; students internalize it from teachers' attitudes and behaviors, classrooms, classmates, and the entire school setting (Anderson, 2002; Myles, 2004; Pinar, Reynolds, Slattery, & Taubman, 2002). As Weiss (2006) argues, "learning is the process whereby knowledge is created through the transformation of experience" (p. 4) and knowledge comes in many forms and for different purposes (Dewey, 1938). Therefore,

when educators create school curriculum, they consciously plan all course objectives they would like students to achieve (Wren, 1999). However, students are not only learning from curriculum that educators plan, but they are also learning from their life experiences and social interactions (Pinar, et al., 2002; Weiss, 2006). As Myles notes, "The hidden curriculum also includes idioms, metaphors, and slang—things most people 'just pick up' or learn through observation or subtle cues, including body language" (p. 4). According to Apple (2004), "the hidden curriculum in schools [includes] the tacit teaching to students of norms, values, and dispositions that goes on simply by their living in and coping with the institutional expectations and routines of schools day in and day out for a number of years" (p. 13). The hidden curriculum is usually not hidden but is often too obvious for educators or students to notice (Anderson, 2002; Gair & Mullins, 2001; Myles, 2004; Weiss, 2006).

Recognizing the hidden curriculum is important not only because it is dangerous, but because students are unconsciously learning from it (Duncum, 1999). Students change their values, morals, and attitudes in response to the hidden curriculum (Snyder, 1971). Greater understanding of the hidden curriculum helps educators and students avoid unconscious learning and helps reach the final goal of education (Myles, 2004; Wren, 1999). People respond to and make sense of what they experience as they accommodate new experiences to old ones (Dewey, 1934; Taylor, 2000). As Taylor (2000) states, "Everything that we create somehow affects everything around us. Therefore, everything we do, read, and create plays a part in our experience" (p. 380). And because of a person's past experiences, what he or she notices and is aware of will be different from that noticed by others; furthermore, what people think, desire, and receive will be different as well (Dewey, 1934).

Meaning is made by people from the same culture; therefore, meanings can also be "submitted to disassembly, reassembly, investment, and exchange" within the same culture (Harasim, 2006, p. 109). Every culture's stability depends on how residents understand the meanings of the experiences circulated in their culture. As Jamieson (2007) notes, people overtly or covertly learn from particular cultural circumstances. Different cultures guide people to different interpretations.

VISUAL LEARNING IN THE VIRTUAL WORLD

Second Life (SL) is an online community where people socialize, communicate, and connect to each other. As in the real-world, SL users communicate not only through oral speech or typed text but also through images. "[H]uman communication is limited; it depends on creating an image in the other of what is trying to be communicated. However, the analogies are always limited and subject to various forms of distortion. Human communication requires interpretation" (Stern & Robinson, 1994, p. 34). In other words, even if an image viewed in SL is one that may help its viewer reproduce the same concept as was intended by the creator of that image, without support in interpreting the viewer may never reach the intended meaning of the image.

"Reality is constructed from what we sense based on our experience, emotional condition, beliefs, and so forth" (Miller & Burton, 1994, p. 66). Human perception of the virtual world also follows this theory. The first time people see a new thing, they may not notice it. However, if that new thing is a very noticeable visual image, they may have emotional feelings about it and even be curious about it. If they do notice an image the first time, when they see it a second time, they may not notice it, or they may feel excited about it because they have seen this image before. If this image does not have a strong connection with them, after several times their feelings about this image will substantially decrease. In other words,

people's ways of seeing are not consistent because of different time, environment, personal experiences and emotional conditions, people may get used to the images they perceive easily, without really noticing them.

Because people may misunderstand others through stereotyped images, stereotyping is another issue that should be considered. "A stereotype is a generalization based on inadequate or incomplete information, because one must select among available information about a person, place, or situation, there is no choice but to make judgments on incomplete or inadequate information" (Stern & Robinson, 1994, p. 44). Despite its potential for misinformation, stereotyping is a necessary means of building up people's knowledge and understanding of images. Without stereotypes, when a partly unfamiliar thing is mentioned, people's mind will be unable to create an image, and the communication will fail. As Morgan and Welton (1992) state, "A degree of stereotyping is inevitable in any figurative median. To communicate, you need a vocabulary of readily understood signs. Personality and attitude can be conveyed by emphasizing certain features" (p. 95).

For Dake (1999), "Visual mind is more than a communication system. Visual mind is also a valuable cognitive system" (p. 9). Through human beings' visual sense, people are not only watching, looking, and seeing, but are also learning from what they see.

In SL, everything is created by users; in other words, everything has a maker and a meaning behind it. There are also many commercial activities in SL. Because the prices of virtual items are much cheaper than those of real-world items, and because the limitations of physical reality do not need to be considered, what people decide to buy primarily depends on how things look. Appearance becomes more important in SL than in real-life.

Along with the increased presence of synchronized communication, voice chat, and fully animated environments in people's lives, the role of virtual worlds has grown. Virtual worlds are now being adopted for use as educational environments. In the virtual world of Second Life, academic institutions construct their learning environments as virtual campuses where the boundary between classroom, campus, and the rest of the virtual world environment is not obvious. Anywhere imaginable can become a learning environment in the virtual world: classes can be held in a garden, in the sky, or under water. Instructors can easily take students off campus for field trips or students can travel outside the campus independently. The whole virtual world can be seen as a learning environment.

Miller and Burton (1994) contend that communication is the exchange and understanding of information between two or more people. However, people in the virtual world of Second Life use avatars to represent themselves, and these avatars can be made to resemble anything from the users' imagination. The gender, age, race, and species of an avatar may be completely different from that of its user in real-life. In other words, when education takes place in the virtual world, who the instructor is and who the students are is not as obvious as in a real-life educational environment.

Communication takes place when viewers are receiving, learning, and understanding the intended meaning of images, and automatic cognition can only help build new knowledge based on prior, regional experience. Therefore, people may not automatically make sense of this global culture because of the regional limitations of their prior experience. Moreover, all human-made images contain meaning, but in different cultures, the same shapes, colors, and compositions may carry different meanings. According to Arnheim (1970), human beings are eager for visual sensations; however, people may also perceive the same images from different perspectives. Visual communication can only be successful if those communicating connect the same meanings to the same images, and if the viewers of those images are knowledgeable about this intended meaning. Without access to this shared understanding, viewers must construct their own meaning. Therefore,

when people who are communicating visually do not have similar cultural or personal backgrounds, their communication may fail.

Second Life (SL) is an online community in which people socialize, communicate, and connect to each other. As in the real-world, in SL "human communication is limited, it depends on creating an image in the other of what is trying to be communicated. However, the analogies are always limited and subject to various forms of distortion. Human communication requires interpretation" (Stern & Robinson, 1994, p. 34). In other words, even if an image viewed in SL is one that may help its viewer reproduce the same concept as was intended by the creator of that image, without support in interpreting the image, the viewer may never reach the intended meaning of the image. The visualized virtual world has become part of the distance learning tools. However, few educators have noticed the importance of the hidden curriculum of imagery. Therefore, the purpose of this research was to help instructors and students become conscious of how they are constantly learning from the images and environments embedded in curricula of the virtual world. Revealing the didactic character of the visual virtual world should allow educators and students to become more open-minded about the visual culture of the virtual world and should enable them to critically decode the images they see.

Observation, Survey, and Interviews

The purpose of this research was to help instructors and students become conscious of how they are constantly learning from the images and environments embedded in curricula of the virtual world. Revealing the didactic character of the visual virtual world should allow educators and students to become more open-minded about the visual culture of the virtual world and should enable them to critically decode the images they see.

The researcher used "simple random sampling" (Robson, 2002, p. 261) to collect the observation location data. The researcher conducted a search, using "Education" as a key word, in the "Second Life Search" window of places in the eleven Second Life (SL) classifications: Linden location, adult, art and culture, business, educational, gaming, hangout, newcomer friendly, parks and nature, residential, and shopping. Many categories produced no results. The researcher then conducted a search of the same eleven SL classifications using "art" as the key word. In categories where more than one result was found, the researcher used place names to sort the results alphabetically and selected the first one in each category as the initial observation target.

The researcher used a survey accompanied by an interview as her methods for addressing research sub questions. The survey questions were divided into four sections. Section one covered the participant demographic information, including computer hardware and software capabilities. Section two included participant site selection and preferences. Section three included the participant learning from visual experiences. Survey section four included the motivation and process of learning. Semi-structured interviews helped the researcher answer the research questions. By combining the data of the surveys and interviews, the researcher was able to find more authentic answers to her research questions.

Visual Learning in Second Life

In response to the interview question, "Have you learned something in Second Life from what you have seen?" only 9% of interviewees said no; 91% all agreed that they learned something from what they saw in Second Life. Some interview participants stated they learned about other religions and cultures in Second Life. In other words, most survey participants consciously knew they were learning from their sense of vision. As Stephen (2007) notes, virtual world interactions can be seen as real experiences that provide an opportunity for people to sensitize their visual perception.

Most survey participants indicated they did not learn about Second Life from books; they stated that they learned to use Second Life by themselves, followed by learning from other avatars. Survey participants indicated that they learned primarily by finding visual clues, followed by reading hover texts and note cards. In other words, texts were not the first choice for survey participants in their process of learning. These data support the assertion that images are perceived more rapidly and readily than texts (McFee & Degge, 1977; Pettersson, 1993). As Freedman (2003) states, when viewing an unfamiliar image or "hidden unit," the brain accesses knowledge stored in the memory to decode this image. Therefore, when relying only on visual clues and without access to previous experiences and memories as referents, people will not be able to fully understand the meaning of the mixed cultural imagery of the virtual world. According to Barry (1997), Hoffmann (2007), and Kellogg (1995), even images people have perceived unconsciously, if viewed repeatedly, will be stored in long-term memory and will influence how similar images are perceived in the future and how viewers are able to manipulate these images in the future. In other words, when the survey participants viewed imagery that exists only in Second Life, their cognitive process helped them to reinforce the visual experience and store it in their long-term memory.

In order to understand the meaning of imagery that exists only in Second Life, survey participants tried to find clues in Second Life, in surrounding areas, from friends in Second Life, or by searching the Internet. They did not tend to ask their real-life friends or they chose to ignore them. These tendencies suggest that Second Life users are curious about the images around them in the virtual world. They will spend time figuring out the meaning of images. However, their preference to not ask real-life friends about the imagery in Second Life shows that, when they are in the virtual world, they have more connections with virtual-world friends than with real-life friends.

When responding to open-ended questions, survey participants explained that, because Second Life is a realistic environment, visual content enhances their learning and because of this formal visual quality, they can learn well in Second Life, paralleling Dake's (1999) contention that images teach people, and people learn from images constantly. Interview participants also agreed that Second Life is a great platform for distance education because in Second Life they can see things as they learn about them and they can see who they are talking with and watch demonstrations. One interview participant pointed out that because Second Life is visually appealing, he likes to stay in Second Life—something he does not do in other text-based chatroom environments. His comment illustrates how the visual environment and online social networking opportunities in Second Life attract more participation than traditional text-based chatrooms without imagery. Second Life is an environment that enables users to visualize abstract knowledge and, through the images, also draws viewer interest.

One survey participant stated that he enjoyed learning about "academic campuses in other countries." However, some survey participants felt that academic campuses were desolate and were just "a replica of a RL [real-life] campus." Survey participants benefitted from learning about other countries' campuses from those reconstructed in Second Life, while other participants wanted to see academic campuses influenced by imagination. In this situation, the hidden curriculum of virtual campuses is formed by site designers. A realistic building in Second Life might not be a reconstructed real-life building. Visitors learned the hidden message of the atmosphere of a school by visiting the virtual campus.

Some of the interview participants who are also educators agreed: "Universities… using SL for teaching really need to be careful of who their neighbors are." In keeping with Gestalt theory, people never view an image alone; their eyes always add other images or texts next to the main image to their perception, or they even add their own mental images to the image they are looking at Groom, Dewart, Esgate, Gurney, Kemp,

and Towell (1999). Therefore, students are not only learning from the environment provided by educators but also learn from imagery near the learning environment.

Some interview participants do not question what they see in Second Life and think they have learned something from their visual perception. Moreover, people do assume that, because all information includes imagery, educational places in Second Life should be accurate representations. These presumptions highlight two things. First, some people do not question what they see in the virtual world but absorb all the information by which they are surrounded. Second, when building educational environments in Second Life, site designers should be aware of what kind of visual environment they provide their visitors. Therefore, when educators employ images in educational environments to stimulate student learning, how students understand images and how educators can teach students to understand images become critical issues. Visual communication, as Kellner (2006) states, "not only teaches students to learn from media, to resist media manipulation, and to use media materials in constructive ways, but is also concerned with developing skills that will help create good citizens and that will make them more motivated and competent participants in social life" (p. 250).

Hidden Curriculum in Second Life

About 57% of survey participants gave a response of neutral, agree, or strongly agree when asked if their own cultural imagery had been misused, misrepresented, or misunderstood in SL. These data suggest that most people think the visual environment of Second Life contains false visual information. In response to an open-ended question about the interpretation of cultural imagery, survey participants pointed out misused, misrepresented imagery, including "political information," "simplified cultural imagery," "liberal bias," "only represented builders' imaginations," and "builders came from different cultural environments and misused cultural imagery." Images are always propagating in the virtual world; builders can easily manipulate images to deliver their political stance (Sturken & Cartwright, 2004). When users are building their idealized world in the virtual environment, the hidden curriculum of imagery in the virtual world becomes no longer authentic but propagates builders' ideologies.

Most research participants confirmed that they learned more in Second Life by finding visual clues or observing than from texts; however, few did not think they learned from didactic imagery in Second Life. In other words, some Second Life users did not realize they were unconsciously communicating and learning through their visual experiences. As Vygotsky states, repeated experience develops internalization; therefore, people depend on cognitive ability to understand abstract knowledge from the world of imagery (as cited in Efland, 2002).

According to the interview participants, they had seen their own cultural imagery (European, Irish, Korean, American, New Zealand, Maori, German, Greek, and Italian) represented in Second Life. Interviewees were not sure if people from countries with different cultural backgrounds would be able to understand the cultural imagery. As Frechette (2002) notes, people from different cultural backgrounds view the same image from different perspectives and have different rational and emotional reflections consciously or unconsciously. The interview participants' statements explained cultural imagery in Second Life as being built by different users with different understandings about their own or other cultures and noted the accuracy of the imagery and point of view may not be correct or neutral. Therefore, when visitors come with different cultural backgrounds, with little or no understanding about the history of other cultures, they may only understand their perspective of the culture but not the meaning of the imagery. "The message [may be] deliberately ambiguous precisely to foster the use of differ-

ent codes by those who, in different times and places" (Eco, 1990, p. 140) will encounter the communication.

In response to the survey question "Have you ever learned about other cultures in SL?" 66% of the survey participants agreed that they consciously learned about other cultures just by being in Second Life. However, very few survey participants actually asked other avatars when learning about other cultures; they mostly learned from what they saw. Sturken and Cartwright (2004) remind us: "there are both conscious and unconscious levels of looking. We engage in practices of looking to communicate, to influence and be influenced" (p. 10). It is possible that the remaining survey participants were also exposed to other visualized cultural environments but did not acknowledge their impact.

Petterson (1993) notes that in different parts of the world, different parts of the country, and different socioeconomic groups, visual communications have their own language and grammar. Images are not only for communication; images also carry metaphysical meanings of which viewers may or may not be aware. However, as interview participants responded: when in an educational place, users assume the images found there to be correct representations and will not question the images they see. The interview participants believed they learned about Buddhist culture from being in this environment. When the researcher observed the place with Buddhist icons, she understood from the note card the builder had designed this site as an educational place for Tibetan Buddhist culture. However, the researcher noticed many cultural images being misused (as shown in Figure 1). First, the gong in front of the Buddha displays an inverted Chinese character. In Chinese, people may sometimes invert characters to show that the meaning of the inverted word is "arriving," and usually the inverted word is a single character. For example, Chinese invert the word "good fortune" to represent the coming of good fortune. However, in this situation, the meaning of these two inverted characters in the image does not make sense. In addition, Tibetans have their own language and symbols; in Tibetan Buddhism, a ritual instrument might be inscribed with Tibetan symbols and would never use a Chinese character. Second, the Buddha should always sit in a lotus to show purity of spirit. Third, pools of water are never found inside a temple. Pools only exist outside the temple to remind people they must cleanse themselves before entering. Fourth, torches are never used in any temple, only candles. Finally, incense should never be placed in vases and never at the Buddha's side; incense should only be placed in front of the Buddha because incense is the medium through which messages are sent from people to the Buddha. These mis-combinations of imagery give viewers a misunderstanding of Buddhist culture. As in Gestalt theory, two and two will not equal four. In this case, each of the pieces distracts from the successful presentation of Buddhist culture.

As the synthesized survey and interview data show, although most participants agreed the imagery in Second Life is fictional, the survey and interview data show that participants do learn from imagery in the virtual world. The visual environment of Second Life becomes a hidden curriculum for its users. As Duncum (1999) stated, the importance of hidden curriculum is

not that it is hidden but because people are unconsciously learning from it. Therefore, educators should teach students visual communication to encourage "critical thinking, practicing critique, and self-criticism, putting in question our assumptions, discourses, and practices" to foster students' visual literacy skills (Kellner, 2006, p. 258). As Masalela (2005) states, "For communication to be meaningful, we need … to construct and approach how other people in other cultures experience their world" (p. 146).

Solutions and Recommendations

Most interview participants agreed that the formal visual quality of Second Life did influence and enhance their own or their students' learning. Higher quality, good visualization, and detailed imagery gave a real sense of presence for students in the virtual learning environment. One interviewee reflected that "what you cannot go out and see… comes to you on SL and so far, the quality seems to be quite good." Another interviewee said: "SL could provide students with a better understanding of… history, reenactment, role playing… providing them with real-world experiences." As Burbules (2006) states, "virtual experience actively engages people's senses, and they may even feel as if an experience is happen-

Figure 1. Tibetan Buddhist culture in second life

ing directly to them." When students learn in the virtual world, they have both physical and psychological experiences with technological tools (Anderson, 2002; Mason & Moutahir, 2006). In short, some educators believe that the Second Life visual environment can be seen as a real-world experience for students; therefore, the following recommendations for site designers, educators, and learners should be considered.

Site Designers

Users in Second Life believe in the accuracy of visual information provided by the educational sites; therefore, designers of educational sites should carefully consider the information they provide, particularly the information delivered through images. Historical or cultural research of the imagery used at sites is necessary.

Educators

It is crucial to teach students the perspective of visual communication when educators use virtual worlds such as Second Life. Without understanding visual communication, students may consciously or unconsciously learn from the hidden curriculum of the imagery in the virtual world. Teaching visual communication reveals the hidden curriculum of imagery in the visualized virtual world. After students have learned about visual communication, they will be able to consciously and critically look at images, and identify and evaluate the hidden curriculum of the imagery.

Learners

Learners should understand that the visual information provided by non-academic educational sites may not be neutral or authentic but may be based on site designers' personal knowledge, imagination, or interests. Learners should also know that academic educational environments in Second Life may not be built by educators who have

researched the educational environment; the visual information presented at sites may not always be authentic. Only by critically evaluating what they encounter will learners be able to consciously see and learn in the visualized virtual world.

FUTURE RESEARCH DIRECTIONS

Based on the research findings, virtual worlds that have been adapted as learning environments contain diverse cultural meanings and learner are learning from what they see. Suggestions for future research directions are described below.

One area of investigation that requires attention is how site builders design and build in virtual worlds, how visitors react when site builders are based on a different culture than that of site viewers, and how visitors from different cultural backgrounds perceive and think about a site. This research direction would help art educators understand the development and direction of virtual world visual culture.

A second option could investigate how builders in Second Life learn from the virtual environment through vision versus how non-builders learn from the virtual environment through vision. This research direction would help educators understand if the process of hands-on building helps virtual-world learners develop strategies for learning from the imagery of the virtual world. If research findings are positive, it will be advisable to teach students basic building along with teaching visual communication.

CONCLUSION

The results of this study show that users learning from their visual sense in the virtual world prefer to learn from images rather than texts. In the visual virtual world, users are curious about other cultural imagery and learn about other cultures by visiting and observing culturally specific sites. Users in the visualized virtual world can look critically at the sites that contain their own cultural imagery; however, when they see cultural images that are not familiar to them and have no reference from which to critically interpret the images, they instead absorb the image and the message they have received from the imagery. Therefore, teaching visual communication in the animated virtual world will help virtual world users to critically look at the images around them, whether they are familiar with the imagery or not.

Images are not innocent (Mirzoeff, 1999) but contain meanings, and human engagement with images includes not only viewing but also interpretation. As Rogoff (2005) contends, "images convey information, afford pleasure and displeasure, influence style, determine consumption, and mediate power relations" (p. 25). As Pettersson (1993) argues, most people think visual communication is concrete and easily understood; however, images not only resemble the thing they represent, they may be more metaphorical than spoken or written language. How well addressees understand a message depends on how the addresser gives the message, through what kind of media as well as with what content it is delivered, and where, when, and how the message is received. Images in the visualized virtual world are not only representational but offer a hidden curriculum for all virtual world residents to learn from.

REFERENCES

Anderson, T. (2002). Revealing the hidden curriculum of e-learning. In Glass, G., & Vrasidas, C. (Eds.), *Distance Education and Distributed Learning* (pp. 113–115). New York, NY: Information Age.

Apple, M. W. (2004). *Ideology and curriculum.* New York, NY: RoutledgeFalmer.

Arnheim, R. (1970). *Visual thinking.* London, UK: Faber.

Aukstakalnis, S. (1991). *Silicon mirage: The art and science of virtual reality.* Berkeley, CA: Peachpit Press.

Barry, A. (1997). *Visual intelligence: Perception, image, and manipulation in visual communication.* Albany, NY: State University of New York Press.

Barry, A. M. (1994). Perceptual aesthetics and visual language. In *Visual Literacy: A Spectrum of Visual Learning.* New York, NY: Tech Publishing.

Berger, J. (1977). *Ways of seeing.* New York, NY: Penguin.

Burbules, N. (2006). Rethinking the virtual. In Weiss, J. (Ed.), *The International Handbook of Virtual Learning Environments* (pp. 37–58). New York, NY: Springer. doi:10.1007/978-1-4020-3803-7_1

Burnett, R. (2004). *How images think.* Cambridge, MA: The MIT Press.

Chandler, D. (2008). *Visual perception.* Retrieved November 2008, from http://www.aber.ac.uk/media/Modules/MC10220/lectures.html

Dake, D. M. (1999). A natural visual mind: The art and science of visual literacy. *Journal of Visual Literacy, 27*(1), 7–28.

Darts, D. (2004). Visual culture jam: Art, pedagogy, and creative resistance. *Studies in Art Education, 45*(4), 313–327.

Davenport, M. (2003). Using simulations to ground intercultural inquiry in the art classroom. *Art Education, 56*(5), 13–18.

Dewey, J. (1934). *Art as experience.* New York, NY: Penguin.

Dewey, J. (1938). *Education and experience.* New York, NY: Macmillan.

Didactic. (2010). *Oxford english dictionary.* Retrieved May 31, 2010, from http://dictionary.oed.com/

Duncum, P. (1999). A case for an art education of everyday aesthetic experiences. *Studies in Art Education, 40*(4), 295–311. doi:10.2307/1320551

Eco, U. (1990). *Travels in hyper reality*. Fort Washington, PA: Harvest Books.

Finnegan, R. (2002). *Communicating: The multiple modes of human interconnection*. New York, NY: Routledge.

Frechette, J. D. (2002). *Developing media literacy in cyberspace pedagogy and critical learning for the twenty-first-century classroom*. Westport, CT: Praeger.

Freedman, K. (2003). *Teaching visual culture*. New York, NY: Teachers College Press.

Freedman, K., & Wood, J. (1999). Reconsidering critical response: Student judgments of purpose, interpretation, and relationships in visual culture. *Studies in Art Education, 40*(2), 128–142. doi:10.2307/1320337

Gair, M., & Mullins, G. (2001). Hiding in plain sight. In Margolis, E. (Ed.), *The Hidden Curriculum in Higher Education*. London, UK: Routledge.

Groom, D., Dewart, H., Esgate, A., Gurney, K., Kemp, R., & Towell, N. (1999). *An introduction to cognitive psychology*. Hove, UK: Psychology Press.

Harasim, L. (2006). A history of e-learning: Shift happened. In Weiss, J. (Ed.), *The International Handbook of Virtual Learning Environments* (pp. 59–94). Dordrecht, The Netherlands: Springer. doi:10.1007/978-1-4020-3803-7_2

Hoffmann, M. (2007). Learning from people, things, and signs. *Studies in Philosophy and Education, 26*(3), 185–204. doi:10.1007/s11217-007-9027-5

Jamieson, H. (2007). *Visual communication: More than meets the eye*. Chicago, IL: University of Chicago Press.

Kellner, D. (2006). Technological transformation, multiple literacies, and the re-visioning of education. In Weiss, J., Nolan, J., Hunsinger, J., & Trifonas, P. (Eds.), *The International Handbook of Virtual Learning Environments*. Dordrecht, The Netherlands: Springer. doi:10.1007/978-1-4020-3803-7_9

Kellogg, R. T. (1995). *Cognitive psychology*. Thousand Oaks, CA: SAGE.

Linden Lab. (2007). *Website*. Retrieved May 2, 2007, from http://lindenlab.com/

Marshall, C. M. (2007). Cultural identity, creative processes, and imagination: Creating cultural connections through art making. *Journal of Cultural Research in Art Education, 25*, 1–12.

Marshall, J. (2004). Articulate images: Bringing the pictures of science and natural history into the art curriculum. *Studies in Art Education, 45*(2), 135–152.

Masalela, R. K. (2005). Electronic literacies in virtual classrooms: Is this a one size fits all? Visual literacy and development an African experience. In *Proceedings of IVLA*. IVLA.

Mason, H., & Moutahir, M. (2006). Multidisciplinary experiential education in second life: A global approach. In *Proceedings of the Second Life Education Workshop at the Second Life Community Convention*, (pp. 30-34). San Francisco, CA: Second Life Community.

McFee, J. K., & Degge, R. M. (1977). *Art, culture, and environment: A catalyst for teaching*. Belmont, CA: Wadsworth.

McMillin, D. C. (2007). *International media studies*. Oxford, UK: Blackwell.

Metros, S. (1999). Making connections: A model for on-line interaction. *Leonardo, 32*(4), 281–291. doi:10.1162/002409499553433

Miller, H. B., & Burton, J. K. (1994). Images and imagery theory. In Moore, D. M., & Dwyer, F. M. (Eds.), *Visual Literacy: A Spectrum of Visual Learning* (pp. 65–83). Englewood Cliffs, NJ: Educational Technology Publications.

Mirzoeff, N. (1999). *An introduction to visual culture*. New York, NY: Routledge.

Morgan, J., & Welton, P. (1992). *See what I mean: An introduction to visual communication*. Oxford, UK: Oxford University Press.

Myles, B. (2004). *The hidden curriculum: Practical solutions for understanding unstated rules in social situations*. Shawnee Mission, KS: Autism Asperger Publishing.

Pettersson, R. (1993). *Visual information*. Englewood Cliffs, NJ: Educational Technology Publications.

Pinar, W. F., Reynolds, W. M., Slattery, P., & Taubman, P. M. (2002). *Understanding curriculum: An introduction to the study of historical and contemporary curriculum discourses*. New York, NY: Peter Lang.

Robson, C. (2002). *Real world research: A resource for social scientists and practitioner-research*. Malden, MA: Blackwell.

Rogoff, I. (2005). Studying visual culture. In Mirzoeff, N. (Ed.), *The Visual Culture Reader* (pp. 24–36). New York, NY: Routledge.

Snyder, B. R. (1971). *The hidden curriculum*. New York, NY: Alfred A. Knopf.

Stephen, J. (2007). Virtually sacred: The performance of asynchronous cyber-rituals in online spaces. *Journal of Computer-Mediated Communication*, *12*(3), 1103–1121. doi:10.1111/j.1083-6101.2007.00365.x

Stern, R. C., & Robinson, R. S. (1994). Perception and its role in communication and learning. In Dwyer, F. M., & Moore, D. M. (Eds.), *Visual Literacy: A Plectrum of Visual Learning*. Englewood Cliffs, NJ: Educational Technology Publications.

Sturken, M., & Cartwright, L. (2004). *Practices of looking: An introduction to visual culture*. Oxford, UK: Oxford University Press.

Tavin, K. M. (2003). Wrestling with angels, searching for ghosts: Toward a critical pedagogy of visual culture. *Studies in Art Education*, *44*(3), 197–213.

Taylor, P. G. (2000). Madonna and hypertext: Liberatory Learning in art education. *Studies in Art Education*, *41*(4), 376–389. doi:10.2307/1320680

Weiss, J. (2006). Introduction: Virtual learning and learning virtually. In Weiss, J., Nolan, J., Hunsinger, J., & Trifonas, P. (Eds.), *The International Handbook of Virtual Learning Environments*. Dordrecht, The Netherlands: Springer. doi:10.1007/978-1-4020-3803-7

Williams, R. (2006). Theorizing visual intelligence: Practices, development, and methodologies for visual communication. In Hope, D. S. (Ed.), *Visual Communication: Perception, Rhetoric, and Technology* (pp. 32–42). Cresskill, NJ: Hampton Press.

Wren, D. J. (1999). School culture: Exploring the hidden curriculum. *Adolescence*, *34*(135), 593–596.

ADDITIONAL READING

Anderson, T. (2002). Revealing the hidden curriculum of e-learning. In Glass, G., & Vrasidas, C. (Eds.), *Distance Education and Distributed Learning* (pp. 115–113). New York, NY: Information Age.

Aukstakalnis, S. (1991). *Silicon mirage: The art and science of virtual reality.* Berkeley, CA: Peachpit Press.

Barry, A. (1997). *Visual intelligence: Perception, image, and manipulation in visual communication.* Albany, NY: State University of New York Press.

Burbules, N. (2006). Rethinking the virtual. In Weiss, J. (Ed.), *The International Handbook of Virtual Learning Environments* (pp. 37–58). New York, NY: Springer. doi:10.1007/978-1-4020-3803-7_1

Eco, U. (1990). *Travels in hyper reality.* Fort Washington, PA: Harvest Books.

Freedman, K. (2003). *Teaching visual culture.* New York, NY: Teachers College Press.

Kellner, D. (2006). Technological transformation, multiple literacies, and the re-visioning of education. In Weiss, J., Nolan, J., Hunsinger, J., & Trifonas, P. (Eds.), *The International Handbook of Virtual Learning Environments.* Dordrecht, The Netherlands: Springer. doi:10.1007/978-1-4020-3803-7_9

Mason, H., & Moutahir, M. (2006). Multidisciplinary experiential education in second life: A global approach. In *Proceedings of the Second Life Education Workshop at the Second Life Community Convention*, (pp. 30-34). San Francisco, CA: Second Life Community.

Sturken, M., & Cartwright, L. (2004). *Practices of looking: An introduction to visual culture.* Oxford, UK: Oxford University press.

Weiss, J. (2006). Introduction: Virtual learning and learning virtually. In Weiss, J., Nolan, J., Hunsinger, J., & Trifonas, P. (Eds.), *The International Handbook of Virtual Learning Environments.* Dordrecht, The Netherlands: Springer. doi:10.1007/978-1-4020-3803-7

Williams, R. (2006). Theorizing visual intelligence: Practices, development, and methodologies for visual communication. In Hope, D. S. (Ed.), *Visual Communication: Perception, Rhetoric, and Technology* (pp. 32–42). Cresskill, NJ: Hampton Press.

KEY TERMS AND DEFINITIONS

Didactic Images: The definition of "didactic" in the Oxford English Dictionary (2009) is: "adj. Having the character or manner of a teacher or instructor; characterized by giving instruction; having the giving of instruction as its aim or object; instructive, perceptive." In this research, the term 'didactic images' denotes any images from which people may consciously or unconsciously learn.

Hidden Curriculum: Hidden curriculum indicates what students may learn in the educational environment, which is not included in the planned school curriculum. According to Wren (1999), the hidden curriculum will impact students' behavior. As Gair and Mullins (2001) state, "the hidden curriculum is not something that people must look behind or around in order to detect; in most cases it is plainly in sight and functions effortlessly" (p. 23). Students learn from what they see, regardless of whether it is in the real-world teaching environment or the virtual world. The term 'hidden curriculum' in this research chapter focuses on how and what images can become hidden curricula in the virtual world and on how students will be influenced by those hidden curricula.

Second Life (SL): Second Life is open software that users can download for free from the Internet. The Second Life browser that the researcher used for this research is the "Second Life 1.23.5" version. Second Life is a Computer-Mediated Communication (CMC) Role Play Game (RPG) with which users can do synchronous communication. SL was founded in 1999 in San Francisco by Philip Rosedale and was developed by Linden Lab (Linden Lab, 2007). In Second Life, everything is visualized and designed by the users. From avatars to the whole environment, it is a user-generated environment. Therefore, this 3D virtual environment is wholly visualized.

Virtual Learning Environment (VLE): The virtual learning environment in this research specifically indicates the online 3D animated virtual world that has been adopted as an educational environment. However, this research is not only limited to the educational environment in the virtual world, but also considers the whole world of Second Life (SL) to be a learning environment. Different educational sites in the virtual world can be seen as different classrooms in real-life. In addition, the whole virtual world can be seen as a parallel to the whole school setting in Real-Life (RL). In both RL and SL, students not only learn in the classroom, but also learn outside of class and through all school activities.

Virtual World: The virtual world in this research does not mean the world of virtual reality; in the virtual world users do not need to wear a head-mounted display or motion tracker for access. The only things users need to access this world are a computer and an Internet connection. The virtual world also does not mean text-based cyberspace. Cyberspace includes websites, blogs, and messengers. The virtual world in this research only includes the 3D animated virtual world: Second Life.

Visual Communication: Masalela (2005) states that "every person's mental life is a reflection of the cultural reality s/he knows. People cannot be complacent that technology is neutral and can be used as an international language" (p. 142). "We must learn to read symbols for both content and form, for concrete and metaphoric meaning. Visual communication, therefore, is using visual symbols to express ideas and convey meaning" (McFee, 1969, p. 108). In this research, visual communication emphasizes how images communicate in the virtual world as it has been adopted as an educational environment. This visual communication includes why users make certain objects and how users perceive them.

Section 2
Social Learning

Chapter 7
Gaming as a Woman:
Gender Difference Issues in Video Games and Learning

Kristen B. Miller
Tuskegee University, USA

ABSTRACT

This chapter reports the findings of two surveys taken by players of the video game Rock Band. The purpose of the surveys was to determine what differences, if any, exist between the ways that males and females learn to play the game, are motivated to improve, interact with other players both online and in real life, and interact with other players in online communities for the game. This study suggests that while females do not appear to learn to play this game much differently from males, they are motivated differently and interact with other players differently, and ultimately they have a harder time than males finding a place in the affinity groups that exist for the game, and these findings provide starting points for teachers who intend to use video games and virtual worlds for educational purposes in guarding against creating a "gender gap" between males and females.

INTRODUCTION

Much of the recent scholarship in video games has been concerned with the connections between video games and learning, either how video games could be used to teach (DeMaria, 2007) or how quality classroom teaching could be modeled after how video games teach (Gee, 2003; Selfe & Hawisher, 2007). Much of why video games serve as a model of good teaching is because

they inspire a lot of motivation, dedication, and willingness to fail on the part of the player. If you can bottle up what it is that inspires a player to work hard and excel at a video game and apply it in the classroom, imagine the improvements to education. Little attention, however, has been given to whether or not males and females learn and play video games differently. Beyond one essay in Selfe and Hawisher's *Gaming Lives in the Twenty-First Century*, most attention I've found

DOI: 10.4018/978-1-4666-2670-6.ch007

given to gender differences in these type of works has concerned the content of the games—their portrayal of women—rather than how female players might engage with them differently, and the subsequent effect this might have on work that seeks to model classroom teaching after video games. That one essay, "Gender Matters: Literacy, Learning, and Gaming in One American Family" by Pamela Takayoshi (2007), addresses one primary aspect of women learning video games, that of the role of affinity groups. Takayoshi makes the observation that video games are more of a communal experience for females than for males, and yet at the same time observes that females are much more cut off from the larger gaming community. That the communal experience of it is central for females fits well with the work of Elizabeth Flynn, who argues in "Composing as a Woman" (1988) that, at least in writing, the male wants to set himself apart from others while the female wants to make connections with others. In this study, I set out to see what differences, if any, exists between the way males and females play one particular video game, Rock Band, a music simulation game that allows players to play along as guitar, bass, drums, or vocals to rock songs at difficulties ranging from easy to expert. Overall, the results of this study fit the findings of Takayoshi and Flynn, suggesting that females tend to focus on and be motivated by the connective aspects of this video game, and yet at the same time, do not seem to feel as welcome in the larger Rock Band or general gaming community, and these are issues that must be taken into account in any attempt to include video games or even instruction modeled after video games in an educational setting.

BACKGROUND

In his 2003 work *What Video Games Have To Teach Us About Learning and Literacy*, James Paul Gee makes the suggestion that video games should become a tool for improving education.

Gee makes the case that playing and improving at video games is a literate practice that follows patterns similar to learning real-life skills, and that many games are designed well enough to motivate the player through many failures in order to acquire the skills necessary to succeed. Cynthia Selfe and Gail Hawisher follow up on Gee's ideas with their 2007 collection *Gaming Lives in the Twenty-First Century*, which looks at individual gamers from many demographics "to offer historical and cultural analyses of their literacy development, practices, and values" (p. 1). Together, through their examination of gaming as a type of literacy, these works suggest two primary purposes to this vein of inquiry: modeling our teaching methods after those utilized in the design of video games and actually using games and similar virtual worlds to teach.

In *Reset: Changing the Way We Look at Video Games* (2007), Rusel DeMaria likewise discusses the potential for using video games in education, but focuses primarily on the latter of these possibilities, using games to teach, while still providing a thorough examination of those elements of games that provide such potential for adaptation to educational purposes: motivation, self-assessment, repetition, and experimentation. Regarding motivation, DeMaria lists the seven motivational factors identified in 1987 by M.R. Lepper and T.W. Malone—"challenge, curiosity, control, fantasy, competition, cooperation, and recognition"—and singles out control as "one of the most powerful and unique aspects of video games" (p. 50). It would seem that video games have the potential to offer all seven of those motivational factors, demonstrating the appeal of using them in an educational setting. DeMaria further explains that he believes that "video games have found a powerful formula for motivating people" and that "the basic elements of this formula are goals, challenges, and rewards" (p. 51). Focusing in particular on the element of challenge, he believes that because they acknowledge the "human propensity to seek and resolve challenges" that "video game designers are masters of motivation" (p. 52). Fostering motivation to improve is a necessary element of any quality education, be it through actually using games that strongly motivate players or attempting to emulate such motivational tactics in classroom instruction. In either case, video games have much to offer in improving the role of motivation in education.

Gee points out in *What Video Games Have to Teach Us About Learning and Literacy* (2003) that "learning is or should be both frustrating and life enhancing. They key is finding ways to make hard things life enhancing so that people keep going and don't fall back on learning and thinking only what is simple and easy" (p. 6). DeMaria feels that games meet this need by providing an environment with lower stakes in which to experiment and practice skills: "Because of the very experimental and nonthreatening nature of video games, we are motivated toward success, rewarded frequently on the way, and allowed to achieve mastery" (p. 54), and he explains further that "where repetition can deepen learning, experimentation—learning from both failure and success—can promote much deeper understanding, especially if the player stops to consider the underlying causes at work" (p. 71). DeMaria also champions the use of games in education because of their inherent encouragement of self-assessment of the player (or learner). Self-assessment "refers to the ability of people in learning environments to predict how well they will perform in various tasks based on their current level of mastery or understanding" and also that person's ability to "assess his or her progress and reflect on what needs improvement" (p. 69). This is, of course, an ideal element of education and skill acquisition and improvement, but is also, according to DeMaria, an element built into the design of games:

Game designers expect players to be continuously assessing their own current abilities, predicting their likely successes, and reassessing results as they move through a game. In fact, game playing

is all about metacognition as learning theorists think of it, and although probably few game designers and even fewer game players know the term, they understand the principle instinctively (p. 69).

Thus, as he outlines the ways in which video games are designed to motivate and encourage practice, experimentation, and self-assessment, DeMaria makes a strong case for tapping this potential of games and utilizing it in education.

The aforementioned works make a strong case for the viability of utilizing video games and virtual worlds in some way for the purposes of improving education. At least one of the two primary options—either utilizing games themselves or modeling teaching practices after game design—would seem a possibility for virtually any subject being taught. However, with games often being considered more of a male than female activity, it would make sense to look at the implications of whether or not either or both of these means of utilizing games in education would privilege males over females. While this would seem an obvious consideration to undertake in discussions of video games and learning, the issue has been instead given very little discussion. Both DeMaria and Gee make brief mention of the issue of gender but quickly dismiss it as a point of further discussion. DeMaria's short mention of gender only addresses the issue of portrayal of women within video games. Gee makes a declaration early in *What Video Games Have to Teach Us About Learning and Literacy* (2003) that he does not intend to take on either violence or gender in video games in his work, and in his brief explanation of what he means by gender, clarifies that he conceives of it, like DeMaria, as a content issue as opposed to one of males and females interacting with games differently from one another.

Because of its effort of collect information on the practices of gamers from a variety of demographics, it is Selfe and Hawisher's collection *Gaming Lives in the Twenty-First Century* (2007) that does begin to address the issues of differences between male and female experiences of gaming and the possible implications for use of video games in teaching. The issue is most specifically addressed by Pamela Takayoshi in "Gender Matters: Literacy, Learning, and Gaming in One American Family" (2007). This essay reports the findings of Takayoshi's case study of four of her female family members (sister Allison, fifteen-year-old niece Jordan, and twenty-one and nineteen-year-old stepdaughters Meghan and Emily) and their interactions with games, motivation for playing and improving, and how they learned to play and improve. The first of Takayoshi's findings in this study is that female gamers lack female role models for their gaming. Allison served as such a role model for all three of the girls during their growing up years, and sisters Meghan and Emily often served as advisors to one another, but all reported preferring other females to teach them over males. As Emily reports of her experience of learning to play a first-person-shooter game, Halo, "sometimes [guys] won't give you a chance to figure out what you're doing, and they just keep killing you" (p. 242). All four women separately concluded that males are more competitive about their video game play than females. Allison notes a preference for playing with her daughter Jordan over her son George, who is more bossy and competitive, and according to Allison, will even ask for her help but then inform her that she is doing it wrong. In her remarks about guys being more competitive than girls, Jordan expresses the belief that girls are more playing for fun, and that when she and her friends play, "it's more of a thing to do and to get past a certain level," (p. 242), thus more about sharing an activity with others and with achieving larger goals together than beating one another.

Through these findings, Takayoshi suggests that males conceive of video games as primarily a competitive medium while females conceive of them instead as a connective medium. However, at the same time, they feel cut off from the larger gaming community: "faced with gendered cultural messages about gaming and gamers… they did not identify themselves as gamers and thus, did not associate themselves with gaming culture" (p. 247). While affinity groups certainly exist for the games that these girls play and could provide them with information and feedback to improve their play, they instead prefer to form their own affinity group, even if it means access to less information and experience. Affinity groups are an important aspect of the learning and literacy process outlined by Gee, but here is a strong suggestion that females are less inclined than males to participate in them, be that based on assumptions that they will not be welcome, a sense that they desire different things from their game play, or one of many other possible reasons. Overall, though, it is ironic that females both appear to desire connection to others through their games and yet do not feel welcome in or comfortable joining the larger communities for those games.

While Takayoshi provides the most direct address of the differences that may exist between male and female gamers, there are still some other useful studies that examine issues of gender differences in video games or education (but not both together). One field that seems to be especially interested in applications of video games and their design in teaching is the field of writing and composition, likely because of both the usefulness of video games and their design principles in teaching skills (and the goal of composition as also teaching and honing skills), and also because much of the discussion of the usefulness of video games in education is made through parallels between gaming and literacy, which would also appear to fall under the umbrella of writing instruction.

One well-known work in the field of composition that addresses issues of gender differences is Elizabeth Flynn's "Composing as a Woman" (1988). In this qualitative study performed by Flynn at Michigan Tech, she examines "narrative descriptions of learning experiences" (p. 554), comparing those written by males to those written by females. Similarly to what Takayoshi observes in gaming habits, Flynn finds that males seem to tend toward finding ways to set themselves apart from others while females tend toward finding ways to connect to others: "The narratives of the female students are stories of interaction, of connection, or of frustrated connection. The narratives of the male students are stories of achievement, separation, or of frustrated achievement" (p. 554). What Flynn found in comparing the work of males and females supports what Nancy Chodorow defined as typical masculine versus feminine identification processes: "Masculine identification processes stress differentiation from others, the denial of affective relation, and categorical universalistic components of the masculine role. Feminine identification processes are relational, whereas masculine identification processes tend to deny relationship" (qtd. in Flynn, 1988, p. 553). Thus, as Flynn looks toward the implications for such differences between males and females in personality and meaningful experiences, and thus attempting to instruct both in writing, she is pointing out some concerns that would likewise be helpful to consider in any attempts to use video games and virtual worlds in an educational setting, should differences between the genders and their interactions with games exist. When she writes that:

We must not assume that males and females use language in identical ways or represent the world in a similar fashion. And if their writing strategies and patterns of representation do differ, then ignoring those differences almost certainly means a suppression of women's separate ways of thinking and writing (p. 559),

her warning is every bit as valid when applied to other ways of teaching and other subjects and skills being taught.

Another useful study, in this case looking at gender differences in game preferences but not necessarily for the purposes of education, is reported by Hartmann & Klimmt in "Gender and Computer Games: Exploring Females' Dislikes" (2006). Hartmann and Klimmt's studies are based in Germany, where data suggest there is an even wider gap between playing rates of males and females than in other places in the Western world. The primary issues they surmise are responsible for females' lesser interest in video games are the gender stereotypes presented in games, which "could impede identification with the female characters or even cause cognitive conflicts and annoyance" (Research on Gender and Computer Games section, para. 2); the presence of violence, because "females tend to display a very low preference for observing or participating in conflicts and their resolutions through violence" (Research on Gender and Computer Games section, para. 3); and the few opportunities for social interaction (actual or simulated) allowed through single-player games. Along with these content issues, Hartmann and Klimmt feel the competitive structure of games is also a deterrent to female interest in them. In order to examine the role of these issues in females' disinterest in video games, Hartmann and Klimmt conducted two studies. The first recorded females' responses to several fictional games, asking them to express their interest in playing games that appeared to have different levels of gender stereotyping, violence, and social interaction. Of these three content issues, the study revealed that the most important factor for female interest in the game was the level of social interaction, while the level of gender stereotyping seemed to be the least of their concerns. These results would appear to support the similar findings of Takayoshi and Flynn, showing the female desire for connection to others manifesting in their content preferences in the games they are willing to play. Hartmann and Klimmt's other study examined females' levels of competitiveness as compared to males and found that the females did, as expected, report themselves as less competitive, placing less value on winning and also demonstrating less confidence in their ability to play well in competitive situations. Overall, Hartmann and Klimmt's findings suggest that the lesser interest in video games shown by females could be explained by both content that is less appealing to them and a lack of interest in competition while most games are designed to be competitive. These differences in what males and females desire to get out of video games are certainly worth consideration as educators prepare to include video games and virtual worlds in their instruction. On top of this, Hartmann and Klimmt provide a warning that likewise holds relevance to possible consequences of failing to address these gender differences; as they warn that "If computer games are more attractive to boys than to girls, they perpetuate gender imbalance in access to modern information technologies" (Introduction section, para. 6), so could it be true that if video games and implementation of their design principles in classroom instruction are more effective in reaching males than females, a consequence could be widening an education gap between the genders.

GENDER DIFFERENCES IN ROCK BAND PLAYERS

Although the numbers are different in different countries, such as in Germany where Hartmann and Klimmt conducted their study, the Entertainment Software Association (2010) reports that in the U.S., 40% of people who play video games are female. It is important to note that this includes a broad definition of video games, not simply console games. Video games *are* being played by women, but as the previously mentioned studies would suggest, females are drawn to different content and play for perhaps different reasons. If games, or at the very least their design principles, are going to be used for educational purposes, some additional questions need to be answered

or at least explored further. First, do males and females actually learn to play the games differently from one another? If games are going to be used to teach skills and males and females learn to play these games differently from one another, the result could be one gender being more likely to find the games an ineffective instructional tool. Because of games' ability to motivate the player so effectively and encourage persistence, another important issue to examine is whether or not males and females tend to be motivated differently. If the motivational techniques provided by games are more effective for males than females, an achievement gap could emerge between the genders. A third important issue is gender differences in group settings, be they cooperative play settings or affinity groups. Using others as resources and forming communities is an important aspect of the literacy-gaining process outlined by Gee, and if females do not, as Takayoshi suggests, feel as welcome in such groups, this important step of increasing literacy could be lost for them.

The Surveys

In order to learn more about whether such gender differences exist, I conducted two surveys of players of the music video game *Rock Band* in May 2009. I chose *Rock Band* for several reasons. The first was simply an issue of practicality—it is the game I play most and am most familiar with, and I am well acquainted with the various online communities surrounding the game, and thus able to get the survey to a wide audience. These practical issues aside, *Rock Band* seemed a good choice for such a study because unlike many other popular games, it is not a violent game nor especially masculine in content and is intended to be played in groups; thus, it does not contain many of the issues identified by Hartmann and Klimmt as deterrents to female interest. Using this game decreases the likelihood of being able to explain away gender differences as being rooted in the content of the game.

The first survey used for this study was linked from the discussion boards of three major *Rock Band* online communities: the official *Rock Band* website, a score-tracking website for *Guitar Hero* and *Rock Band* called ScoreHero, and the website of a gaming clan for female gamers called the PMS Clan. I also linked it from my YouTube account (subscribed to by many other *Rock Band* players) and passed it along to people I knew played the game through Facebook and email, desperately seeking less-serious players to fill it out along with the competitive players. In a little under a week, it had received 650 responses, at which point I closed the survey. This survey in no way reflects accurately the numbers of people who play on which difficulty, nor, I would guess, the true proportion of male to female players, since I could not find an effective way to get it to more casual players who would be less likely to frequent online communities related to the game. I also sent a second, follow-up survey to 40 male and 40 female respondents, asking more narrative questions about how they learned to play the game, and also trying to match the distribution of competitive players in the two groups as evenly as possible to attempt to give casual players equal representation. While serious players are certainly over-represented in these surveys, some of the results of this survey and the differences between male and female players that they suggest are especially interesting considering that most of the respondents, including most of the female respondents, are serious or competitive players.

The Respondents

The responses to this survey do not come close to matching the ESA (2010) statistics of the proportion of the gaming community that is female. Rather than 40% of the respondents being female, female respondents comprised only 8.3% (54) of the 650 responses. Likewise, within the *Rock Band* community, females comprise a very small percentage of competitive or elite players. It could be

the case that the real number of *Rock Band* players is closer to 40% female but that a majority of those female players are only interested in casual play or stay away from the online communities for the game. Regardless, female participation in these online communities, and thus participation in this survey, is quite low. The issue of participation in affinity groups will be discussed in more depth later; I bring it up here to both stress that this is a small pool of female respondents, but also that those females who did respond are for the most part serious and competitive players. In fact, along with this survey being most accessible to people serious enough about the game to participate in its online communities, the results themselves reveal the seriousness with which most respondents play the game. A vast majority reported playing the game at least once or twice a week, with most playing it somewhere between several hours a week and several hours a day, every day. In addition to time spent on playing the game, a majority of respondents also reported playing at least one instrument on expert, and even when playing on expert, indicating that they feel they should still be improving. Even with this group of serious players as respondents, there are still some pointed differences between the genders and their interactions with this game revealed through these responses.

Number-Focus vs. Goal-Focus

One major difference I found between males and females is that males seem to be more focused on numbers than females. In his article "Mastering the Game," Charles Soukup pinpoints the idea of the quantification of action, boiling down one's actions to a score and the consequent drive to improve or achieve a perfect score, as a major contribution to one's motivation to learn and improve at video games. In his article, he is describing how the content of video games reinforces patriarchy through their focus on domination through violence and force, but he also spends time discussing the draw of mathematical mastery. He does not make as strong a claim that this is more of a masculine tendency, but I do see the suggestion through survey responses that males are more drawn to numbers or scores than females. Both male and female respondents were equally likely to restart songs or replay them multiple times to improve their scores on songs, but females seem to be far less likely to "score track" than males. I saw this echoed in narratives on the follow-up survey in which I asked respondents what their most frustrating and most rewarding experiences with the game had been. Males were more likely to report frustration with trying to achieve a specific score or to get 100% on a song, for instance this story from a top-ranked guitarist on the game:

Probably my most frustrating times were not when I was going for FCs, but on songs like Painkiller. I think I got 94% on the first solo on guitar at least 40 - 45 times before I hit the 95% mark for the bigger score bonus.

In contrast to this focus on numbers, females tended toward reporting more big-picture frustrations like physical limitations with drums and guitar, or with passing a certain difficulty. Responses regarding rewarding moments were largely similar across the genders except males were more likely to mention achieving specific ranks on leader boards, which females did not mention. Males were significantly more likely to check their rankings on the online leader boards than females were. Overall, four males and no females mentioned specific numbers or scores in their most frustrating moments, and ten males to four females mentioned numbers in their most rewarding moments (with females' use of numbers most often referring to getting 100% on a song rather than scores or other percents or leader board ranks like the males included). Based on these responses, it does seem that numbers hold at least somewhat more meaning for male players than female players.

Competitiveness

As I mentioned before, Takayoshi observed that video games are more a connective medium for females, as opposed to the competitive medium they seem to be to males, and Hartmann and Klimmt likewise found that females demonstrated less competitive tendencies and desire to win than males. This also fits with Flynn's work in composition studies regarding females' focus on building connections and males' focus on setting themselves apart. The results of my survey echo this: both genders reported being "self-competitive" (58% of males and 67% of females selected this option) while males reported being competitive with others at a significantly higher rate than females, with 54% of males classifying themselves this way as compared to 33% of females. Interestingly, the few times that female respondents mentioned feeling competitive with others in their narrative responses, it was almost always with other females. For instance, one woman talks about how, when she was learning to play *Guitar Hero* (a precursor to the game *Rock Band*), she describes it as being "all about the fun" and "being better than the girls I played with." At the time, she was quite content to play on medium, but when *Guitar Hero III* was released, she was motivated by the ability to play online against others and by the progress of a friend who also played the game:

I was previously content to play on Medium, one of the girls was already playing on Hard. Such a thing was not to be. I was not to be outshone be a stay-at-home wife, even if she DID play 4 to 5 hours a day. It was pure outrage that got me serious about becoming a better player.

Another female respondent in her narrative remarked about noticing how female players either tend to form bonds with one another because of being in the minority, or they become more viciously competitive, trying to establish themselves as the best female player. So overall, even among serious players, it seems that males are more competitive with others than females, but both are competitive with themselves, and females may be sparked into being competitive through an urge to be the best of their minority group.

Behavior in Group Settings

Respondents' narratives of learning to play the game were fairly similar across genders. The biggest difference seemed to be that males were more likely to recount specific ways they found to solve a problem or get past an obstacle, while females were more likely to mention getting help or encouragement from others along the way, again echoing Flynn's claim that males tend to focus on setting themselves apart while females focus on connections with others. Females were more likely to mention working on a different instrument instead or leaving the game itself alone for a while when becoming stuck. On the other hand, one of the places where the biggest differences between male and female players emerged was in mostly self-reported behavior in group play. Overall, you see females being more motivated to improve when it is for a group rather than themselves, being more likely to give up the more popular instruments to others, showing more concern for how others will feel in multiplayer settings, and overall more support of other people.

First, though it was not an option on my follow-up survey, several female respondents wrote in to explain that at least part of their motivation to improve comes from wanting to play well for their bands, or for their clan mates in the case of PMS Clan members. Along with the suggestion that wanting to improve for the sake of others is a consideration for the female players, descriptions of band atmospheres from both male and female players suggests that female presence in bands tends to create a more supportive group. As females describe playing in mixed-gender bands, they tend to talk about becoming friends outside of the game and also discuss feeling responsible for lightening the mood and being supportive. As one respondent describes,

I'm usually the only female in a band, and when the guys get competitive and act like jerks, I tend to over-compensate by praising parts where they did well, and giving out advice for where they could improve. I just can't stand to see someone put down because they messed up. We all had to start somewhere. If the jeering gets too bad, I'll leave, or if I'm the leader, I'll kick the offending player. I don't care if you're the best player in the world, I don't want to hear that crap. If there is another female in the band, it seems most of the time, she and I will collaborate to keep things light. Makes it more fun.

Another female describes taking on a similar role in the top-ranked band for which she is the vocalist:

Being the vocalist, my job was the 'easiest' of the other instruments, so more often than not I was the voice of reassurance for the others. 'It's okay, we'll get it next time.' 'Let's quit that song and try it another day.' Etc.

As males discuss being in mixed-gender bands, they either say that they don't find it much different from playing in an all-male band (stressing that if you are good at your instrument, you are good at your instrument - gender doesn't matter), while others seconded the female description of a supportive atmosphere and being friends outside of the game. In male descriptions of participating in all-male bands, there are descriptions of both supportive atmospheres ("The experience was overall very positive. Everyone was very understanding of mistakes, chokes, or 'off' days, and, especially in the case of chokes, we would often laugh and joke about it afterward") and of serious, business-like atmospheres ("and for the most part we were not very supportive and more sarcastic than anything. Not really something I would prefer to do again"). As one respondent described it, he and his band mates "weren't really supportive, more like understanding" of "off" days and mistakes. However, there were no descriptions of mixed-gender bands being extremely businesslike, while numerous all-male bands were described this way.

Likewise, males and females report substantially different responses to certain scenarios in group play. In cases of other players failing out of songs in group play, females are slightly more likely to be supportive and understanding and to protect the struggling players by conserving "overdrive" so save them if they fail out. Males report being more likely to kick players who are struggling in between songs, quit themselves, suggest the struggling players drop a difficulty level, or refuse to save them if they fail out. In cases of the respondents themselves failing out, females are more likely to drop a difficulty for the next song. Males are more likely to quit during or after the song and to keep the same difficulty if they stay. Females also report being less frustrated with players who pick lower difficulties than they do.

Overall, most of the females in the *Rock Band* community who are well known are well known for being vocalists, but most female respondents to this survey do still play other instruments on expert, though primarily guitar and bass. However, these same females seem to either feel obligated to give up the more prestigious or challenging instruments (guitar and drums), or at the very least, are more willing than males to take the less-desired parts of vocals and especially bass. A common

problem one runs into in group play with *Rock Band* is that few people want to play bass; almost everyone prefers lead guitar. This is backed up by responses to my survey; few people choose to play bass when playing alone. It makes sense that more people would play bass in groups simply because when four people are playing, someone is going to have to take it. What is interesting is how much more often females report playing bass in group settings than males. The adjustment to frequency of playing bass is similar to a bell curve for males (see Figure 1).

Females, however, seem far more willing (or feel more obligated) to give up guitar to other people, with quite a different adjustment to their willingness to play bass in multiplayer settings as compared to male respondents (see Figure 2).

Females do show a higher preference for playing bass in solo play than males, but they are still disproportionately taking this part in group play. These reflect a tendency of females, and in this case, females who are fairly serious and competent players of this game, to relegate themselves to playing the easier or less interesting part of bass as opposed to guitar. If the players' choice of instrument in solo play can be taken to be their general preference, females are not getting to play their preferred part in multiplayer settings.

I also asked respondents on the follow-up survey how it makes them feel if they pick a higher or

Figure 1. Frequency of playing bass guitar, solo vs. multiplayer (male)

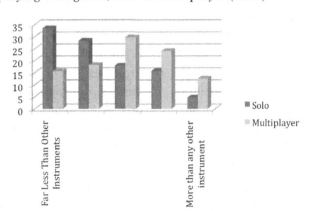

lower difficulty than the people, they are playing with (which, in the case of these respondents, almost always meant playing at a higher difficulty than the people around them). Both males and females reported feeling unwanted or undeserved attention for playing on expert, and both genders report still playing their best regardless. About even numbers also reported enjoying excelling or feeling good about playing on the higher difficulties. The biggest difference was that two separate females specifically mentioned either playing their worst instrument, playing badly on purpose, or dropping a difficulty to more closely match what other people are doing. One male respondent, while not playing worse than he is capable of, did say that he prefers to sit back and let others play for a while before he joins in so he does not scare them off. These responses, though from a small pool, suggest that females are a little more worried about others' feeling like they are not good enough and that they are more willing to feign a lack of ability for the sake of other people, again supporting this notion of their seeking video games to be a connective medium.

Participation in Affinity Groups

However, while females more than males seem to be looking for connections with others as they play the game, there remain many ways that females feel unwelcome in this gaming community. Narratives from females and from males who are mistaken for females in online play illustrate how females are treated quite differently from males in online gaming. The major themes in this seem to be females (and males thought to be females) getting hit on, receiving more friend requests, and being sent more messages, but in addition to this extra attention, also being singled out, particularly in first person shooter games, for being harassed and/or killed (or in the case of *Rock Band*, harassed or kicked from multiplayer sessions). Several females report trying to give the impression that they are male by using male

avatars and not speaking through the microphone so they do not get treated any differently. The situation seems the same regarding online communities for *Rock Band*. The three biggest ones are the ones I mentioned earlier: the official *Rock Band* forums, which cater more to the casual players; Scorehero, which tends to attract the most competitive players; and the PMS/H2O Clan site, a site for multiple games which is competitive but aims at creating a place where females are encouraged to play and where males can play with those females as equals. Males generally favored the official site and Scorehero, while females in this survey favored Scorehero and the PMS clan site. Scorehero, because of its being comprised of serious players but not specifically aimed at including females, provides the best illustration of the troubles females encounter when trying to join these affinity groups. Multiple females described joining Scorehero and becoming involved but feeling conflicted about whether or not to reveal their gender, such as this story relayed by a female respondent:

When I first started posting on ScoreHero though, most people assumed I was a male because my avatar was of a male guitar player (my favorite guitarist), and my username and other details didn't give any indication as to my gender. Being a "mediocre" player by ScoreHero standards, I did feel like it was hard to get anyone's attention, whereas I perceived that new female posters of similar (or even lesser) skill who came right out and announced their gender seemed to get more. For a couple months I felt a little uncomfortable because I knew people assumed I was male (saying things like "thanks man!" or "i agree, dude") but I wasn't sure whether I should "come out" and make some kind of public announcement considering I didn't think it was really relevant to the game. However I eventually made a few connections and over time I participated in enough discussions of non-game related things that some people eventually figured out I was

Figure 2. Frequency of playing bass guitar, solo vs. multiplayer (female)

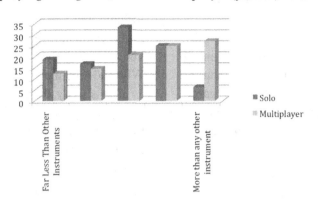

female. After Rock Band came out and I started posting videos of my singing on YouTube, even more people figured out I was female who hadn't already, and I started to get more attention then. That could have been due to the fact that I was a better vocalist and was doing something unique at the time (there were not many people making vocal videos then), not necessarily because of my gender, but that's something that's impossible to know for certain.

Another female respondent shared a similar experience of the consequences of *not* outright telling others she was female:

On ScoreHero when it started to come to light that I was a female, my perception was actually that some people felt a little betrayed, even though I'd never done anything to indicate my gender. I believe there was actually another female poster who was a little irked by the fact that I hadn't announced it earlier, being of the opinion that female gamers shouldn't have to hide their gender. I suppose the way I saw it was that I had never "hidden" it—I just didn't think there was a reason to announce it and then people just assumed.

These and other stories of behavior both in online communities and playing online indicate that many female players feel like they will be taken more seriously as players if they do not

reveal their gender, but feel like they are lying to people by not revealing it. At the same time, they didn't want to reveal that they were female because they didn't want to get attention just for being female, as they saw less skilled players get attention simply based on gender. It seems a shame that this is the choice so many female players feel like they must make, but this comes from them being received as outsiders by so much of the gaming community; there doesn't seem to be a way to keep gender from being an issue. Experiences like these could be responsible for causing or perpetuating the tendency noted by Takayoshi for female gamers to avoid the traditional and popular affinity groups for the games they play. Overall, females report either getting very positive or very negative reactions from male players, but also, on the whole, report feeling that male players are supportive of them, or, as one respondent describes it, "I would generally say 'more supportive' but in a mildly condescending, 'women are supposed to suck' kind of way." In short, even these serious and competent gamers feel like intruders at least some of the time, and such feelings are important to consider if we are going to use video games and virtual worlds for educational purposes, as interaction with other players and sharing of knowledge is an essential aspect of learning and improving at games, and obstacles to full participation in such groups would be detrimental.

Solutions and Recommendations

The results of this survey of Rock Band players points to several specific differences in the tendencies of male and female players, and all could be considered in both the design of games for educational purposes, decisions regarding what games to use, or emulation of game design in educational tactics.

Narrative responses regarding frustrating and rewarding experiences revealed that males were more likely than females to include numbers in their descriptions of these experiences. Males also revealed more interest than females in numbers through their tendency to track scores and check their ranks. This could simply stem from increased tendencies toward competitiveness, and in a score-based game, the numbers would be an essential part of the competition. However, it could also be that the numbers themselves hold more interest for the male players, while females, not unlike Jordan in Takayoshi's study, are more concerned with achieving larger milestones and less concerned with the minutiae. In either case, it suggests that in order to maintain the interest of and keep motivated both males and females, video games and teaching methods emulating them should deliberately include both broad measures of progress and specific, number-based ones. Many games already do this, including *Rock Band*, but sacrificing one and using only the other could render some of the players or students less motivated than the others, with this split possibly occurring along gender lines.

The issue reflected in female respondents' tendency to take less desirable instruments and feign lesser abilities is one that is not new to education. We have been searching for a solution to female students' tendencies to hide their intelligence in the classroom for many years, and while progress has been made, it still appears to be an issue, and in video game settings as well. On the one hand, it is difficult to fault someone for trying to be supportive of others, let others have their way, or avoid making others uncomfortable, but particularly if they are being used for educational purposes, females should not be holding themselves back for the sake of others. With video games conventionally being viewed as male activity, the danger of this would seem to be especially high. The best solution may come the same way that improvement has come in the traditional classroom setting: teacher awareness and active encouragement of females to perform up to their best abilities.

Effective use of groups may also help alleviate some of this tendency of females to underperform, as most of the other issues of gender difference suggested by this study are also concerned with behavior in groups. If females are drawn to the connective aspects of games, as other studies in addition to this one have agreed, then group settings, such as playing cooperatively or being put into groups to behave as affinity groups, would seem to be an effective way to keep females involved and engaged. When solving problems and getting past obstacles, males in this study tended to find their coming up with solutions most memorable while females were more likely to recount connections with and help from others along with a desire to improve for others; assuring group interaction rather than isolation would seem to allow for the game experience to be memorable for both genders. Comments about experiences playing with bands comprised of all males versus males and females together suggest that having a female in a group tends to increase the likelihood of a supportive atmosphere, perhaps more strongly when there are multiple females in the same group. So not only should group interaction be a part of efforts to incorporate games in education, but deliberately mixing genders in the groups could help make it a more positive experience for everyone, and at the very least discourage females from becoming disengaged with the use of video games.

Whether or not the issue suggested by both this study and Takayoshi's case study with females feeling welcome in affinity groups for the games they play should be a major concern for an educator utilizing games in their instruction depends on the nature of the game being used and the location of the affinity groups. In online affinity groups like ScoreHero, part of the female players' difficulty feeling engaged in the community stems from the anonymity that comes from it being an online community and uncertainty as to whether sharing their gender with others is necessary. They feel dishonest if they don't but then have to worry that their treatment if they do share that they are female is based simply on their gender. All the while, male community members do not have to make such a decision because the assumption is always that they are male unless they give reasons for people to suspect otherwise. Feeling dishonest or suspecting inauthentic attention and praise are both barriers to feeling part of a community.

If the affinity groups for the purposes of games in education are face-to-face rather than online and anonymous, the above barrier could be removed, but not the barriers suggested by Takayoshi's study, that video games are a male domain and that the males are automatically the experts in such groups, or that males and females, seeking different types of fulfillment in the games they play, do not have much to offer one another in the same affinity group. The former could be alleviated simply based on the games being used; if the games are unfamiliar, male students should have less claim to expertise over female students, beyond perhaps general gaming experience. The latter of these issues seems as though it should be able to be alleviated through careful explanation and encouragement by the instructor to keep use of games balanced between competitiveness and connection. If competitiveness with others is appropriately downplayed or kept in check and cooperation encouraged, then males and females should be able to bring their own strengths to a group setting without feeling like their own desires for how to utilize their gaming are in conflict with the others.

FUTURE RESEARCH DIRECTIONS

While this study does point to a few important considerations regarding gender differences to be incorporated into educational use of games, this is certainly no exhaustive list. A much more complete picture could be offered by doing similar examinations of motivation factors, competitiveness, and group behavior with players of several different sorts of games, such as MMORPG games, first person shooters, sports games, simulation games, and perhaps even Facebook games. In addition to examining behavior in recreational use of games, once more teachers have begun to incorporate games into their curricula or even simply model their teaching methods to emulate game design principles, studies that examine these practices for potential gender-based disparities would seem a fruitful line of inquiry. Using video games and virtual worlds for educational purposes appears to offer rich possibilities for improving the quality of instruction provided to students, but we need to be vigilant in examining our implementation of this and guard against lowering the quality for some groups as we raise it for others. Those groups may be gender-based, as has been my concern here, or based on other issues such as race, age, or economic status.

CONCLUSION

My examination of *Rock Band* players and the differences between male and female players of the game supports the prior work of Pamela Takayoshi regarding video games and of Elizabeth Flynn regarding the differences in males and females that manifest in their writing. Females more than males in this study showed more interest in making connections with others than standing out from others, whether through their direct answers or through the types of stories and details they would focus on in their narrative answers. They also tended to show more awareness of others and their feelings when describing their own behavior in multiplayer situations. And yet in contradiction to their focus on connecting with others through the game, female players seem to have a hard time finding a place within the community without making an issue of their gender, tending to receive either overly positive or negative attention because of their gender when it is known, or feeling deceitful if they do not make their gender known. This demonstrates how gaming is still largely a male-dominated place, despite what statistics may say about how many females are playing games. Some of these differences may be counteracted by the instructors who are using video games in their instruction, such as through careful construction and use of groups, attention to the types of goals and rewards offered students as they play, and discouragement of females hiding their abilities. Further, it is important that, once teachers begin utilizing games in their instruction, that they are attentive to ways that they may be privileging one gender, age, race, or economic group over another, both through awareness of this potential and further study.

REFERENCES

DeMaria, R. (2007). *Reset: Changing the way we look at video games*. San Francisco, CA: Berret-Koehler Publishers.

ESA. (2010). *Industry facts*. Retrieved January 14, 2011 from http://www.theesa.com/facts/index.asp

Flynn, E. A. (1988). Composing as a woman. *College Composition and Communication, 39*(4), 423–435. doi:10.2307/357697

Gee, J. P. (2003). *What video games have to teach us about learning and literacy*. New York, NY: Palgrave Macmillan. doi:10.1145/950566.950595

Hartmann, T., & Klimmt, C. (2006). Gender and computer games: Exploring females' dislikes. *Journal of Computer-Mediated Communication, 11*(4), 910-931. Retrieved January 14, 2011 from http://jcmc.indiana.edu/vol11/issue4/hartmann.html

Selfe, C. L., & Hawisher, G. E. (Eds.). (2007). *Gaming lives in the twenty-first century: Literate connections*. New York, NY: Palgrave Macmillan. doi:10.1057/9780230601765

Soukup, C. (2007). Mastering the game: Gender and the entelechial motivational system of video games. *Women's. Studies in Communications, 30*, 157–179.

Takayoshi, P. (2007). Gender matters: Literacy, learning, and gaming in one American family. In Selfe, C. L., & Hawisher, G. E. (Eds.), *Gaming Lives in the Twenty-First Century: Literate Connections* (pp. 229–249). New York, NY: Palgrave Macmillan.

ADDITIONAL READING

Alexander, J., McCoy, M., & Velez, C. (2007). A real effect on gameplay: Computer gaming, sexuality, and literacy. In Selfe, C. L., & Hawisher, G. E. (Eds.), *Gaming Lives in the Twenty-First Century: Literate Connections* (pp. 167–190). New York, NY: Palgrave Macmillan.

Belenky, M. F., Clinchy, B. M., Goldberger, N. R., & Tarule, J. M. (1997). *Women's ways of knowing: The development of self, voice, and mind*. New York, NY: BasicBooks.

Bunce, M., Herbert, M., & Collins, J. C. (2007). Taking flight: Learning differences meet gaming literacies. In Selfe, C. L., & Hawisher, G. E. (Eds.), *Gaming Lives in the Twenty-First Century: Literate Connections* (pp. 229–249). New York, NY: Palgrave Macmillan.

Cassell, J., & Jenkins, H. (Eds.). (1998). *From Barbie to Mortal Kombat: Gender and computer games*. Cambridge, MA: MIT Press.

Chodorow, N. (1978). *The reproduction of mothering: Psychoanalysis and the sociology of gender*. Berkley, CA: University of California Press. doi:10.1177/0959353502012001551

Corbett, S. (2010, September 15). Learning by playing: Video games in the classroom. *The New York Times*. Retrieved from http://www.nytimes.com/2010/09/19/magazine/19video-t.html

Gee, J. P. (2007). *Good video games and good learning*. New York, NY: Peter Lang.

Gilligan, C. (1983). *In a different voice: Psychological theory and women's development*. Cambridge, MA: Harvard University Press.

Griffin, J. (2007). Relationship gaming and identity: Stephanie and Josh. In Selfe, C. L., & Hawisher, G. E. (Eds.), *Gaming Lives in the Twenty-First Century: Literate Connections* (pp. 133–142). New York, NY: Palgrave Macmillan.

Jones, G. (2002). *Killing monsters: Why children need fantasy, super heroes, and make-believe violence*. New York, NY: Palgrave.

Koster, R., & Wright, W. (2004). *A theory of fun for game design*. Scottsdale, AZ: Paraglyph.

McNamee, S. (1998). Youth, gender, and video games: Power and control in the home. In Skelton, T., & Valentine, G. (Eds.), *Cool Places: Geographies of Youth Culture* (pp. 195–206). New York, NY: Routledge.

Michael, D., & Chen, S. (2006). *Serious games: Games that educate, train and inform*. Boston, MA: Thomson Course Technology.

Ray, S. G. (2003). *Gender inclusive game design: Expanding the market*. Hingham, MA: Charles River Media.

Salen, K., & Zimmerman, E. (2003). *Rules of play: Game design fundamentals*. Cambridge, MA: MIT Press.

Shaffer, D. W. (2008). *How computer games help children learn*. New York, NY: Palgrave Macmillan.

Walkerdine, V. (2009). *Children, gender, video games: Towards a relational approach to multimedia*. New York, NY: Palgrave Macmillan.

Yee, N. (2006). Motivations for play in online games. *Cyberpsychology & Behavior*, 9(6), 772–775. doi:10.1089/cpb.2006.9.772

Young, J. (2010, January 24). 5 teaching tips for professors—From video games. *The Chronicle of Higher Education*. Retrieved from http://chronicle.com/article/5-Lessons-Professors-Can-Learn/63708/

KEY TERMS AND DEFINITIONS

Affinity Group: A group formed around a common interest or goal. As it relates to video games, a group or community that plays a common game or type of game and shares knowledge and strategy with one another.

Avatar: A visual representation of a person used in an online or virtual space, which may or may not be a realistic portrayal of that person.

Band: In *Rock Band*, players can form teams of up to four players (with each playing either the guitar, bass, drums, or vocal part) to play songs together either in person or online through the *Rock Band* game; occasionally groups of four will form a standing band and compete with other bands for high scores.

Clan: A group or team of players who play computer or console games online together.

Expert: The highest difficulty in *Rock Band* as of the time of this study (*Rock Band 3* has since added "pro mode" as an additional difficulty above expert).

FC ("Full Combo"): In music games, this is hitting 100% of the notes in a song on a particular instrument without any extra hits in between notes.

Kick: *Rock Band 2* introduced the capability of kicking other players out of group play sessions. A player who is continually failing out of songs, picking songs that other players do not like, or otherwise being disagreeable may be kicked from the session by any of the other players there.

Leaderboards: Online scoreboards that, if one is connected to the Internet, will record one's score and show one's relative rank to other players. *Rock Band* leaderboards are broken down by song and instrument but can also reflect total score across all songs.

Overdrive: Bonus energy a *Rock Band* player picks up, which may be used to either double one's score for a short period of time or to save a band mate if he or she fails out in full band play. It can also be deployed in either solo or multiplayer modes to help an individual player pass a difficult part of a song without failing. In band play, it is courtesy to use it at the first opportunity to save a member who has failed out, but some respondents report deliberately not using it if someone is consistently trying to play above his or her skill level.

Scoretracking: Tracking one's scores either through online leaderboards, one's own records (such as spreadsheets), or scoretracking websites like ScoreHero.

Chapter 8
Instructional Design Meets Politeness Issues in Virtual Worlds

Yueh-Hui Vanessa Chiang
University of Texas at Austin, USA

Diane L. Schallert
University of Texas at Austin, USA

ABSTRACT

Attempts at incorporating emerging and innovative instructional technology, like virtual worlds, into educational settings requires efforts to understand new discourse patterns that may develop and bring in a learner-centered instructional design that takes the affordances and constraints of the new technology into consideration. These efforts can contribute to an effective and positive learning experience for learners. Drawing upon observations of different types of learning activities held in Second Life, an increasingly popular virtual world, this chapter aims at initiating a discussion interweaving the concerns for politeness, reflecting learners' psychological needs during their interactions with fellow learners and technology, with considerations of instructional design in a virtual world as a new learning context. Such a discussion has the potential of more effectively exploiting what new immersive environments can offer for learning.

INTRODUCTION

The emergence and development of virtual world technology has led to an increasing interest in integrating virtual worlds into learning and teaching. Such integration creates a new learning culture, bringing with it a need for careful documentation of the learning taking place in such environments as well as attention to careful design of educationally relevant and effective activities. Simply because the technology seems particularly dazzling is no reason to reduce the importance that educational technologists have traditionally given to good instructional design

DOI: 10.4018/978-1-4666-2670-6.ch008

of learning activities. In this chapter, we want to offer insights and suggestions about the use of virtual worlds in learning based on two projects that involved researching (1) graduate students' use of discourse and face-saving strategies when they gathered with team members in Second Life to complete several computer-supported collaborative learning projects, the CSCL project (see Figure 1), and (2) how professional journalists from various countries in Latin America improved their strategies and decision-making skills in the event of a crisis by participating in simulation and role-taking activities in Second Life, the journalism project (see Figure 2). Drawing from a series of in-world observations of different types of learning activities held in Second Life for these two projects, we want to offer insights about important instructional design considerations, about issues of discourse strategies particularly relevant to the affordances and constraints provided by Second Life, and about areas that we believe need further exploration.

This chapter is organized in five parts. We will provide (1) background information about relevant constructs and ideas that impinge on our work, (2) a brief description of the two projects, the CSCL and the journalism projects, informing this chapter, (3) some instructional implications for designing and holding learning activities in virtual worlds, (4) a description of the discourse

issues associated with politeness and face work in learning activities held in virtual worlds, and (5) a discussion of what needs further investigation and development in educational uses of virtual worlds and in research on such worlds.

BACKGROUND

In this section, we provide an overview and definition of three main topics relevant to this chapter: virtual worlds, instructional design, and discourse strategies.

Virtual Worlds

Immersive Three-Dimensional (3D) virtual environments, called *virtual worlds* or *MUVEs* (Multi-User Virtual Environments), are of increasing interest to education for their potential to broaden instructional possibilities. As of 2009, over 300 educational institutions had a presence in Second Life (Jarmon, Traphagan, Mayrath, & Trivedi, 2009). Many universities and institutions worldwide have conducted classes and had field trips with their students in virtual worlds (Lamb, 2006; Graves, 2008). The idea of using virtual worlds for education is growing, perhaps simply because the virtual world environment is itself growing (FitzGerald, 2007; Keegan, 2008)

Figure 1. Team conference area in the CSCL project

Figure 2. The flooded town simulation area in the journalism project

and the number of people using virtual worlds is increasing as well. As Gartner Research predicted, by 2011 "80 percent of active Internet users will have a 'second life'" (Pettey, 2007). The term *second life* here refers to being a participant or having an avatar in such virtual world environments as Second Life, World of Warcraft, Club Penguin, Kaneva, or Sun Microsystems' MPK20 virtual workspace.

The presence of a virtual world as an educational environment changes the nature of social interactions in computer-mediated online learning by means of involving more contextualization cues (Schiffrin, 1994) when compared to purely text-based online discussion formats. Schiffrin (1994) defined *contextualization cues* as "aspects of language behavior (verbal and nonverbal) that relate what is said to the contextual knowledge (including knowledge of particular activity types) that contributes to the presuppositions necessary to the accurate inferencing of what is meant (including, but not limited to, the illocutionary force)" (pp. 99-100). Although virtual worlds are different from games (New Media Consortium and EDUCAUSE Learning Initiative, 2007), some of the positive instructional effects of games are still likely to apply to virtual worlds such as accommodating learning preferences of Net Generation students, enhancing student motivation and engagement, facilitating collaboration, and providing immersive, experiential learning opportunities unavailable

in traditional learning environments (Gee, 2003; Kirriemuir & McFarlane, 2003; Dede, Clarke, Ketelhut, Nelson, & Bowman, 2005; Prensky, 2006; Jarmon, et al., 2009).

Additionally, there are positive effects that have been suggested for virtual worlds such as abundant opportunities for social interactions, an increased sense of shared presence and experience, affordances for free exploration and discoveries, and the capacity for user creation, appropriation, and redistribution of the environment, data, and media content (Craig, 2007; Jenkins, 2007; cited in Craig, 2007; FitzGerald, 2007; Lamb, 2006; New Media Consortium and EDUCAUSE Learning Initiative, 2007). Consequently, researchers (Dickey, 2005; Bronack, Riedl, & Tashner, 2006; Rosenman, et al., 2007; DiPaola, 2008; Jarmon, et al., 2009) have suggested that virtual world environments like Second Life are particularly suitable for collaborative learning, grounded in social constructivist views of learning (Vygosky, 1978), and supporting experiential learning processes (Kolb, 1984). In addition, when used for learning purposes, virtual worlds have been analyzed from the perspective of Massively Multiplayer Online Gaming (MMOG; Steinkuehler, 2004, 2006) and as a literacy practice, drawing on Gee's (1996) theory of D/discourse.

Previous studies have explored the educational effectiveness of virtual worlds empirically. Barab and colleagues (Barab, Hay, Barnett, & Keating, 2000; Barab, Hay, Barnett, & Squire, 2001) reported that the use of 3D modeling software to develop virtual worlds helped learners become "knowledgeably skillful (gain conceptual understanding and practical skills together)" by affording them opportunities to experience learning content directly. Dede, Ketelhut, and Reusss (2003) used *River City*, a virtual world for students, to form and test hypotheses on causes of illness, and found that although the use of this tool did not result in statistically significant content test score improvements for all students, it did so for low-achieving students. A simulation of the outbreak and spread of a virtual epidemic among students' avatars, using *Whyville,* also helped students understand better the nature of infectious disease (Neulight, Kafai, Kao, Foley, & Galas, 2007). A recent ethnography conducted by Fields and Kafai (2009) explored how knowledge was shared and diffused among teenagers across virtual world (*Whyville*), home, and classroom spaces. Hudson and Degast-Kennedy (2009) led students in a simulated experience in *Second Life* for Canadian border training. Through role-play activities with three groups of students in various roles in a simulated border situation, the students were able to perform and learn at the same time while going through the experience. Conducting a project-based learning course in *Second Life*, Jarmon et al. (2009) asked students about their learning expectations, their experiences, and their feelings about the platform before and after the course, and concluded that Second Life was helpful in facilitating project-based experiential learning in interdisciplinary communication. Barab and colleagues (Barab, Dodge, Ingram-Goble, Volk, Peppler, Pettyjohn, & Solomou, 2009; Thomas, Barab, & Tuzun, 2009) conducted a series of studies to explore students' learning from pedagogical, motivational, and social interactional aspects when they engaged in transformational play in a 3D virtual world gaming environment, *Quest Atlantis*. Soukup (2004), in an ethnographic study of

a virtual space called *Palace,* discovered that the ability to construct the environment collectively enhanced participants' sense of social community.

In sum, virtual worlds, as emerging learning technologies, provide new affordances and are promising in increasing the effectiveness of educational contexts, as new learning environments shaped by new technologies introduce new learning opportunities.

Instructional Design in the 21st Century

A second area relevant to our consideration of virtual worlds for educational purposes is that of instructional design. Traditionally linked with the use and development of educational technology, instructional design has always emphasized a process beginning with careful planning to develop, deliver, evaluate, and revise instruction that can fulfill a group of targeted learners' needs for learning a specific topic. Like many occupations that depend on design, such as architectural design, software design, graphic design, industrial design, and so on, careful planning before development is seen as pivotal for the success of the instructional design process. Over the years, a variety of instructional design models consisting of different individual phases and suggesting different sequences in the process have been offered. Yet, many of these share the premise that the instructional design process starts with identifying the learning goals that the developing instruction aims to accomplish (Cennamo & Kalk, 2005). Thus, instructional design is at its heart learner-focused and represents an attempt to consider the systemic influences one can control in achieving the desired outcomes.

The origin of the discipline of instructional design can be traced back to World War II when psychologists were called in to help design instruction for the millions of soldiers needing to be trained quickly. Influenced by the dominant learning theory of the time, behaviorism, early instructional designers emphasized the use of behavioral objectives (Skinner, 1938; Ferster & Skinner, 1957), a focus that has continued to be central to instructional design even when transformed and translated into instructional goals, learner needs, and outcomes. During the 1970s, many influential instructional design models were published (Dick & Carey, 1978; Gagne & Briggs, 1974; Kemp, 1971), and the practice of needs assessment was added to the identification of learner goals or outcomes.

In the 1980s, the emergence of personal computers introduced a change in what was required of instructional designers. Now designers were expected to develop effective and replicable instruction that could be delivered via computer technology. As computer technology continued to develop, multimedia-based instructional products became feasible and affordable. Meanwhile, cognitive psychology as a developing learning theory began to influence the practices of instructional design (Cennamo & Kalk, 2005; Schallert & Martin, 2003). During the 1990s, due to the prevalence of Internet technology, instructional designers now incorporated distance education and Web-based instruction into their set of tools for designing instruction. The concept of providing just-in-time information to learners also began to replace the idea of training learners to perform certain observable behaviors. Nowadays, the practices of instructional design continue to be influenced by contemporary learning theories, such as sociocultural theory (Vygotsky, 1978; Wertsch, 1991), situated learning (Brown, Collins, & Duguid, 1989; Greeno & van den Sande, 2005), and cognitive constructivism (Piaget, 1985).

Most important to instructional designers in the 21st century are three core values. First, learner-centered instruction, which includes the idea that learning is goal-driven, is the key element of instructional design. As Cennamo and Kalk (2005) suggested, there are five essential elements for instructional design: Learners, Out-comes, Activities, Assessments, and Evaluation. These five elements influence and are influenced by each other, but at their core is the element of Learners, the center of the relationship among these five elements. When designing instruction, instructional designers always need to consider learners' information needs, prior knowledge, previous experiences, existing beliefs, and values relevant to the topic of instruction. Representing a second core value, modern instructional design models, such as the rapid prototyping model (Dorsey, Goodrum, & Schwen, 1997) and the spiral model (Cennamo & Kalk, 2005), emphasize the design and development of instruction from a systems view, which entails that it is not as linear as implied by the classic ADDIE (i.e., Analysis, Design, Development, Implementation, and Evaluation) instructional design model (Dick, Carey, & Carey, 2001). A systems view of instructional design highlights its iterative and recursive nature as the design and development of instruction evolve. Finally, instructional design is a collaborative practice among learners, instructional designers, subject matter experts, and other members of an instructional design project team. Team members with diverse expertise contribute to different aspects of instructional design to complete effective instruction tailored to learners' needs.

Discourse Strategies

A third construct relevant to our work, *discourse strategies*, relates to the kinds of strategies students use as they interact in virtual worlds. Gee (1996) defined *Discourse* as "a socially accepted association among ways of using language, other symbolic expressions, and 'artifacts,' of thinking, feeling, believing, valuing, and acting that can be used to identify oneself as a member of a socially meaningful group or 'social network,' or to signal (that one is playing) a socially meaningful 'role'" (p. 131). (Gee distinguished *Discourse* from *dis-*

course, with a lower case *d*, referring to "connected stretches of language which hang together so as to make sense to some community of people" [p. 90].) Based on Gee's definition, Discourse is highly context-related and is more than simply the language encountered in a situation. Discourse analysis, in his view, is not centrally focused on language as an abstract system, but instead deals with what happens when people draw on the contextual knowledge they have about language, situated knowledge based on their memories of things they have said, heard, seen, or written before, to do things in the world (e.g., exchanging information, expressing feelings, making things happen, creating beauty, entertaining themselves and others, and so on). Discourse is both the source of this situated knowledge and the result of it.

Discourse strategies are the ways interlocutors use discourse in an interpersonal social event to serve one (or more) social purpose(s). One social purpose endemic to any interpersonal event is the goal of being polite in order to be sensitive to the "face needs" of self and others. Sociologist Goffman's (1967) work on "face" was the grounds for Brown and Levinson's (1987) Politeness Theory. According to Goffman, the term *face* is associated with the social-emotional notions of being embarrassed or humiliated. Drawing on Cupach and Metts's (1994) definition of *face* as the "concept of self that each person displays in particular interactions with others" (p. 3). Walsh, Gregory, Lake, and Gunawardena (2003) defined *face* as one's conception of one's self-image while participating in interpersonal interactions. Face can be lost, maintained, or enhanced when individuals participate in any interpersonal interaction. Generally speaking, when people interact with others, they not only pay attention to saving their own face (i.e., concerns for self-face), but also attend to helping others not lose face (i.e., concerns for other-face) because face is mutually vulnerable (Ting-Toomey & Kurogi, 1998). Goff-

man's notion of face emphasized its universality. Accordingly, Brown and Levinson (1987) assumed that concerns with face represent wants that all competent adult members of a society have and know each other to have.

Expanding on Goffman's (1967) face work, Brown and Levinson defined two types of face: positive face and negative face. *Positive face* means "the positive consistent self-image or 'personality' (crucially including the desire that this self-image be appreciated and approved of) claimed by interactants" (p. 61). *Negative face* refers to "to freedom of action and freedom from imposition" (Brown & Levinson, 1987, p. 61). In short, *positive face* refers to individuals' desire to be needed; whereas *negative face* refers to individuals' desire for freedom from impingement (Morand & Ocker, 2003). Given the assumption of the universal wants of face in a society, whenever individuals engage in interpersonal interactions, some acts have the potential to threaten face. These acts are called "Face-Threatening Acts" (FTAs) (Brown & Levinson, 1987; Morand & Ocker, 2003). Because many potential FTAs may occur while individuals interact with each other, Brown and Levinson (1987) claimed that individuals will employ strategies to avoid or minimize the threat when they realize that they are likely to perform an FTA. Brown and Levinson's strategies are similar to the later notion of *facework* proposed by Oetzel, Ting-Toomey, Yokochi, Masumoto, and Takai (2001), that is, the communicative strategies individuals use to enact self-face and to interact with other-face.

In accordance with Brown and Levinson (1987), politeness strategies are linguistic/verbal acts used to redress the intrinsic FTAs. They categorized politeness strategies into positive and negative politeness strategies, in accordance to which aspect of face the individuals want to save. Positive politeness strategies refer to moves "showing an appreciation of something that the speaker believes the listener would like to hear," while negative politeness strategies refer to moves "attempting to reduce any imposition on the hearer" (Yang, et al., 2006). It is important to note that in this usage, negative politeness is not the oppositeness of positive politeness, somehow on a "rudeness to good manners" continuum. Instead, these two kinds of strategies represent the kinds of face, positive or negative, they address.

Studying students' use of discourse strategies for politeness purposes can be particularly important because politeness is a universal principle grounding human interaction with a variety of viable expressions and interpretations depending on context (Brown & Levinson, 1987). The term *universal* does not describe the form and function of actual politeness strategies, but instead, reflects the psychological needs that human beings carry into all of their interactions with their world. Neither is politeness universal because of its static stable nature. Instead, as contexts shift and as individuals find themselves in new kinds of encounters, their ways of enacting politeness principles need to adapt. New situations make face needs vulnerable, and as individuals adapt to the innovations they encounter, they adjust their interpretations and expressions of politeness, even as the underlying face needs remain as solidly entrenched as ever. This is why politeness matters in learning situations.

In addition to allowing for an ever-adapting awareness of face-saving concerns, studying politeness in learning contexts can contribute to informing educators and students of the need for tolerance for diversity and the cultivation of empathy. In a learning context where learners interact with each other, one action or utterance could have multiple possible intentions and viable interpretations, and could trigger various reactions that become another action or utterance with multiple intentions and interpretations, creating a cycle that evolves gradually into a distinctive

learning experience that participants retrospectively evaluate as positive or negative. To avoid negative learning experiences and to foster a positive learning atmosphere, particularly during activities at high risk of threatening face (as when group members need to give each other constructive criticism), awareness, and appreciation of the necessary face work and tolerance for diversity become pivotal. Keeping in mind a tolerance for differences of perspectives and diversity expands people's understanding and consideration, and possibly increases their empathy. Merely having benign intentions is not enough; politeness strategies matter because human interactions, with learning representing one type of human interaction, entail the importance of addressing human needs. Humans have needs: the need to be respected, the need to be needed, the need to be free from imposition by others, the need to be liked, the need to be listened to, and so on, and Brown and Levinson's (1987) politeness theory grounded in Goffman's (1967) face work suggests ways to address these human needs.

In terms of how these lofty goals relate to our concerns here with politeness in virtual worlds from the perspective of instructional design, we see instructional technology, in its service of facilitating, scaffolding, and improving learning, as continually subject to change, to innovation. Incorporating new technology into instructional settings creates new learning contexts. Politeness conventions are not rigid. Because politeness is particularly context-dependent, studying politeness in emergent learning contexts not only contributes to enriching the fundamental theory, but also to helping prepare learners to engage in new immersive learning environments with comfort with the ways of fostering awareness of other's and self's face concerns, cultivating tolerance for differences, increasing the ability to handle face-threatening situations with empathy, and reducing frustration. Thus, we come back full circle to the learner-centered core value of instructional design as concerns for politeness in interacting with fellow learners can allow one more effectively to exploit the potential of new immersive environments for learning.

THE PROJECTS INFORMING OUR RECOMMENDATIONS

Having described key conceptual foundations to our work, we turn next to descriptions of particular learning activities that made use of immersive virtual worlds, in our case Second Life. These activities came from two projects, the CSCL project that was focused on the group processes of several collaborative assignments for a graduate course, and the journalism project that was focused on role-play activities in crisis simulations for journalist training.

The first research site was a graduate-level Computer-Supported Collaborative Learning (CSCL) course in a public university in the southwest of the United States. This course included several authentic projects requiring the students to work collaboratively as a team online throughout the semester to complete their projects. The objective of the course was to provide students with opportunities to learn and employ diverse communication tools as these applied to educational settings by reading about and engaging in comprehensive and intensive online collaborative learning experiences. In a sense, the teacher was using a "learn by doing" approach as the students were learning about how to design activities that involved collaborative online learning by being involved themselves in projects that required increasingly sophisticated computer-mediated collaboration.

Except for monthly face-to-face gathering sessions (Webcast for off-campus students), students conducted all course activities collaboratively through online communication. The course mate-rial was mainly delivered via a course website, providing students with the course schedule, course content, relevant resources, and the instructions for the activities and assignments. A conference system called TeachNet was the main tool for asynchronous online communication and provided for both private email and public discussion via a board that remained available throughout the course. A 3D virtual world system, Second Life, was used for synchronous online communication via voice chat, text chat, and avatars. Other tools that allowed for public postings on a bulletin board (via Blackboard), for blogging (via WordPress), and for collaborative writing (via Wikipedia) were introduced to the students throughout the semester based on the requirements of each collaborative learning activity. The 18 graduate students enrolled in this course were divided into four teams 4 teams; two teams consisted of 4 students each, and two teams with 5 students each. The course consisted of four learning modules involving the use of Second Life and requiring different degrees of collaboration.

The second project included three training sessions serving as pilot studies for the development of training of professional journalists using the virtual world to simulate different field experiences. The goal of the training was to help the journalists improve their strategies and decision-making skills needed to cover a crisis situation when it first happens and how this training can help improve their news stories. Twenty-eight journalists were recruited from various countries in Latin America and given a 2-hour training, all done in Spanish, in Second Life by a professional journalist from Argentina. The training was broken out into three parts. The first part involved a 30-minutes lecture by the instructor on the basics of covering crisis situations. The second part involved the journalists breaking out into two groups each to perform a role-play activity on a given crisis situation. The participants were assigned to the roles of interviewees, journalists, observers, and victims. After 30 minutes, the third part began and involved the journalists regrouping with the instructor and discussing the exercise and strategies they had implemented during the role-play activity.

In the rest of this section, we provide a brief description of the learning activities involved in these two projects, dividing these activities into four types based on their major use of Second Life.

Second Life as a Place to Hold Academic Discussions of Ideas

Both projects included learning activities that used Second Life as a place to hold academic discussion of ideas. One of the learning modules in the CSCL project used Second Life as a place where students discussed assigned academic readings and made sense of relevant academic topics. In this learning activity, academic readings and relevant resources were provided online to the students, and students' task was to discuss their emerging understanding of these concepts with their teammates in their virtual conference area, equipped with a conference table surrounded by chairs, in Second Life. By contrast to the student-led discussions in the CSCL project, the first part of the training session in the journalism project was a virtual lecture given by the instructor and the third part was a teacher-led discussion reflecting on the previous role-play activity. For these, the virtual classroom included several sofas arranged in a U-shaped form, with a big screen placed at the front of the area on which the instructor's avatar could show the presentation slides of the lecture.

Although still new in their delivery format due to the students' relative unfamiliarity with virtual worlds, these learning activities (e.g., a lecture, a teacher-led discussion, and a student-led discussion) were nevertheless quite similar to learning activities that commonly occur in most classroom settings.

Second Life as a Conferencing Tool for Project Management Meetings

As a second type of activity, Second Life made it possible for participants to hold meetings during which they could to discuss how to proceed on team projects. For example, in the CSCL project, one module required the students to participate in some collaborative writing. The objectives of this module were to have students understand and effectively use the strategies and techniques for collaboratively authoring a document, to understand Wikis and use them effectively as a means of supporting online collaborative learning, to explore and use online tools for collaborative writing, to understand current research related to collaborative writing, and to work effectively as a member of a collaborative learning team. Students were asked to collaborate in composing a Wikipedia entry on a CSCL-related topic with their team members, with the Wikipedia entry serving as their team product. A second example, again from the CSCL project, involved strategies for collaborative online inquiry. The objectives of this module were to enable students to understand strategies and techniques for collaborative Web-based inquiry, to understand the purpose and structure of a WebQuest, and to design a WebQuest collaboratively that met stated criteria. A WebQuest is a collaborative activity in which learners are presented with a problem, question, scenarios, or tasks, and are required to analyze and synthesize information to come up with their own creative solutions, using primarily information from the Web (Dodge, 2007). Each team was asked to design and develop a WebQuest, which stood as the team product for this module.

Even though the team products for these two modules were different, students' use of Second Life was similar: they met in Second Life to chat about their projects, to discuss their topic and scope, set up a timeline, divide, and assign tasks to team members, schedule the next meeting, and so on. For this type of learning activities, the implementation of team products did not occur in Second Life. In this case, Second Life served the function of a conferencing tool for project management discussions. Students scheduled time with their team members to meet virtually in Second Life in accordance with each team's needs and the progress of their project.

Second Life as a Gathering Place for Debates

One of the learning modules in the CSCL project asked the students to conduct academic debates with their team members in Second Life. The objectives of this module were to enable students to navigate and communicate effectively through the use of avatars in a virtual environment, to carry out substantive dialogue and discourse in the virtual environment, to use strategies effectively to introduce and critique important points related to an academic issue or topic, and to understand the potential benefits and limitations of virtual worlds like Second Life in supporting collaboration, dialogue, and discourse. Students needed to read several online articles to learn the theoretical and practical background knowledge related to the activity. Each team was asked to select an issue to serve as the focus of the academic controversy debate. The team was then divided into two groups and assigned to pro or con positions on the selected issue. Each group needed to develop its position and the supporting information and arguments, to do research using the Web or other sources (e.g., textbook, library, personal experience) to support its position, to prepare a series of persuasive arguments to support its position, and to prepare a persuasive document to be given to the opposing group. Then, a debate session was held synchronously via Second Life. After the first debate session, groups in a team were asked to reverse their positions to have a second debate session. Unlike the second type of learn-

ing activities, the team product for this learning activity was not built outside of Second Life, but instead, the debates themselves taking place in Second Life were the learning products.

Second Life as a Simulation Area

Finally, Second Life could act as a site to simulate a real-life event. In the journalism project, one part of the training was a role-play activity occurring in two areas in Second Life simulating two types of crisis situations. The first simulation was a flooded town that had been hit by a tropical storm that had extensively damaged the office buildings, homes, and businesses in the community. The students were given 30 minutes to explore and gather information and facts from the area as they played the role of victim, journalist, or official source as part of covering a news story about the flood. The other simulation was a medical center in a community that had been hit by a health pandemic similar to the H1N1 virus, with patients crowding the center and continuing to arrive in a steady stream. The students' tasks were to explore the medical center, obtain information from the patients, and role-play the parts of patient, official source, and reporter as they went through the simulation.

For this type of learning activities, Second Life, as a virtual world, provides essential affordances to simulate crisis situations that would not be desirable or feasible to create in the real world simply for training purposes. Students stated openly that they thought Second Life offered them the opportunity to perform practical tasks they would do in real-life such as interviewing during a crisis situation:

It seems to me that it is a great use of the platform to do interviews and implement in crisis situations. In certain circumstances, it may be more than helpful.

INSTRUCTIONAL DESIGN CONSIDERATIONS IN CREATING VIRTUAL WORLD ENVIRONMENTS FOR LEARNING

Embracing immersive technology, for all its appeal, does not necessarily guarantee the effectiveness and efficiency of learning and teaching. New instructional technology can create new learning contexts that may require new concerns that need to be taken into consideration when designing and delivering instruction. Without an appropriate instructional plan and design in place, it is likely that new instructional technology may lead to less than optimal experiences for both learners and teachers. Thus, informed by field observations collected in the two projects described above, interviews with participants, and online surveys filled out after learning activities, we provide instructional implications for using virtual world technology in educational settings with the hope of highlighting the contributions that instructional design can bring to the use of virtual worlds in educational settings.

"Why Don't We Use Skype?"

By comparing the learning activities involved in the two projects, we can offer guidelines about the use of virtual worlds along several lines. The most important concern is that not every academic field or learning situation can benefit from the features afforded by virtual world technologies. For example, we were asked by some of the students in the CSCL project "Why don't we use Skype for our group discussions?" Though quite different in terms of their learning objectives and topics of discussion, the types of learning activities involved in the CSCL project, such as academic discussions of ideas, project management meetings, and debates, were alike in seeming not to require the 3D simulation of a virtual world to proceed. Students seemed to treat Second Life as a varia-

tion on a synchronous online communication tool, for which many other options, such as Skype or purely text-based chatting tools, could have fulfilled their needs. The appealing visual and audio features of Second Life were not essential to the learning activities in the CSCL modules, offering many more affordances than the students needed to complete the learning activities. However, for the journalism project, the role-play activities in the simulations depended highly on the 3D visual features afforded by Second Life. Students had no doubt about why they were taken into a virtual world and appreciated that Second Life provided them with opportunities to practice their interviewing skills in a more authentic environment.

In sum, given that one of the five essential elements of instructional design (Cennamo & Kalk, 2005) includes learning activities, we strongly suggest that instructional designers take into consideration the degree to which affordances of Second Life are exploited and essential when designing a virtual world learning activity. Given the costs that come with entering a virtual world, it would seem important to consider whether the pay-off does or does not depend essentially on what the virtual world can offer that no other venue can. Once an instructional designer has decided that virtual world technology is truly warranted, there are more instructional design considerations that need attention. We will discuss these concerns organized by the three phases of an activity: pre-activity, activity, and post-activity phases.

Pre-Activity Phase

With its focus on preparing for an activity, the pre-activity phase consists of two stages serving different but prerequisite objectives: an orientation stage and an environment set-up stage. The orientation stage should be designed to provide learners with skills in the basic operations of Second Life, such as flying, walking, sitting down, standing up, talking via voice or typing, gesturing, changing one's avatar's appearance and outfit, navigating in the virtual world with search and teleport functions, and so on. The following excerpt from a participant when self-reflecting on the anticipated learning experience in the journalism project highlights the importance of the orientation stage in learners' becoming accustomed to Second Life.

Really for me it will be a challenge course, since it not only involves adequate knowledge about the specific topic, but for me it will be a double learning experience related to the specific use of Second Life for this purpose. The truth is I have no clear idea of how it will be, but at the same time, this is what attracted me to the project. Finally, since I received the invitation, I have been practicing in Second Life, although I still consider myself a beginner level and hope it does not affect my development in the course.

In addition, in the orientation stage, it is important to ascertain that students know how to find and return to the particular Second Life space where the learning activities will occur as well as to confirm the time of a meeting, keeping in mind students' local time when they inhabit regions belonging to different time zones.

The stage of setting up the environment aims at preparing a ready-to-go learning environment for each individual learner. Although every learner may have his/her own unique equipment settings, some general guidelines still need to be communicated to learners along with the orientation stage to foster their awareness of the importance of this preparation stage.

1.   Checking computer system capacity to see if it fits with the system requirements recommended by the Second Life official website (http://secondlife.com/support/system-requirements/?lang=en-US). Note that the information provided by Second Life

is subject to change. Checking regularly or a check-in before the learning activity may be recommended.

2.   The recommendation for Internet connection listed on the official website is mainly concerned with Internet speed and bandwidth. As for concerns about the stability of Internet connection, particularly for voice chat, wired connection is preferable to wireless.

3.   Updating Second Life software regularly. Even though there is no need to do this every time, checking if there is a latest update available before the scheduled learning activity when there is still enough time could avoid delays in joining the learning activity.

4.   Using headsets rather than the system built-in microphone and speaker could avoid voice feedback. We also recommend testing the headset in Second Life before the learning activity starts.

5.   The push-to-talk mode can help avoid voice feedback when it is not one's turn to talk but the microphone is still active, causing feedback of the voice coming out from the person's speaker. In addition, toggling off the talk button when not talking to one's interlocutors in Second Life could avoid the embarrassing situation that a conversation with someone in one's real life is transmitted to Second Life via the microphone.

The following excerpt from a participant's self-reflection on the learning experience emphasizes the importance of setting up the environment before the learning activity taken place.

In my personal case, I had to change my computer because it did not respond because of my laptop, and it could not perform the necessary interactions to complete tasks. Fortunately from my home I have the resources to enter Second Life, but in universities and newsrooms they do not have powerful equipment to use this tool.

In sum, the importance of the preparation phase before the learning activity cannot be overemphasized because it serves to reduce distraction during the learning activity.

During Activity Phase

During the learning activity, learners need to pay close attention to all that is involved, and that is the primary reason why the pre-activity phase is so important. However, there still are a few recommendations that we can make to help learners benefit from the activity and avoid unnecessary distractions.

1. Paying attention to the white dot above each avatar's head. This white circle indicates the avatar's voice. When one is talking and the volume is normal, there are green waves emanating from the white circle. In the case that the volume is so loud that the speaker's voice will be distorted, the white circle is surrounded with red waves, and this is when the avatar's owner needs to adjust his/her microphone volume.

2. Remembering to toggle off the Talk button when not talking to avoid feedback and possibly embarrassing moments of inadvertently sharing conversations with off-world individuals.

3. Assigning someone to act as a monitor in the Second Life space where the learning activities are taking place to deal with any unexpected and possibly distracting situation. For example, in the journalism project, the Second Life space was set to be open to the public. During one training session, the monitor noticed a stranger who had entered the simulation area and seemed to be attempting to set fire to objects placed in the simulation. After confirming that the stranger was not a late-arriving student, the monitor blocked the stranger out of the space to ensure that students would not be distracted.

4. Dealing with such issues as unexpectedly low attendance rate with poise. Our recommendation is to stay on schedule and adjust the learning activities for the students who attend on time. Second Life is a virtual world affording persons around the real world to come together via Internet technology. However, events occurring in the real world can definitely impact students' ability to show up in Second Life on time, and it is difficult to predict or prevent everything that can happen to persons physically present in another region of the globe, even with a detailed instructional plan in advanced. For example, one of the training sessions of the journalism project was planned for a particular Saturday afternoon. Unfortunately, the planners had not noticed that the agreed-upon date was Carnivale in one of the Latin American countries. All students living in that country did not show up on time for the session due to the festival. Another example was that a storm occurring in another Latin American country interrupted Internet access. Students from that country all suddenly disappeared from Second Life. The influence of severe weather conditions during learning activities is even less predictable and less manageable than human cultural factors. Also, all of these real-world unexpected events can occur to the instructor as well, and back-up systems of communication are crucial to ensure the success of learning activities.

Post-Activity Phase

Learning takes place not only during an activity but after it has ended as well. Self-reflecting on the learning experience after an activity has been found frequently to enhance learning (Boud, Keogh, & Walker, 1985; Lave & Wenger, 1991).

This is as much true for activities taking place in virtual worlds as it is in more traditional classroom environments. One advantage of online learning activities is that it is usually relatively easy to record what took place during the activity and to review voice or visual files when prompted to do so for a reflection activity. Such captured video and audio recordings of Second Life sessions could provide a scaffolding resource for learners to reflect on their interaction process. For example, one student in the CSCL project expressed a need to review the videotaped recordings of his group's online sessions, stating:

People have to review their conversations because when you were doing a conversation, you remembered a lot of "you said, I said, he said"…and there was a flow, but when you go back to listen to your conversation again, you realize, "that was the way I sounded?" You really need to reflect on how you were coming across, because, when you were talking, you were just talking. Of course you listened, but when you look at that from a different view, you are seeing a totally different person.

This excerpt not only stresses the importance of reflecting on the learning process and discourse taking place in a collaborative learning context, but also brings up the need for providing this kind of scaffolding resource to learners.

In sum, we have offered several considerations when designing virtual world learning environments that are guided by the core values of learner-centered design held by contemporary instructional designers. Our design suggestions center on how to give learners a positive learning experience and how to reduce the possibilities of learners' frustration in virtual worlds. After taking learners' needs, prior knowledge, and previous experience of virtual worlds into account, if learners do not seem ready for learning in Second Life, it is recommended either to choose other learning technologies to hold the learning activities or to offer a more comprehensive orientation of Second Life if allowable.

DISCOURSE ISSUES ASSOCIATED WITH PSYCHOLOGICAL NEEDS OF LEARNERS IN VIRTUAL WORLDS

Participating in learning activities held in virtual worlds typically involves interpersonal social interaction, bringing with it what we introduced earlier as the face work aspect of face-to-face human social exchanges. In any learning context where learners must interact with each other, the language that constitutes these interactions, the discourse, often expresses multiple intentions and is open to several viable interpretations, each of which always has the potential of threatening a learner's own face as well as others.' As learners continue to interact, the play of different politeness strategies creates a cycle evolving gradually into a distinctive learning experience that individuals come to see as helpful to different degrees. Taking learners' psychological needs into consideration can help avoid negative learning experiences and foster a positive learning atmosphere. Particularly for occasions when there is a risk of threat to learners' face, an awareness of face work becomes pivotal in making learning constructive and productive.

Thus, in this section, we describe new issues related to face concerns that arise when virtual world instructional technology is introduced in educational settings. With the goal of addressing learners' psychological needs when interacting with peers, teachers, and technologies, we discuss what kinds of phenomena have the potential to threaten learners' face in Second Life, what kinds of discourse strategies may be used to redress face threats, and how students may benefit from a discussion of politeness issues over and above the more typical consideration of netiquette. We summarize five points pertinent to politeness issues emerging from our projects and exemplified with students' discussion transcripts.

Need to be Responsive: "Got It" as a Politeness Move

When chatting in Second Life, learners can experience an unusual discourse situation that requires special face work not typically experienced in other interaction situations. Because the virtual world does not allow interlocutors to see each other in person, there are no direct clues that allow a speaker to know if hearers are attending and following what the speaker is saying. This was particularly an issue at the beginning of the CSCL project because students were still quite inexpert in getting their avatars to gesture. Thus, rather than having their avatar nod, they felt the need to give a signal, usually a short verbal utterance like "Got it" or "Ok," to let speakers know their utterances had been received, a politeness move showing attention to speakers' needs. In this situation, this politeness move is not meant to redress a face threat act that has already occurred; instead, it is a politeness move to prevent a potential face threat resulting from lack of response to the others' utterance. Instead of simply remaining quiet throughout a speaker's long utterance, hearers very frequently used these short responses, highlighting the unique communication nature of Second Life environments.

The following example demonstrates how the failure to provide this signal can cause a face threat situation and may require many subsequent face saving moves the redress the threat. In the beginning of a chat session, while George, Bill, and Yi-Jun waited for the other two members of their group to arrive, they chatted about Bill's children.

George: You have a couple of kiddos?

Bill: Yeah, I have an older son. He is 22.
George: Wow
Yi-Jun: Wow wow
Bill: And I have a daughter who is 15 now.
George: They keep you very busy.

At this point, Bill did not respond. After a few seconds, George asked Bill another question but still no response.

George: Do they live in the Austin area, Bill?

Bill's lack of response seemed to create a face threat for George, for which he made two attempts to save face. The first was to attribute the situation to communication media problem by checking with Yi-Jun to see if she could hear his voice.

George: Yi-Jun, can you still hear me?
Yi-Jun: Yeah, I can hear you.
George: Okay, I wanna make sure of that.

Having established that the problem was not caused by communication media, George's second attempt was to seek other reason for Bill's lack of response.

George: Are you still there, Bill?

Only after a few more moments of silence did Bill finally respond, redressing the situation by explicitly describing he had been doing when he had been unresponsive to George's questions.

Bill: Yeah, I was just talking to Younghee. He's having some tech problem, but he says in 5 minutes, he will be in.

In face-to-face conversation, being unresponsive can be viewed as an impolite behavior. However in Second Life, and perhaps also with other kinds of computer-mediated communication, a lack of response can be caused by many other factors that are not meant to be intentionally rude (i.e., a dropped phone call, a computer crash, and so on).

When students accustomed to face-to-face communication conventions are first introduced to Second Life, any lack of responsiveness can be disconcerting and act as potential face threats. We recommend that instructors discuss with learners the many different ways that they may need to indicate their presence and reception of each other's messages in Second Life. Tolerance and an assumption that most likely a group member does not mean to be rude will both go a long way to reduce the potential face threat of many communication situations in virtual worlds.

Reading Each Other's Mind: Supplementing Others' Utterances

As in face-to-face conversation, one interlocutor engaged in a Second Life voice chat can jump in to "fill in the blank" when the other party seems unable to choose or remember a specific word to complete his/her utterance. Although such a move can be interpreted as rude, it can also be seen as a helpful act, one that shows how the hearer is on the same page as the speaker. In the following example, George stated that he would be available for a chat, and Yi-Jun needed to check if he meant voice chat.

George: And if we're available for the chat and I'll be glad to do that as well.
Yi-Jun: voice chat?

Then, George wanted to express that both voice chat and text chat would be fine but it seemed that the phrase "text chat" had slipped his mind. Yi-Jun jumped in with the proper word.

George: Any of them. Voice chat or |uh uh uh|
Yi-Jun: |text chat|

George: I prefer voice chat over text.

Although such a situation may be viewed as an interruption by Yi-Jun of George's utterance, a face threat act, it can also be seen as a politeness move showing how Yi-Jun is aware of George's needs. Especially because Yi-Jun did not continue to hold the floor with this interruption, her supplementary utterance seemed to function as a face saving move, saving George's face from showing that he could have such a simple word slip his mind. Because this kind of politeness move presupposes that the interrupter has knowledge of the speaker's needs, it may also imply a shorter social distance between interlocutors. Again, a discussion with students of the different ways to interpret interruptions can help them adjust to a new environment in which they may use and encounter different communication strategies new to them.

Media Problems: "Can You Hear Me?"

One kind of frequently encountered conversation in Second Life was about problems with the communication media. Students frequently asked "Can you hear me?" to make sure that other team members could hear their voice, pointing to the poor quality of sound delivery. For example, in one group session, it seemed that after Younghee had joined the Second Life chat, the group experienced many sound problems. Sometimes, Younghee's volume was too loud and his voice distorted.

Younghee: CAN YOU HEAR ME? [very loud]
George: You have to turn your volume own a little bit, Younghee.
Katrina: When the distortion happened, I could not understand what you said.

Sometimes, when Younghee turned on his voice chat function, team members experienced a loud feedback noise and an echo at each their computers, as Bill explained to Katrina when she first joined the group.

Bill: *We have problems with feedback and echo [echoing].*
Katrina: *Uhmm…Even when you use the headset?*
Bill: *I think when Younghee came, there was a lot of echo.*

Interestingly, we found that when the conversation topic was about media problems, students tended to make their utterances more straightforward, rarely using politeness moves to soften their utterances. This was true even though what they were saying certainly had the potential to threaten others' face, as when Bill directly attributed the sound problems they were experiencing to Younghee's presence. This is consistent with previous literature indicating that factors other than simply the degree of face threat will also influence the decision to use politeness strategies (Brown & Levison, 1987; Morand & Ocker, 2003; Schallert, Chiang, et al., 2009). When other factors outweigh face saving concerns, interlocutors tend to strive for clarity and use more direct and to the point language (Brown & Levison, 1987). In the Second Life voice chat, sound problems could even halt the conversation entirely because no one can have a conversation when they cannot hear others' voices clearly. Therefore, the concern with solving such major communication media problems seemed to outweigh concerns for face saving. And, interestingly again, all members of the groups seemed to accept that they were in an emergency situation that required short, direct speeches and that all issues of face threat and face saving were temporarily tabled.

Our general recommendation is twofold. First, voice chat communication is currently very susceptible to technical problems. Helping students adjust their computer's sound system and prepare before any activity so as to be heard is extremely important. Second, we return to the recommendation to enjoin students to be tolerant in the face of all kinds of problems that may occur in virtual world communication.

Whose Avatar Are You? Misidentifying Others

No matter in which type of communication, misidentifying someone by calling an individual by the wrong name can be a face-threatening act. However, communicating via an Internet tool relatively new to interlocutors can provide other possible interpretations of such a situation, particularly in the case of Second Life voice chat with its reliance on an avatar to create or supplement a presence in group work. The following example shows such a situation between Yi-Jun and George. When Younghee joined his group members' chat, he saw everyone but Katrina. He asked, "Where is Katrina?" Just as he asked the question, Yi-Jun's avatar suddenly got up onto the conference table for no apparent reason. Misidentifying Yi-Jun as Katrina, George said, "Oh, here she is. Oh no, that is Yi-Jun."

From a politeness perspective, we can view this situation as face threatening because George not only failed to recognize Yi-Jun's avatar but also did not notice Yi-Jun's name appearing directly above her avatar. However, a broader interpretation would bring in the effect of the context of Younghee's question followed by Yi-Jun's unexpected operation of her avatar and George's unfamiliarity with Second Life. Thus, the subsequent reaction of team members to this situation, they simply ignored it and went on talking about something else, seemed appropriate. Returning to politeness theory, what the team members did was to go "off record." According to Brown and Levinson (1987), a decision to go off-record is chosen when the danger to face is high, concerns for saving both the hearer's and speaker's faces are high, and the necessity to clear up and explain the situation is low. It seems that the George misidentification of Yi-Jun fit these three conditions well.

Again, the implication we draw from this example is the need for instructors to discuss with students how to pay attention in Second Life to the identity of their interlocutors, how to develop strategies for keeping track of fellow team members, but mostly, how to be tolerant when they are misidentified as such misidentifications are common in virtual worlds.

"Where Did Yi-Jun Go to?" Disappearance in Second Life

Suddenly vanishing into thin air during an interaction is not possible in face-to-face communication, but in online communication, disappearance without any notification is not only possible it happens frequently. Such disappearance can seem rude to one's interlocutors. Particularly in Second Life, when one's avatar disappears in the middle of conversation, others notice it. Usually, this disappearance is caused by technology problems, something that may not dawn on those who are relatively new to Second Life. In the following example, Yi-Jun disappeared in the middle of a conversation without informing Bill and George in advance. In reaction, George used a joke, what Brown and Levinson would identify as a positive politeness strategy, to redress this situation.

[Yi-Jun disappears]
George: *Where did Yi-Jun go to?*
Bill: *I don't know. She vanished.*
George: *Haha. She just left us.*

When Yi-Jun later returned, she used two politeness moves, an apology and providing a reason for her disappearance, to redress the situation.

Yi-Jun: *Sorry, sorry. Something wrong with my Internet.*

George also tried to save Yi-Jun's face by using politeness moves of his own, telling her she had not caused a big problem and minimizing the imposition.

George: *Not a problem. I'm just glad we can talk to each other today.*

After a while, Yi-Jun's Internet problem occurred again. This time, she notified her team members with a text message, "let me restart SL… be right back," before she vanished, and her team members expressed no surprise with this situation.

Although the types of communication problems we have described may not be limited to virtual worlds, the fact that a voice chat function is coupled with an avatar represents a new way of combining features of both face-to-face oral conversation and traditional text-based online discussion, bringing with it potentially new situations unlike any experienced by students before. Communicating via any new Internet technology needs to be approached like entering a new culture. Interlocutors may need time and special effort to acculturate and to become accustomed to new conversational norms, and instructors or students who will teach or learn in the virtual world would do well to approach these new environments just as they might prepare themselves for visiting a new country. Attention to how face concerns may need to be addressed is not simply a matter of niceties but rather, as suggested by Yang et al. (2006), such concerns can have an impact, either positive or negative, on individuals' learning process. Face threats occurring in collaborative learning situations can damage a sense of community among group members leading to a poor collaboration. Being aware of the potential face threat pitfalls in Second Life can help students avoid or redress face threat situations they encounter, be more comfortable in Second Life, and focus on their teaching/learning.

LACUNAE IN RESEARCH ON INSTRUCTIONAL USES OF VIRTUAL WORLDS

Finally, having provided some recommendations of how to design learning activities in a virtual world for to help manage issues and problems we had encountered in our own previous projects, we want in this section to move from the minutia of design to the more global concerns that researchers and instructional designers may have about the use of virtual world in educational settings. We have two suggestions to make for future research on the use of virtual worlds that takes into account good instructional design principles. First, more experimental studies are needed that test whether the introduction of learning activities in virtual worlds are beneficial in improving learning performance. Again, such intervention studies can address instructional design considerations in terms of what kinds of learning activities in which domain field are best suited to the application of virtual worlds for learning.

Second, in addition to evaluating the effect of the inclusion of virtual worlds on learning performance, educators may be interested in understanding students' learning processes in such new immersive learning environments. In addition to outcome studies, more research focused on the learning process occurring in virtual worlds is recommended. With Vygotsky's (1978) dictum in mind that learning happens through the course of engaging in learning activities, Wells (2001) suggested that educators should not only look for learning products as evidence of learning after students have received input from teachers' instruction or textbooks. Rather, we should pay attention to the learning process occurring as students participate in the activities that make up the curriculum. As Schallert, Reed, Kim, Beth, Chen, Yang, and Chang (2004) reported, students give evidence of their learning even as

they are involved in online discussions. The use of in-world observation as an integral component of ethnographic research methods makes possible the collection of relevant and informative data. However, because of the inclusion of auditory/oral and visual online communication afforded by the multimedia features in 2D/3D virtual worlds, observing the virtual field inevitably introduces additional challenges to researchers and program evaluators, when compared with collecting data in pure text-based computer-mediated learning contexts and traditional face-to-face instructional settings. We will discuss ethical concerns and technical challenges we have encountered when conducting in-world observations in Second Life, and offer some possible solutions.

Ethical Concerns

To understand students' learning processes in both projects, the voice chat and participants' avatar movements in Second Life were videotaped using a screen-and-voice capture software (Camtasia). Of course, such recording of what students do and say as they engage in learning activities requires as much attention to obtaining informed consent as it would in real-world situations. An ethical issue we faced was how to observe a session and how to continue to capture it for Camtasia unobtrusively. Simply to observe learners in Second Life, one needs an avatar positioned judiciously to see and hear others. Typically, as observers, we would log on to Second Life, adjusting our avatar's view to ensure that the participants' voices could be heard and each participant's avatar could be viewed on our recording computer. After each session, the Camtasia recordings were saved and converted to portable video files as a data source to extend field observation notes. One disadvantage of collecting data in this way was that a researcher's presence in the conference area might pose some degree of obtrusiveness to the participants. One solution was to adjust the researcher's avatar in Second Life so as to be less noticeable (e.g., a small dog), and another was to remain on the periphery where an observer's avatar may distract the students less.

Technical Challenges

As researchers conducting a naturalist study to explore participants' interactions, collecting data that could demonstrate students' online discourse in Second Life was a continuously emerging challenge. The software that captured students' interactions in Second Life could produce videos that included students' voice and avatar movements. However, just like videotaping a normal face-to-face classroom discussion, we encountered some difficulties when videotaping the chat sessions in Second Life. These difficulties influenced the quality of the video recordings and even the availability of this data source. We categorize the difficulties into two types: problems occurred on the researcher's end and those on the students' end. Unsurprisingly, the problems occurring on the students' end also influenced students' participation in the learning activities. Therefore, the solutions discussed below to the problems occurring on the students' end can also serve as instructional suggestions for future uses of Second Life.

Problems occurring on the researcher's end: One challenge we encountered in videotaping students' interactions in Second Life for the CSCL project was when two teams were scheduled to meet in Second Life at the same time. Second Life does not allow one avatar login twice at the same time. To solve this issue, we prepared two computers to videotape simultaneous Second Life conversations and created two avatars (two separate accounts) in Second Life. However, simultaneous videotaping of two conversations in Second Life led to another problem. Whichever avatar entered Second Life first would lose voice connection when the other avatar entered Second Life. At the time of data collection (2008), Second Life only allowed one avatar login from computers connected to the same DSL modem, such as is true with a common DSL setting in one's household. Thus, even though a router is used to split the service to allow multiple computers access to the Internet, the outgoing Internet connection still occupies only one IP address. It seemed that different avatars entering Second Life from the same IP address caused a conflict in voice connection. One solution (the one we tried) is to purchase an additional type of Internet service, a 3G wireless connection card.

Another challenge encountered was that running both Second Life and Camtasia on a computer required enormous system resources. Even when we used powerful computers to do the recordings, still when the length of recording ran over one hour, Camtasia became unresponsive, and all systems on the computer were very likely to crash.

Problems occurring on the students' end: The first challenge students encountered was when two teams had chat sessions in Second Life simultaneously, they could sometimes overhear the other team's conversation even though the team conference areas were separated by some distance. The solution to this situation was that team members of one team muted the voice of the avatars of the other team. This is a function provided by Second Life interface to filter out voices a user does not need to hear in Second Life.

In spite of solving the issue of overheard voices, voice-related problems continued to interfere with students' conversations. The volume was the first problem. Because each avatar had a different level of volume and students did not know how their voices sounded to other team members, they needed to remind each other when they found that one member's voice was too soft or too loud. It usually took a while for them to adjust the volume to the correct level. Moreover, after they became used to the Second Life interface, they noticed the white circle above each avatar's head when the avatar's voice chat function was enabled. When the avatar talked, the white circle would become green with ripples around the circle. The range of the ripples expanding indicated the level of volume. In the case that the volume was too loud, the circle, and the ripples would even turn red. By paying attention to the voice indicator above their own avatar's head, team members could have a general sense of their volume level.

Furthermore, sometimes, the voice could become distorted and team members would hear voice feedback or an echo. This situation interrupted the conversation badly because no one could hear others. The feedback occurred whenever team members used built-in microphones and speakers; the voice coming out from the speaker of one person's computer would be re-captured by the microphone. Thus, using a headset was the solution. Such voice-related issues took students a long time to solve throughout the whole project, and seemed to recur at the beginning of each chat session.

The next observed challenge related to students' Internet connections. Some team members' avatars would suddenly disappear in Second Life or look like a mist even as the conversation was taking place. When this occurred, the students would have to re-log in to solve the problem, causing them to miss part of the team conversation. One of the reasons causing this problem may have been the unstable Internet connection, usually in the case of using a wireless Internet connection. Therefore, the solution to this issue was to ask students to switch to a wired Internet connection if possible.

Last but not least, as we mentioned earlier, embarrassing moments could occur in the Second Life voice chat session when students forgot to toggle off the talk button after they had finished talking, and others could hear background voices from a student's real-world location. When one forgot to do this, a baby crying could be overheard or a side conversations between the student and a family members. In these cases, a private text message can be sent or a quick comment made to remind the student to toggle off the talk button. In addition to avoiding possibly embarrassing moments, toggling off the talk button could also reduce the possibility of getting feedback.

CONCLUSION

The adoption of new immersive virtual worlds as an instructional technology in educational settings can create a new type of learning context, which introduces new opportunities as well as new challenges for learning. How to augment the utility of new opportunities and address or overcome the challenges becomes an interest to educators as a trend for teaching and learning in virtual worlds develops. Reflecting on our project experiences of holding learning activities in Second Life, this chapter serves as an effort to initiate an ongoing conversation about the need for thinking of learners when designing an instruction involving learning activities in virtual worlds (i.e., learner-centered instructional design). The use of new instructional technology needs to expand instructional design considerations to accommodate the affordances and constraints offered by the new technology. A set of guidelines for instructional design was provided as a starting point to invite more input for the future beneficial application of virtual worlds in teaching and learning.

Moreover, to deepen our understanding of the concept of learner-centered instructional design, we highlighted the importance of politeness concerns in addressing learners' face needs as they interact with each other in such new learning environments. We believe that interacting in a new learning context calls for adjusting or modifying established discourse conventions to reflect the distinct features of the new context as well as to serve for the universal psychological face needs. Our goals for this discussion were to increase awareness of the potential pitfalls for face threat caused by the unfamiliarity with the new learning environment and to expand the understanding of and considerations for politeness concerns when learning in virtual worlds in order to foster positive learning experiences for all learners.

Lastly, we recommend that more research be conducted on the application of virtual worlds to teaching/learning situations. We particularly encourage more studies revealing the learning process when learners engage in virtual world learning activities. We believe that by understanding the learning process more deeply, educators can acquire more insights in terms of how to improve the instructional design of virtual world activities. To contribute to this aspect, we shared the challenges we faced and the solutions we used or suggested. As technology is subject to change and to improvement, it is very likely that some of the problems we encountered may not exist in the coming future, and some solutions we mentioned above may be replaced with better and newer solutions. However, we believe the innovation of technology is always based upon endeavors to solve past challenges. It is worth our efforts to accumulate a record of past experiences to create a new future as information technology evolves.

REFERENCES

Barab, S. A., Dodge, T., Ingram-Goble, A., Volk, C., Peppler, K., Pettyjohn, P., & Solomou, M. (2009). Pedagogical dramas and transformational play: Narratively-rich games for education. In Iurgel, I. A., Zagalo, N., & Petta, P. (Eds.), *Interactive Storytelling* (pp. 332–335). Heidelberg, Germany: Springer. doi:10.1007/978-3-642-10643-9_42

Barab, S. A., Hay, K. E., Barnett, M., & Keating, T. (2000). Virtual solar system project: Building understanding through model building. *Journal of Research in Science Teaching, 38,* 70–102. doi:10.1002/1098-2736(200101)38:1<70::AID-TEA5>3.0.CO;2-L

Barab, S. A., Hay, K. E., Barnett, M., & Squire, K. (2001). Constructing virtual worlds: Tracing the historical development of learner practices. *Cognition and Instruction, 19*(1), 47–94. doi:10.1207/S1532690XCI1901_2

Boud, D., Keogh, R., & Walker, D. (1985). *Reflection: Turning experience into learning*. London, UK: Routledge.

Bronack, S., Riedl, R., Tashner, J., & Greene, M. (2006). Learning in the zone: A social constructivist framework for distance education in a 3D virtual world. In *Proceedings of Society for Information Technology and Teacher Education International Conference 2006,* (pp. 268-275). IEEE.

Brown, J. S., Collins, A., & Duguid, P. (1989). Situated cognition and the culture of learning. *Educational Researcher, 18*(1), 32–42.

Brown, P., & Levinson, S. C. (1987). *Politeness: Some universals in language use*. Cambridge, UK: Cambridge University Press.

Cennamo, K., & Kalk, D. (2005). *Real world instructional design*. Belmont, CA: Thomson Wadsworth.

Craig, E. (2007). *Meta-perspectives on the metaverse: A blogsphere debate on the significance of second life*. Paper presented at ED-MEDIA World Conference on Educational Multimedia, Hypermedia & Telecommunications. Vancouver, Canada.

Cupach, W. R., & Metts, S. (1994). *Facework*. Thousand Oaks, CA: Sage.

Dede, C., Clarke, J., Ketelhut, D., Nelson, B., & Bowman, C. (2005). *Fostering motivation, learning, and transfer in multi-user virtual environments*. Paper presented at the American Educational Research Association Conference. Montreal, Canada.

Dede, C., Ketelhut, D. J., & Reuss, K. (2003). *Motivation, usability, and learning outcomes in a prototype museum-based multi-use virtual environment.* Paper presented at the Fifth International Conference of the Learning Sciences. New York, NY.

Dick, W., & Carey, L. (1978). *The systematic design of instruction.* Glenview, IL: Scott Foresman.

Dick, W., Carey, L., & Carey, J. O. (2001). *The systematic design of instruction* (5th ed.). New York, NY: Longman.

Dickey, M. J. (2005). Three-dimensional virtual worlds and distance learning: Two case studies of active worlds as a medium for distance education. *British Journal of Educational Technology, 36*(3), 439–451. doi:10.1111/j.1467-8535.2005.00477.x

DiPaola, S., Dorosh, D., & Brandt, G. (2008). *Ratava's line: Emergent learning and design using collaborative virtual worlds.* Unpublished manuscript. Retrieved March 1, 2008 from http://ivizlab.sfu.ca/research/colabdesign/dipaolaF1.pdf

Dodge, B. (2007). *What is a WebQuest?* Retrieved from http://webquest.org/index.php

Dorsey, L. T., Goodrum, D. A., & Schwen, T. M. (1997). Rapid collaborative prototyping as an instructional development paradigm. In Bills, C. R., & Romiszowski, A. J. (Eds.), *Instructional Development Paradigms.* Englewood Cliffs, NJ: Educational Technology.

Ferster, C. B., & Skinner, B. F. (1957). *Schedules of reinforcement.* New York, NY: Appleton-Century-Crofts. doi:10.1037/10627-000

Fields, D. A., & Kafai, Y. B. (2009). A connective ethnography of peer knowledge sharing and diffusion in a tween virtual world. *International Journal of Computer-Supported Collaborative Learning, 4*(1), 47–68. doi:10.1007/s11412-008-9057-1

FitzGerald, S. (2007). *Virtual worlds - What are they and why do educators need to pay attention to them?* Paper presented at E-learning Networks June Online Event Retrieved July 13, 2007, from http://seanfitz.wikispaces.com/virtualworldsenetworks07

Gange, R. M., & Briggs, L. J. (1974). *Principles of instructional design.* New York, NY: Holt, Rinehart & Winston.

Gee, J. P. (1996). *Social linguistics and literacies ideology in discoures.* New York, NY: Routledge-Falmer.

Gee, J. P. (2003). *What videogames have to teach us about learning and literacy.* New York, NY: Palgrave Macmillan.

Goffman, E. (Ed.). (1967). *Interaction ritual: Essays on face-to-face behavior.* Garden City, NY: Anchor Books.

Graves, L. (2008, January 10). A second life for higher ed: A virtual world offers new opportunities for teaching. *US News and World Report Online.* Retrieved October 2, 2008 from http://www.usnews.com/articles/education/e-learning/2008/01/10/a-second-life-for-higher-ed.html

Greeno, J. G., & van de Sande, C. (2005). *A situative perspective on conceptual growth.* Paper presented at the Annual Meeting of the American Educational Research Association. Montreal, Canada.

Hudson, K., & Degast-Kennedy, K. (2009). Canadian border simulation at Loyalist College. *Journal of Virtual Worlds Research, 2*(1). Retrieved July 1, 2009 from https://journals.tdl.org/jvwr/article/view/374/449

Jarmon, L., Traphagan, T., Mayrath, M., & Trivedi, A. (2009). Virtual world teaching, experiential learning, and assessment: An interdisciplinary communication course in second life. *Computers & Education*, *53*(1), 169–182. doi:10.1016/j.compedu.2009.01.010

Keegan, V. (2008, October 2). We'll all be citizens of virtual worlds. *Guardian*. Retrieved October 5, 2008 from http://www.guardian.co.uk/technology/2008/oct/02/virtual.worlds

Kemp, J. E. (1971). *Instructional design: A plan for unit and course development*. Belmont, CA: Fearon.

Kirriemuir, J., & McFarlane, A. (2003). *Literature review in games and learning*. Retrieved August 10, 2006, from http://www.futurelab.org.uk/research/lit_reviews.htm#lr08

Kolb, D. A. (1984). *Experiential learning: Experience as the source of learning and development*. Englewood Cliffs, NJ: Prentice-Hall.

Lamb, G. M. (2006). Real learning in a virtual world. *The Christian Science Monitor*. Retrieved from http://www.csmonitor.com/2006/1005/p13s02-legn.html

Lave, J., & Wenger, E. (1991). *Situated learning: Legitimate peripheral participation*. Cambridge, UK: Cambridge University Press. doi:10.1017/CBO9780511815355

Morand, D. A., & Ocker, R. J. (2003). Politeness theory and computer-mediated communication: A sociolinguistic approach to analyzing relational messages. In *Proceedings of the 36th Hawaii International Conference on System Sciences*. IEEE Press. Retrieved June 1, 2007, from http://ieeexplore.ieee.org/xpl/freeabs_all.jsp?arnumber=1173660

Neulight, N., Kafai, Y. B., Kao, L., Foley, B., & Galas, C. (2007). Children's participation in a virtual epidemic in the science classroom: Making connections to natural infectious diseases. *Journal of Science Education and Technology*, *16*(1), 47–58. doi:10.1007/s10956-006-9029-z

New Media Consortium and EDUCAUSE Learning Initiative. (2007). *The horizon report*. Retrieved March 20, 2007, from http://www.nmc.org/pdf/2007_Horizon_Report.pdf

Oetzel, J. G., Ting-Toomey, S., Masumoto, T., Yukochi, Y., Pan, X., Takai, J., & Wilcox, R. (2001). Face and facework in conflict: A cross-cultural comparison of China, Germany, Japan, and the United States. *Communication Monographs*, *68*, 235–258. doi:10.1080/03637750128061

Pettey, C. (2007, April 24). Gartner says 80 percent of active internet users will have a 'second life' in the virtual world by the end of 2011. *Gartner.com*. Retrieved October 2, 2008 from http://gartner.com/it/page.jsp?id=503861

Piaget, J. (1985). *The equilibration of cognitive structures: The central problem of intellectual development*. Chicago, IL: University of Chicago Press.

Prensky, M. (2006). *Don't bother me, mom, I'm learning! How computer and video games are preparing your kids for 21st century success and how you can help!* St. Paul, MN: Paragon House.

Rosenman, M. A., Smith, G., Maher, M. L., Ding, L., & Marchant, D. (2007). Multidisciplinary collaborative design in virtual environments. *Automation in Construction*, *16*(1), 37–44. doi:10.1016/j.autcon.2005.10.007

Schallert, D. L., Chiang, Y., Park, Y., Jordan, M. E., Lee, H., & Cheng, A. (2009). Being polite while fulfilling different discourse functions in online classroom discussions. *Computers & Education*, *53*, 713–725. doi:10.1016/j.compedu.2009.04.009

Schallert, D. L., & Martin, D. B. (2003). A psychological analysis of what teachers and students do in the language arts classroom. In Flood, J., Lapp, D., Squire, J. R., & Jensen, J. M. (Eds.), *Handbook of Research on Teaching the English Language Arts* (pp. 31–45). Mahwah, NJ: Lawrence Erlbaum Associates.

Schallert, D. L., Reed, J. H., Kim, M., Beth, A. D., Chen, Y., Yang, M., & Chang, Y. (2004). *Online learning or learning on the line: Do students learn anything of value in sa CMD?* Paper presented at the meeting of the National Reading Conference. San Antonio, TX.

Schiffrin, D. (1994). *Approaches to discourses*. Malden, MA: Blackwell Publishing.

Skinner, B. F. (1938). *The behavior of organisms*. Upper Saddle River, NJ: Prentice Hall.

Soukup, C. (2004). Multimedia performance in a computer-mediated community: Communication as a virtual drama. *Journal of Computer-Mediated Communication, 9*(4). Retrieved July 24, 2007, from http://jcmc.indiana.edu/vol9/issue4/soukup. html

Steinkuehler, C. A. (2004). Learning in massively multiplayer online games. In Y. B. Kafai, W. A. Sandoval, N. Enyedy, A. S. Nixon, & F. Herrera (Eds.), *Proceedings of the Sixth International Conference of the Learning Sciences,* (pp. 521–528). Mahwah, NJ: Erlbaum.

Steinkuehler, C. A. (2006). Massively multiplayer online videogaming as participation in a discourse. *Mind, Culture, and Activity, 13*(1), 38–52. doi:10.1207/s15327884mca1301_4

Thomas, M. K., Barab, S. A., & Tuzun, H. (2009). Developing critical implementations of technology-rich innovations: A cross-case of the implementation of quest Atlantis. *Journal of Educational Computing Research, 41*(2), 125–153. doi:10.2190/EC.41.2.a

Ting-Toomey, S., & Kurogi, A. (1998). Facework competence in intercultural conflict: An updated face negotiation theory. *International Journal of Intercultural Relations, 22,* 187–225. doi:10.1016/S0147-1767(98)00004-2

Vygotsky, L. S. (1978). *Mind in society: The development of higher psychological processes*. Cambridge, MA: Harvard University Press.

Walsh, S. L., Gregory, E., Lake, Y., & Gunawardena, C. N. (2003). Self-construal, facework, and conflict styles among cultures in online learning environments. *Educational Technology Research and Development, 51*(4), 113–122. doi:10.1007/BF02504548

Wells, G. (2001). The case for dialogic inquiry. In Wells, G. (Ed.), *Action, Talk, and Text: Learning and Teaching through Inquiry* (p. 184). New York, NY: Teachers College Press.

Wertsch, J. V. (1991). *Voices of the mind: A sociocultural approach to mediated action*. Cambridge, MA: Harvard University Press.

Yang, M., Chen, Y., Kim, M., Chang, Y., Cheng, A., & Park, Y. … Jordan, M. (2006). Facilitating or limiting? The role of politeness in how students participate in an online classroom discussion. *Yearbook of the National Reading Conference, 55,* 341-356.

KEY TERMS AND DEFINITIONS

Discourse: Along with linguistic/verbal expressions of languages, other forms of symbolic expressions, such as body language, facial expressions, silence, actions, and so on, are included which are meaningful and socially accepted by a group of people in the given context.

Discourse Strategies: Ways that interlocutors use discourse in an interpersonal social event to serve one (or more) social purpose(s).

Face: A self-image held by every individual and presented to others in any interpersonal social event that is vulnerable to threat and may arouse social-emotional reactions.

Instructional Design: A process beginning with careful planning to develop, deliver, evaluate, and revise instruction that can fulfill a group of targeted learners' needs for learning a specific topic.

Learner-Centered Instructional Design: A core value of instructional design highlighting that the process of instructional design should center on learners by attending to the learners' information needs, prior knowledge, previous experiences, existing beliefs, and values relevant to the topic of instruction.

Politeness Strategies: Discourse strategies used to address interlocutors' politeness concerns, serving to save self's or others' face, in any interpersonal social interaction.

Second Life: An application of virtual world technology, created and maintained by Linden Lab since 1999, provides a 3D virtual environment, enabling its users to communicate and to interact via text chats, voice chats, and avatars' body movements and gestures.

Virtual Worlds: Immersive 3D/2D virtual environments that afford visual and/or audio features, allowing in-world interpersonal interaction.

Chapter 9
More than just Logging In:
A Case Study of Learner Engagement and Immersion in Cross–Curricular Events in Second Life

Kae Novak
Front Range Community College, USA

Chris Luchs
Front Range Community College, USA

Beth Davies-Stofka
Front Range Community College, USA

ABSTRACT

This case study chronicles co-curricular activities held in the virtual world Second Life. The event activities included standard content delivery vehicles and those involving movement and presence. Several international content experts were featured and allowed students to meet and discuss ideas on a common ground with these experts. When developing these events, the researchers wondered, could an immersive learning environment be provide a deeper level of engagement? Was it possible to have students do more than just logging in? During the events, the students discovered a whole new way of learning. Chief among their discoveries was the realization that in these virtual world educational events, students, scholars, and faculty can all be mentors as well as learners. In virtual worlds, the expert-on-a-dais model of teaching is rapidly replaced by a matrix of discussion, collaboration, and movement that quickly generates a pool of ideas and knowledge.

DOI: 10.4018/978-1-4666-2670-6.ch009

INTRODUCTION

The group had just finished listening to the panel and were about to fly to the next event. All of a sudden, the participants froze in place and everything faded to grey. The rolling restart had begun. Luckily, there had been a ten-minute warning and the participants had been provided with evacuation and re-entry instructions. As the team waited in the Real World, they thought about the day so far. Lecturers vanished in mid-presentation. Monsters flew through the air. Participants' heads exploded, and a cataclysmic event forced total evacuation. This was not your typical classroom. That is, unless your classroom is in a virtual world.

Virtual worlds are cutting-edge pedagogical tools when used well. In the 3-D environment, educators can immerse students in learning by engaging them in exciting ways that are still quite new to their experience. The potential of learning in virtual worlds reaches far beyond asking students to create avatars that simply sit in replications of their on-campus real-life experiences. Handled creatively, virtual worlds enable students to become agents of their own learning through active contributions to the learning environment.

This case study chronicles events held on the Front Range Island in Second Life, *The Fine ARRRRRT of Being a Pirate* and *Met@Morph: The Second Life Web Comics Comic-Con*. These events were used to enhance the content of Humanities, Philosophy, Women's Studies, and Accounting classes at Front Range Community College. The event activities included orientation to Second Life, tours, raiding and looting, lectures, roundtables, contests, and even evacuation during an unplanned rolling restart. Community college students attended presentations, discussed academic papers and concerns, and socialized with scholars from five countries.

During these events, the researchers wondered, could Second Life be used to actively engage online students in learning? Could an immersive learning environment be created that is different than the real world campus environment? Could faculty, instructional designers, and students create an immersive learning environment? Could a virtual world provide the level of engagement called for by Prensky (2005) and others? Was it possible to have students do more than just logging in?

BACKGROUND

In the fall of 2008, a team of faculty and instructional designers at Front Range Community College hosted events in Second Life designed to expose to students to a wealth of international and offbeat scholarship while teaching them the skills they would need to complete assigned learning activities in Second Life in the spring of 2009. The first event, called *The Fine ARRRRRT of Being a Pirate*, was scheduled for Saturday, September 20, 2008 (a tie-in to International Talk like a Pirate Day), and attracted roughly 25 participants.

The site was the Front Range Island in Second Life, and the event provided a combination of play-acting and scholarly presentations as seen in Figure 1.

Students learned to navigate and communicate in Second Life by learning how to speak and gesture as pirates. A Renaissance-era Venetian banker dueled with a rogue swordswoman on and above a pirate ship, and all who were assembled attended lectures on an island floating in shark-infested waters. Chris Luchs, accounting faculty, asked the assembly, "Who were pirates?" "Scoundrels!" "Rogues!" "Thieves!" said the assembly. "Did Pirates have accounting?" asked Luchs. "No!" replied the crowd. "Wrong!" said Luchs, appearing as the 16th-century Venetian banker. Luchs proceeded to introduce students to basic accounting principles by outlining the society and culture of a pirate ship, highlighting the need to avoid violence and thwarted self-interest by carefully accounting for every item on the ship. Stu-

Figure 1. Agenda for the fine arrrrrt of being a pirate

Noon to 1pm	**Boarding Party**
	We'll guide you in navigating Orientation Island and Help Island and then reporting (teleporting) to Front Range Island.
1pm to 2pm	**Getting Your Sea Legs in a Virtual World**
	On Front Range Island you'll go through pirate indoctrination to include a movement workshop – sit, jump, fly, use gestures and of course etiquette.
2 pm to 3pm	**Articles of the Ship (Human Resources 4 Pirates)**
	Pirate Accounting by Abacus the Acrimonious (Wages & Benefits)
	Women Pirates by Melinda the Merciless (Diversity)
	The Real Captain Morgan by Iron Tom Flint (Employee of the Month Program)
3pm to 4pm	**Raiding Party**
	Lethal Lady Leedale & Captain Que the VisiGoth lead participants on Port Calls to faraway islands with SWAG (stuff we all get) and other freebies

dents also enjoyed a lecture on the feminist women pirates of the 18th and 19th centuries, and another on the real Henry Morgan.

Before and after the lectures, faculty and instructional designers dedicated themselves to teaching students how to use Second Life. Beth Davies-Stofka, philosophy faculty, discovered that at the beginning, her students tended to cling to her, unwilling to move their avatars to any significant physical distance from hers. This was rapidly overcome by a group decision to take the students shopping. The team provided students with L$100.00 each, and took off at an astonishing pace. Students floundered at first in this sink-or-swim environment. Of necessity, they discovered just how useful the IM and teleport functions in Second Life could be. They quickly grasped that they were never more than a short message or a click of a button from their teacher, no matter how far afield they might explore.

It was at that point that the fun started, as students began teleporting at will, buying new clothes and hair, finding and visiting interesting philosophy or world religions sites, and sending evaluations to each other and their teacher via chat. Much to the team's surprise, the hour budgeted for teaching students and faculty how to use Second Life was unnecessary, as students caught onto the basics in a mere five minutes. They discovered that they could move at will and without limits through the vast space of Second Life, guiding and directing each other, and discovering interesting resources for their studies.

The Pirate event served as a dry run for the next event, the *Met@Morph: Second Life Web-Comics Con and Conference*, co-sponsored by the *Center4EduPunx*, *The Comic Book Bin*, and the *Institute for Comics Studies*. Having noticed that Second Life shares numerous attributes of Web comics, the team decided to break new ground by hosting a convention in Second Life that would be similar to the San Diego Comic-Con or the various regional Wonder Cons, all of which have academic tracks. Shortly after the team began organizing, national fuel prices went through the roof, and many comics professionals had to curtail their visits to Real Life cons in order to conserve dwindling cash resources. This made the Second Life conference doubly attractive, for being green and for being free to attend.

Since the burdens of real world travel are entirely excised from Second Life gatherings, the team was pleased and surprised to receive proposals from presenters in many parts of the world. In the end, the program presented a mixture of scholars and professionals largely from the United States and Canada, but also from Wales, Spain, and South Africa. The team also solicited participation from several Second Life "natives," such as Sabine Reljic of the *Second Life Social Presence Center*, and Botgirl Questi, a digital artist who uses Second Life as source matter for both the art and themes of her original comics, which she displays on the Web and in Second

Life. In short, students were exposed through-out the day to seasoned comics professionals, including scholars, teachers, and creators, along with scholars from multiple points on the globe, and were able to mingle with them informally in between sessions. Students found they could lend their Second Life technical expertise to the comics experts, and even more revealing, could hold their own in debates over ideas.

The day-long *Met@Morph* event (Figures 2 and 3) began with a call to meeting from Hervé St-Louis, owner and publisher of *The Comic Book Bin*.

This was followed by a social event designed to get people involved and having fun by experi-menting with the motion capabilities of their avatars. The Kool-Aid icon ran through the crowd. Avatars in dramatic dress battled with swords and sabers. Participants were invited to "Make like an Action Figure!" and emulate the iconic superhe-roes of the comics. Sabine Reljic from the *Second Life Social Presence Center* along with partners from the *Center 4 EduPunx* led the activities, setting an example of creative and uninhibited motion while teaching the basic rules of Second Life etiquette.

During the conference's morning session, scholars from around the world presented papers on various aspects of comics research and study on Front Range's floating island. Most took advantage of the large flat-screen TV's capability to display PowerPoint slides containing images from their comics research, and Second Life's capacity to enable lectures to be delivered over an audio chan-nel was a big hit. Conference attendees reported that it was easy to forget that they were in their home offices, so convincing was the simulation. It was easy to imagine that we were at a real life academic conference!

Easy, that is, unless the conference experienced events that were literally impossible to duplicate in the real world. One presenter had difficulty with a DSL line that was bouncing. Several times

during his lecture, he vanished from the stage. One audience member jokingly noted that this would never happen at a real life lecture, others speculated about the rumored Christian "Rapture," and another kept the group hugely entertained by repeatedly blowing up his head while the lecturer re-connected with Second Life. This did not seem to disturb our engagement with the lecturer's research; quite the contrary. We spent the time discussing what he had already presented, using voice and chat. This review of points already made actually clarified the content of the lecture, and fixed it much more firmly in our minds.

The mid-day session was a roundtable discus-sion about college and university comics classes. What should appear on the syllabus of a survey course in comics? Can comics be taught without placing them in the context of comics scholar-ship? What is more critical to a syllabus: comic history, or cartooning? Should a comics course be cross-listed to multiple departments? Which department should host a comics course, English, Art, or another? Participants were amazingly passionate about these questions, reaching into their hard drives to produce and circulate syl-labi. Websites supporting comics scholarship were posted, and crucial points in the discussion were captured and temporarily posted to Flickr. In a turn of events that surprised everyone, stu-dents, faculty, and comics professionals debated as confident peers. There was no sense that one person was more entitled to define the course of discussion and the importance of conflicting claims than another. The team felt that this was in part attributable to the anonymity afforded by the use of avatars, and in part attributable to the crowded and busy roundtable setting in Second Life, in which it was difficult to remember—and be intimidated by—real life identities. Frankly, real life just did not seem that important by this time.

The afternoon was spent in the Front Range art gallery enjoying presentations by artists. Some were Web comics artists who came to the gallery

Figure 2. Agenda for Met@Morph second life web-comics con and conference, October 3, 2008

8:00 to 8:30 am	Welcome from Hervé St.-Louis, Owner and Publisher, The Comic Book Bin
8:30 to 9:00 am	Make Like An Action Figure: Hosted by the Social Presence Center and Friends from the Center for EduPunx
9:00 to 10:00 am	Panel One: Web Comics Marking Transition - the work of Neal von Flue, Hanli Geyser, University of Witwatersrand, South Africa
	Web comic as engaging tool: The best of this: it wasn't an activity, Ruth Martinez, Madrid, Spain
10:15 to 11:00 am	Roundtable One: Giving Them Their Props: What Needs to be in a Survey of Comics Class
	Facilitator: José Garcia-Paine, Front Range Community College Discussant 1: David Accampo Discussant 2: Leonard Rifas, Seattle Central Community College
11:00 to 11:30 am	Social Time: Conversation, and Nudging and Bumping, and Dancing if you like!
	Make Like An Action Figure! Hosted by the Social Presence Center and Friends from the Center for EduPunx
11:30 to 12:30 pm	Panel Two: Scholarship on Comics Freedom within Boundaries: The Theory and Practice of Constraint in Comics, Derik Badman, Temple University
	How Comics Mean: A Look at How We Understand the Medium, Robert N. O'Nale, Jr., Henderson State University
	Alan Moore – cartoonist, Andrew Edwards, Sequart and Wrexham, Wales, UK

to discuss their work, providing insight into the history of Web comics, the process of creating Web comics, the economics of the profession, and sources of inspiration. One presenter, Botgirl Questi, a digital artist, uses both the visual aspects of SL and the curious relationships of avatars to create comics probing the relationship between humans and avatars. By meeting Botgirl Questi, students encountered something rare in the academic world: a genuinely new paradigm of thought.

Pete Coogan of the *Institute for Comics Studies* dismissed the assembly at the end of the day, but it was a bit hard to leave. Many of the participants expressed an interest in staying, reluctant to see the day end. Philosophy students who had already participated for 6 hours or more convinced the team to host a second "Make like an Action Figure!" session, and gained more confidence and security in the deployment of their avatars into inspired activities, unrestrained by the normal constraints of physics and gravity.

Novak, the lead instructional designer, reflected on the event in a blog hosted by RezEd. She noted three different "A-ha!" experiences:

For first timers – the Aha was "I'm at home but also in a virtual conference with people across the U.S., Canada, Wales, Spain and South Africa – how cool is this!" Those of us who have been in-world awhile expect this. As long as we take the Time Zone issues into consideration we expect international participation.

For those who had been in world for a little bit longer their Aha was, "this roundtable discussion around the MystiTool table is even better than in person, because even if there is someone else talking you can text and the conversation is fast and furious."

But the third Aha was for those of us who have been here for awhile. The college librarian Jeff Wahl commented, "I'm sure you realized this already... but this (being in-world) is like being in a comic book." He said this after attending the Center for Social Presence's "Make Like an Action Figure!" The session presented by Sabine Reljic was more than just an orientation on how to sit, walk, and fly. It translated the physics of being in a virtual world to how you relate to people in Second Life. Reljic showed people how to move and engage the environment—bumping avatars, doing backflips, and dance. My favorite was the All Blacks' haka. But really it's the next step in teaching in a virtual

Figure 3. Agenda for Met@Morph second life web-comics con and conference, October 3, 2008, continued

12:45 to 1:15 pm	Quick Web 2.0 Comics Creators, Kate Hagerty, The Center for EduPunx
1:15 to 2:00 pm	Roundtable Two: College Comics Clubs in the Meatspace and in the Metaverse
	Facilitator: Lauren Nagle, President of the Front Range Community College Comic Book Club
	Discussant 1: Que Jinn, Centre for EduPunx
	Discussant 2: Beth Davies-Stofka, The Comic Book Bin
2:00 to 3:30 pm	Creators' Commons Host: Christopher Moshier, Writer and Editor, The Comic Book Bin
	Creators: Botgirl Questi, Second Life Comics Creator
	Anthony Fontana, Machinima and Mash-up Creator
	Tim Volpe, Web Comics Creator
	Mireille Massue, A short introduction to the use of comics in communication and training
3:30 to 3:45 pm	Closing Comments by Pete Coogan, Institute for Comics Studies

world—how do you relate and teach when you are not in front of the students lecturing. What if all types of movement were possible; even movement that is not possible in real life?"

In the feedback obtained by surveys, it became clear that there is wide interest in further such events.

MAIN FOCUS OF THE CHAPTER

Issues, Controversies, Problems

The instructional team for these events consisted of five faculty members from the Accounting, Philosophy, Humanities, and Multimedia and Graphic Design disciplines, two Instructional Designers, and a student worker. In addition to this core group of individuals, two staff members of the campus Information Technology department also assisted in the implementation and support of these events.

The team had student engagement in a cross-curricular event as their main objective. They relied on educational research and their own experience as educators to choose this as the main objective. Additional objectives included increasing students' critical thinking and problem solving skills, which are known to support their autonomy and agency as students and citizens, and to prepare them for further virtual worlds-based activities that are designed to teach content related to specific courses.

Educational theory and research findings together show that students who are engaged learn more, so instructional best practices encourage student engagement (Skinner & Belmont, 1993). As has been reported in the literature, engagement is generated through stimulating and challenging experiences that involve enjoyment, fun and play (Douglas & Hargadon, 2000; Read, MacFarlane, & Casey, 2002). The ultimate goal is *flow* (Csik-szentmihalyi, 1990), where the students is so engaged in the learning activity that they experience total immersion.

Cross- curricular and interdisciplinary curricula challenge students to look at subject matter in new ways and question assumptions relating to just one discipline (Jones & Merrit, 1999). The events were planned with the themes of pirates and comics with the goal of having students look at these subjects critically and from multiple perspectives.

Challenges

The instructional team wanted to enhance student learning beyond the use of the Learning Management System (LMS). Courses in traditional LMSs are like silos in that there is minimal ability for students from one class to interact with another class. Traditionally, students login and only interact with one instructor and the other 25-30 students in the class. To interact with students from another class, they must be enrolled in that class. Due to design of the traditional LMS or issues of student authentication, major corporate LMSs do not allow for easy access for cross-curricular events. It is easier to have students create an avatar and go into a virtual world than make a separate course shell and enroll students from all the participating classes. The team also believed that having students participate in a synchronous event where immersion in a virtual world was possible would also be more engaging for the students.

Second Life was chosen due to the practicality of the environment and its ability to allow students and subject matter experts to all gather in the same place. Using a virtual world also allowed all participants to immerse themselves in the environment and the activities. These activities included "Don't Just Talk like a Pirate: Be the Pirate!" and "Make like an Action Figure!" The objective was to provide richness in content and immersion through the virtual world and permit role-play informed by the psychomotor domain of learning (Bloom & Krathwohl, 1956). Harris defines immersion as "a metaphorical term derived from the physical experience of being submerged in water" (Harris, 1998). The instructional team hoped that all participants would feel submerged, especially when they went diving for treasure in the haunted shipwreck on the island.

In community colleges, there has been a call for "engagement by design" since community college students are more likely to have responsibilities of full time work and be the primary caretaker for their family (McClenney, 2007). The Online Learning department at Front Range Community College is no different than most community colleges. It has almost 5,000 students enrolled in online classes. The online student population is 70% female and a majority of the students are at least 25 years old. The students may be taking one class online or taking full-time credit online. A majority of students taking online classes either

work full-time or are the primary caregiver of children in their household. Given these limitations, the instructional team wanted to develop a set of events that would provide for the highest level of engagement in the content material and in the technical tools available through an immersive virtual environment.

Currently, the college online learning policy does not allow mandatory synchronous attendance. Online Students are always provided with additional options. In order to remain consistent with policy, online courses offered these events as a LMS discussion post options, project options, and extra credit opportunities. Students who attended these events were assessed through the grading of these means and direct interaction with instructors.

Solutions and Recommendations

These events were designed to encourage cross-curricular engagement and collaborative learning in an immersive virtual world. The team's motivation was to design an event that was engaging and immersive enough to ensure the learning would endure (Wiggins & McTighe, 2005). Cross-curricular content from *The Fine ARRRRRT of Being a Pirate* and *Met@Morph* covered abstract and often misunderstood facts and ideas. The focus was to allow students to interact with content from multiple perspectives.

The design of the events was developed to ensure that students benefited from the established pedagogical practices while taking advantage of additional practices inherent in an immersive learning environment. The instructional design framework was informed by:

- The Dick and Carey Systems Approach Model for Designing Instruction (Dick & Carey, 2005)
- The Seven Principles for Good Practice (Chickering & Gamson, 1987)
- The three learning domains—cognitive, affective, and psychomotor (Bloom, 1956;

Harrow, 1972; Anderson & Krathwohl, 2001)
- New Media Literacy Skills (Jenkins, et al., 2006)

The student and guest lecturers had not previously used a virtual world application. All of the students did have the technical skills to navigate and communicate using the college's LMS.

The Seven Principles for Good Practice in Undergraduate Education (Chickering & Gamson, 1987) provided a background for the development of these events. The events were designed to encourage synchronous collaboration between instructors, students, and subject matter experts. The utilization of a virtual world allowed for the development of reciprocity for instructors, student and subject matter experts. Each took turns teaching and then learning. The team also incorporated Chickering and Gamson's principle of communicating high expectations and instructors did inform students of these prior to the events.

These events were designed to engage students in all three of the learning domains—cognitive, affective, and psychomotor (Bloom & Krathwohl, 1956). In the cognitive domain, students were expected to recall the information and summarize the information in the weekly discussion posts. They were also responsible for taking questions from their classmates who did not choose the option to go into Second Life. In the affective domain, there were two specific learning tasks. The first learning task was immersion in a virtual environment and the second task was to value the subject content of the events. Students were introduced to a new technology that immersed them in an entirely new culture. In *The Fine ARRRRRT of Being a Pirate*, the goal was to receive the phenomena. The goal of the second event, *Met@Morph*, was for the student to respond to the phenomena. They were able to participate in both events. In *The Fine ARRRRRT of Being a Pirate*, they could question the instructors. At the roundtable at *Met@*

Morph they were expected to participate and to question concepts and models in order to fully understand them.

The most interesting type of learning that virtual worlds may have to offer is in the psychomotor domain. While not identical to the real world, avatars provide for movement, coordination, and use of motor-skills in a virtual world. Development of these skills in a virtual world requires practice. These skills are evaluated in terms of speed, precision, distance, and technique, and may be simple, compound, or complex.

In the psychomotor domain students must use perception to choose, detect and identify (Harrow, 1972). These skills are absolutely necessary to navigate in Second Life. The first event was set up to include a guided response based on imitation of the instructor and trial and error. This is only established through practice. By the end of the second event, it was hoped that basic movement could be performed with confidence and proficiency. The workshop in the second event was developed for students to move into the realm of non-discursive communication with the "Make like an Action Figure!" session. The performance objectives from the psychosocial domain were:

The Fine ARRRRRT of Being a Pirate – Students will be able to sit, stand, fly, teleport, buy items, instant message and communicate using the local chat function.

Met@Morph – Students will be able to use gestures, utilize the in-world white board, and follow an audio/visual presentation with back channel communication.

The instructional team decided utilizing new media literacy skills situated in the subject matter content would provide the richest learning experience. The interaction embedded in the events allowed students to test and form their constructs with other students, instructors, and subject matter experts. The team focused on designing activities and sessions that would involve development of new media literacy skills that would involve play, performance, multitasking, distributed cognition, and negotiation (Jenkins, et al., 2006). Virtual worlds where students have the ability to create have an inherent advantage over a traditional LMS. Virtual worlds allow students to build and experiment with their surroundings. The creation of an avatar and customization allow students to try on alternative identities and continue to play. The multimodal streams of communication—chat, audio, instant messaging, and non-discursive communication such as gesturing, encourage students to multitask, scanning the environment for builds, objects and movement not possible in the real world. Several of the sessions were specifically developed for distributed cognition such as avatar customization and gesturing. The Looting Party and subsequent teleport trips were designed to have students visit diverse communities respecting the traditions and norms of the different sites.

FUTURE RESEARCH DIRECTIONS

Directions for future research include the investigation and development of scenarios and experiences for students that are not possible in real life. A virtual world can create an experience for students that allows them to interact, problem solve and reflect in ways not possible from watching a video. A learning scenario in a virtual world can be visual, auditory, and immersive. Virtual worlds can be thought of as problem solving learning environment. Faculty and instructional designers can see how the environment can be developed to allow learner to interact, problem solve and reflect.

Second Life is not the only possible platform. Research should continue in Open Sim, Unity3D, and the other virtual worlds and 3D platforms that allow for content creation. Additional research would allow educators and instructional designers to make more informed decisions on whether this type of learning environment is useful for their learners. A comparison of the virtual worlds based

done by researchers who are building and utilizing instructional modules in multiple virtual worlds would allow for informed report of the affordances and constraints of both.

CONCLUSION

These events encouraged active learning to the extent of even utilizing psychomotor skills in the real world and as an avatar in Second Life. Both events were designed to have portion where students were living the experience not merely talking about the experience. Active learning is the area in which virtual worlds can vitally expand learning.

Based on direct observation and review of the chat transcripts, the instructional team did believe that the cognitive engagement was achieved by the students. The team was able to record the behavior using the transcripts of the communication history from the Second Life events and video using Camstudio screen capture. Cognitive engagement was demonstrated by their sustained engaged attention to activities requiring new learning and mental activities (Corno & Mandinach, 1983). The team also reported instances of play, fun, and enjoyment.

Throughout these events, the instructional team and participants concluded that:

1. SL is a powerful platform for cost-effectively connecting large groups of people.
2. The interaction between people is special – SL handled our style, which is dynamic, lively, and satisfying.
3. Learning was enhanced by the fun and the free-for-all chat windows.
4. SL worked as a central point for the meeting of people, their Flickr accounts, their URLs, their PowerPoint presentations, their blogs, and their art.
5. Students were connected to scholars from around the world.

6. Students were connected to industry professionals.
7. Students were connected to artists.
8. Students were empowered to mentor scholars and professionals, in both scholarship and in digital literacy skills.

All participants—students, instructors, and subject matter experts—were able to negotiate and test the immersive environment and the knowledge presented. Current educational practices support the use of instructional methods that make student active learners. Compared to the traditional LMS, virtual worlds allow online students more active learning opportunities.

Second Life can be used to create a learning environment based on current educational theory and practice. However, why stop there? Second Life is also a powerful immersive application with a huge selection of features, more added regularly. The events led the team to wonder, why limit ourselves to recreating a real life setting? Using these features, we found, is fun. They inspire students to play, engaging, and immersing them in interpersonal interaction, ideas, and critical thinking. The experience is enormously satisfying to the professional lives and goals of faculty, instructional designers, and IT staff. As a result of the positive experiences of these events, the team has been conducting other cross-curriculum events for two years.

Instructors and Instructional designers need not limit the learning environment in virtual worlds to recreations of real life setting. At the same time, the team is now exploring some fresh questions. First, is play a legitimate pedagogical tool? If we call it "play," will we alienate students who might conclude we are not taking their learning objectives seriously? If the class objectives do not include creation of the learning environment, the use of all three learning domains, and participatory culture, then a locked-down simulation may be a better fit for the class.

Second, what is the role of the instructor in the virtual environment? Should the instructor be a master controller, in charge of defining the environment? Does learning slip away when the instructor releases the reins to the student? What would the student say? Through participation in these events, Front Range students discovered a whole new way of learning. Chief among their discoveries was the realization that in these Second Life educational events, students, scholars, and faculty can all be mentors as well as learners. In Second Life, the expert-on-a-dais model of teaching is rapidly replaced by a matrix of discussion, collaboration, and movement that quickly generates a pool of ideas and knowledge to which everyone has contributed and over which everyone feels a sense of ownership and pride.

While it has been reported that the role of educator has changed in the online environment (Conceicao, 2006), we believe the role of the instructor will continue to evolve in immersive virtual worlds, moving beyond the cognitive and affective learning domain to include the psychomotor domain.

To the team's surprise and delight, all participants returned from the unplanned rolling restart. Everything was where they had left it; that is what is different about a cataclysmic event in a virtual world. The group enjoyed the rest of the afternoon events. As the session drew to a close, many returned to real life musing over the day's experiences and blogging on them. However, they realized that some things never change, even in a virtual world. It is never a good idea to take candy from a stranger. In Second Life, the candy was good, until your head exploded.

REFERENCES

Anderson, L. W., & Krathwohl, D. R. (Eds.). (2001). *A taxonomy for learning, teaching and assessing: A revision of Bloom's taxonomy of educational objectives: Complete edition.* New York, NY: Longman.

Bloom, B. S., & Krathwohl, D. R. (1956). *Taxonomy of educational objectives: The classification of educational goals, by a committee of college and university examiners: Handbook 1: Cognitive domain.* New York, NY: Longmans.

Chickering, A. W., & Gamson, Z. F. (1987). Seven principles for good practice in undergraduate education. *The American Association for Higher Education Bulletin.* Retrieved from http://www.uis.edu/liberalstudies/students/documents/seven-principles.pdf

Conceicao, S. C. O. (2006). Faculty lived experiences in the online environment. *American Association for Adult and Continuing Education, 57*(1), 26–45. doi:10.1177/1059601106292247

Corno, L., & Mandinach, E. B. (1983). The role of cognition engagement in classroom learning and motivation. *Educational Psychologist, 18*(2), 88–108. doi:10.1080/00461528309529266

Csíkszentmihályi, M. (1990). *Flow: The psychology of optimal experience.* New York, NY: Harper and Row.

Douglas, Y., & Hargadon, A. (2000). The pleasure principle: Immersion, engagement, flow. In *Proceedings from ACM Hypertext 2000* (pp. 153–160). New York, NY: ACM Press. doi:10.1145/336296.336354

Harris, J. H. (1998). *Hamlet on the holodeck: The future of narrative in cyberspace.* Cambridge, MA: The MIT Press.

Harrow, A. (1972). *A taxonomy of psychomotor domains: A guide for developing behavioral objectives.* New York, NY: David McKay.

Jenkins, H., Clinton, K., Purushotma, R., Robison, A. J., & Weigel, M. (2006). *Confronting the challenges of participatory culture: Media education for the 21st century.* Chicago, IL: The MacArthur Foundation. Retrieved December 30, 2008 from http://www.digitallearning.macfound.org/atf/cf/%7B7E45C7E0-A3E0-4B89-AC9C-E807E1B0AE4E%7D/JENKINS_WHITE_PAPER.PDF

Jones, P. C., & Merritt, Q. (1999). The TALESSI project: Promoting active learning for interdisciplinary, values awareness and critical thinking in environmental higher education. *Journal of Geography in Higher Education, 23*(3), 335–348. doi:10.1080/03098269985281

McClenney, K. M. (2007). Research update: The community college survey of student engagement. *Community College Review, 35*(2), 137–146. doi:10.1177/0091552107306583

McMahan, A. (2003). Immersion, engagement, and presence: A method for analyzing 3-D video games. In Wolf, M. J. P., & Perron, B. (Eds.), *The Video Game Theory Reader* (pp. 25–46). New York, NY: Routledge.

Novak, K. (2008). RezEd: The hub for learning in virtual worlds. *Social Presence Effects Group.* Retrieved on January 13, 2009 from http://www.rezed.org/forum/topics/2047896:Topic:6518?groupUrl=socialpresenceinvirtualworlds&id=2047896%3ATopic%3A6518&groupId=2047896%3AGroup%3A6392&page=6#comments

Prensky, M. (2005). Engage me or enrage me: What today's learners demand. *EDUCAUSE Review,* 60-64. Retrieved January 3, 2009 from http://net.educause.edu/ir/library/pdf/erm0553.pdf

Read, J., MacFarlane, S., & Casey, C. (2002). Endurability, engagement and expectations: Measuring children's fun. In *Proceedings of the International Workshop on Interaction Design and Children,* (pp. 189-198). Eindhoven, The Netherlands: Shaker Publishing.

Skinner, E. A., Wellborn, J. G., & Connell, J. P. (1990). What it takes to do well in school and whether I've got it: A process model of perceived control and children's engagement in school. *Journal of Educational Psychology*, 82, 22–32. doi:10.1037/0022-0663.82.1.22

Wiggins, G., & McTighe, J. (2005). *Understanding by design* (2nd ed.). Upper Saddle River, NJ: Prentice Hall.

Chapter 10
Online Behavior of the Social Media Student

Alan J. Reid
Old Dominion University, USA

Kate Prudchenko
Old Dominion University, USA

ABSTRACT

A survey of 100 undergraduates and 30 post-secondary faculty members was conducted in order to examine the current attitudes and perceptions of both groups toward the integration of social media sites such as Facebook and Twitter in education. Results indicate that both parties are willing to incorporate these social media sites into academics but caution that digital identities are not necessarily representative of face-to-face behavior, thus suggesting the need for an awareness of social presence for online interaction between students and faculty. Social cognitive theories are applied to the use of social media as an instructional tool and a set of best practices for implementing social media in academics is proposed.

INTRODUCTION

Educators are teaching a new generation of students. Unlike generations X, Y, or Z, the Social Media Generation is not determined by the year in which a person is born but by the amount that person interacts with others through social media tools. As a result, the Social Media Generation includes all ages and backgrounds. Kindergartens, elementary schools, the Queen of England and the Pope have Facebook pages. This year, Mark Zuckerberg, the founder of Facebook, beat out the President of the United States, thirty-three Chilean miners, Afghanistan's President Hamid Karzai, and the Tea Party for *Time Magazine*'s Person of the Year. This speaks volumes to the relevance social media has in our society and suggests that social media is much more than a temporary fad. This all-encompassing Social Media Generation lives in an environment where communication is instant, connectivity is expected, and digital identities and relationships mimic real world actualizations. As a result, more and more educators and educational institutions are integrating social

DOI: 10.4018/978-1-4666-2670-6.ch010

media with academics in the hopes that doing so will relate to students and keep them engaged in learning, but are these two worlds compatible?

The mission of this chapter is to survey current post-secondary undergraduates and faculty located throughout the country in order to take a pulse on the attitudes and perceptions of social media in education, and to reconcile these attitudes with common and acceptable online behaviors. Through the lens of social learning theories, the authors explore how students construct and maintain multiple digital identities in order to interact with social, business, and academic networks. Accordingly, a set of guidelines and recommendations for the use of social media in education is drafted.

BACKGROUND

Social Media

The term *social media* generally refers to the big three networking sites: Facebook, MySpace, and Twitter, but can be expanded to include microblogging sites, wikis, social bookmarking, blogs, content management systems, and any other type of consumer-generated material. Of these tools, Facebook and Twitter are the most commonly used in academia. Though MySpace still boasts 57 million unique U.S. users, the number of active users is dwindling and, as a result, MySpace is often left out of the conversation of integrating social media with education (Owyang, 2010).

With over 550 million (and counting) users, Facebook is the largest proprietor of all social media and serves one out of every twelve people on the planet. The website is accumulating approximately 700,000 new accounts per day (Grossman, 2010). Statistically speaking, it is a good possibility that you own a Facebook page and understand how it operates. Users can create a free account on Facebook, which requires only

an e-mail address. The profile page allows users the option to customize sections such as birthday, relationship status, schools attended, interests, political views, religion, a short biography, and favorite quotations among others. Additionally, photos and videos are staples of most Facebook accounts. Once the profile is created, friends may be accumulated through importing contact lists from the user's email account, or searching for friends by name or institution. Moreover, Facebook continually suggests friends with similar profiles and establishing friendships involves either sending or accepting a "friend request." More information regarding Facebook can be found at the following sites:

- http://news.cnet.com/newbies-guide-to-facebook/
- http://www.mahalo.com/how-to-use-facebook
- http://www.facebook.com/help/

Facebook is used a variety of ways in academia. Most educational institutions have a Facebook page, which is often used to recruit new students and update current students and alumnae. In addition, Green and Bailey (2010) loosely identify five uses of Facebook in education. These include sharing and discussing homework and answers (mostly unique to K-12 students), interacting on study group pages (mostly unique to post-secondary students), creating group pages for school-related clubs and organizations, creating individual pages for academic and degree programs, and communicating with the instructor (both formally and informally) via individual instructor pages.

The second most popular social media site in education is Twitter, a microblogging application that allows users to send bursts of information to its followers in 140 characters or less. As of September 2010, Twitter's population of 105 million is growing at an exponential rate of approximately 300,000 per day (Facult Focus, 2010). While it does not cultivate a platform for social interactivity, as Facebook does, Twitter's popularity in academia has been nevertheless steadily increasing, and is most commonly used to communicate with students and disseminate information. A survey of 1,362 higher education professionals shows that more than one third of them are currently using Twitter in some fashion, and over half (56.8%) expect to increase their usage over the coming academic year (Faculty Focus, 2010). As with Facebook, Twitter is highly conducive to a mobile environment as a result of smartphone applications. Smartphones, such as the Android and iPhone, enable instructors to interact with students at a higher level through real-time updates and immediate communication. Reid, Houchen-Clagett, and Browning (2010) integrated Twitter into the community college classroom for two semesters and found that 59% of the 117 participants reported an increase in course motivation and engagement, despite an initial hesitation to join Twitter. While Twitter is not as popular as Facebook, its uses may be more advantageous as an instructional resource and tool for information disbursement. An associate professor at Lock Haven University notes a common student perception of the two: "Facebook is where I go to socialize, and Twitter is where I go to work" (Chapman, 2010).

Other social media such as wikis, blogs, and YouTube are also often implemented into courses as instructional resources and assessment tools, but the debate regarding the educational value of social media remains focused on Facebook and Twitter, due to their commanding popularity of the social networking sphere. Because social media is easily accessible, free, and comes with a built-in audience, instructors often implement Facebook or Twitter as supplemental tools without considering the instructional design necessary to validate these tools. For these reasons, and to keep the conversation relevant, the use of the phrase *social media* will refer mainly to the applications Facebook and Twitter.

When the social and academic worlds of post-secondary students collide, there are many issues that may arise. These issues may be, in part, due to the notion that undergraduates often create multiple identities to accompany the situation in which each one may be appropriate or desired. The social media world may encourage the student to project a digital identity that is inconsistent with their academic lives and identities portrayed in the traditional face-to-face classroom. More-over, social media giant Facebook was created specifically for students to connect with fellow constituents within their college or university. Instructors attempting to cross into this virtual world may risk the credibility as a professional. Mazer, Cheri, and Simonds (2007) warn that by implementing social media such as Facebook, instructors "may violate student expectations of proper behaviors and run the risk of harming their credibility" (p. 3). Additionally, their study refers to Facebook as "student-based territory," and that invading this space will "have negative effects on students" (p. 14). At its core, this discussion over the viability of social media as an instructional tool hinges on fundamental social-cognitive theories and the widely accepted notion that learning is social in nature.

Theoretical Frameworks

In essence, a social network is an online community in which the user creates a digital identity and builds a network of friends. It is no wonder why educators are so anxious to employ social media as another facet of their instruction; if instruction is injected into a pre-existing Social Web, then learning is bound to be a byproduct, right? But there are many circumstances under which social media could impede or obstruct a learner's performance and affective perceptions of the course or even the instructor.

Albert Bandura's (1977) social learning theory posits that human behavior is influenced and directly affected by observation and experiences (pp. 11-12). Users of social media applications often interact with others observationally; that is, they view the postings and updates that are visible to friends, but do not necessarily interact through direct communication with that friend. Moreover, Vygotsky's social development theory builds on Bandura's work, proposing "every function in the child's cultural development appears twice: First, on the social level, and later, on the individual level…[a]ll the higher functions originate as actual relationships between individuals"(Vygotsky, 1978, p. 57). If educators can harness this social climate, learning is facilitated. The problem is that oftentimes, students behave differently online than they do in a traditional classroom setting. Their behavior online has to correspond with the digital identity that they have created for themselves, which may be wildly unlike their personality in real life or in school.

Social presence theory (Short, Williams, & Christie, 1976) is defined as the "degree of salience of the other person in a mediated communication and the consequent salience of their interpersonal interactions" (p. 65). In other words, Short et al. hypothesized that the medium of communication dictates the behavior of its users. Though Gunawardena and Zittle (1997) add, "[i]n spite of the characteristics of the medium, student perceptions of the social and human qualities of CMC [Computer-Mediated Communication] will depend on the social presence created by the instructors/moderators and the online community" (p. 23). User behaviors are shaped and cultured through the medium by which communication is being delivered *and* through observations and interactions with others: Instructors and classmates.

Biocca, Harms, and Burgoon (2001) offer a broader definition of social presence to include three categories: 1) Co-presence, co-location, and mutual awareness, which include the sense of togetherness and being with others socially, 2)

psychological involvement, which includes the salience of others, formation of identity through the constellation of nonverbal cues, and mutual understanding (Short, et al., 1976; Savicki & Kelley, 2000), and 3) behavioral engagement, which is the extent to which individuals can interact with others in a virtual reality (Heeter, 1992). Just as in real world environments, selves consist of multiple identities. Individuals select an identity to use for work, for school, for family, for friends, even for strangers. In most social media, the owner creates one profile that is projected to all connections. As a result, social media sites may potentially conflict with an intersection of academic and social identities. While this inconsistency in identities may be tolerable for some, it can be problematic for others.

Vazire and Gosling (2004) equate online profiles, such as those created on social media sites, as representations of real-world environments. For instance, a poster in a dorm room of Albert Einstein could convey the importance of intellectual values without direct communication (p. 124). Likewise, postings, statuses, photos, videos, "likes," and "dislikes" can influence others through simple observation of the user's profile. This reflection of personality based on the environment is referred to as "behavioral residue" (Vazire & Gosling, 2004, p. 124). Behavioral residue can be both constructive and detrimental to the user's digital identity. In a social media site such as Facebook, the user creates a single profile page; all acquaintances, friends, and groups are linked to that one profile. Thus, the profile that a user would display for a group of friends may not coincide with a profile desirable for professionals such as instructors and classmates to view. In fact, the user does not even have to behave inappropriately; behavioral residue left by friends' comments and photos on the Facebook page may form an unwanted impression of the owner. Walther, Van Der Heide, Kim, Westerman, and Tong (2008) reinforced earlier findings that "other-generated descriptions are more truthful to observers than target-generated claims" (p. 45). Importantly, behavioral residue left from friends, falsified or not, is more powerful in the impression formation process than what the profile owner projects. "Because online impressions are controllable" they are "often suspect" (Walther, et al., 2008, p. 32).

SOCIAL MEDIA IN ACADEMIA

Survey Methodology

The survey was distributed to 100 undergraduate students and 30 faculty members across a number of educational institutions during October and November 2010. The students were contacted randomly via e-mail, which contained a link to the online survey and explained the rationale and objectives of the anonymous survey. The majority of student respondents (68%) came from Brunswick Community College, a two-year college in Supply, North Carolina, with approximately 1,500 students. The next leading institution was Old Dominion University (29%), a four-year institution located in Norfolk, Virginia with approximately 23,000 total students. Other respondents included students from the University of North Carolina at Wilmington, Niagara University, and Anne Arundel Community College in Arnold, Maryland. Faculty members were randomly chosen to complete a similar survey online. Major respondents included current teaching faculty from Brunswick Community College, Old Dominion University, University of North Carolina at Greensboro, Arizona State University, Tufts University, and Rochester Institute of Technology.

The online surveys were created using Survey Monkey. The student-issued survey consisted of thirty-six multiple-choice and open-ended questions (See Appendix A), and the faculty-issued survey consisted of nineteen questions (See Appendix B).

Survey Results

Student respondents are predominantly female (72%), and the primary age range of those surveyed is 18-25 (66%), though 79% of all respondents are under the age of thirty. The faculty respondents were split (15 men and 15 women), and the predominant age range is 36-40 (20%), though the second highest recorded age group is 61 and over (13.3%). The number of individuals who own smartphones with Wi-Fi access was relatively equal between the groups, with 49% of the students and 43.3% of faculty, but there is a discrepancy between the number of e-reading devices such as Kindle and Nook between students (21%) and faculty (81.8%). Though this information suggests both groups possess a high level of technological competency, given their adoption of technological tools, and their participation in a computer-based survey, this is fairly representative of the general population.

As expected, the majority of students (48%) selected text messaging as their primary form of communication with friends. This further reinforces the characteristics of the social media generation and the superseding of technology over more personal forms of interaction. This is compared to the 28.3% of students who prefer face-to-face communication, and the 18.2% who mainly correspond via phone. Only 1% and 7.1% primarily communicate with friends using email and social media sites, respectively. In particular, 70% of faculty and only 57% of students agreed that social media was effective communication tool for interacting with one another. The reluctance to use social media as a primary communication tool could be due to the fact that text messages are private and direct, whereas the main purpose of social media is to post information to an array of friends using a shotgun approach. Moreover, communicating on-the-go through text messaging is not inhibited by Internet connectivity as in the case of using social media. Despite students' strong preference for text messaging as a primary form of communication, only 30% of faculty members indicated they use texting to correspond with students. Results indicate that while faculty members do not typically text students, 36.8% do feel more comfortable using social media to communicate with students informally about topics not necessarily related to class.

Results from the survey also show that both faculty and students are open to integrating social media into education and both groups view it as a viable form of communication. 92.9% of students indicated that they maintain a social media account and 71% thought of social media as a viable educational resource. While the number of faculty with a social media account was slightly less (76.7%), their attitudes were comparable. 73.3% indicated that social media was a viable educational resource. However, students and faculty had differing attitudes regarding the permanence of social media in our culture. While 50% of students think of social media as a temporary fad, 86.7% of faculty members disagreed.

In terms of usage, 73% of students and 73.9% of faculty indicated that they checked their social media account one or more times per day. Furthermore, 51% of the students agree that they check their social media account more often than their school email. An additional 25% selected "neutral." Of the faculty, 50% reported that they use social media in an educational setting and 36.3% reported that they use social media to communicate with students outside of the educational setting. Additionally, no faculty respondents (0%) agree that higher education institutions should block social media sites. 86.4% of faculty members use their social media accounts to primarily communicate with friends/faculty/colleagues, and no one (0%) strongly disagreed with this statement.

Students were asked about common behaviors on social media sites. The majority of students (63.3%) agreed that it is common to see swearing or cursing. Since cursing appears commonplace, it is also likely that social media sites feature nega-

tivity towards one another. In particular, 62.2% of students indicate that negativity is common while only 12.2% disagree with this statement. When asked whether they choose to intervene when someone is speaking negatively towards someone else, the majority (37.8%) of students indicated that it "depends on how well they know the person." Furthermore, 32.2% of students indicated that they never intervene, 24.4% sometimes intervene, and a meager 5.6% always intervene.

In terms of student online behaviors, 74% reported that they post pictures of themselves online and 66% post pictures of others. Survey results suggest that most pictures tend to be appropriate in that 70% disagreed with the statement "it is common to post pictures of others or myself without a shirt on my site." Findings are also similar in terms of pictures that feature alcoholic beverages and kissing; 60% disagree with the statement "it is common to post pictures of others or myself with alcohol or in a bar." Moreover, 60% disagree with the statement that it is common to post pictures of themselves or others kissing. Students were also inquired as to whether they perceived "drunk updates," or updating statuses while clearly intoxicated, to be common: 24.4% strongly disagreed, 24.4% disagreed, 21.1% neutral, and 26.7% agreed. Only 3.3% strongly agreed with the statement. These findings are contrary to the assumptions of the authors.

The survey also explored the most commonly discussed issues on social media sites. Student respondents were asked to rate the issues based on their frequency of appearance on social sites. The findings discovered the following issues most often discussed: Friends (70%), parties (63.3%), school (60%), family (58.9%), and sex (27.8%). To summarize, the survey found that students use social media sites to primarily discuss friends and parties, sometimes discuss family and school, and rarely discuss sex.

Because school is a common topic being discussed, it is no wonder that the majority (52.1%)

of students agreed with the statement that social media can be used for instruction and other educational purposes, and 49% agreed that it could be an effective tool to communicate with instructors. However, only 33.3% of students granted that they are open and excited about using social networking in the classroom for instructional purposes and a large portion (32.3%) remains neutral. This is likely an indicator of the uncertainty of social media as a credible academic resource.

Fewer students than faculty members are convinced of whether or not potential employers and schools preview social media sites to investigate their behavior prior to employing or accepting them. Yet, the majority of students (66.7%) agree that one should be held responsible for what he or she says and does on a social media site.

Since students feel that they and others are responsible for their online social presence, it was expected that students would view a correlation between their online and real world identities. Many students agreed (68%) with the statement that their online identities were representative of their face-to-face identity. These findings are considerably different from those of the faculty: Only 26.7% believe that students' online presence is representative of their classroom presence. Interestingly, though, 65% of students indicated that they do not use their social media accounts to communicate with their parents, which begs the question, if digital identities are truly representative of real-world identities, why do so few students engage with their parents online?

Student Comments

The following comments were derived from the open-ended questions on the survey distributed to post-secondary undergraduate students. The question asked: Do you feel as though you have a "digital identity?" In other words, do you behave differently online than you do in person? Because the question was not required to complete the sur-

vey, it is assumed that the students who voluntarily responded feel strongly toward the topic of using social media in education.

I think I am a more open person online.

Facebook should only be used for personal reasons.

I have seen people's pages, and the way they act at work or school is totally different.

I need a social forum that is different from school.

I'm sure people don't represent themselves accurately because [Facebook] is private. Or so they think.

I do have an online identity, from my pictures and stuff that I say to my friends, you would think I was loud and liked to be the center of attention, but really, I'm shy and kind of quiet.

I act the same online as I do in person.

Yes, I do have an online identity. I behave differently by leaving responses on different issues. In other words, speaking my mind when [I was] not asked.

Discussion

Because of the limited sample size of this study, the findings may not be generalized to the entire academic population. However, the results do provide an insight into current perceptions of post-secondary students and faculty members regarding the integration of social media into education. Access to the Internet and its technological tools is rapidly increasing (Grunwald Associates LLC, 2010), and while the term *social media* does not pertain solely to one particular application such as Facebook or Twitter, the concepts of online collaboration, communication, and digital citizenship remain engrained in the social media generation. The danger, however, lies in compromising instructional values, student security, or learning outcomes in order to adopt the newest, shiniest social media tool.

From this survey, it is apparent that an alarming number from both groups already maintain social media accounts in some capacity, whether recreationally or for instructional purposes. Generally, students and faculty are open to implementing social media in education, and view this medium as an effective tool for communication. This is significant in that the skills required for using social media in a classroom environment are, in most cases, preexisting. Consequently, less time is needed to train students on using social media applications and more time can be devoted to instruction-related topics.

Contrary to recent studies and the authors' expectations, this survey identifies student online behaviors on social media sites as being relatively appropriate. Though the respondents admitted that vulgar language and negativity is common, few acknowledged to posting what Kolek and Saunders (2008) refer to as "socially objectionable" images that feature partying, drinking, or scantily clad individuals. This is divergent from previous studies of Facebook profiles, which revealed a high percentage of profiles referencing these very behaviors (Kolek & Saunders, 2008; Watson, Smith, & Driver, 2006). This finding may point to the assertion that students are either unaware of how they are portraying themselves online, or that there is disconnect among the standards of what is considered to be socially objectionable in an online environment.

Importantly, this survey highlights an often-overlooked aspect of social media: Digital identities. The formation of this identity is critical. In many cases, students' online personalities on social media sites are more indicative of their desirable self and not accurately representative of their actual self. This may cause problems when social

media operates as both a social, informal forum, and an educational, formal environment for the student. In most social media applications where the user creates one profile for everyone to see, the student is conflicted with trying to uphold a social identity in addition to the identity he or she wishes to convey to the instructor. A common objection to implementing social media in academia is that "students do not like teachers or parents in 'their' space" (Boon & Sinclair, 2009). Teacher immediacy is the distance an instructor maintains between himself and his students' space. If there is not appropriate distance in teacher immediacy, students may experience discomfort and their satisfaction and performance in the course will suffer (Boon & Sinclair, 2009; Hewitt & Forte, 2006; Mazer, Murphy, & Simonds, 2007).

There is a wide array of social media tools, and the level at which these tools are utilized may vary. Implementing a blog site as an informal way to engage and communicate with students is quite different from using Facebook as the sole vehicle to deliver instruction. Social media has many applications to academia; it can be a means for disseminating information, assessing student performance, collaborating with peers, creating clubs and organizations, developing instructor-student relationships, among many other uses. Social media can help foster an environment conducive to learning through boosting teacher immediacy and, ultimately, student satisfaction (Moore, Masterson, Christophel, & Shea, 1996; Richardson & Swan, 2003). However, each scenario warrants its own set of heuristics that augments learning.

Aside from the classroom, social media is currently being used in all facets of education: The admissions process, institution profiles, campus events, and marketing, among others. Academia is adapting to the wants and needs of its constituents, which means social media and education are becoming more intertwined. It is crucial that this partnership remain positive, for social media was originally designed for sharing, collaborating, and communicating, not education; it just so happens that these variables are essential to education as well as our social lives. To ensure social media is properly utilized in the classroom, some fundamental guidelines should be followed. The following recommendations are derived from the findings of this survey, and should, at minimum, be employed when social media is integrated into education:

The 7 Best Practices for Integrating Social Media

1. Notify administration before implementing social media sites.
2. Establish clear policies and consequences.
3. Clearly define ethical boundaries for socially objectionable behavior.
4. Set privacy settings to highest level of security.
5. Avoid overuse of applications (employ a maximum of three per class).
6. Do not require the use of social media if it exceeds the expectations for class participation.
7. When possible, social and academic profiles should be independent of one another.

FUTURE RESEARCH DIRECTIONS

Because social media is fluid and constantly evolving, so are the uses and attitudes towards its role in education. The objective of this survey was to identify current attitudes and perceptions of postsecondary students and faculty members toward the integration of social media in academia. Though limited in terms of size, the findings confirm the high usage of social media among students and faculty, and suggest openness to using social media as a supplement to instruction. Future research should investigate the effects of social media on student performance and achievement of learning outcomes. Further, research that explores the impact of social media on students and their digital identities would be beneficial to the case for social media in education.

The fusion of characteristics typical of social media and asynchronous learning platforms is becoming apparent. Emerging Learning Management Systems (LMSs) are incorporating more and more features formerly distinctive of social media sites: Instant messaging, virtual chat rooms, and the capability of users to create and maintain profiles. It is the assertion of the authors that social media and LMSs will continue to blend until a hybrid model becomes commonplace in education. This will benefit K-12 educators who wish to use social media, but are confined by privacy and security issues of their students. These attributes of social media that students endear may eventually be synonymous with course platforms. The desire to integrate social networking sites such as Facebook may begin to dwindle as similar education-specific programs are developed.

Another aspect of social media that appeals to its users is its accessibility on mobile devices. Mobile learning is an emerging trend in education, and with over 100 million iOS devices in the hands of users (Chen, 2010), this demand for just-in-time learning remains an untapped resource for educators. The development of mobile educational applications is another expectation of the Social Media Generation, and another area of endless opportunities.

CONCLUSION

Learning is a social process. Interacting with others enhances cognitive development and is imperative to education. We have countless tools at our fingertips that will assist educators in this endeavor, but we have to use them with caution. Understanding student behavior in an online environment is critical to effective instruction, and making the assumption that online and face-to-face identities are synonymous can be detrimental.

The Social Media Generation consists of digital immigrants and digital natives who have come to expect instantaneous communication and feedback, engaging content, and accessibility. Education must compete with this mentality, but must maintain its instructional values, worth, and credibility in doing so. This chapter intends to make the case for using social media in education, but cautions being overzealous. Learning outcomes, quality instruction, and effective teaching should never be supplanted with social media or other technological tools. Instead, the reasoning for integrating social media into education should be to enhance the value of the instruction, cultivate relationships with students, and foster communication skills. Following the best practices that the authors have proposed will facilitate student satisfaction and engagement in the course, which will ultimately lead to better performance and cognitive development. After all, this is the goal of an educator.

REFERENCES

Bandura, A. (1977). *Social learning theory.* Englewood Cliffs, NJ: Prentice-Hall.

Boon, S., & Sinclair, C. (2009). A world I don't inhabit: Disquiet and identity in Second Life and Facebook. *Educational Media International, 46*(2), 99–110. doi:10.1080/09523980902933565

Chapman, P. (2010). More professors are using Twitter – But mostly not for teaching. *The Chronicle of Higher Education.* Retrieved from http://chronicle.com/blogs/wiredcampus/more-professors-are-using-twitter-but-mostly-not-for-teaching/27354

Chen, B. (2010, June 18). Analyst: iPhone sales to surpass 100 million by 2011. *Gadget Lab.* Retrieved from http://www.wired.com/gadget-lab/2010/06/analyst-iphone-sales-to-surpass-100-million-by-2011/

Ewins, R. (2005). Who are you? Weblogs and academic identity. *E-learning, 2*(4), 368–377. doi:10.2304/elea.2005.2.4.368

Faculty Focus. (2010). *Twitter in higher education 2010: Usage habits and trends of today's college faculty.* Madison, WI: Faculty Focus.

Green, T., & Bailey, B. (2010). Academic uses of facebook: Endless possibilities or endless perils? *TechTrends, 54*(3), 20–22. doi:10.1007/s11528-010-0398-z

Grossman, L. (2010, December 15). Person of the year 2010: Mark Zuckerberg. *Time.* Retrieved from http://www.time.com/time/specials/packages/article/0,28804,2036683_2037183,00.html

Grunwald Associates LLC. (2010). *PBS annual survey report.* Retrieved from http://www.grunwald.com/reports/

Gunawardena, C. N., & Zittle, F. J. (1997). Social presence as a predictor of satisfaction within a computer-mediated conferencing environment. *American Journal of Distance Education, 11*(3), 8–26. doi:10.1080/08923649709526970

Heeter, C. (1992). Being there: The subjective experience of presence. *Presence (Cambridge, Mass.), 1*(2), 262–271.

Hewitt, A., & Forte, A. (2006). Crossing boundaries: Identity management and student/faculty relationships on the Facebook. In *Proceedings of the ACM 2006 Conference on Computer Supported Cooperative Work.* Banff, Canada. Retrieved from http://wwwstatic.cc.gatech.edu/~aforte/Hewitt-ForteCSCWPoster2006.pdf

Kolek, E., & Saunders, D. (2008). Online disclosure: An empirical examination of undergraduate Facebook profiles. *National Association of Student Personnel Administrators Journal, 45*(1), 1–25.

Mazer, J. P., Murphy, R. E., & Simonds, C. J. (2007). I'll see you on "facebook": The effects of computer-mediated teacher self-disclosure on student motivation, affective learning, and classroom climate. *Communication Education, 56*(1), 1–17. doi:10.1080/03634520601009710

Moore, A., Masterson, J. T., Christophel, D. M., & Shea, K. A. (1996). College teacher immediacy and student ratings of instruction. *Communication Education*, *45*, 29–39. doi:10.1080/03634529609379030

Owyang, J. (2010, January 19). A collection of social networking stats for 2010. *Web Strategy*. Retrieved from http://www.web-strategist.com/blog/2010/01/19/a-collection-of-social-network-stats-for-2010/

Reid, A., Houchen-Clagett, D., & Browning, J. B. (2010). *Integration of microblogging in post secondary courses*. Manuscript submitted for publication (copy on file with author). Unpublished.

Richardson, J., & Swan, K. (2003). Examining social presence in online courses in relation to students' perceived learning and satisfaction. *Journal of Asynchronous Learning Networks*, *7*(1), 68–88.

Savicki, V., & Kelley, M. (2000). Computer mediated communication: Gender and group composition. *Cyberpsychology & Behavior*, *3*(5), 817–826. doi:10.1089/10949310050191791

Short, J., Williams, E., & Christie, B. (1976). *The social psychology of telecommunications*. London, UK: John Wiley and Sons.

Vygotsky, L. S. (1978). *Mind in society*. Cambridge, MA: Harvard University Press.

Walther, J. B., Van Der Heide, B., Kim, S., Westerman, D., & Tong, S. T. (2008). The role of friends' appearance and behavior on evaluations of individuals' Facebook profiles: Are we known by the company we keep? *Human Communication Research*, *34*, 28–49. doi:10.1111/j.1468-2958.2007.00312.x

Watson, S., Smith, Z., & Driver, J. (2006). Alcohol, sex and illegal activities: An analysis of selected Facebook central photos in fifty states. *Online Submission*. Retrieved from EBSCOhost.

ADDITIONAL READING

Aragon, S. (2003). Creating social presence in online environments. *New Directions for Adult and Continuing Education*, *100*, 57–68. doi:10.1002/ace.119

Dunlap, J. C., & Lowenthal, P. R. (2009). Tweeting the night away: Using Twitter to enhance social presence. *Journal of Information Systems Education*, *20*(2), 129–135.

Ellison, N. B., Steinfeld, C., & Lampe, C. (2007). The benefits of Facebook friends: Social capital and college students' use of online social networking sites. *Journal of Computer-Mediated Communication*, *12*, 1143–1168. doi:10.1111/j.1083-6101.2007.00367.x

Gunawardena, C. N., & Zittle, F. J. (1997). Social presence as a predictor of satisfaction within a computer-mediated conferencing environment. *American Journal of Distance Education*, *11*(3), 8–26. doi:10.1080/08923649709526970

Joyce, K. M., & Brown, A. (2009). Enhancing social presence in online learning: Mediation strategies applied to social networking tools. *Online Journal of Distance Learning Administration*, *12*(4).

Kehrwald, B. (2008). Understanding social presence in text-based online learning environments. *Distance Education*, *29*(1), 89–106. doi:10.1080/01587910802004860

Kleck, C. A., Reese, C. A., Behnken, D. Z., & Sundar, S. S. (2007). *The company you keep and the image you project: Putting your best face forward in online social networks*. Paper presented at the Annual Meeting of the International Communication Association. San Francisco, CA.

Manzo, K. K. (2009). Twitter lessons in 140 characters or less. *Education Week*, *29*(8), 14.

Messner, K. (2009). Pleased to tweet you: Making a case for Twitter in the classroom. *School Library Journal, 55*(12), 44–47.

Morris, L. V., & Finnegan, C. L. (2009). Best practices in predicting and encouraging student persistence and achievement online. *Journal of College Student Retention: Research. Theory into Practice, 10*(1), 55–64.

Parks, M. R. (2007). *Personal networks and personal relationships*. Mahwah, NJ: Lawrence Erlbaum Associates.

Parrot, T. V., & Tipton, S. (2010). Using social media "smartly" in the admissions process. *College and University, 86*(1), 51–53.

Picciano, A. G. (2002). Beyond student perceptions: Issues of interaction, presence, and performance in an online course. *Journal of Asynchronous Learning Networks, 6*(1), 21–40.

Rimskii, V. (2010). The influence of the internet on active social involvement and the formation and development of identities. *Russian Education & Society, 52*(8), 11–33. doi:10.2753/RES1060-9393520802

Rourke, L., Andersson, T., Garrison, D. R., & Archer, W. (1999). Assessing social presence in asynchronous text-based computer conferencing. *Journal of Distance Education, 14*(2), 50–71.

Russo, T., & Benson, S. (2005). Learning with invisible others: Perceptions of online presence and their relationship to cognitive and affective learning. *Journal of Educational Technology & Society, 8*(1), 54–62.

Swan, K., & Shih, L. F. (2005). On the nature and development of social presence in online course discussions. *Journal of Asynchronous Learning Networks, 9*, 115–136.

Tagtmeier, C. (2010). Facebook vs. Twitter: Battle of the social network stars. *Computers in Libraries, 30*(7), 6–10.

Tom Tong, S., Van Der Heide, B., & Langwell, L. (2008). Too much of a good thing? The relationship between number of friends and interpersonal impressions on Facebook. *Journal of Computer-Mediated Communication, 13*, 531–549. doi:10.1111/j.1083-6101.2008.00409.x

Tu, C.-H. (2000). On-line learning migration: From social learning theory to social presence theory in a CMC environment. *Journal of Network and Computer Applications, 23*, 27–37. doi:10.1006/jnca.1999.0099

Tu, C.-H. (2001). How Chinese perceive social presence: An examination of interaction in an online learning environment. *Educational Media International, 38*(1), 45–60. doi:10.1080/09523980010021235

Turkle, S. (1995). *Life on the screen*. London, UK: Weidenfeld and Nicholson.

Walther, J. B., Van Der Heide, B., Kim, S., Westerman, D., & Tong, S. T. (2008). The role of friends' appearance and behavior on evaluations of individuals' Facebook profiles: Are we known by the company we keep? *Human Communication Research, 34*, 28–49. doi:10.1111/j.1468-2958.2007.00312.x

Young, J. R. (2010). Teaching with Twitter: Not for the faint of heart. *Education Digest: Essential Readings Condensed for Quick Review, 75*(7), 9–12.

Zhao, S., Grasmuck, S., & Martin, J. (2008). Identity construction on Facebook: Digital empowerment in anchored relationships. *Computers in Human Behavior, 20*, 1816–1836. doi:10.1016/j.chb.2008.02.012

KEY TERMS AND DEFINITIONS

Behavioral Residue: The impression a person leaves as determined by the interactions and relationships with others.

Computer-Mediated Communication (CMC): The interaction and contact an individual has with another in an online, computer-based environment.

Digital Identity: The persona constructed by an online user. Digital identities may be accurate representations of real-world qualities or fictive portrayals of desired characteristics.

Online Behavior: The manners and conduct of an individual in an online environment. These behaviors may be appropriate, inappropriate, representative, or non-representative of real-world behaviors.

Social Media: Any Internet application that allows user-generated material and media to be shared among other users.

Social Presence: The level of existence an individual conveys in an online setting. This can be transmitted through written text, photos, videos, or simply being present or absent.

Teacher Immediacy: The perceived distance an instructor is in relation to the student in an online environment in terms of communication and interactivity.

APPENDIX A

STUDENT SURVEY

Name of your institution:

Demographics

1. Select One: *Male, Female*
2. Select One: Age *18-25, 26-30, 31-35, 36-40, 41-45, 46-50, 51-55, 56-60, 60+*
3. My primary form of communication with friends is: *face-to-face, texting, e-mail, phone, social media sites.*
4. Do you own a smartphone with Internet capabilities? *yes/no*
5. Do you own an e-reader? (this includes iPod Touch and iPad). *yes/no*

Usage

Using the scale: *I don't have one, never, once a month, once a week, once a day, more than once a day, hourly.*

6. I use my social media account:
   a. If you answered "I don't have one" jump to Attitudes section.
7. I check my social media site more than my school email account.
   strongly disagree, disagree, neutral, agree, strongly agree
8. My social media site is: *public (open to anyone), private (open to just friends), I'm not sure*

   Using the scale: s*trongly disagree, disagree, neutral, agree, strongly agree*

9. I join charities and organizations/causes through social media sites.
10. I connect with local events through my social media site.
11. I communicate with my parents on my social media site.
12. I visit businesses' social media sites before or after using their services.

Behaviors

Using the scale: s*trongly disagree, disagree, neutral, agree, strongly agree*

13. It is common to see curse words/swearing on a social media site.
14. It is common for people to speak negatively towards others on social media sites.
15. I post pictures of myself on my social media site.
16. I post pictures of others on my social media site.
17. It is common to post pictures of:
    a. Myself or others in a bikini or shirtless on my site

     b.   Myself or others with alcoholic beverages or in a bar

     c.   Myself or others kissing

18.   It is common to see "drunk updating" or updating statuses while intoxicated.

19.   When someone is speaking negatively towards someone else, I: *never intervene, sometimes intervene, always intervene, it depends on how well I know the person.*

Using the scale: *never discussed, rarely discussed, neutral, sometimes discussed, often discussed.* Rate the following issues that are discussed on a social media site:

20.   School

21.   Sex

22.   Family

23.   Friends

24.   Parties

Attitudes

Using the scale: s*trongly disagree, disagree, neutral, agree, strongly agree*

25.   Social media sites are a temporary fad.

26.   Social media can be used for instruction and other educational purposes.

27.   Social media sites can be effective communication tools with instructors.

28.   Social media sites can be effective networking tools for jobs/careers.

29.   One should not be held responsible for what he/she says/does on a social media site.

30.   Employers and schools search social media sites to investigate behavior.

31.   My online personality or identity is representative of who I am in face-to-face environments.

32.   I would be open to/excited about using social networking in the classroom for instructional purposes.

Open-Ended Questions

33.   What type of behavior is unacceptable for a social media site?

APPENDIX B

FACULTY SURVEY

Name of your institution:

Demographics

1. Select One: *Male, Female*
2. Select One: Age *18-25, 26-30, 31-35, 36-40, 41-45, 46-50, 51-55, 56-60, 60+*
3. Do you own a smartphone? *yes/no*
4. Do you own an e-reader? (this includes iPod Touch and iPad). *yes/no*

Usage

Using the scale: s*trongly disagree, disagree, neutral, agree, strongly agree*

5. I use a Learning Management System (Moodle, Blackboard, etc.) in my course.
6. Mobile devices (smartphone, iPad, iPod, e-readers) are permitted in my class for educational use.
7. I use text messaging as a communication tool with my family/peers.
8. I use text messaging as a communication tool with my students.
9. I have a social media account (MySpace, Facebook, Twitter). *yes/no*
    a. If you answered "no," jump to Attitudes section.
10. I use my social media account: *rarely, once a month, once a week, once a day, more than once a day, hourly.*
11. I use social media to communicate with friends/family/colleagues.
12. I use social media to communicate with students informally (not related to class).
13. I use social media to communicate with students in an educational setting (related to class).

Attitudes

Using the scale: s*trongly disagree, disagree, neutral, agree, strongly agree*

14. Social media sites are a temporary fad.
15. Social media can be used in higher education for educational purposes.
16. Higher education institutions should block social media sites on computers.
17. Social media sites can be effective tools for communicating with students.
18. Students' online personalities/identities are representative of their personalities in class.

Chapter 11
Teaching Social Skills in Virtual Worlds:
A Primer for Extending Existing Social Science Education to Business Management

András Margitay-Becht
Saint Mary's College of California, USA

Dana R. Herrera
Saint Mary's College of California, USA

ABSTRACT

The process of teaching business is rather complex, as it inherently combines a large number of different tasks, approaches, and techniques. On the one hand, business students have to be taught the basics of rational decision-making, accounting, business planning, and other similar "hard" topics. On the other hand, however, they also have to be prepared to deal with other humans and their myriad diverging desires. In this chapter, the authors propose that some inherently immersive virtual worlds can be used as educational sandboxes that allow business students to practice their business tools. They provide a set of examples as to the specific kinds of knowledge they can attain and practice in the virtual environment, and conclude with sample lesson plans for enterprising professors.

INTRODUCTION

Innovative approaches for teaching business and management extend beyond the traditional textbook assignment. Puffer's (2004) *International Management: Insights from Fiction and Practice*, for example, juxtaposes fictional prose to business articles as a means of illustrating complex lessons. Kameda's "Englishes" in *Cross-Cultural Business Communication* (2004) presents facts and figures about the use of English in the business world followed by strategic recommendations about communicating with non-native speakers. In the same volume, Nobel Prize winning author

DOI: 10.4018/978-1-4666-2670-6.ch011

Gabriel García Márquez's *One of These Days* (2004) captures the power dynamics between a small town dentist and a notorious Mayor with a mouth abscess. Both pieces are suitably thought provoking. "Englishes" highlights a practical concern that professors can easily use for testing students' problem solving abilities; how would a student, for example, reconstruct a business' communication culture for ease of international discourse? *One of These Days* inspires a multi-level approach. Rather than a simple tale of a man with a toothache, *One of These Days* asks the reader to consider the nature of power and authority within the framework of a fictional interaction. In a classroom, both professors and students would then be tasked with applying the observations to real-world business scenarios.

Other approaches infuse new media practices with traditional pedagogy. Russow's *Digital Technology in Teaching International Business* explores a variety of ways in which modern computing, the Internet, and digital resources are changing the classroom. For example, Agami's *Using Internet Resources in Teaching Financial Reporting and Analysis of Multinational Enterprises* (2003) lauds the availability of digital corporate financial information through the Internet and explores the advantages and disadvantages of using these resources. *Using Information Technology to Promote Multi-Cultural Case Teaching: A Pedagogical Framework* (Benbunan-Fich & Stoever, 2003) argues for utilizing the latest computer mediated communication technologies for bringing together internationally diverse groups of students and teachers to work on collaborative projects. Finally, Miller's (2003) *Teaching Business Strategy for an Emerging Economy: An Internet-Based Simulation* refers to a computer simulation designed to teach MBA students about analyzing a (fictional) company's entry into an emerging economy.

This chapter focuses on what we consider one most innovate methods for teaching business management: participation in virtual worlds.

VIRTUAL WORLDS

Edward Castronova (2007), economist and leader in the field of virtual world research, defines virtual worlds as "massive multiuser online environments where millions of people live out a collective fantasy existence" (p. 5). World of Warcraft, Second Life, and Eve Online are only some of the more popular computer generated realities where millions of people from around the world participate in activities or otherwise socialize with one another. Because of the investment of time, emotion, energy, and skill of the participants, virtual worlds (as further discussed and expanded upon below) are an ideal tool for teaching.

Authors such as Shaffer (2006) and Gee (2007), for example, describe how the combination of computers, simulations, games, and interactions with others (both virtually and in real life) can improve learning. In our own research (Herrera & Margitay-Becht, 2008; Herrera & Margitay-Becht, 2010b), we discuss how student participation in virtual worlds as a core assignment for our respective classes actually improved students' retention and application of key economic ideas or anthropological theories. We also observed and analyzed how the collaborative nature of virtual world exercises strengthened group dynamics. Similarly, other scholars suggest that virtual worlds may also be useful in business where "groups of employees...must accomplish their tasks by working with teammates who are physically dispersed" (Bowers, Smith, Cannon-Bowers, & Nicholson, 2008, p. 408). Bowers et al. (2008) utilize the specific virtual world of Second Life for illustrating how virtual environments improve the "behaviors" (p. 413), "attitudes" (p. 416), and "cognitive performance" (p. 418) of teams who are not in the same physical location.

We argue that the dual strengths of the virtual world business education are in the 1) immersion into initially unknown multicultural situations and 2) immersion of students into an environment where every participant is invested in the world and the outcomes.

Business Education in Virtual Worlds

In traditional business management textbooks, the issue of dealing with other (real-life) cultures is considered so significant entire courses are devoted to discussing these interactions. Anthropologist and former Harvard Business School professor Edward T. Hall pioneered the early work in dealing with cross-cultural communication in business, writing several texts for businesspeople and students. His categories for understanding others was an attempt to distinguish how "each cultural world operates according to its own internal dynamic, its own principles, and its own laws—written and unwritten" (Hall & Hall, 1989, p. 3). Hall and Hall's (1989) analyses of doing business with the French, German, and Americans included distinguishing how each group dealt with "fast and slow messages" (pp. 4-6); different notions of space (pp. 10-12); "time" (pp. 13-23); "information flow" (pp. 22-24); "action chains" (pp. 24-26); "interfacing" (pp. 26-27); "releasing the right responses" (pp. 27-29); and the oft-quoted "high and low context" of each cultural group (pp. 6-10). They summarize their work by stressing that:

in organizations everything management does communicates; when viewed in the cultural context, all acts, all events, all material things have meaning...The cues around which these corporate and cultural messages are organized are as different as the languages in which they are associated. Most important, their meaning is deeply imbedded and therefore harder for management to change when making the transition from one country to another (Hall & Hall, 1989, p. 29).

Many others have since expanded and added to Hall's work (cf. Lane, Maznevski, Deetz, & DiStefano, 2009; Punnett, 2010; Thomas, 2002), underscoring the urgency of this particular issue.

Therefore, assigning students directed exercises in virtual worlds adds a layer of extra complexity to their learning. What does it mean to carry out business exercises in a virtual culture? Because virtual worlds are populated with real-life participants from around the world, people can and do interact with others who might be their neighbor from around the corner, to someone on the other side of the planet. Barring any significant language barriers, virtual world citizenship consists of living/working in a multicultural, multilingual virtual society complete with class, gender, political, and other social markers (cf. Herrera & Margitay-Becht, 2010a). Therefore, students who engage in virtual world activities are potentially thrust into situations where culture, and understanding culture, matters for arriving at sound decisions—much like real-life scenarios.

For example, a student might be asked to recruit other participants into an online guild, for the purposes of completing complex group activities in the virtual environment of Azeroth (World of Warcraft). This mimics the real-world task of putting together a team for a business project. While a real life project manager may recruit from within his or her own company, recruiting from a virtual world, however, adds extra complexity to the task. The student "Guild Leader" must potentially choose from a group of people he has never met. Over eleven million people hailing from most of the real world's regions (e.g. North and South America, Asia, Europe) work and play in virtual Azeroth and the only experience the Guild Leader has with them is on-line. How does a Guild Leader build a stable team with to successfully complete tasks with such a multicultural group? As Hall and Hall (1989) suggests, an awareness of cross-cultural business differences can positively influence the selection process of guild members (this, and other considerations, will be further addressed below). The second strength of using virtual worlds in pedagogy involves the investment of participants in their respective environments. In a landmark study, anthropologist Tom Boellstorff (2008) spent more than two years immersed in the virtual world of Second Life. Part of his work,

Coming of Age in Second Life: An Anthropologist Explores the Virtually Human (Boellstorff, 2008) details the intensity with which people live their virtual lives. Weddings, friendships, group activities, trade, gambling, establishing business—these activities, and more, demonstrated the vibrancy of the various communities within Second Life itself. In World of Warcraft, the citizens of Azeroth display a similar investment.

Previous Experience

As social scientists, it is difficult not to notice the relationship between virtual worlds and the real world, and its potential for educational uses. Traditional social science and management models were created to tackle the complexity of real-world institutions; to explain and teach concepts complex enough to be baffling to students and researchers alike (see Figure 1).

The operators of virtual worlds use these models to try to understand how the real world works, and then create a virtual mapping of many of the social structures and business phenomena. Their goal in re-creating the "real" in the virtual is to increase the experience of immersion as people participate in the virtual worlds, but educators can use this very same mapping for educational purposes. Economists have been using the Marshall Cross and perfectly competitive

market models to explain how the desire to buy and ability to produce certain goods will determine the amount produced and the price of the said good. Using the same theoretical models one can also explain some of the activities seen in the virtual worlds. However, the models will not explain everything one can observe in the virtual marketplace. Using the observations in the virtual worlds, it is then possible to explain both the workings of the theoretical constructs, and also their failings. Thus, utilizing the virtual we not only provide an alternative to the existing teaching approaches, but can enrich the student experience.

At St. Mary's College of California we offered a set of experimental courses teaching the students economics, anthropology, business processes and programming. We discovered that using virtual worlds had pedagogical advantages: we could increase student participation, retention and the ability to apply specific theories to various scenarios. To be able to measure improvement objectively, we prepared a detailed questionnaire about various topics in anthropology and economics. This survey then was given to the students at the first and the last class as well, and we analyzed how they performed. The improvement was significant in both subjects. Since the course enrolled students who previously studied anthropology and economics we could also assess how those new to the

Figure 1. The relationship between theory, practice, and virtual

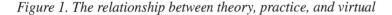

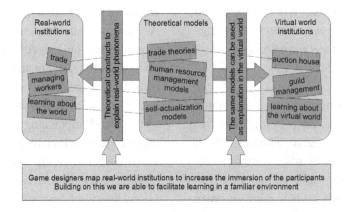

subjects performed compared to those who were already familiar with the field. We found that in both subjects, without exception, those who never studied the field performed better by the end of the semester, than those who already studied the field did at the beginning. We argue that this is evidence that our approach leads to deeper understanding than the traditional methods. (For more on the methodology and the results refer to Herrera & Margitay-Becht, 2008). In the remainder of this chapter, we will explain how similar technologies can be used to tackle some of the harder topics in business management; namely those that deal with the "imperfections" caused by having to operate with real-world people.

VIRTUAL MANAGEMENT SCENARIOS

From the above examples, it is clear that on the one hand virtual worlds can be used effectively to teach various social sciences; on the other that business education could also take advantage of such an approach by using virtual worlds to teach the students about certain motivation-based and social skills. This chapter contains a few examples about concrete occurrences in virtual worlds that have potential pedagogical uses.

Group Management Examples

One of the most difficult things to teach business students is how to operate effectively as a group; how to be leaders and how to resolve the potential conflict of interest between personal and group goals. Using Massively Multiplayer Online Role-Playing Games (MMORPGs) to address these issues, the textbook theories can be put to practice. This is crucial since dealing with real-life people is usually much more complex than it first appears.

One of the great lures of MMORPGs is their social nature: people feel that their accomplishments matter more if they have a virtual peer-group

appreciating it (cf. Kutner & Olson, 2011). To facilitate this, the game designers include many incentives for the participants to group together and tackle larger tasks together. Sometimes these tasks require only a few people; at other times, dozens or in some cases even hundreds of them work together for a shared goal. Sometimes the goal of such activities is to defend pre-programmed obstacles (content that is frequently referred to as Player versus Environment, or PvE; and the larger-scale versions dubbed "raids"), while at other times two groups of participants are pitted against each other to see who will emerge victorious (Player versus Player or PvP encounters).

When dealing with computerized obstacles (e.g. virtual monsters with great strength), content designers attempt to create encounter mechanics that ensure that players have to coordinate their actions among themselves. A frequent technique is to have players fulfill different roles; some are skilled at inflicting damage, others are good at surviving, while yet others are providing various support activities for the rest. As these groups consist of four to five participants to as many as forty individuals, coordinating these groups is akin to managing small companies. The management has to deal with the different personalities that form the group. Who is agreeable? Who is prone to cause trouble? Do their performance characteristics offset potential personality issues? What is the motivation for each individual? Are they there to participate, have fun, become more powerful, or to gain renown?

When handling challenges that focus on overcoming other humans (PvP), the management tasks become more complicated as the leaders are responsible for reacting to the actions of the opposing team, thereby changing the behavior of their team, and ensuring continued success.

Just as in a company, the management must deal with promotion and layoff issues. How are people motivated to strive for improvement and avoid making mistakes? How are those who consistently perform well rewarded? How are those who are a hindrance punished or eliminated? What are the benefits and disadvantages of choosing between consistent but average "workers" and exceptional but erratic ones?

After over 15,000 hours of research in virtual environments, the authors conclude that there is a very strong correlation between management styles and group performance in a virtual worlds as well. Professional groups (or as they are most frequently referred to in the virtual worlds, "guilds") usually have a much stronger management structure, greater incentives for good performance, and tackle problems better. Even the most professional of the guilds, however, can rapidly fall apart if they lose their leaders. It does not help that there is an established corporate culture—without the proper management team performance will falter, and the group will suffer. Guilds that are less focused on completing the most difficult tasks in the virtual environment (the so called "casual guilds") focus more on interpersonal relationships, and are frequently the virtual extensions of real-life friendships or shared interests. In these collectives, being "civil" and "nice" is more important than performance—and consequently performance usually suffers.

These educational points are easy to understand in theory, but practicing them is usually problematic. What is the appropriate tone to talk to different kinds of people? How can one avoid causing offense? When does it become inevitable to offend some people? How do I, the manager, feel about such decisions? Can I make the hard calls? To tackle these issues, many business schools use specialized "simulation sessions" where the students engage education specialists who attempt to re-create real-life situations that the students must navigate. While this approach is widely popular and successful, it emphasizes the business side of things at the expense of the unpredictable "human side." There is a "good way" of dealing with the emerging situations and the teaching professionals attempt to guide the students to this solution while they themselves remain emotionally detached. Because the train-

ing professionals behave according to a script, it is much easier to anticipate the correct problem solving answer. If, however, such practices are enriched with participation in virtual worlds, the management trainee has to deal with real personalities who genuinely care about the outcome of the management decisions, and might react in an erratic, illogical, but lifelike manner. This way the students experience some of the aspects of corporate management that they would not have been able to encounter in the simulated sessions.

Business Management Examples

Managing a business is a set of complicated tasks, which could be difficult to fathom based on nothing but textbook examples. It would be very beneficial for students to try their hand in actively managing their own business, but that would involve such financial burden and timeframe that is usually not acceptable or applicable in a classroom setting.

A way of handling this dilemma is utilizing virtual worlds. Second Life, for example, is a prominent virtual environment that is devoid of the standard "themes" present in most of the other worlds. It is nothing else but a huge virtual landscape where real-world entities can purchase land. Using the built-in construction tools, they can create everything from virtual clothing and small items to industrial complexes. The operators of this virtual world prefer giving complete freedom for the participants, and allowing them to fully express themselves beyond what is possible in the real world. This, of course, provides a business opportunity that some participants gladly take advantage of: designing, creating and selling virtual items is not only possible but also greatly supported. To facilitate this trade, Linden Labs, the operators of Second Life provide a marketplace for the virtual goods, and their own currency, Linden Dollars, can be exchanged to real world currency in their marketplace.

To be successful in the virtual business of Second Life, participants have to tackle a wide variety of tasks. Just as with any business, they have to come up with an idea first: what is their core business? They must ensure that they have the production management professionals able to find "workers" or talent who can either build their goods or are willing and able to learn how to do so. Then they have to tie a business plan to the idea that includes market research and strategic planning. The distribution channels must also be managed: purchase or rental of property, construction of storefronts, or alternative distribution channels must be created. While some of these tasks (like the actual construction part) involves some virtual-world specific knowledge, the majority of the business operation has to do with tasks that are also present in the real world. Although most business classes do some sort of simulation exercise to practice business decisions, whether these are computerized or have real-life "actors" participate the task is obviously educational in nature. As a supplement or alternative to these approaches, the students can be tasked with constructing and operating a business and make it successful among other participants in Second Life. As these others are there on their own volition and are not part of the business exercise, their reactions and the overall success of the endeavor can provide crucial feedback about how to handle the above management tasks. Did we become successful? Could we have become more successful? Is our product comparable? Did we price it properly? Do the potential buyers know about it? Did we make it accessible enough? These and a host of other questions can help the students make their virtual business successful, and teach them about business management basics at the same time.

Negotiating New Environments Examples

When entities, whether they are human people or corporations, encounter a new environment, they have a set of strategies regarding how to negotiate these environments. A new participant in a virtual world has limited to no knowledge about their surroundings. Similarly, a new hire knows little about a corporation's inner workings—just as a fresh entry to an industry might have only partial knowledge of its operation. The negotiating new environments examples describe how these entities develop techniques for adapting to environments of which they have only limited knowledge. One of the most challenging things to teach in business education is how to do this. The basic ideas are not necessarily complex; the difficulty comes from encouraging the application of these strategies.

In the next few pages, we discuss how participants negotiate the World of Warcraft, and how they learn about the opportunities and the constraints of the environment. As members of a new "reality," they have to learn about their possible and expected roles, potential and "desirable" actions. They have inherently no knowledge of their surroundings, the mechanics of the environment, the topography, the lore, the culture or even how their virtual representation (their avatar) functions. Anthropologists, accustomed to navigating these types of new cultures and environments, have developed specific perspectives for operating in new environments, which can be helpful for analyzing new participants in virtual worlds. Robben and Sluka (2012), for example, anthologize the seminal writings of early anthropologists whose studies in different cultures lay the groundwork for specific methodologies. Essays in Angrosino's (2007) *Doing Cultural Anthropology* outline some of these methods such as "working with numerical data" (p. 109), "carrying out a structured observation" (p. 91), "planning and moderating focus group research" (p. 115), and, most importantly, "becoming a participant observer" (p. 9). Considered "the foundation of cultural anthropology," (Bernard, 2011, p. 256) participant observation is the primary avenue through which anthropologist immerse themselves in new environments. Bernard's (2011) widely used textbook *Research Methods in Anthropology* explains:

Participant observation involves going out and staying out, learning a new language...and experi-

encing the lives of the people you are studying as much as you can...Participant observation involves immersing yourself in a culture and learning to remove yourself every day from that immersion so that you can intellectualize what you've seen and hear, put it into perspective, and write about it convincingly. When it's done right, participant observation turns fieldworks into instruments of data collection and data analysis. The implication is that better fieldworkers are better data collectors and better data analyzers (p. 258).

Bernard (2011) also describes associated practices (e.g., "getting to know the physical and social layout of your field site" [p. 269]) which ultimately help anthropologists refine their research questions while collecting pertinent data.

Interestingly, the methods of participant observation parallels the behaviors of people new to virtual worlds. We discovered that like anthropologists, members choose different strategies for dealing with the uncertainty of a new environment, with the end goal of participating more fully in a new culture for positive effects. These behavioral patterns can form the basis for new ideas and strategies for dealing with the challenges of a new work environment or a new competitive marketplace. One way of describing the different levels of engagement and investment is our BESOR framework below:

1. **BROWSE:** The participants simply wander around, enjoy the scenery, react to things happening.
2. **EXPERIMENT:** They *actively* try to figure out how things work, and experiment with an "optimal" solution using the information available within the environment.
3. **STUDY:** The participants move outside the environment, gather information available to the public, copy the "accepted" "best way" to do things.
4. **OPTIMIZE:** *Based on the accepted best practices*, they make use of already existing optimization tools to improve performance.

5. **RESEARCH:** These participants move past using the tools others create, analyze the inner workings of the environment and develop their own optimization tools.

As we mentioned before, the majority of the user experience in a virtual world focuses on defeating either computerized enemies or organized groups of opposing players. To be able to tackle these challenges, however, new participants of the virtual world must first learn to negotiate the environment, fit into the culture and learn about how to effectively operate their avatars. The framework above is based on our participant observations regarding the five major levels of involvement new entrants to virtual worlds can do to achieve those goals. Most new players start out at the BROWSE pattern, freely roaming the new environment, "taking in" the world. They explore various areas of the world (jungles, deserts, cities, towns, etc.), visit virtual shops, and speak with others. The more inquisitive ones even during the introduction phase will utilize the EXPERIMENT pattern, trying to figure out the workings of the world, i.e., understanding the underlying mechanics of the environment. Eventually, as challenges become more and more complex, participants leave the world to gather information on official or fan-run websites. What is the best way for me to operate my avatar? How do I defeat the evil dragon? What techniques do successful teams use to win certain player versus player challenges? By following the best practices, the STUDY pattern promises "average chance" of success and average performance—the theoretical zero economic profit. Those who want to move beyond the average usually use special optimization tools that allow them to tweak their personal performance. These individuals, following the OPTIMIZE pattern, put in the extra effort to go beyond the average, but this effort is mostly focusing on adopting or adapting techniques that others developed (in essence, they are the early adopters). The last (and smallest) group of participants are those who actively try to RESEARCH newer and newer ways of doing things. They are the true innovators, who come up with both the best practices used in the STUDY pattern and the new technologies copied in the OPTIMIZE pattern. They take extra amount of effort for potentially extra rewards; in the game world, they are the usually well-paid electronic sports participants: those who can make a real world living from participating in a virtual world.

It is clear that the above strategies are greatly different based on the amount of effort invested and the potential outcome. It is also easy to see that some or most of these steps are followed by any entity negotiating a new environment. The initial BROWSE pattern is best suited to the new discovery of the environment and often evokes the "thrill of exploration." The initial motivation to participate in virtual worlds come from this very thrill, the same excitement that makes watching movies or reading books appealing. In the case of a motivated employee, this pattern can be the entry-level pattern as well, although at times the very real external pressure for performance might prevent browsing for fear of appearing unmotivated. For corporations, starting at the BROWSE pattern can lead to certain failure, as the intensely competitive nature of the industrial environment does not allow for the leisurely timeframe required for this pattern to work. Just as in the real world, where we suggest that this pattern would be inefficient, also in the virtual worlds following this pattern (or following it too long) will render the participant to perform below average, frequently leading to failure. The term "noob," referring to clueless participants, developed from the fact that usually *newer* members of a virtual community are still stuck at the BROWSE stage and their performance is sub-par.

The next pattern, EXPERIMENT is used as a transitional pattern by those who wish to excel, or as an entry-level pattern by the intellectually curious. Once they have accumulated sufficient knowledge about the environment on their own, they will attempt to *organize* that information in a manner that aids their performance. As discussed above, part of the lure of virtual worlds

is that they mimic real world societies, and this mimicry leads to rather complex workings. Even though the designers usually spend a great deal of time making the learning curve flat, if they want to create an environment that will keep the participants enthralled for years, they must create intricate enough environments that will entertain long-time participants as well. Because of this, advancing to the EXPERIMENT step is required to succeed in the virtual world—an important lesson with a real world implication. As members of large corporate organizations, the success or failure of an individual does not only depend on their professional and social skills, but also on their ability and willingness to understand the workings of their environment and adapt to it. Attaining the EXPERIMENT pattern in a virtual world exercise drives that point home: to become better, you need to actively try to figure out the workings yourself and internalize your findings. In the corporate setting, even though this strategy is a clear improvement over the BROWSE pattern, the pace of learning is still too slow. For a corporation to have a chance of success, they have to start at the next pattern.

In case of personal development, the STUDY pattern is frequently the ultimate stage in performance improvement. Those following this pattern will study and analyze how experts of their role behave, and try to imitate their activities. In a virtual world setting this means that participants access available information about the given topic or role, and attempt to copy the pre-described formula they find. Even those participants who do not themselves follow the STUDY pattern will frequently adhere to "common knowledge" by simply mimicking the behavior of those who do follow it (so the STUDY pattern becomes heavily imprinted on the EXPERIMENT pattern). The real-world equivalent of this behavior is the prevalence of industry-wide "best practices" that promise on successful execution a performance *close to* the average performance of the industry as a whole. A similar unspoken promise of this also appears in the virtual worlds.

The OPTIMIZE pattern takes a significant step beyond the STUDY pattern in that followers utilize preexisting analytical tools to modify the generally accepted best-practice approaches. These activities serve to optimize for a specific task, a group of other participants or to the preferences of the participant herself. To make this pattern work one has to familiarize themselves with all the information accessible through the STUDY pattern, and also access and learn how to utilize some of the readily available optimizing tools. This approach can provide results *better* than the average—like in the real world. Early adopter corporations that abandon the "known paths" and "best practices" of an industry to follow innovators and apply their innovations can become more successful than their peers, but they also take on additional risks by leaving the known paths. Practicing the OPTIMIZE pattern and comparing it with the STUDY pattern in a virtual world will give acute awareness of the potential gains and dangers when leaving the known path, and will internalize the understanding that a lot of groundwork is required when one wants to improve on the generally accepted approaches.

The last pattern is a further deviation from the norm. Those who follow the DEVELOP pattern not only use readily available optimization tools but also will actually research the workings of the environment. They will use reverse engineering to gather some of the information, and conduct extensive tests to figure out what is not available through other means. Members of this community are usually the people to prepare the tools or practices used in the OPTIMIZE pattern, and have the deepest understanding of how the environment works. The parallel to this behavioral pattern is exhibited by members of the research community who try to improve the efficiency of organizations or industries—sometimes from the outside, sometimes from within. Whether their research deals with technological details or is organizational in nature, these individuals not only resist the industry standards as the way to do

things, but they want drastic improvements on core concepts and workings in the field. The greatest results can come out of this mentality—but just as in the virtual worlds, so in the real world it represents large risks of failure and requires the greatest amount of resources to follow this path.

The negotiating new environments examples serve two purposes. One, the participants of virtual worlds can learn about and experience how the various personal performance behavioral patterns affect their efficiency, but they also are able to discern the difference in the relative economic cost of each approach. The other, similarly important take-away from this could be the understanding that these practices apply to the corporate level as well.

Value Chain Examples

Another aspect of many of the populated, themed virtual worlds is the existence of the so-called "trade professions." These allow the participants' avatars to create items usable by others—a parallel to the manufactures (and corporations) of real world. Usually there are two kinds of professions, the harvesting professions tied to the generation of raw materials, and crafting professions, which are used to transform the raw materials to final products.

The participants must make many decisions about these professions. First, they have to decide which professions to practice, as there is usually a limit to how many an avatar can be proficient in (in case of World of Warcraft, this is two). Then there are the decisions related to "honing one's skill" in the given profession; it is frequently required that participants practice their skill in order to improve at the given profession. In these cases the decision is: how to best practice? What materials should I use? What materials should I create? How do I get the materials? Do I pair my crafting profession with a harvesting profession? Do I buy up the raw materials in the marketplace? What is the market value of the produced good?

Can it be used by other professions? Does it have intrinsic value due to its attributes? What substitutes does this product have? Can the end product be harvested for different kinds of raw materials? Finally, once they have reached mastery in their profession, they must make decisions about how to use that profession. Similar questions arise as during the practicing phase, regarding the usability, substitutability, and cost of our product.

The perfect market model frequently employed by economists uses the premise of perfect information, and stipulates that if all information is shared, and there are a large numbers of buyers and sellers of a homogenous good, an equilibrium price will emerge. The simulated marketplaces of virtual worlds are usually much closer to the real-world markets than the "perfectly competitive" markets: while the goods are inherently homogenous (since the designers of the worlds determine what can be produced—though introduction of randomness can ease even this constraint), the information is far from perfect, and there are distinct situations when the buyers and/or the sellers are in limited supply; creating temporary monopolies or oligopolies that can and sometimes do transform into more competitive market structures.

The observed behavior of participants highlight behavioral discrepancies which are differently rational than predicted by the standard economic models. One such apparently strange behavior is when the finished product is being sold for prices significantly lower than the cost of the raw materials required to produce the item, essentially making the activity a negative-profit production. In some cases, this behavior can be explained by the "practice" activities: high quality goods can only be crafted by master craftsmen. Some of the traders decide to "invest in Research and Development" to be able to create the more complicated and expensive products. In many cases, however, this motivation cannot explain the cost discrepancies: top-level products are being sold for 80-90% of the material costs. The usual problem in this case is that those crafters who also double as harvesters (thus have a completely internalized production chain) consider the raw material need for their end product as something that they need to harvest themselves, and then once they have spent the (usually quite extensive amount of) time required to gather the raw materials they just jump ahead, create the product and then price it by undercutting other producers. Since there is no internal check about pricing, they do not realize that selling the unprocessed raw materials might be more profitable than trying to sell the added-value final product. This pattern eerily parallels decisions in larger corporate structures where exact accounting of each activity is obfuscated or is inefficient: such internal inefficiencies can hide the true reason for limited profitability.

An interesting new teaching tool is currently in development by one of the major participants in the virtual world business. In their upcoming new virtual reality, Blizzard Entertainment will provide participants with two distinct way of buying and selling products (Diablo III Auction House Overview, 2011).One of these ways will be the by-now traditional auction house model employed by most of the virtual worlds. However, they will also provide an alternate auction house that will not use the world's own currency but actual real-world money. This will enable participants to try and earn or spend real-world currency on virtual items—a practice that currently is illegal (as it violates the end-user licensing agreement) yet is quite widespread. It will be interesting to see how this utilization of real currency will change buyer and seller behavior, but we suggest the impact will be little: those who do not seem to follow their self-interest in the current environment will be hard-pressed to "smarten up" by the additional constraint of having to pay for things.

It is our firm belief that by subjecting the students to an environment where the apparent buyer and seller behavior cannot be explained by traditional models, the kind of thinking required to avoid and tackle such problems can easily be internalized.

SAMPLE LESSON PLANS FOR BUSINESS EDUCATION

Having seen that virtual worlds provide great training ground to business students, we want to conclude with some sample lesson plans for the enterprising education professional.

Virtual Business in Second Life

As discussed in the business management example, Second Life provides a vast virtual landscape where potential businesses can be opened. Incorporating this into the standard classroom projects could not only enrich the learning experience but also provide the students with valuable feedback.

At the beginning of the semester, the students could be invited to form groups that will serve as the foundation for their businesses. At the start of the learning process, the students have to tackle their "personal performance" evaluation: learn about the world in the ways they deem appropriate, and then at a later time discuss their approach with their group, and finally with the whole class. How did they go by exploring the world and gathering information?

As the major task, each group has to handle a number of jobs: figure out a base product; do the market research to ensure that there is demand for it and to see the potential competition; determine how it should be produced; decide on and manage the distribution channels; select and purchase storefronts, manage sales etc. At the end of the semester the performance of the various businesses can be compared to each other and/or to a preset benchmark, and students can learn not only from their own experiences but also from what the other participants observed.

While this approach has the huge advantage of being very lifelike, it is so lifelike that business students might run into the problem of managing the production side of the class (as one would need at least one person in the group who is willing to learn the item-creation interface to do the actual production of goods—unless they want to act as distributors of already existing goods). To solve this issue one could create a cross-class assignment, where engineering, arts, or computer science students would form the "worker" component of the teams, while business students would oversee the management tasks. Although this approach requires some extra coordination on the part of the professors, the students receive further valuable life lessons: what is it to manage real-life "workers," or on the artists' side, what does it feel to have business professionals set targets for them. Setting up such a course is complicated, but the rewards for all participants are well worth the effort.

Group Dynamics in World of Warcraft

An alternative approach that avoids the actual skill of producing something desirable is to have business students participate in some of the group tasks in a themed virtual world, like World of Warcraft. In that environment even at a very early stage such opportunities present themselves: after about an hour or two of presence the individuals can generate a virtual representation, an "avatar" that is suitably equipped to tackle either preset challenges of the entry level PvE dungeons or participate in objectives against other human-controlled players in PvP. Just as with the Second Life lesson plan, this one also starts with the "personal performance" part: everyone is left to explore on their own, and then they share their methods and findings with the others.

After the initial "explore the world" the students are invited to participate in the group activities, determine their roles and functions, establish communication among the members, come up with motivation plans, etc. To facilitate the learning experience the groups should have rotating leadership responsibilities. This way the students within the group can learn from each other: who does the coordination best, what is their secret, how could we all improve and the like.

A later task could involve dealing with the issues described in the value chain example. Task the students to make a certain amount of money, an amount they cannot tackle without some sort of in-game professions, and then have them document their progress. Have weekly – bi-weekly sessions of public discussion of their progress and their techniques, and see if they improve over time. Do they learn from their past experiences? Do they learn from each other?

The great advantage of this kind of lesson structure is that they require no special skills to make it work. All they need to know is to familiarize themselves with the virtual world itself—a task that is integral to the learning-process. At the same time, some of the key lessons the Second Life class could provide will be lost with this approach.

CONCLUSION

In a recent Forbes article, Elliot Noss, chief executive of Tucows, Inc., extolled the virtues of participating in virtual worlds such as World of Warcraft to improve business acumen: "You have these events [in "World of Warcraft"] that are very leadership-driven...when you're in a raid that's poorly led, it's really easy to see how valuable are skills like managing the social dynamic, making sure there was the right level of preparation and making sure that there was a clear hierarchy in terms of who is performing what roles" (Chiang, 2010). Noss subsequently takes the leadership lessons from working in WOW and incorporates them into the corporate culture. Training for the business world can therefore begin in the classroom where cost effective virtual world participation can

mimic real-world scenarios and produce measurable gains. Rather than dismissing virtual worlds as a space defined only for fun, these environments can be used as tools for enhancing social science, humanities, and STEM classroom techniques.

REFERENCES

Agami, A. (2003). Using internet resources in teaching financial reporting and analysis of multinational enterprises. In Russow, L. C. (Ed.), *Digital Technology in Teaching International Business* (pp. 115–131). Binghamton, NY: International Business Press. doi:10.1300/J066v14n02_08

Angrosino, M. V. (Ed.). (2007). *Doing cultural anthropology: Projects in ethnographic data collection*. Long Grove, IL: Waveland Press Inc.

Benbunan-Fich, R., & Stoever, W. A. (2003). Using information technology to promote multi-cultural case teaching: A pedagogical framework. In Russow, L. C. (Ed.), *Digital Technology in Teaching International Business* (pp. 13–27). Binghamton, NY: International Business Press.

Bernard, H. R. (2011). *Research methods in anthropology: Qualitative and quantitative approaches*. Lanham, MD: AltaMira Press.

Boellstorff, T. (2008). *Coming of age in second life: An anthropologist explores the virtually human*. Princeton, NJ: Princeton University Press.

Bowers, C., Smith, P. A., Cannon-Bowers, J., & Nicholson, D. (2008). Using virtual world to assist distributed teams. In Zemliansky, P., & St. Amant, K. (Eds.), *Handbook of Research on Virtual Workspaces and the New Nature of Business Practices*. Hershey, PA: IGI Global. doi:10.4018/978-1-59904-893-2.ch029

Castronova, E. (2007). *Exodus to the virtual world: How online fun is changing reality*. New York, NY: Palgrave Macmillan.

Chiang, O. (2010). *How playing video games can boost your career*. Retrieved August 20, 2011 from http://www.forbes.com/2010/07/19/career-leadership-strategy-technology-videogames.html

Diablo III Auction House Overview. (2011). *Website*. Retrieved August 20, 2011 from http://us.blizzard.com/en-us/company/events/diablo3-announcement/index.html#auction:auction-summary

Gee, J. P. (2007). *What video games have to teach us about learning and literacy*. New York, NY: Palgrave Macmillan. doi:10.1145/950566.950595

Hall, E. T., & Hall, M. R. (1989). *Understanding cultural differences*. Yarmouth, ME: Intercultural Press, Inc.

Herrera, D. R., & Margitay-Becht, A. (2008). Fun is learning: A case study of gaming as education in virtual worlds. In Nygaard, C., & Holtham, C. (Eds.), *Understanding Learning-Centered Higher Education* (pp. 95–110). Copenhagen, Denmark: Copenhagen Business School Press.

Herrera, D. R., & Margitay-Becht, A. (2010a). Cyber-diasporas: The affects of migration to virtual worlds. In DePretto, L., Macri, G., & Wong, C. (Eds.), *Diasporas: Revisiting and Discovering* (pp. 287–298). Oxfordshire, UK: Inter-Disciplinary Press.

Herrera, D. R., & Margitay-Becht, A. (2010b). Do-it-yourself learning: Case studies of gaming as education in virtual worlds. In Riha, D. (Ed.), *Videogame Cultures and the Future of Interactive Entertainment* (pp. 33–42). Oxfordshire, UK: Inter-Disciplinary Press.

Kameda, N. (2004). Englishes in cross-cultural business communication. In Puffer, S. M. (Ed.), *International Management: Insights from Fiction and Practice* (pp. 67–75). Armonk, NY: M.E. Sharpe.

Kutner, L., & Olson, C. (2011). *Grand theft childhood: The surprising truth about violent video games and what parents can do*. New York, NY: Simon & Schuster.

Lane, H. W., Maznevski, M., Deetz, J., & DiStefano, J. (2009). *International management behavior: Leading with a global mindset*. Hoboken, NJ: Wiley.

Márquez, G. G. (2004). One of these days. In Puffer, S. M. (Ed.), *International Management: Insights from Fiction and Practice* (pp. 173–174). Armonk, NY: M.E. Sharpe.

Miller, V. V. (2003). Teaching business strategy for an emerging economy: An internet-based simulation. In Russow, L. C. (Ed.), *Digital Technology in Teaching International Business* (pp. 99–114). Binghamton, NY: International Business Press.

Puffer, S. M. (Ed.). (2004). *International management: Insights from fiction and practice*. Armonk, NY: M.E. Sharpe.

Punnett, B. J. (2010). *Experiencing international business and management: Exercises, projects, and cases*. Armonk, NY: M.E. Sharpe.

Robben, C. G. M., & Sluka, J. A. (2012). *Ethnographic fieldwork: An anthropological reader*. Malden, MA: Blackwell Publishing.

Russow, L. C. (Ed.). (2003). *Digital technology in teaching international business*. Binghamton, NY: International Business Press.

Shaffer, D. W. (2006). *How computer games help children learn*. New York, NY: Palgrave Macmillan. doi:10.1057/9780230601994

Thomas, D. C. (2002). *Essentials of international management*. Thousand Oaks, CA: Sage Publications, Inc.

ADDITIONAL READING

Aldrich, C. (2005). *Learning by doing: A comprehensive guide to simulations, computer games, and pedagogy in e-learning and other educational experiences*. San Francisco, CA: Pfeiffer.

Aldrich, C. (2009). *Learning online with games, simulations, and virtual worlds: Strategies for online instruction*. San Francisco, CA: Jossey-Bass.

Bainbridge, W. S. (2010). *The Warcraft civilization: Social science in a virtual world*. Cambridge, MA: The MIT Press.

Beckwith, R. T., Chaput, H., & Slator, B. M. (2006). *Electric worlds in the classroom: Teaching and learning with role-based computer games*. New York, NY: Teachers College Press.

Bloch, S., & Whiteley, P. (2007). *How to manage in a flat world: Get connected to your team-- Wherever they are*. Boston, MA: FT Press.

Blume, A. (2010). *Your virtual success: Finding profitability in an online world*. Franklin Lakes, NJ: Career Press.

Brake, T. (2009). *Where in the world is my team: Making a success of your virtual global workplace*. San Francisco, CA: Jossey-Bass.

Castronova, E. (2005). *Synthetic worlds: The business and culture of online games*. Chicago, IL: The University of Chicago Press.

Chatfield, T. (2010). *Fun Inc.: Why gaming will dominate the twenty-first century*. Amsterdam, The Netherlands: Pegasus.

Chorafas, D. N., & Steinmann, H. (1995). *Virtual reality: Practical applications in business and industry*. Upper Saddle River, NJ: Prentice Hall.

Czerniawska, F., & Potter, G. (2001). *Business in a virtual world*. West Lafayette, IN: Purdue University Press.

de Mesa, A. (2009). *Brand avatar: Translating virtual world branding into real world success*. New York, NY: Palgrave Macmillan.

Gee, J. P. (2007). *Good video games + good learning: Collected essays on video games, learning, and literacy*. New York, NY: Peter Lang.

Gibson, D., Halverson, W., & Riedel, E. (2007). Gamer teachers. In Gibson, D., Halverson, W., & Riedel, E. (Eds.), *Games and Simulation in Online Learning: Research Development Frameworks* (pp. 175–188). Hershey, PA: IGI Global.

Heiphetz, A., & Woodill, G. (2009). *Training and collaboration with virtual worlds: How to create cost-saving, efficient and engaging programs*. New York, NY: McGraw-Hill.

Kopf, S., Scheele, N., Winshcel, L., & Effelsberg, W. (2005). Improving activity and motivation of students with innovative teaching and learning technologies. In *Proceedings of the International Conference on Methods and Technologies for Learning,* (pp. 551-556). Southampton, UK: WIT Press.

Lindsell-Roberts, S. (2011). *New rules for today's workplace: Strategies for success in the virtual world*. Boston, MA: Houghton Mifflin Harcourt.

Mahar, J., & Mahar, S. M. (2009). *The unofficial guide to building your business in the second life virtual world: Marketing and selling your product, services, and brand in-world*. New York, NY: AMACOM.

Malaby, T. (2009). *Making virtual worlds: Linden lab and second life*. Ithaca, NY: Cornell University Press.

McGonigal, J. (2011). *Reality is broken: Why games make us better and how they can change the world*. New York, NY: The Penguin Press HC.

Molka-Danielsen, J., & Deutschmann, M. (2009). *Learning and teaching in the virtual world of second life*. Toronto, Canada: Tapir Academic Press.

Pearce, C., & Artemesia. (2009). *Communities of play: Emergent cultures in multiplayer games and virtual worlds*. Cambridge, MA: The MIT Press.

Reeves, B., & Read, J. L. (2009). *Total engagement: Using games and virtual worlds to change the way people work and businesses compete*. Boston, MA: Harvard Business School Press.

Shaffer, D. (2006). *How computer games help children learn*. New York, NY: Palgrave Macmillan. doi:10.1057/9780230601994

Taylor, T. L. (Ed.). (2006). *Play between worlds: Exploring online game culture*. Cambridge, MA: The MIT Press.

Wankel, C., & Kingsley, J. (2009). *Higher education in virtual worlds: Teaching and learning in second life*. Bingley, UK: Emerald Group Publishing Limited.

KEY TERMS AND DEFINITIONS

BESOR-Model: Our 5-step model in describing how an individual engages a new environment.

Business Simulation: Specialized practices—computerized or otherwise—explicitly designed to facilitate business education.

Group Management Tasks: All the assorted activities that deal with getting a set of individuals follow a single group goal.

Immersion: The characteristics of virtual worlds that they are engaging for the participants.

Motivation Hazard: The problem that people running a business simulation are not emotionally invested in it.

Value-Chain Discrepancies: The apparent behavior of some participants in virtual or real world economies where some steps of the value chain have a negative added value.

Virtual World: A computerized 3-dimensional simulation with real-world participants.

Section 3
Future Trends

Chapter 12
Virtual Worlds in the Context of Competence Development and Learning

Albena Antonova
Sofia University, Bulgaria

ABSTRACT

Recently, different researchers and practitioners provided new evidence for successful implementation of Virtual Worlds (VW) in educational context. Virtual worlds propose an immersive environment and sophisticated technology infrastructure and stimulate active learning and complex learning scenarios. At the same time, many educators and learning institutions are still hesitating to adopt VW in their educational models. Statistics show that the public interest in VW is declining and users spend less time in-world. VW is still a highly dynamic market, and many of them close operations. Should educational institutions join VW? What will be the future of VW in education? The present chapter aims to discuss the challenges behind VW implementation in the educational process from three main perspectives. First, how virtual worlds can enhance knowledge acquisition and development of key competences, increasingly needed by new generations, is analyzed. The second perspective discovers if and how virtual worlds can be used to practically transform the educational process, developing a new set of learning and training experiences. Finally, virtual worlds will be discussed from a disruptive technology point of view, discovering its strengths and limitations for education. At the end, the discussion will provide a general framework for assessing the VW benefits for education and its expected further development.

INTRODUCTION

Just few years ago, virtual worlds emerged with the promise to transform the Internet and the future of communication and collaboration. In 2007, virtual worlds gained attention of the business community, press, researchers and universities, public administration and international organizations. Millions of people joined the VW platforms and took part in building amazing 3D environments on the edge of human imagination, forming virtual communities and exploring new

DOI: 10.4018/978-1-4666-2670-6.ch012

virtual experiences. Huge investments in money and time have been made, inventing sophisticated VW applications in various domains—business, research, education, entertainment, healthcare, politics, social care, art, and even there have been established virtual embassies. There emerged virtual economy, virtual goods and virtual money, allowing virtual trade and virtual business models. Virtual meetings, virtual company trainings, and virtual conferences proposed an alternative way of bringing people together, not just replacing telephone calls and physical meetings, but providing new dimensions and richness of interactions. Virtual worlds became a way of self-expression, business opportunity, and entertainment channel, as well as mode of life for millions. According to forecasts of Gartner in 2007, VW would soon dominate the Internet use, reaching 80% of active Internet population by 2011.

However, only few years later, the future of virtual worlds and their universal application is not so obvious. Statistics are proving that the interest toward VW is declining (Brenner, 2012). As discovered by some reports of Internet use, VW is one of the least popular Internet activities in 2010, used by less than 4% of all Internet users in USA, and VW are not popular among younger generations (Zickuhr, 2010). The reasons of this are numerous. On one side, companies behind VW had to survive the recent global financial and economic crises. Some of the VW have closed operations (Vivid®), while the others had to slow down their activities and technology development, neglecting some of the customer services and going on unpopular measures as raising prices. So what will be the future of VW? Will the implementation of virtual worlds in education remain an isolated experience from the first decade of 21st century?

The future of VW will be certainly a combination of many social, economical and technology factors. For example, Flavin (2012) makes an analysis of technologies used in higher education and concludes that although the high number of technological solutions used officially or non-

officially in educational institutions, their success widely vary. His findings reveal that more bottom-up and less top-down approach is more likely to lead to the enhanced and successful adoption of educational technologies. Every user in education creates own meanings for technologies implementation. So how these findings will reflect on the use of Virtual Worlds?

Along with other Internet applications and social media solutions, educational use is not the primary concern for VW development. Thus, it is possible even very successful VW implementations in education to be endangered from VW closing or policy changing, thus putting all investments in educational infrastructure and learning content at risk. In the context of fast changing economic, social, and technological paradigms, it is extremely difficult for educational institutions and academia to adapt and follow the emerging trends. What trends will be persistent? What investments and how much investment should be made in VW and in any other technology in education? What will be the future trends in education?

Education institutions and academia need to change and modernize in order to meet the increasing public expectations. Adopting new styles of learning, new methodologies of learning and new technologies for learning or applying overall innovations in learning is somehow expected by students, by the society and even by the lecturers. However, it is difficult to predict which technological or social trends will persist and what type of innovations should be implemented. The process of knowledge acquisition and learning cannot change substantially because of the fixed human cognitive processes. Therefore, any application of new technologies in learning should be coherent to the objectives of the basic knowledge acquisition. Thus, the present chapter aims to discuss the phenomena of adopting virtual worlds in education from three main perspectives. The first part will review how virtual worlds can enhance knowledge acquisition and develop key competences, increasingly needed by new generations, according to the key competences frameworks, adopted by main political organizations. The second perspective will discover what type of learning processes can be facilitated by virtual worlds. The third perspective will analyze if virtual world can become disruptive technology in education. VW are proposing many technological benefits to transform the educational process, adopting new set of learning and training experiences outside the limitation of space, time, geographical location, or cost. Thus, an appropriate framework for analysis will be proposed to assess the practical benefits of using VW applications in specific educational context. Finally, there will be proposed analysis and some conclusion thoughts of further development of VW in educational process.

BACKGROUND

Virtual Worlds (VW) can be defined as synchronous, persistent network of people, represented as avatars and facilitated by networked computers (Bell, 2008). This definition is based on three main components—real time and avatar-based immersive communities within computer networks, and allow differentiating VW from other platforms as Social network sites. Considering "virtual worlds" as philosophical concept, Bittarello (2008) proposes "visual" definition of virtual worlds as "digitally constructed environments, where peer-to-peer interactions can take place," opposed to more "imaginative" and broad view of virtual worlds, exploited in text-based narratives, literature, religion and art since the beginning of human development. Schroeder (2008) highlights the function of virtual worlds as "...persistent virtual environments in which people experience others as being there with them—and where they can interact with them...."

Historically, virtual worlds are closely related to development of video and computer games. As defined by Messinger (2008), open or unstructured virtual worlds represent a blending of the elements of immersive 3D gaming environments, together with elements of online social networks. Thus, VW are shaped based on experience of arcade games, console systems, LAN games, unstructured games, and games with player generation of content, matching with social network sites. Thus, VW emerged from the entertainment and gaming industry and their ultimate objective is to provide enjoyable on-line social experiences. In literature there are used also terms as 'metaverse,' 'synthetic world,' Massively Multiplayer Online Games (MMOG) and Multi-Users Virtual Environments (MUVE) in place of 'virtual world.'

VW Characteristics and Typology

Today, an increasing number of virtual worlds and multiplayer online games (MMOG) are in operations and more specifically, according to industry-focused Web sources, their number is close to 577 (http://www.mmorpg.com, retrieved October 2012). Therefore, it is necessary to distinguish different types of VW. Some authors identify structured and unstructured (open) virtual worlds (Mannecke, 2008). Closed worlds are predefined structures and environments, where users need to follow strict role-play. Open virtual worlds rely on social interaction among people and their avatars and occur in a 3D immersive environment, with user-chosen objectives, user-generated content and social networking tools. Open virtual worlds consist of massively multiplayer gaming platforms with unstructured objectives, user-generated content, immersive 3D virtual reality shared environments, and social networking elements used between people through their avatars (Messenger, 2008). In these worlds people can form relationships, create objects that can be sold or given to other people. Bittarello (2008) describes the key features of a virtual world as: underlying rules (physics), user representation (graphical representation, avatars), real time interaction, shared world, and world persistence. VW are fully-fledged alternative realities, as the only new element in technology-based VW is interactivity (Bittarello, 2008).

Other authors state that virtual worlds consist of four components (Sivan, 2009): "...real virtual worlds arise from the integration of 3D, Community, Creation, and Commerce...." Virtual worlds should include presence in space, real-time interaction, persistent environment and objects and representation of avatar. On his turn, Messenger (2008) propose a typology of VW, extending the typology of virtual communities of Porter (2004). The authors identify 5 key elements that differentiate VW: purpose, place, platform, population and profit model. The purpose is the content of interaction (strategic, tactic, or thematic), place can be collocated or geographically displayed, platform determines the level of immersion, synchronous or asynchronous communication, population is the number of participants, and the profit model describe the sustainable business model of VW provider (Messinger, 2008). However, even rooting the development of the virtual worlds from the game industry, VW have been widely adopted spaces for research, education, politics, and work.

VIRTUAL WORLDS IN THE CONTEXT OF KNOWLEDGE ACQUISITION AND COMPETENCE BUILDING

One of the main reasons to adopt virtual worlds in education is to enhance knowledge acquisition and competence building. As discovered earlier, virtual worlds naturally belong to entertainment industry and thus many educators doubt about their contribution for educational process. However, in the emerging "life-long learning" way of living, people need to reassess what is knowledge and how competence building can be enhanced by technological tools. Today, knowledge evolves faster and faster transforms practically all aspects of life. Thus continuous knowledge acquisition and competence development become increasingly important not only for individuals but as well for social prosperity. So how can virtual

worlds implement knowledge acquisitions and competence development? Within the next paragraph there will be provided some theoretical overview of knowledge and competences in the context of learning.

Knowledge and Knowledge Acquisition

Knowledge is defined as complex and abstract concept, associated with personal experience and acquired mental models for understanding and processing facts and information within an application context. One of the most popular definitions states that: 'knowledge is a fluid mix of framed experience, values, contextual information, and expert insights that provides a framework for evaluating and incorporating new experience and information' (Davenport & Prusak, 1998). Moreover, knowledge is often described as "expectation or assumption about the reality, acquired trough number of trial and errors experiences" (Popper, 1999). Two main types of knowledge are identified: explicit, conscious knowledge, that can be easily articulated in formal language and transmitted with electronic tools, and tacit knowledge, which is sub-conscious knowledge embedded in individual experiences, difficult to formalize and articulate, and developed through a process of trial and error encountered in practice (Tiwana, 1999). Knowledge is "justified true belief" built upon personal mental models for understanding and assessing the world (Davenport & Prusak, 1998). Another concept is that knowledge is a human product, socially and culturally constructed and individuals create meaning through their interactions with each other and with the environment they live in (Kim, 2001). Therefore, experience, context, and social interactions are crucial factors for knowledge acquisition and influence the knowledge transformation from explicit to tacit knowledge and from tacit to explicit knowledge.

Learning enables people to acquire competences, skills, and knowledge in order to cope with challenges and to make rational decision.

Learning is considered a social process and occurs when individuals are engaged in social activities (McMahon, 1997). Moreover, learning forms attitudes, perspectives, insights, and understandings, enabling learners to perform desired functions with proficiency (Wiig, 1999). Personal experience and method of trial and errors represent substantial component of learning and knowledge acquisition. A general model of acquiring knowledge is getting declarative knowledge, or adding facts to create mental model of the phenomena (Waterworth, 1999). In the process of building declarative knowledge, the learner adds procedural knowledge or knowledge how to do things (functional knowledge). The expert reaches an autonomous stage, where task skills performs automatically and tasks become easier and faster to perform with less errors. Waterworth (1999) outline some differences between perceptual and conceptual learning, discovering that conceptual learning is theoretical and generalized learning about "there and then," while perceptual learning concerns present "here and now." Perceptual learning is closer to learner and transform faster the knowledge from conscious to unconscious (and thus to expertise, tacit knowledge). According to Waterworth (1999), the general learning process is split on 3 main phases: coding-retention-activating. The first phase consists of picking up information, processing it and coding it into memory, the second stage is retention and coding the information in long-term memory, and finally the activating phase consists of applying information when the stored knowledge is retrieved (Waterworth, 1999). On opposite, the Kolb's learning cycle proposes an alternative learning model, focusing on learning by doing and evaluation of learning experiences (Kolb, 1994). The Kolb model comprises 4 stages: gain experience; review of experience and reflection on outcomes and feedback; theorizing about what happened and why, exploring options and alternatives; planning what to do differently next time, looking for practical applications of ideas, finding opportunities to implement (Kolb, 1994). The Kolb model responds better on the fast chang-

ing environment and life-long-learning approach, where learning is problem-based, situational, and experiential. Thus, the most powerful learning comes from direct experience (Senge, 2005), and proactive, experience-gaining learning is better than reactive and passive learning (Bennet, 2004). Thus, the theories of active learning are increasingly gaining attention on inquiry-based learning, problem-based learning, role-playing learning and other types of activities in learning (Misirlaki & Paraskeva, 2011). Therefore, in order to enhance knowledge acquisition and learning, VW should be implemented in active learning scenarios.

Competence Building and Key Competences

Competences can be defined as the ability to perform activities to the standards required in employment, using an appropriate mix of knowledge, skill, and attitude. Thus improving competence building is not about increasing the knowledge acquisition, but include understanding of context of knowledge application; personal skills and attitude for knowledge application within specific professional context. Virtual worlds can be thus used in many aspects for building professional skills and special competences, including simulations, social interactions, and scenario exploration.

The concept of "key competences" designates some common and context-independent competences, applicable and effective across different institutional settings, occupations, and tasks (Winterton, 2005). They represent the ground for further knowledge acquisition and professional competences building. These typically include basal competences, such as literacy, numeracy, general education; methodological competences, like problem solving, IT skills; communication skills, including writing and presentation skills; and judgment competences, such as critical thinking. EU has recently identified a framework for key competences, determining that: "...key competences are those which all individuals need for personal fulfillment and development, active citizenship, social inclusion, and employment" (EU, 2007). OECD (2005) has selected a small set of key competences in its DeSeCo Project, determining that each of them must contribute to some valuable outcome for societies and individuals; to help individuals to meet important demands in a wide variety of contexts; and are important not just for specialists but for all individuals. Initiating a national debate for development of intellectual capital, the US Metiri group defined "21st Century Skills" including key skills, needed by students and workers in the digital era. In order to develop common understanding about key competences, Table 1 discovers competences and key skills provided by the three main organizations: EU, OECD, and Metiri.

Table 1 provides a reference list of key skills and competences for 21st century generations, as defined by main political organizations (OECD, 2005; EU, 2007; Metiri Report, 2000). Although slight variations, there can be outlined three basic competency domains: ability to communicate, ability to acquire and process complex information and knowledge and ability to realize personal plans and projects and to express personality. These new competences are admitted as basic skill set for 21st century society and require new framework of methodological approaches, including adoption of new teaching and learning methods and tools. These new competences need to be developed and trained using pro-active and student-centered flexible learning approaches, rather than traditional and unified systems. Therefore, adoption of VW can be directly linked to the development of these specific competences and abilities, based on accumulating experiences and personal reflections.

EDUCATIONAL PROCESSES IN VIRTUAL WORLDS

Virtual worlds represent a new form of learning environment that can provide a new simulated learning situation, rather than simply replicat-

ing traditional classroom experiences (Walker, 2009). In this section, there will be made some reflections and examples about learning experience and educational processes within VW. As it is reported in increasing number of case studies, VW can be applied in various educational fields and scenarios (Antonova & Martinov, 2010). The interest in VW for education is proved as well by impressive number of university campuses and educational institutions installations and activities within Virtual Worlds.

Investigating different learning processes, occurring in VW, Lim (2009) identified the following learning models:

- **Learning by exploring:** Learning by exploring consists of learning through exploration of installations, communities, and landscapes, already present in VW. The exploration task can include as well some additional features as observations, gathering, and collection of data or subsequent analysis of different fieldwork within virtual world. Exploration is intrinsic to the presentation of information in space but implies presence. Exploration is type of experiential learning facilitating both knowledge acquisition and synthesis of contextual and situational knowledge (Waterworth, 1999).

- **Learning by collaborating:** VW supports learning from collaboration and working in teams, or learning on problem solving and decision-making in interactive and group settings. The focus here is to help learners to increase their meta-cognitive habits, and their understanding of distributed cognition and social dynamics of groups (Lim, 2009). This means that VW contribute to learning collaboratively as opposed to learning competitively.

- **Learning by being:** VW enforce learning of exploration of self and of identity. Entering in different identities can enlarge individual perception of situation, leading

Table 1. Comparison of key competences, according to OECD, EU framework, and Metiri report

Key competence	EU Competence Framework (2007)	OECD (2005)	21st Century Literacy (2000)
Communicate and work in groups	Communication in mother tongue; Communication in foreign languages; Social and civic competences;	Interact in heterogeneous groups -Relate well to others -Co-operate, work in teams -Manage and resolve conflicts	Interactive Communication -Team collaboration -Personal and social responsibility -Interactive communication
Understand complexity	Mathematical competence and basic competences in science and technology; Digital competence; Learning to learn;	Use tools interactively -Use language, symbols and texts interactively; -Use knowledge and information interactively; -Use technology interactively)	Digital Age Literacy -Basic, scientific, technological literacy -Visual and information literacy -Cultural literacy and global awareness Quality, State-of-the-Art Results -Effective use of real-world tools
Express personality	Sense of initiative and entrepreneurship; Cultural awareness and expression.	Act autonomously -Act within the big picture -Form and conduct life plans and personal projects -Defend and assert rights, interests, limits and needs)	Inventive Thinking -Adaptability/ managing complexity and self-direction -Curiosity, creativity and risk-taking -High-order-thinking and sound reasoning -Prioritizing, planning, and managing for results

to improved cognitive and communication skills. "Learning to be" can be reinforced by role-playing, using different avatars, entering in different scenarios.

- **Learning by building:** VW allow learners to build objects or script them. This expands the ability of learners to conceive 3 dimensional objects, involving better visualization of theoretical issues in mathematics and physics. It leads naturally to art and design skills, but also includes information technology skills and abilities.

- **Learning by championing:** VW can propose a unique tribune to attract interest of wider communities of peoples. Learning by championing could be facilitated by many of the opportunities in VW to build installations and raise awareness, to educate and inform general public about particular causes, and to use the right setting or expressions that might be meaningful to them.

- **Learning by expressing:** Lim (2009) make observation that virtual worlds can facilitate building of expression competences, externalizing experiences from

in-world to the real world; Some of these experiences can include storyboarding, report activities, movies and pictures and others.

The observed learning models are usually adopted in combination, meaning that learners get complex experiences while exploring, communicating, role-playing, and building objects within specific learning scenarios. This comes to show that VW support mainly active learning, requiring learners to be involved in educational activity, rather to receive information in explicit form.

It can be stated that the main benefits of VW are that they employ popular "entertainment" approach to build experience in stimulating, user-centered environment and motivate learners to achieve better results. Learners "invest something of themselves in a learning experience as they fully engage with the role" (Sivan, 2009). This 'personal investment' is a critical factor in achieving high-level learning experience (Antonova & Todorova, 2010). For example, Putz (2012) summarizes the results of an empirical study with approx. 100 students and reveal that it leads to higher energetic activation, more positive emotions, more positive attitudes towards learning content, and more efficient knowledge transfer than a conventional case study approach.

Among the multiple evidences of the benefits of VW for education, Carpenter (2009) provides a short summary of observations from adopting of VW for learning.

- Virtual worlds are playful, engaging and interactive alternatives to more passive media, involve learners in educational content, and they learn more.
- The learner is becoming creator and has control over elements of a world.
- Virtual world helps to create mental maps, exploring and understanding new world and its systems.
- Learners get more responsibilities and develop social skills.
- VW provide tools for self-expression and improve computer literacy.
- VW enable learners with physical and communicative needs, make passive learners more active.
- VW remove barriers for learning for learners with difficulties in traditional learning.
- VW allow collaboration and sharing of knowledge.
- VW better illustrate some concepts of complex processes.
- High degree of entertainment.
- VW have abilities to implement context and relationships, not achievable in traditional learning setting.

However, considering learning outcomes, there are reported several problem areas from the practical implementation of VW in learning. Kirriemuir (2008) reports that VW can be very distractive and time-consuming. Walker (2009) discovers that there can be observed slight difference in performance of students, using VW (Second Life), and the other students, taking face-to-face course.

The author reports that students highly appreciated the increased opportunities for live-media rich interaction, afforded by VW (SL), in order to enhance their understanding and application of the course content, but they opposed to technological learning curve challenges that overwhelm the course content. Moreover the majority of learners reported that VW (SL) didn´t help them to learn more on the course. Lee (2009) reported almost the same problems with VW, assuming students' observations that VW are time consuming, they have moments of feeling losts and distracted. All practitioners highlight that technology issues remain still an issue and can harm VW experiences, due to problems with incompatible hardware and software, requirements for enhanced video-cards and sound cards, slow Internet connection and high possibility of crashes. Campbell (2009) discovers that students need to acquire a number of VW specific skills (walking, building, scripting), that can be platform-dependent, and create additional cognitive challenge.

VIRTUAL WORLDS AS DISRUPTIVE TECHNOLOGY IN EDUCATION

Disruptive technologies are technologies that disrupt established practices, and bring to market a very different value proposition (Christensen, 1997). Products based on disrupt technologies are usually cheaper, simpler, smaller, and, more convenient for use. Disruption, therefore, emerges from usage of these technologies, and disruptive technologies are opposed to sustained technologies (Christensen, 1997). The main question in front of the educators and educational institutions today is whether VW are disruptive technology for education?

This question still does not have a single answer, as revealed by Kirriemurier (2012) in his last snapshot on virtual world activity in UK high education in August 2012. After summarizing his work on VW adoption in UK universities and colleges for the last 5 years, he concludes that while some universities and lecturers are in-world already for 5 years and more, others university close VW operations or just hold-on their activity there, waiting for new arguments (or better technologies) to further reconsider its use. Actually, there can be considered two main aspects to what extend virtual worlds can be identified as disruptive technology for education:

1. The value proposition of VW and how they can disrupt educational process,
2. The context of VW implementation.

Today technologies still have not changed fundamentally traditional training/teaching models. As reported by Prensky (2001) technologies are more frequently applied in education to disseminate training content or to improve content delivery and communication process (both ways: lecturer-learner and learner-learner). Simulations and complex scenarios for new active-based training methods are still in the phase of pioneering. While VW can enhance value proposition in activity learning models, they have sharp learning curve, and cannot be assumed as simpler or more convenient for use than other learning instruments. Moreover, it should be mentioned that the application of virtual worlds in traditional type of lecturing is not efficient. Traditional lecturing and presentations delivery can be used only to limited extend in VW, because VW cannot transmit the full expression of the oral presentation of the lecturer, including his non-verbal expressions—gestures, lips synchronization, and mimics, the monologue soon become boring, leading to group distractions and lost attention. The author experienced different lectures in the VW Second life, where the avatar of the lecturer get asleep and become inactive while his talking and presenting. Thus, VW cannot be applied as extended presentation tool, because of the limited capacity to make a proper presentation, to show lecture slides or to insert a video presentations. Therefore, in the

case of traditional lectures other technologies as teleconferencing, combination of desktop sharing and VoIP or video streams are more convenient.

VW can add value only in case of specific activity-based models of learning. VW proposes new complex learning environment that need to be explored, populated, and contextualized by students and learners. In VW, learners should have the leading role as they have to be involved in complex open-ended cognitive activities. At the same time, educators have less control over the classroom dynamics and teaching sessions and thus they can less influence the end-results. Thus, their role should transform from "knowledge providers" to advisers and facilitators, guiding and helping students through first-hand knowledge acquisition activities. Therefore, VW require additional efforts and skills from instructors to attain positive educational experiences, meaning both personal involvement and investments in time, including scenario building, educational simulations, complex task conception, and preliminary preparation (Antonova & Todorova, 2010).

When discussing the context of use, it should be analyzed how VW are used for educational purposes. Often VW imposes specific technology requirements and need to be installed on desktop computers with substantial hardware characteristics, where additional software applications and good Internet connection is in place (this is the case for one of the most used VW in education—Second Life). In university computer labs, lecturers often do not have the authorization to install software, some university firewalls block the VW platforms, and this imposes additional efforts concerning software installation, administrative permissions, and additional hardware devices and PC periphery needs. Moreover, organizing the class experiments in-world can become a risky experience, because of multiple technology crashes. After experimenting different situations in the VW Second life (open lectures, public presentations, VW explorations, and exhibitions), the author estimates that technology constraints of running

VW in educational environment are substantial and are still hardly predictable. Moreover, different experience in VW can result from class activity, or from individual experience.

In order to summarize its own finding and the outcomes of the literature review of VW adoption in education (more often in SL), the author proposes the following framework for VW adoption in educational context (Table 2).

During the active learning scenarios in VW, learners extend their competences to communicate, to acquire and process complex information and knowledge, and to realize their personal plans and projects (Table 2). However, VW learning experiences should be designed as complex learning situations:

- If focusing mainly on group communication, the use of VW can make the communication less efficient, then other technologies;
- If focusing on exploring existing VW environments, simulations, experiments, a detailed instructions should be provided and back-up plans should be envisaged in case of technology problems;

- If focusing only on design/ building activities, more specialized software can be explored more successful as for example for drawing; image processing, 3D-object design, etc.

Therefore, extending the use of VW in education should be conformed to the course objectives, and providing a good mix of communication/ knowledge acquisition and processing/ and project management tasks and activities. Moreover, VW scenarios should both involve in-class involvement and individual experiences.

DISCUSSION

Following the analysis above, it can be observed that VW can successfully contribute for development of key complex competence for 21st century generations. A significant number of researchers report that VW contribute for enhanced communication, teamwork and problem-solving skills, planning skills, creativity, and leadership skills (Campbell, 2009). In particular, MMOGs enhance next generation skills through activities

Table 2. Framework for key competence trainings in VW educational experiences

Key Competences	In-class experience scenarios	Individual experience scenarios
Communication and collaboration competences	- Realization of group projects, group assignments and group evaluations	- Group projects in mixed and open educational environments (open teams, mixed teams) - Industry/education; - Different nationality/ university/faculty/subject expertise teams)
Competence to acquire and process complex information and knowledge	• Exploration of existing VW installations, • Take part in predefined VW experiments and simulations; • Build objects and visualize complex relationships in VW;	• Design VW experiences as events, exhibitions, conferences and others; • Knowledge discovery and assessment – conduct interviews, perform surveys, analyze results; • Active learning scenarios
Competence to realize personal plans and projects	• Work on open-end exploration/ building projects; • Design own educational patterns in VW	• Design and perform educational projects in VW; • Conceptualize his own learning path;

that demand collaboration with different teams of people, creation, sharing, conquest of knowledge through evaluation and infiltration of information, thriving in chaos, critical thinking, and problem solving skills (Misirlaki & Paraskeva, 2011). Immersive technologies and VW allow students not only to memorize the content but also to creatively use, apply and synthesize it, developing complex communication and knowledge processing skills, and building self-confidence. There are identified wide number of interactive application domains of VW for both education and business (Antonova & Martinov, 2010). With adoption of VW, practitioners can replace previously used methods to illustrate learning content as case studies and experiential exercises with student-leaded activities as exploration and experimentation (Lee, 2009).

However, while researchers and educators continue to collect evidences of positive outcomes for learning in VW, statistics discover that VW nowadays loose attractiveness. Different studies report that popularity of VW is decreasing, fewer users connect to VW, users spend less time online in VW, the dynamics in VW is very high, and many VW already closed operations. It is increasingly common to see ghost towns and empty infrastructure, abandoned in VW. So what changed? Why people abandoned these spaces, after huge investments of time and money?

VW still impose many technology constraints. For example, users usually cannot explore VW on mobile (handheld) devices. This contradicts to the recent development of ubiquitous computing, embedded computing, cloud computing applications, and client expectations. A recent survey discovers that more than 60% of young people in USA (18-29) have smart phone and use mobile platforms (as laptops, smart phones, or tablets) as a primary tool to access and browse in Internet, thus substituting desktop computers (Brenner, 2012). The Social Network Sites (SNS) and online video facilities become increasingly popular and attract majority of the Internet users, and especially young generations (Zickuhr, 2010).

Thus, the SNS prove the finding of the Disruptive Technology theory that argues that ease of use is a significant factor in the take up of a disruptive technology. For example, Wikipedia, Google, Facebook, and Twitter have this capacity. SNS prioritize the content and not the form, proposing fast and instant connection to the whole network of social contacts and media-rich content, freely accessible from different devices. SNS allow easy, highly interactive, and media-rich way of expression and status up-dates. On opposite of SNS, mastering VW as Second Life requires more advanced competencies, and the returns for these extra-efforts are not evident. If technologies are kept simple, people are more likely to use them, and today VW are reserved for special community of VW adepts. Many observations report that VW have sharp learning curve, making newcomers to feel uncomfortable while operating (moving, communicating) in-world. Moreover, learning in VW can be time-consuming activity, where many extra efforts are put on technical issues and not on learning and collaboration. Thus in VW the focus is still put on the form and not on the content of interaction. This is why people increasingly prefer alternative technologies for socialization and communication and for self-expression. VW need to propose new sort of interactive experiences that can add real value to users. Dancing or drinking virtual coke could be attractive because of the colorful animations, but visiting virtual life concert or exploring replica of museum, can add different feeling of presence and give additional value of "being there" to personal experience. Having sophisticated VW and 3D environments with avatars, only to chat remotely do not propose meaningful reason.

Educational institutions today usually follow the technological trends of the streamline. On one side, companies looking for competitive advantage and increasing global market shares lead technological innovation growth, exploiting new sophisticated solutions, complex services, and advanced business models. This results in more knowledge-intensive products and services, with shorter life cycle, and increased demands for support and customization. Thus, to retain their market position, companies increasingly need educational institutions. On one side, they need educated employees and customers that are able to use and further develop and support these innovative products and services. On the other side, universities have been expected to deliver high-quality scientific output, accelerating further technological innovations and R&D products. On their turn, educational institutions and academia tried to follow their century-proved mission to serve on the society. Their primary focus is to prepare new generations of professionals, attaining deeper understanding of fundamental knowledge principles, and to enhance knowledge discovery, often not matching to the short-term business objectives of the companies. Sometimes this provokes disappointment both for companies and for graduates. In periods of economic growth, companies accuse academia to be unable to provide quality experts prepared to respond on the increased demand and to fill immediately the new jobs openings. On opposite, in period of crisis fresh-graduates accuse academia for not providing them with right competency set to find fast job on the labor market. Thus, interest in fundamental disciplines is decreasing, while practical aspects of very narrow-focused trainings are highly appreciated by both industry and learners. This controversy provokes many social debates about the objectives of the education and its fundamental mission, about adequacy of education to the social demands and not last, about public funding of education and research as investment for future social prosperity.

VW can have many positive outcomes for education. However, VW require additional efforts and skills from instructors to attain positive educational experiences, meaning both personal involvement and investments in time. Thus, the positive learning outcomes largely depend on how VW are implemented in practice and what is the context of this deployment. Thus, the application of VW in education should be carefully prepared and based on sound methodological principles: the value of technology use for education, resources for its implementation in class, is it fitting with the goals of the curriculum, and how can be evaluated learning outcomes. Trainings in VW should be designed around open-ended learning activities, composed as scenarios, and combining 6 learning processes of Lim (2009). The focus of learning scenarios should be put on the content of the learning process, and not on specific technical skills for using VW. Learners have to be able to benefit from variety of technology tools that can be accessible to them and not limited to specific VW technology applications. Moreover, VW should not be considered as technological solutions along with its technology problems, but as virtual environments beyond physical, geographical, and time constraints.

CONCLUSION

While there are identified more than 570 virtual worlds and multiplayer online games (MMOG) in operations, already more than 187 MMOG have closed or disappeared (MMORPG, 2012). At the end, reflecting about the future of virtual worlds in education, we will focus our attention on recent technology trends. While young generations are migrating to mobile devices, desktop computers will soon be replaced by other more convenient solutions. Embedded computing and Internet of Things will soon contribute to the evolution of sensitive displays, intelligent walls, smart TV set and other intelligent devices that will enhance user experience and will disrupt the way to work and learn with new technologies. Virtual worlds are losing part of their interest because of the emerging applications of augmented reality, the mirror worlds, or mixed realities. The applications of augmented reality are much closer to the learners, as they can approach some of the AR applications via their smart phone. Therefore, from technology point of view, VW should migrate to mobile applications and converge with other new appearing technologies, in order to increase further end-user unique value offering.

From social and cognitive point of view, it should be noted that VW experiences have to be investigated beyond technology platform. Bittarello (2008) compared on one side virtual worlds, based on text and narratives in literature, religious and art and on the other side virtual worlds as technology platforms. He assumes that virtual worlds are spaces, intrinsically different from actual reality, that are unreachable without the help of device (dream, guided use of imagination, technological device). The characters experience such places without leaving behind their body. The virtual world is a space for freedom. Experiences made in mythic spaces are useful because it is sort of training, that can be helpful in everyday life, it can be life changing, and it has real effects. Players (as well as heroes and travelers) perform absolutely ordinary actions but in an extraordinary context.

So virtual worlds, literary, visual or technological can be set up as learning places, not a false copy of reality, but something else, alternative reality, something that have been always existed and expressed through different media (story-telling, literature, art, cinema). VW is about freedom, exploration, experimentation, visual representation, integrated into daily life (Bittarello, 2008).

Virtual worlds have to be applied in education, because new learners need to be prepared better to cope with increasing global challenges. Resource scarcity, climate changes, and demographic issues will be among the urgent topics that will rise within next decades. So new generations should be trained to communicate better to reach global agreements, should be able to understand better complex interdependences and consequences of their actions, should lead better their personal and social plans for more sustainable future. Complemented with new advances in AR, Virtual worlds should be applied as learning places, outside technological limitations, allowing complex simulations, experimentations and role-play, and focused on new complex competences building. Educators should be prepared not to adopt another technology tool in class, but to reach new understanding of VW as places of freedom, where learners have to perform ordinary actions, but in extraordinary context, that will change their life. This way the debate about current level of VW technologies development is left behind. Along with other learning settings, content should be prioritized and not the form. Surviving very dynamic and competitive market, VW will definitely change and evolve. Thus future work will concentrate on how VW can soon become disruptive technologies, transforming traditional learning and extending it to new learning experiences.

REFERENCES

Antonova, A., & Martinov, M. (2010). Educational and business applications of serious games and virtual worlds. In *Proceedings of SAI Conference.* Sofia, Bulgaria: SAI.

Antonova, A., & Todorova, K. (2010). Serious games and virtual worlds for high-level learning experiences. In *Proceedings of S3T Conference,* (pp. 250-255). S3T.

Bell, M. (2008). Toward a definition of virtual worlds. *Journal of Virtual Worlds Research, 1*(1).

Bennet, A., & Bennet, D. (2004). *Organizational survival in the new world.* Burlington, UK: Elsevier.

Bittarello, M. (2008). Another time, another space: Virtual worlds, myths and imagination. *Journal of Virtual Worlds Research, 1*(1).

Brenner, J. (2012). *Pew internet: Mobile.* Retrieved from http://pewinternet.org/Commentary/2012/February/Pew-Internet-Mobile.aspx

Campbell, C. (2009). Learning in a different life: Pre-service education students using an online virtual world. *Journal of Virtual Worlds Research*, 2(1).

Carpenter, S. (2009). Virtual worlds as educational experience: Living and learning in interesting times. *Journal of Virtual Worlds Research*, 2(1).

Christensen, C. M. (1997). *The innovator's dilemma: When new technologies cause great firms to fail*. Boston, MA: Harvard Business School Press.

Davenport, T. H., & Prusak, L. (1998). *Working knowledge: How organizations manage what they know*. Boston, MA: Harvard Business School Press.

Flavin, M. (2012). Enabling disruptive technologies for higher education learning and teaching. In *Proceedings of ECEL*. ECEL.

Kim, B. (2001). Social constructivism. In M. Orey (Ed.), *Emerging Perspectives on Learning, Teaching, and Technology*. Retrieved from http://www.coe.uga.edu/epltt/SocialConstructivism.htm

Kirriemuir. (2008). *Measuring the impact of SL for educational purposes*. New York, NY: Eduserv Foundation.

Kolb, D. A., Rubin, I. M., & McIntyre, J. M. (1994). *Organizational psychology: An experiential approach to organizational behavior* (4th ed.). London, UK: Prentice Hall.

Lee, P. (2009). Using second life to teach operations management. *Journal of Virtual Worlds Research*, 2(1).

Lim, K. (2009). The six learnings of second life. *Journal of Virtual Worlds Research*, 2(1).

Mannecke, B., McNeil, D., Ganis, M., Roche, E., Bray, D., Konsynski, T. A., & Lester, J. (2008). Second life and other virtual worlds: A roadmap for research. *CAIS, 22*, 371-388.

McMahon, M. (1997). *Social constructivism and the world wide web - A paradigm for learning*. Paper presented at the ASCILITE Conference. Perth, Australia.

Messinger, P., Stroulia, E., & Lyons, K. (2008). A typology of virtual worlds. *Journal of Virtual Worlds Research*, 1(1).

Metiri Group. (2000). *Twenty-first century skills*. Retrieved from http://ncrel.engauge.org

Misirlaki, S., & Paraskeva, F. (2011). Massively multiplayer online games as activity systems: The relationship between motivation, performance and community. In *Proceedings of ECGBL*. Athens, Greece.

OECD. (2005). *The definition and selection of key competencies*. New York, NY: OECD.

Parliament, E. U. (2007). *Key competences for lifelong learning: A European framework*. Geneva, Switzerland: European Union.

Partnership for 21st Century Skills. (2008). *21st century skills, education & competitiveness, resource and policy guide*. Partnership for 21st Century Skills.

Popper, K. (1999). *All life is problem-solving*. London, UK: Routledge.

Prensky, M. (2001). *Digital natives, digital immigrants*. Retrieved from http://www.marcprensky.com/writing/prensky%20%20digital%20natives,%20digital%20immigrants%20-%20part1.pdf

Putz, T. (2012). The project mobile game based learning. In *Proceedings of ECEL*. ECEL.

Schroeder, R. (2008). Defining virtual worlds and virtual environments. *Journal of Virtual Worlds Research*, 1(1).

Senge, P. (2006). *The fifth discipline: The art & practice of the learning organization*. New York, NY: Broadway Business. doi:10.1002/pfi.4170300510

Sivan, Y. (2009). *Overview: State of virtual worlds standards in 2009*. Retrieved from http://journals.tdl.org/jvwr/article/view/671/539

Tiwana, A. (1999). *The knowledge management toolkit*. Upper Saddle River, NJ: Prentice Hall.

Walker, V. (2009). 3D virtual learning in counselor education: Using second life in counselor skill development. *Journal of Virtual Worlds Research, 2*(1).

Waterworth, J., & Waterworth, E. (1999). Education as exploration: Being, going and changing the world. In *Proceeding of Didactics of Informatics and Mathematics in Education* (pp. 42–55). IEEE.

Wiig, E., & Wiig, K. (1999). *Conceptual learning considerations*. Retrieved from http://www.krii.com/downloads/conceptual_learning.pdf

Winterton, J., Delamare, F., & Stringfellow, E. (2005). *Typology of knowledge skills and competences*. Research report. CEDEFOP project

Zickuhr, K. (2010)... *Generations (San Francisco, Calif.), 2010*, Retrieved from http://pewinternet.org/Reports/2010/Generations-2010.aspx

Chapter 13
Conversational Metabots for Educational Applications in Virtual Worlds

David Griol
University Carlos III de Madrid, Spain

Zoraida Callejas
University of Granada, Spain

Ramón López-Cózar
University of Granada, Spain

ABSTRACT

Education is one of the most interesting applications of virtual worlds, as their flexibility can be exploited in order to create heterogeneous groups from all over the world who can collaborate synchronously in different virtual spaces. Additionally, they can create opportunities to offer educative contents with the advantages of online courses, but also the feel of "presence" that only virtual worlds can provide. However, the interaction in social virtual worlds usually takes place in text mode, given that usually only textual and chat facilities are provided to communicate with avatars and bots. This makes it difficult for people without enough technical knowledge, or with visual or motor disabilities, to interact with such systems. To solve this problem, the authors propose a methodology for building bots as intelligent embodied conversational agents that can communicate with the users through oral as well as visual modalities.

INTRODUCTION

The contents of the chapter are structured as follows. In Section 1, we introduce the topic of virtual worlds and contextualize the rest of the chapter and our proposal. Section 2 presents the potential of virtual worlds as an educative tool and describes the main experiences carried out recently in the application of these technology to teaching and learning. In Section 3, we center on Second Life, which is one of the most extended virtual worlds, and pay special attention to the

DOI: 10.4018/978-1-4666-2670-6.ch013

specific resources it provides for educational purposes such as Sloodle.

Section 4 examines the barriers that some users may find in using these applications and explains how speech can be useful to address this problem. The section focuses on the so called *spoken dialog systems*, explaining their classical architecture and discussing three applications: learning, assistance to elderly and handicapped users, and virtual environments. Section 5 presents our proposal to integrate voice interaction into Second Life by developing conversational bots for educational purposes in this virtual world. In this section, we propose our own methodology for creating conversational metabots. We describe in detail the architecture of the proposed conversational metabot and the technologies and protocols employed for developing its conversational behavior and its synchronization with the avatar. Finally, Section 6 presents the conclusions derived.

1. INTRODUCTION TO VIRTUAL WORLDS

The stunning increase in the amount of time people are spending socializing online is creating new ways of communication and cooperation. With the advances in the so-called Web 2.0, virtual worlds have grown dramatically over the last decade. These worlds or "metaverses" are computer-simulated graphic environments in which humans, through their avatars cohabit with other users. Traditionally, virtual worlds have had a predefined structure and fixed tasks that the user could carry out. However, social virtual worlds have emerged to emphasize the role of social interaction in these environments, allowing the users to determine their own experiences.

Social Networking has been a global consumer phenomenon during the last few years. According to Nielsen (2009), two-thirds of the world's Internet population visit a social network or blogging site and the sector now accounts for almost 10%

of all Internet time. Member Communities has overtaken personal Email to become the world's fourth most popular online sector after search, portals, and PC software applications. The staggering increase in the amount of time people are spending on these sites is changing the way people spend their time online and has ramifications for how people behave, share and interact within their normal daily lives. The development of so-called Web 2.0 has also made possible the introduction of a number of applications into many users' lives, which are profoundly changing the roots of society by creating new ways of communication and cooperation.

The advance of social networking has entailed a considerable progress in the development of virtual worlds (Arroyo, et al., 2009; Lucia, et al., 2009), in which humans, through their avatars, "cohabit" with other users. This new model is more humane because it simulates the real environments characteristics in which the human being is and has become. For humans, a 3D world is "more real," a world in which we can feel the distance, color, sunset, the presence of our friends, in which we can use the capabilities of our senses and we can interact with objects and avatars that inhabit it. These virtual worlds or metaverses are in fact true social networks and they are useful for interaction between people in different locations. Likewise, in the three-dimensionality context it is very appropriate to develop virtual robots with the same appearance as that of the human-driven avatars. These new virtual robots are called metabots term coined from the contraction of the terms metaverse and robot. A metabot will therefore be a fully capable software completely able to interact in one or more metaverses through one or more avatars.

Metabots, with the same appearance and capabilities that the avatars for human users, thus intensify the perception of the virtual world, providing gestures, glances, facial expressions, and movements necessary for the communication process. Therefore, these virtual environments are very useful to enhance human-machine interaction. This way, virtual worlds have become real social networks useful for the interaction between people from different places who can socialize, learn, be entertained, etc.

Thanks to the social potential of virtual worlds, they have also become an attraction for institutions, companies, and researchers with the purpose of developing virtual robots with the same look and capabilities of avatars for human users. However, social interaction in virtual worlds are usually carried out using only text communication by means of chat-type services. In order to enhance communication in these environments, we propose the integration of dialog systems to develop intelligent metabots with the ability of oral communication and, at the same time, which benefit from the visual modalities provided by these virtual worlds.

A dialog system (McTear, 2004; López-Cózar & Araki, 2005; Griol, et al., 2008) can be defined as an automatic system that are able of emulating a human being in a dialog with another person, in order to complete a specific task (usually providing information or perform a particular task). Two main objectives are fulfilled thanks to its use. The first objective is to facilitate a more natural human-machine interaction using the voice. The second one allows the accessibility for users with motor disabilities, so that the interface avoids the use of traditional interfaces, such as keyboard and mouse. These systems include Artificial Intelligence (AI) and Natural Language Processing (NLP) techniques.

With the growing maturity of conversational technologies, the possibilities for integrating conversation and discourse in e-learning are receiving greater attention. Dialog systems have been developed to meet a wide range of applications in education, including tutoring (Pon-Barry, et al., 2006), question-answering (Wang, et al., 2007), conversation practice for language learners (Fryer, et al., 2006), pedagogical agents and learning companions (Cavazza, et al., 2010), dialog applications for computer-aided speech therapy

with different language pathologies (Vaquero, et al., 2006), and dialogs to promote reflection and metacognitive skills (Kerly, et al., 2008).

Our chapter focuses on three key points. Firstly, since it is very difficult to find studies in the literature that describe the integration of Speech Technologies and Natural Language Processing in virtual worlds, to show that this integration is possible. Secondly, to show a practical application of this integration through the development of a conversational metabot that provides academic information in the virtual world Second Life (http://secondlife.com/). Finally, we promote the use of open source applications and tools for the creation and interaction in virtual worlds, such as OpenSimulator.

2. EDUCATIVE APPLICATIONS OF VIRTUAL WORLDS

Virtual words provide a combination of simulation tools, sense of immersion and opportunities for communication and collaboration that have a great potential for their application in education.

As criticized in Girvan and Savage (2010), many of the existing educative experiences in virtual worlds only replicated traditional approaches into the new environment, such as for example recreating classrooms co-located in a virtual world. Although such direct translation does not leverage all the potential of the technology, it provides an added value in the case of online courses, for example, as a mean of e-assessment for large classes during a course (Perry & Bulatov, 2010) or as mean of recreating face-to-face contact with classmates and teachers.

In these cases, virtual worlds have been usually employed to replicate real world activities, and it has been reported that experiences in the virtual world have a similar effectiveness in terms of learning than in real world (Jarmon, et al., 2009). Nevertheless, field experience is usually needed to obtain more meaningful learning. For example,

Winn et al. (2005) evaluated the oceanographic knowledge obtained in a virtual environment as well as with real visits to the ocean and found that field experience was very important to contextualize learning for students with little prior experience of the topic.

Anyhow, virtual settings that reproduce real situations help to reduce costs or to offer improved learning activities to the students with the same budget. For example, Andrade et al. (2010) used avatar-mediated training in medicine, to teach the students how to deliver bad news. Usually, this is done by hiring actors that play the roles of standardized patients, which is very expensive and also limits the situations that the actors can portray. Avatars can be customized to create a wider range of scenarios and create a richer learning experience.

The described situations do not take full advantage of all the possibilities that virtual environments offer, as virtual worlds benefit from unique characteristics that traditional learning environments do not present and provide opportunities for atypical ways of learning.

Virtual environments allow the creation of learning activities that cannot take place in the real world, thus fostering experiential learning or "learning by doing." In virtual worlds, students can apply and acquire knowledge in an environment without real-world restrictions. For example, Ellison and Matthews (2010) used Second Life to teach eighteenth-century culture to students in an island that resembled the eighteenth-century London. In this setting, the students had to reconstruct spaces with interactive elements with as much historical authenticity as possible and interact within them, with the aim to dismantle the generalizations of scholars who characterize Enlightenment as an individualist period.

In addition, virtual worlds allow creating manageable representations of abstract entities and thus help students to construct mental models by direct observation and experimentation. Mickropoulas and Natsis (2011) identified that science

and technology courses had much more presence in virtual worlds than social studies and argued that this might be because the concepts explained are usually more abstract, unobservable, or far from everyday experience. Thus, such topics can benefit to a greater extent form the representative capabilities of virtual worlds in order to train students in subjects that require spatial abilities and high order thinking skills.

For example, Limniou et al. (2008) provided virtual representations of molecules and chemical reactions, which only exist in a microscopic level and thus are far from the student's everyday experiences. Similarly, Anthamatten and Ziegler (2006) employed a 3D representation of geographic formations using the GeoWall system. This allowed the students to see the correspondence between 2D topographic maps and 3D surfaces and interpret features such as slopes, ridges, and valleys that are difficult to envision in 2D. In the two previous experiences, virtual representations were created using a technology different from virtual worlds and the teacher operated the virtual model and the students could not manipulate it.

Other interesting unique characteristics of virtual worlds which were not exploited in these cases are immersion, manipulability, and first order experience. In some virtual environments, students are immersed in the virtual world; this provides an enhanced interactivity which would be very difficult in a traditional classroom and that makes the students become protagonists of the learning experience (Bailenson, et al., 2008). For example, Bakas and Mikropoulos (2003) report the use of a virtual spacecraft controlled by the students in an astronomy class in primary school. The students usually had problems to overcome previous misconceptions of the planetary phenomena such as the relative distances and sizes of celestial bodies and the movements they describe. Within the virtual world, the students could approach the Earth in their aircrafts and have a situated perspective of the phenomena obtaining a first order experience of the concepts learned.

Such a sense of immersion generally fosters engagement of the students with the tasks and the course, or, in a more general sense, with the formation of their own understanding. According to Mickropoulas and Natsis (2011), most of the educational studies of virtual worlds claim that virtual interaction favors engagement. However, other studies have reported that the virtual world sometimes distracts the attention of the students because of the novelty of the environment, or because of the interruption of avatars of other users of the virtual world, which are not students of the subject. Some authors have taken advantage of these "distractions" to encourage the students to be more explorative. For example, Barab et al. (2007) employed a virtual world to make the students appreciate the complexities of real world problems by exploring different perspectives over the same problem. Concretely, the students discovered that environmental awareness involves balancing ethical, economic, political, and scientific factors.

Virtual worlds also provide new opportunities for collaboration, as they facilitate synchronous and asynchronous communication, supporting and enhancing student-student and teacher-student interaction. Petrakou (2010) reported that the students involved in their research socialized just like they do in real world courses, trying to get to know each other, and also learning to cope with the new environment. They also reported that the student-student interaction continued after the course when some students discussed the assignments and tried to reach a common understanding of them.

Although virtual worlds can be employed as a tool for collaboration and communication to supplement face-to-face communication, the learning curve of using the virtual world might place it in disadvantage compared to other technologies (Andreas, et al., 2010). However, when used for multi-cultural and distributed learning, it can provide important advantages. For example, Kanematsu et al. (2010) report an experience with US, Korean and Japanese students for which they incorporated a language grid to Second Life that allowed multilingual discussion.

In addition, the possibility to communicate with classmates embodied in their avatars can help to develop understanding of civic values and empathy. Park (2010) described the use of Second Life to make the students experience role-playing with different ethnicities and gender roles, which allowed them to better recognize characteristics of male/female gender roles and give them a different perspective.

To fully benefit from all the described characteristics of the virtual worlds, the course contents must be active, project-based and designed following a pedagogical strategy that leverages the unique potential that virtual worlds offer Jarmon et al. (2009). According to Girvan and Savage (2010), social constructivist pedagogies are more appropriate to design effective learning experiences in virtual worlds. This way, knowledge is acquired on the basis of authentic real-world problems, for which the solution is a communal task that must be achieved as the union of the individual efforts in the virtual environment.

In addition, competence in technologies and in particular in the use of the virtual environment has been found to be fundamental. As reported by Petrakou (2010), when the use of the virtual world is a new experience for the students, this technology itself constitutes a collaborative learning activity that contributes to socialization between students. Thus, Petrakou (2010) highlights that the teacher must be aware of the fact that the students need to familiar with the virtual world before it is possible for them to focus on the actual course content. For example, Jarmon et al (2009) required as a condition to get a permission to register in the subject, that students had to meet some pre-class Second Life requirements, set up their accounts and create their avatars, and complete an online tutorial.

Other characteristics of the users such as learning styles, age, or cultural background might play an important role in learning. Some authors have addressed the challenge of identifying relevant features that provide a positive effect on learning and the relations between them. These features are related to many factors such as the characteristics and usability of the virtual world, experience of the interaction (performance and satisfaction), learning and psychological factors, and other the characteristics of the students. A comprehensive study can be found in Lee et al. (2010).

3. TEACHING AND LEARNING IN SECOND LIFE

Second Life (SL) is a three dimensional virtual world developed by Linden Lab in 2003 and accessible via the Internet. A free client program called the Second Life Viewer enables its users, called "residents," to interact with each other through motional avatars, providing an advanced level of a social network service.

There are many aspects in which SL is similar to Massively Multiplayer Online Role Playing Games (MMORPGs). Like an MMORPG, users represent themselves with a customizable, three-dimensional figure that acts like a computer-generated puppet. Users navigate through an online world, encountering strange landscapes and new people. Unlike MMORPGs, residents in SL are not in a game, though there are games inside its virtual environment. They inhabit a virtual world free of predetermined goals or tasks, just like the real world.

Second Life has shown to be appropriate to build educational experiences, as it provides the possibility to create groups and communities to share activities and interests with other Second Life users. Residents can explore, meet other residents, socialize, participate in individual and group activities, create and trade items (virtual property) and services from one another. The stated goal is to create a user-defined world of general use in which people can interact, play, do business, and otherwise communicate.

SL is currently being used with success as a platform for education by many institutions, such as colleges, universities, libraries, and government entities (e.g. Ohio University, Universidad Pública de Navarra, Cervantes Institute, Carlos III University of Madrid, etc.). Figure 1 shows two images of the Carlos III University of Madrid campus in Second Life.

Usually, these communities inhabit an island or "sim," which aspect and constructions can be continuously changed to recreate different spaces which can resemble the real world or be totally non-realistic. Within these spaces, communication between avatars can be carried out by means of voice, chat, videos, presentations, images, and gestures of the avatars.

This way, the islands can be filled with different types of multimedia information that can be shared, such as PDF documents, video, audio, Webs, and images. SL offers the possibility to visualize PDF files by using the Sloodle Presenter utility. Linden Labs offers also a Web browser. In addition, it is possible to upload video files to the inventory of an avatar, which allows uploading and sharing educative videotutorials, which incorporates not only images or screenshots, but

Figure 1. Carlos III University of Madrid in Second Life

also voice, and subtitles with detailed explanations for the students.

Residents can hear and view streaming audio and video inside Second Life, where audio in MPEG and Ogg Vorbis formats are supported. Streaming video requires the user to install Quicktime. Residents can choose to display video on specific surfaces in the land they own. To do this, they designate the surface's texture as a media surface. If any other surface within that resident's land has the same texture, it will also display the streaming video. Since this can cause confusion, residents should make sure the surface they choose has a unique texture within their land.

All the objects in Second Life can be exhibited along with information tags that describe them in detail. Moreover, the objects created within Second Life can be replicated an unlimited number of copies, which eases sharing contents and providing information about their use.

Users can "teleport" by pushing the corresponding button and visit different regions depicted in mini-maps of the virtual islands as the one shown in Figure 2, and interact with the avatars, bots and objects placed in the island. In addition, Second Life provides a search engine to locate resources.

Avatars can get around Second Life by walking, flying, or teleporting to their destination. Residents make their avatars walk around by using the arrow keys; for instance, pushing the up arrow key makes the avatar walk forward. Moving the mouse changes the position of the avatar's head, making it look around. Pie-shaped menus include options that allow residents to interact with other users or objects.

There are different ways in which the residents might communicate with each other, the main ones are: gestures, text messages, and voice. Gestures are animations that can convey a mood or simulate an action. Second Life includes a tool for designing customized gestures, which can also be bought by buying them or trading with another resident. Residents can also use a chat box, which opens a

Figure 2. Second Life map of a sim

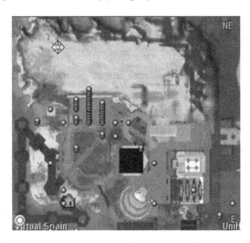

window in which they can type messages. Finally, residents may also opt to use the voice feature, which allows users with microphones to talk to one another in real time.

It is possible to develop script for Second Life using Scratch, a graphical programming language based on constructing programs by snapping together graphical blocks which were developed by the Lifelong Kindergarten group at the MIT Media Lab. Scratch can be installed and freely redistributed and its source code is available under a license that allows modifications for non-commercial uses. This way, it is possible to create custom applications.

Additionally, it is possible to create automatic bots using the Robot tool, which offers different commands to send instantaneous message to an avatar ("*IM | <name of the avatar> | <text>*"), to whisper in the public chat ("*WHISPER | <text>*"), to speak in the public chat ("*SAY | <text>*"), to shout in this chat ("*SHOUT | <text>*"), to verify the bots that are around (*WHO*), to allow that the bot follows to us (*FOLLOW*), to indicate the bot to stop following us (*NOFOLLOW*), to obtain the UUID key of an avatar (*FINDKEY*), to teleport to the position of the bot (*TAXI*), to obtain the contents of the inventory (*INVENTORY*), and to obtain landmark values (*LANDMARK*, landmarks are precise locations in Second Life).

Despite these interesting multimedia communication capabilities, voice communication is seldom employed in SL between avatars and metabots. Usually, metabots only provide information to the users, and thus the communication is unidirectional. In the cases in which a dialog takes place between human users and automatic metabots, it occurs through the chat box interface. Thus, although spoken communication is technically plausible in Second Life, it mainly takes place between human users and not between human users and metabots. Voice communication in SL is optional (it can be activated or deactivated by the users). The owners of each land control the use of the voice in their respective lands.

3.1. Specific Resources for Education in Second Life

Besides the previously described features, Second Life presents several utilities specifically tailored for their use in education; probably the most relevant is Sloodle (Simulation Linked Object Oriented Dynamic Learning Environment), an open source project that integrates Second Life with the Moodle (Modular Object-Oriented Dynamic Learning Environment) learning-management system.

Moodle is a Course-Management System (CMS), which makes possible the creation of virtual courses, delivers exercises, provides forums, carries out exams, etc. Its integration with Second Life makes possible the virtual access to them by means of an avatar, participating in classes and conferences in real time. Figure 3 shows a snapshot of a Sloodle course.

Sloodle provides a range of tools for supporting learning and teaching to the immersive virtual world. Firstly, it allows controlling the user registration and participation in a course thanks to an access checker as depicted in Figure 4. Also new users can register in a course using the so-called Enrol_Booth.

Secondly, there are several tools to create surveys in Sloodle, such as Choice Horizontal, Quiz Chair, or Quiz Pile On (Figure 5). Choice horizontal allows instructors to create and show surveys in the virtual world, compile the information and show the results in a course. With Quiz Chair an avatar can answer questionnaires of a course in SL, while with Quiz Pile On provides a similar functionality with a more amusing format. In Quiz Pile On, questions in the form a text that floats over a pile, the students seat over the correct answer and if the answer is wrong, he falls over.

Thirdly, the Sloodle Presenter tool (shown in Figure 6) allows creating presentations in Second Life, which can combine images, Web pages, and videos and may be configured so that any avatar or only the owner of the corresponding sim controls the display of the presentation.

Finally, there are other interesting tools for object sharing such as the PrimDrop, which allows students to deliver their works by sending objects in Second Life, or the Vending Machine, which can be used to deliver object to the students (Figure 7).

3.2. Alternatives to Second Life

OpenSimulator[1] is an open source multi-platform, multi-user 3D simulator that uses the same standard as Second Life to communicate with their users, and emulates virtual environments independently from the world of Second Life, using its own infrastructure.

OpenSimulator can be used to create a virtual environment, which can be accessed through a variety of clients, on multiple protocols. OpenSimulator also allows virtual world developers to customize their worlds using the technologies they feel work best—we've designed the framework to be easily extensible. OpenSimulator is written in C#, running both on Windows over the .NET framework and on *ix machines over the Mono

Figure 3. Sloodle sim in Second Life

framework. The source code is released under a BSD License, a commercially friendly license to embed OpenSimulator in products.

Out of the box, OpenSimulator can be used to simulate virtual environments similar to Second Life, given that it supports the core of SL's messaging protocol. In fact, OpenSimulator currently uses the Second Life protocol for client to server communication, and is compliant with the Second Life viewer by Linden Lab as well as a range of other virtual world's viewers being developed by the open source community. OpenSimulator community includes end users, content contributors, region owners, grid owners, testers, and developers.

The virtual worlds created with OpenSimulator can be accessed with the regular SL viewers. However, OpenSimulator lacks support for many

Figure 4. Sloodle access checker activated by entering a login zone (left), access checker with a door (middle), and Enrol_Booth (right)

Figure 5. Choice horizontal, quiz chair, and quiz pile on

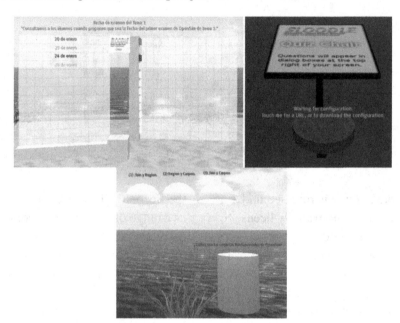

of the game-specific features of Second Life (on purpose), while pursuing innovative directions towards becoming the bare bones, but extensible, server of the 3D Web. OpenSimulator utilizes loadable modules for most of its functionality. These loadable modules are available on the OpenSimulator GForge hosting and can be independently developed to add functionality to the server.

Figure 6. Sloodle presenter

OpenSimulator can operate in one of two modes: standalone or grid mode. In standalone mode, a single process handles the entire simulation. In grid mode, various aspects of the simulation are separated among multiple processes, which can exist on different machines. Standalone mode is simpler to configure, but is limited to a smaller number of users. Grid mode has the potential to scale as the number of users grows. OpenSim also uses an architecture known as "Hypergrid," which allows users to teleport between multiple OpenSim-based virtual worlds by providing a hyperlinked map which indexes public grids. This allows for public grids to retain teleportation links to each other without having to be on the same grid.

The main features of OpenSimulator include the supporting of 3D virtual spaces of variable size within one single instance, realtime Physics Simulation, multiple clients and protocols, in world scripting using a number of different languages (including LSL/OSSL, C#, Jscript, and VB.NET), clients that create 3D content in real time, and the provision of unlimited ability to customize virtual world applications through the use of scene plug-in modules.

OsGrid[2] is a network that allows linking completely free virtual worlds developed using simulators such as OpenSimulator.

The virtual world OpenLife[3] is a grid based on OpenSimulator developed by the team at 3DX. OpenLife rents its lands by paying a cost for the maintenance of the servers.

Wonderland virtual world[4] has been created by Sun Microsystems. Wonderland offers a fully developed set of tools for creating Java 3D collaborative virtual worlds, becoming multiplatform. Its main objective is focused on collaborative work to enable its users to communicate by means of avatars with high fidelity, immersive audio, desktop sharing, real-time applications, and documents in real time, trade, etc. It is a centralized environment with code under GPL license. This way, companies can use it to develop their own virtual world to interact with their customers.

Croquet[5] virtual world is an open-source software technology. Croquet aims to enable collaboration between users, acting as an online conferencing system built over a 3D interface and a P2P network architecture. It can be considered as a sort online operating system with applications shared with other users and with an open architecture.

Croquet integrates a high-end three dimensional sound and graphics, collaboration technologies, simulations and other tools to create a space for sharing, and a great scope for the creation, use of digital content. This project is important for three main reasons: the functionalities that it offers, to promote collaboration and learning environments, and for the way it can teach us about designing new innovative software environments. Croquet represents in our vision a major step of computing as a communication and services provision platform, available anytime, anywhere, and from any device (e.g. PDAs).

Open Cobalt[6] virtual world offers an open-source platform to build, access, and participate in virtual workspaces for research and education. Open Cobalt also allows to hyperlink the created 3D virtual worlds by means of Internet portals to form a large distributed network of collaborative spaces between them. It also enables schools and other organizations to freely set their own 3D virtual networks offering integrated Web, voice

Figure 7. PrimDrop (left) and vending machine (right)

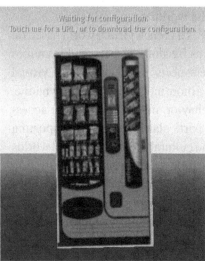

chat, text chat, and access to remote desktop applications.

Open Cobalt has been developed with the main functionality of facilitating the development of secure virtual world for both individuals and organizations. By leveraging the OpenGL-based 3D graphics, it supports highly scalable collaborative visualization of data, virtual learning, and development of problem-solving environments, 3D wikis, online games, as well as privacy and security in virtual environments to facilitate group communication. By means of Open Cobalt, it is possible to have all the network resources (learning management systems, resource management systems, wikis, etc.) in an interactive virtual space. Open Cobalt is intended to stimulate development and collaborative decision making among all its users, and problem solving among members of virtual organizations and distributed educative communities.

The 3rd Rock Grid virtual world[7] is a grid based on OpenSim. It consists of a social community of individuals around the world who interact in a 3D virtual world. Contents, appearance, and presentation of the world are created by its users. This way, it is possible to find in this virtual world homes, businesses, music clubs, playgrounds, parks, museums, and any kind of constructions developed by its members to build the community. It is also possible to meet and talk with people from around the world.

NewWorld[8] is a French virtual world based on human values as freedom, respect, and resources sharing. These aspects make possible the virtual worlds to have a more interactive, social, dynamic, and human behavior, making them more accessible to all, in particular by means of supporting educational and cultural projects in virtual worlds as a communication medium and a collaboration platform. New World is managed by the nonprofit organization Virtus[9], raising funds from its users, volunteers and land rental, in order to actively support this kind of projects.

Open Neuland[10] and Wilder Westen[11] are 3D virtual worlds created by TalentRaspel Ltd. They are based on the open source software Open-Simulator. Virtyou[12] virtual world was founded in 2009. Virtyou GmbH is a German company focused on media convergence in interactive 3D worlds. Alternative Your Life[13] is a multi-user virtual world that allows its users to interact with each other through 3D avatars, which can create and trade virtual properties and services.

The Magazine for Enterprise Users of Virtual Worlds Hyper Grid Business[14] periodically publishes statistics about the evolution in the number of grids of each one of the main virtual worlds. They consider how many more regions, registered users, and active users the grid reported compared to the previous month. Table 1 summarizes this information for December 2010.

According to these statistics, the top 40 grids have more than doubled in size over the past year—in December 2009, they had a total of 7,246 regions.

OpenSimulator grids hit new 15,094 regions on the top 40 grids, an 11% increase from November 2010 (13,564 regions). Meanwhile, total registered users on these grids grew 5% from 140,053 in mid November to 147,565 at the end of December 2010. Figure 8 shows the evolution in number of regions of virtual worlds created with OpenSimulator from November 2009 to December 2010. Te reduction in this number during the summer of 2009 can be explained due to OSGrid conducted a major housekeeping campaign and cleared out thousands of inactive regions during those months.

OSGrid remains the top gainer in terms of regions, growing to a new high of 8,512 regions through a gain of 795 new regions. OSGrid currently has more regions than all other top-40 grids combined, due to the fact that people can connect regions for free if they have the technical skills to run OpenSimulator at home.

OSGrid is also home to the largest user population of any OpenSim grid, with 54,154 total

Table 1. Ranking of virtual worlds taking into account the evolution from November 2010 to December 2010

OSGrid 8512 regions	WorldSimTerra 202 regions	eceCloud 97 regions	GiantGrid 61 regions
Virtual Worlds Grid 813 regions	3rd Rock Grid 171 regions	Oasis World 96 regions	Open Neuland 57 regions
InWorldz 719 regions	SpotOn 3D 166 regions	Role Play Worlds 96 regions	SIM World 52 regions
New World Grid 543 regions	Avination 152 regions	German Grid 87 regions	NZ Virtual World Grid 51 regions
ScienceSim 338 regions	Triton Grid 149 regions	Logicamp 81 regions	Pseudospace 47 regions
AlphaTowne 334 regions	ReactionGrid 144 regions	Avatar Hangout 75 regions	GerGrid 44 regions
Metropolis 304 regions	MyOpenGrid 137 regions	JokaydiaGrid 71 regions	Annuna Grid 40 regions
Meta7 294 regions	VeeSome 133 regions	Craft World 69 regions	PMGrid 40 regions
NexXtLife 272 regions	VirtualLife 114 regions	Twisted Sky 69 regions	SimValley 40 regions
FrancoGrid 215 regions	Virtyou 105 regions	PrimSim 66 regions	Your Alternative Life 38 regions

registered users. OSGrid residents run a variety of freebie stores and event venues, which helps attract visitors. Finally, OSGrid allows hypergrid teleports to other grids, making it appealing for those looking for a jumping-off point from which to explore the metaverse. However, while OSGrid gained the most new regions, InWorldz—a closed, commercial grid—gained the most users.

Virtual World Grid, now in second place in number of regions, is run by Myron Curtis, a IT specialist at Butte College, and is also known as Virtual Worlds College. The grid is home to some installations that require a lot of land—for example, the under-construction Virtual Worlds Galleries is planned to be the single biggest virtual building, spanning 36 regions. That translates to 576 acres of virtual land—about halfway in size between

Figure 8. OpenSimulator virtual world evolution from August 2009 to December 2010

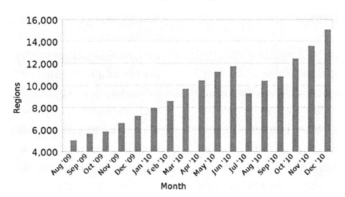

New York's Bronx Zoo (265 acres) and Central Park (843 acres). However, Virtual Worlds Grid is in 34th place by users, with just 279 registered account holders on the grid.

Unlike Second Life—where each region costs $300 a month to run, with a $1,000 setup fee—regions on OpenSim grids are usually free to create and cheap to run, with professionally hosted prices typically ranging from $10 to $100 a month, depending on power and features. In addition, groups with access to low-cost servers, such as research companies or educational institutions, can easily run large numbers of regions at very little cost if they have the in-house technical skills to set up an OpenSim server. As a result, total land area might not be the best indicator of how active a particular grid is.

The growth of these top 40 public OpenSim grids is only a small part of the story, however. There are hundreds of institutions, organizations, and individuals running private grids and mini-grids. In fact, creating a new grid is now as simple as downloading setup files onto a USB stick and popping it in. In addition, many hosting providers (including ReactionGrid, SimHost, and Dreamland Metaverse) run private-label grids and mini-grids for the clients. In addition, the non-profit Immersive Education Initiative offers free hosting and free help for schools and colleges looking to set up their own grids.

4. SPEECH TECHNOLOGIES TO ENSURE DIGITAL EQUALITY IN VIRTUAL LEARNING ENVIRONMENTS

Very recently, Mikropoulos and Natsis (2011) have presented a ten-year review on the educational applications of virtual reality covering more than 50 research studies, and have pointed out that, although virtual worlds support multisensory interaction channels, visual representations predominate. The authors claim for a more detailed study on the intuitiveness of interactivity when no other channels are provided and the impact on the students' learning outcomes. In this section, we present a description of the main barriers that adding oral interactivity can overcome.

4.1. Barriers that Limit User Interaction with Computers

There are a number of barriers that limit user interaction with computers. One is concerned with the devices employed. The classical interaction between users and computers is based on devices such as keyboard, mouse, and screen. This means that the user must have at least a minimum training for using the devices and must not be handicapped by visual or motor disabilities in order to use them. Moreover, the user must have his eyes and hands available for the interaction with the computer, which is not appropriate if they are busy with another task, for example, car driving. In learning environments, these barriers may have important implications since user cannot benefit from automated educational tools.

In order to address these limitations, an alternative and relative new way for interacting with computers is based on the processing of human speech, which allows several advantages in comparison with the classical interaction. Among others, speech offers a greater speed for transmitting information, allows carrying out simultaneously other tasks (liberating the user from the need to use his hands and/or eyes), informs about the identity of the speaker, and allows that some kinds of disable users can interact with the computer. Speech allows a great expressivity; in fact, human beings express ideas and feelings using the language. Speech also allows transmitting information about the state of mind the speaker as well as their attitude towards the listener. Moreover, speech can be transmitted by simple and widely used devices such as fixed and mobile telephones, making it possible the remote access to a variety of speech-based services. In despite of these advantages, speech-based interfaces may become inherently easy to use when computers can actually understand speech like human beings do. Unfortunately, nowadays these interfaces lack the fluency and unlimited language characteristic of human interaction.

4.2. Dialog Systems

Dialog systems can be defined as computer programs designed to engage users in a conversation that aims to be as similar as possible as that between humans. These systems employ a greater or smaller number of interaction modalities depending on their complexity. If the interaction is carried out using speech only, the systems are called *Spoken Dialog Systems* (SDSs). These systems have demonstrated to provide a more natural interaction than traditional GUI-based interfaces, and have a more affordable learning curve for people without enough technical knowledge (McTear, 2004). In fact, nowadays they are typically used for a number of applications, including tutoring (Forbes-Riley & Litman, 2011; Graesser, et al., 2001; Johnson & Valente, 2008), entertainment (Ibrahim & Johansson, 2002), command and control (Stent, et al., 1999), healthcare (Beveridge & Fox, 2006), call routing (Paek & Horvitz, 2004), and retrieval of information about a variety of services, for example, weather forecasts (Maragoudakis, 2007), apartment rental (Cassell, et al., 1999), and travelling (Huang, et al., 1999).

SDSs usually employ five technologies: Automatic Speech Recognition (ASR), Natural Language Understanding (NLU), Dialog Management (DM), Natural Language Generation (NLG), and Text-To-Speech synthesis (TTS). These technologies are used to implemented independent modules as shown in Figure 9.

The goal of ASR is to process the speech signal in order to obtain the sequence of words uttered by the user (Rabiner & Huang, 1993). It is a very complex task as there is much variability in the input characteristics, which can differ largely depending on the linguistics of the utterance, the speaker, the interaction context, and the transmission channel. Linguistic variability involves differences in phonetic, syntactic, and semantic components that affect the voice signal. Inter-speaker variability refers to the big difference between speakers regarding their speaking style, voice, age, sex, or nationality.

The objective of NLU is to obtain a semantic representation of the sequence of words provided by the speech recognizer (Mairesse, et al., 2009). In other words, its goal is to enable the SDS in "understanding" what the user said. This process generally involves morphological, lexical, syntactical, semantic, discourse, and pragmatic knowledge. In a first stage, lexical and morphological knowledge allow dividing words in their constituents, distinguishing lexemes and morphemes. Lexemes are the part of the words that indicate their semantics whereas morphemes

Figure 9. Typical architecture of a spoken dialog system

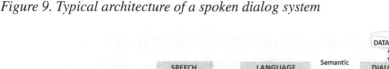
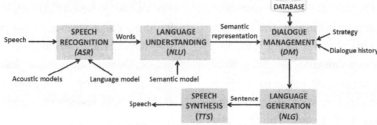

are the different infixes and suffixes that allow obtaining different word classes. Syntactic analysis yields a hierarchical structure of the sentences. However, in spoken language, phrases are frequently affected by disfluencies such as filled pauses, repetitions, syntactic incompleteness, and repairs. Semantic analysis extracts the meaning of a complex syntactic structure from the meaning of its constituents. In the pragmatic and discourse processing stage, the sentences are interpreted in the context of the whole dialog.

The third technology involved in the implementation of a SDS is Dialog Management (DM). In accordance with Traum and Larsson (2003), DM involves four main tasks: 1) updating the dialog context, 2) providing a context for interpreting the user input, 3) coordinating other modules, and 4) deciding the information the system must convey to the user and when to do it. Thus, the dialog manager of a SDS must deal with different information sources, such as the output of the NLU module, results of database queries, knowledge on the application domain, knowledge about the users, and data about the previous dialog history. The complexity of this module depends on the difficulty of the task, the dialog flexibility and the type of initiative desired for the dialog (either system-directed, user-directed, or mixed).

Natural Language Generation (NLG) can be defined as the process for obtaining a text message, written in natural language, from a non-linguistic representation of information (Seneff, 2002). This task is usually carried out in five steps: content organization, content distribution in sentences, lexicalization, generation of referential expressions and linguistic realization. It is important to note that the generated messages must not only be correct from a syntactic and semantic point of view, but also be natural in the context of a conversation. This requires using referring expressions (anaphora), omitting words if they are available in the context of the conversation (ellipsis), and adapting the vocabulary to the linguistic competence of the users. The simplest

method for NLG typically uses predefined text messages, for example, to create computer's error messages and warnings.

The goal of Text-To-Speech synthesis (TTS) is transform the output of the NLG module into speech (Utama, et al., 2006). Typically, a TTS system is comprised of two parts: front-end and back-end. The front-end carries out two major tasks. Firstly, it converts the raw text created by the NLG, which may contain numbers and abbreviations, into their equivalent words. Secondly, it assigns a phonetic transcription to each word, divides the text, and marks it in terms of prosodic units, e.g., phrases, clauses and sentences. The back-end (often referred to as the synthesizer) converts the symbolic linguistic representation into speech.

Multimodal Dialog Systems (MMDSs) are another type of dialog system, which is much more complex than spoken dialog systems. They are based on the fact that human-to-human communication relies on the use of several communication channels to transmit and receive information from the conversation partner, e.g., speech, lip movements, body gestures, and gazes (López-Cózar & Araki, 2005). Imitating this human procedure, MMDSs can use several input modalities to obtain data from the user, and a number of output modalities to influence several senses of the user simultaneously. An advantage of having this wide range of devices available is that the user can select the most appropriate devices considering environmental conditions (e.g. in terms of noise) as well as his preferences or needs. For example, handicapped users many not be able to use some modality but yet use another. The user can also select the interaction modalities considering the type of task to be carried out. For example, while driving a car it is safer to use a modality that allows having the hands and eyes free, for example, speech. On the contrary, in a place requiring silence (e.g. a library) or when providing personal data to the system, speech may not be the best option.

4.2.1. Dialog Systems for Learning Applications

A very challenging application of dialog systems is to automated tutoring systems that aim to elicit human-like conversations with students. These systems have a number of advantages in comparison with real tutors. As practice is essential for learning, automated tutoring systems provide chances for practicing which are only limited by technological resources. A second aspect is that some students may feel more comfortable interacting with an automated tutoring system, as they may feel embarrassed of making the same mistakes repeatedly. A third point is that these systems can provide additional material, such as examples or explanatory images, with less effort than a human tutor (Engwall, et al., 2004).

Initial tutoring systems enabled interaction by means of natural language in text format, i.e., students did not talk to the systems but used a keyboard. For example, Evens et al. (2001) presented a system that was able to conduct conversations with students to help them solve problems in cardiovascular physiology dealing with the regulation of blood pressure. The Rimac project[15] focused on the development of an enhanced version of the Andes physic tutoring system in order to address the following limitation of classical text-based tutoring systems: they are interactive in the sense that they try to elicit explanations from students instead of lecturing to them, but they do not reuse parts of the student's dialog turns in their own turns.

In the next level of complexity, we can find speech-based automated tutoring systems. It is believed that these systems can be even more effective for teaching because spontaneous self-explanations by students improves learning gains during human-to-human tutoring (Chi, et al., 1994). Moreover, this type of explanation occurs more frequently in spoken tutoring than in text-based tutoring (Hausmann & Chi, 2002). A number of studies can be found in the literature on the application of SDSs to tutoring applications.

For example, Martins et al. (2008) developed a system that helps to cook a recipe. The main challenge for this system was the change of classical paradigm: instead of the system being driven by the user, the user was instructed by the system. Another examples is Litman and Silliman (2004), which presented ITSPOKE, a system that engages the user in a spoken dialog to provide feedback, correct misconceptions and elicit more complete explanations about Physics.

4.2.2. Dialog Systems for Elderly and Handicapped Users

Another challenging area of research in the field of dialog systems is concerned with the target users: elderly and handicapped. This area is very important as most dialog systems are designed for the general population. As we get older, our perception is lessened, our attention is narrowed, and our memory is limited. This makes it extremely difficult for us to listen to and use the information that dialog systems provide. Thus, it is very important to develop SDSs that produce language that best maximizes our comprehension while also encouraging our independent behavior. Several studies have been carried out to address the specific features of these users. For example, Raux et al. (2003) worked on the Let's Go project in order to improve the performance of a SDS that provides bus schedule information, paying special attention to elderly and non-native speakers of English.

Multimodal Dialog Systems (MMDSs) provide important advantages for elderly and handicapped users because, as discussed above, they allow replacing one interaction modality with another if the former is not suitable for the user or the interaction context. For example, blind users cannot see the device's display whereas deaf users cannot speak to the system. Therefore, these systems enable a greater adaptation to the user needs. An application domain of high interest for MMDSs is concerned with pedestrian navigation systems. For example,

Strothotte et al. (1996) developed a dialog system to provide mobility aid for blind people, which assists travelers in exploring information about the localities to which they wish to travel. The dialog manager of the system deals with the special needs that different users may have by employing a user model and a knowledge base. Also concerned with this application domain, Helal et al. (2001) presented a system that integrates several technologies, including wearable computers, speech recognition and synthesis, wireless networks, Geographic Information System (GIS) and Global Positioning System (GPS). The system augments contextual information to the visually impaired and computes optimized routes based on user preferences, temporal constraints (e.g., traffic congestion) and dynamic obstacles (e.g., ongoing groundwork or road blockade for special events).

Dealing with another application domain, Beskow et al. (2009) presented the MonAMI reminder, a multimodal dialog system to assist elderly and disabled users in organizing and initiating their daily activities. The system can carry out the following tasks: adding, leafing through them and editing events in a calendar in a familiar way, asking about the contents of the calendar, and being reminded of events in the calendar in an efficient and unobtrusive manner.

4.2.3. Dialog Systems for Virtual Environments

Dialog systems have recently started to be applied to virtual environments (e.g., Second Life). For instance, Griol et al. (2010) presented a spoken dialog system that communicates with a metabot in Second Life in order to provide academic information. To do so, the metabot interacts with a previously developed spoken dialog system that provides information about subjects, professors, PhD courses and university registration (Callejas & López-Cózar, 2008).

Concerned with a different application domain, Benotti et al. (2010) presented a dialog system that automatically generates instructions to help a user to carry out a given task in a 3D virtual environment. The system guides the user through interconnected rooms in order to find a trophy hidden in a safe. In order to achieve this goal, the system instructs the user to perform several subtasks, for example, deactivating alarms, and opening the safe by pressing a sequence of bottoms on the walls of the rooms.

Hofs et al. (2010) presented a multimodal dialog system represented by an ECA (Embodied Conversational Agent) that can help users to find their way in a virtual environment, while adapting its affective linguistic style to that of the user. In addition, the system detects the level of politeness of the user in real-time, and aligns its own language to that of the user employing different politeness strategies.

5. A PROPOSAL FOR INCLUDING SPEECH IN VIRTUAL LEARNING ENVIRONMENTS

We propose a methodology that can be used to develop avatars in SecondLife and also in our own virtual world generated with OpenSimulator, an open source alternative which uses the same standard as SecondLife. With it, it is possible to take advantage of the possibilities of Sloodle to create Moodle contents and courses, not only in SecondLife but also in other freely accessible environments. The section will describe these possibilities in detail and present a thorough evaluation of the behavior of the avatar in both cases.

Our approach extends the typical architecture of dialog systems: speech recognition, language understanding, dialog management, database access, and generation of oral response, with the visual appearance of a metabot and the pedagogic strategies for the learning environment.

We decided to use Second Life as a testbed for our research for several reasons. Firstly, because it is one of the most popular social virtual worlds available: its population is nowadays of millions of enthusiastic residents from around the world. Secondly, because it uses a sophisticated physics engine, which generates very realistic simulations including collision detection, vehicle dynamics and animation look and feel, thus making the avatars and the environment more credible and similar to the real world. Thirdly, because SL's capacity for customization is extensive and encourages user innovation and participation, which increases the naturalness of the interactions that take place in the virtual world. We own an island in Second Life called TESIS, in which we built its Virtual facilities in which numerous educational activities are performed. Figure 10 shows an image of the TESIS island.

We have developed a conversational metabot that facilitates academic information (courses, professors, doctoral studies, and enrollment) based on the functionalities provided by a previously developed dialog system (Callejas & López-Cózar, 2005, 2008). The information provided by the metabot can be classified into four categories: subjects, teachers, doctoral studies, and registration, as shown in Table 2. As can be observed in this table, the system must ask the user for different pieces of information before producing a response.

The system has been developed using the typical architecture of current spoken dialog systems previously described in Figure 9, including a module for automatic speech recognition, a dialog manager, a module for access to databases,

data storage, and the generation of an oral response through a language generator and a text to speech synthesizer, as described in the previous section.

We defined a semantic representation for the task, in which one or more concepts represent the intention of the utterance, and a sequence of attribute-value pairs contains the information about the values given by the user. In the case of user turns, we defined four concepts related to the different queries that the user can perform to the system (*Subject, Lecturers, Doctoral studies, Registration*), three task-independent concepts (*Affirmation, Negation*, and *Not-Understood*), and eight attributes (*Subject-Name, Degree, Group-Name, Subject-Type, Lecturer-Name, Program-Name, Semester*, and *Deadline*). An example of the semantic interpretation of an input sentence is shown in Box1.

The labeling of the system turns is similar to the labeling defined for the user turns. A total of 30 task-dependent concepts were defined:

- Task-independent concepts (*Affirmation, Negation, Not-Understood, New-Query, Opening*, and *Closing*).
- Concepts used to inform the user about the result of a specific query (*Subject, Lecturers, Doctoral-Studies*, and *Registration*).
- Concepts defined to require the user the attributes that are necessary for a specific query (*Subject-Name, Degree, Group-Name, Subject-Type, Lecturer-Name, Program-Name, Semester*, and *Deadline*).
- Concepts used for the confirmation of concepts (*Confirmation-Subject, Confirmation - Lecturers, Confirmation-DoctoralStudies*,

Box 1.

User Turn:
I want to know information about the subject Language Processors I of Computer Science. **Semantic Representation:** (*Subject*) *Subject-Name*: Language Processors I *Degree*: Computer Science

Figure 10. An image of the TESIS island in Second Life

Confirmation-Registration) and attributes (*Confirmation-SubjectName, Confirmation-Degree, Confirmation GroupName, Confirmation-SubjectType, Confirmation-LecturerName, Confirmation-ProgramName, Confirmation-Semester*, and *Confirmation-Deadline*).

Figure 11 shows the architecture developed for the integration of conversational metabot both in the Second Life and OsGrid virtual worlds. The conversational agent that governs the metabot is outside the virtual world, using external servers that provide both data access and speech recognition and synthesis functionalities.

The speech signal provided by the text to speech synthesizer is captured and transmitted to the voice server module in Second Life (SLVoice) using code developed in Visual C#.NET and the SpeechLib library. This module is external to the client program used to display the virtual world and is based on the Vivox technology, which uses the RTP, SIP, OpenAL, TinyXPath, OpenSSL and libcurl protocols to transmit voice data. We also

Table 2. Information provided by the academic conversational metabot

Category	Information provided by the user (names and examples)		Information provided by the system
Subject	Name	Compilers	Degree, lecturers, responsible lecturer, semester, credits, Web page
	Degree, in which it is taught in case that there are several subjects with the same name	Computer Science	
	Group name and optionally type, in case he asks for information about a specific group	A Theory A	Timetable, lecturer
Lecturers	Any combination of *name* and *surnames*	Zoraida Zoraida Callejas Ms. Callejas	Office location, contact information (phone, fax, email), groups and subjects, doctoral courses
	Optionally *semester*, in case he asks for the tutoring hours	First semester Second semester	Tutoring hours
Doctoral studies	Name of a doctoral program	Software development	Department, responsible
	Name of a course if he asks for information about a specific course	Object-oriented programming	Type, credits
Registration	Name of the deadline	Provisional registration confirmation	Initial time, final time, description

use the utility provided by Second Life lipsynch to synchronize the voice signal with the lip movements of the avatar.

In addition, we have integrated a keyboard emulator that allows the transmission of the text transcription generated by the conversational avatar directly to the chat in Second Life. The system connection with the virtual world is carried out by using the libOpenMetaverse library. This .Net library, based on the Client/Server paradigm, allows accessing and creating three-dimensional virtual worlds, and it is used to communicate with servers that control the virtual world of Second Life.

Speech recognition and synthesis are performed using the Microsoft Speech Application Programming Interface (SAPI), integrated into the Windows Vista operating system. To enable the interaction with the conversational in Spanish using the chat in Second Life, we have integrated synthetic voices developed by Loquendo.

Using this architecture user's utterances can be easily recognized, the transcription of these utterances can be transcribed in the chat in Second Life, and the result of the user's query can be communicated using both text and speech modalities. To do this, we have integrated modules for the semantic understanding and dialog management implemented for the original dialog system,

which are based on grammars and VoiceXML[16] files. Figure 12 shows the developed metabot providing information about tutoring hours of a specific professor.

A set of 150 dialogs was acquired with the conversational metabot by means of its interaction with students and professors of our university. Figure 13 shows an example of a dialog extracted from this corpus and translated from Spanish to English. Turns with S refer to system turns, and turns with U refer to user turns.

We considered the following measures for the evaluation:

1. **Dialog success rate (% success):** This is the percentage of successfully completed dialogs in which the metabot provides the correct information to each one of the required questions.
2. Average number of turns per dialog (nT).
3. **Confirmation rate (%confirm):** It was computed as the ratio between the number of explicit confirmations turns (nCT) and the number of turns in the dialog (nCT/nT).
4. **Average number of corrected errors per dialog (nCE):** This is the average of errors detected and corrected by the dialog manager of the conversational metabot. We have

Figure 11. Architecture defined for the development of conversational metabot for the interaction in virtual worlds

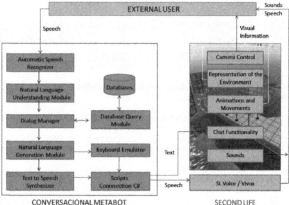

Figure 12. Conversational metabot developed to interact in virtual worlds

considered only those errors that modify the values of the attributes and that could cause the failure of the dialog.

5. **Average number of uncorrected errors per dialog (nNCE):** This is the average of errors not corrected by the dialog manager. Again, only errors that modify the values of the attributes are considered.

6. **Error Correction Rate (% ECR):** The percentage of corrected errors, computed as nCE/ (nCE + nNCE).

The results presented in Table 3 show that the developed conversational can interact correctly with the users in most cases, achieving a success rate of 94%. The dialog success depends on whether the system provides the correct data for every objective defined in the scenario. The analysis of the main problems detected in the acquired dialogs shows that, in some cases, the system did not detect that the user wanted to finish the dialog. A second problem was related to the introduction of data with a high confidence value due to errors generated by the automatic speech recognizer that were not detected by the dialog manager. However, the evaluation confirms a good operation of the approach since the information is correctly provided by the metabot in the majority of cases, as it is also shown in the value of the error correction rate.

In addition to the capability of providing information by means of the dialog interaction with the developed automatic conversational metabot, it started to be applied at the end of the academic year 2009-2010 in the Computer Science Degree at the Carlos III University of Madrid to interact with the students by presenting them a set of questionnaires about this subject. The subject Compilers was selected for the elaboration of the different test questionnaires including questions concerning theoretical contents as a review of methodologies and concepts. These questionnaires were implemented using the different tools previously described for Sloodle, like Presenters,

Figure 13. Example of a dialog acquired with the interaction of the system with real users

S1: Hi! You can ask me for information about subjects, lecturers, doctoral studies and registrations.
U1: I want to know information about subjects in Computer Science.
S2: Which subject do you want to consult?
U2: Language Processors I.
S3: Here you can consult the information of the subject. Anything else?
U3: Can you inform me about the schedules of Group D?
S4: I give the information for the Group D of Language Processors I: Monday 9:00-11:00, Wednesday 11:00-13:00. Anything else?
U4: Can you tell me the name of the lecturer?
S5: I give the information for the Group D of Language Processors I. The name of the lecturer is David Griol. Anything else?
U5: No, thank you.
S6: Bye!

Table 3. Results of the objective evaluation of the conversational metabot

	%success	nT	%confirm	%ECR	nCE	nNCE
Conversational Metabot	94%	11.6	28%	93%	0.89	0.06

Table 4. Results of the subjective evaluation of the conversational metabot

	Q1	Q2	Q3	Q4	Q5	Q6	Q7	Q8	Q9	Q10
Average Value	4.6	2.8	3.6	3.8	3.2	3.1	2.7	2.3	2.4	3.3
Maximum Value	5	3	4	5	5	4	3	3	4	4
Minimal Value	4	1	2	3	2	3	2	2	1	3

(1=worst, 5=best evaluation)

Quiz Chair, Quiz Pile On, Choice Horizontal, and PrimDrop. The different questions were implemented by means of VoiceXML files.

Figure 14 shows an example of a VoiceXML form for the multimodal presentation of a specific question, collect the student's response, and provide it to the Natural Language Understanding Module in the EducAgent platform. As it can be seen, each VoiceXML file corresponding to a specific question includes an initial grammar, manages of help events, and deliveries the student's answer to the Language Understanding module in the conversational agent.

A total of 110 questions, practical cases, and problems were elaborated for the subject. We evaluate these questions by proposing them to students. It should be emphasized that the total of questions were answered by 89% of students. 86% of students expressed the usefulness of the provided cases and problems to facilitate the achievement of the objectives of the course, enhance their learning and facilitate knowing the degree of understanding of the different contents.

The indicators about the operation of the conversational metabot that we want obtain at the end of the current academic year include the complete evaluation of the different modules and educational contents for the subject, the evaluation of their reliability and usability, the validation of the acceptation degree of the different contents, and the definition and evaluation of technological parameters associated to the specific operation of each one of the modules in the platform.

Figure 14. Example of a VoiceXML form to generate a specific question in the conversational bot

```
<?xml version="1.0" encoding="UTF-8"?>
<vxml version="2.0" xmlns="http://www.w3.org/2001/vxml"
xmlns:xsi="http://www.w3.org/2001/XMLSchema-instance"
xsi:schemaLocation="http://www.w3.org/2001/vxml
http://www.w3.org/TR/voicexml20/vxml.xsd">
<form id="Lexical Analysis">
<block>Please, answer now the following question.</block>
<field name="PAL-03">
<prompt>Do you think that regular expressions can be used
to recognize tokens? </prompt>
<grammar src="pal-03.grxml" type="application/srgs+xml"/>
<catch event="help">
You have to select one of the possible answers shown at your screen.
if it is possible to recognize tokens by means <reprompt/>
</catch>
</field>
<submit next="/servlet/analisis/pal" namelist="pal-03"/>
</block>
</form>
</vxml>
```

In addition, we have already completed a preliminary evaluation of this functionality of the conversational metabot based on questionnaire to assess the students' subjective opinion about the metabot performance. The questionnaire had 10 questions: 1) Q1: State on a scale from 1 to 5 your previous knowledge about new technologies for information access.; 2) Q2: How many times have you accessed virtual worlds like Second Life?; 3) Q3: How well did the metabot understand you?; 4) Q4: How well did you understand the messages generated by the metabot?; 5) Q5: Was it easy for you to get the requested information?; 6) Q6: Was the interaction rate adequate?; 7) Q7: Was it easy for you to correct the metabot errors?; 8) Q8: Were you sure about what to say to the system at every moment?; 9) Q9: Do you believe the system behaved similarly as a human would do?; 10) Q10: In general terms, are you satisfied with the metabot performance?

The possible answers for each one of the questions were the same: Never, Seldom, Sometimes, Usually, and Always. All the answers were assigned a numeric value between one and five (in the same order as they appear in the questionnaire). Table 4 shows the average, minimal and maximum values for the subjective evaluation carried out by a total of 15 students from one of the groups in the subject.

From the results of the evaluation, it can be observed that students positively evaluates the facility of obtaining the data required to fulfill the complete set of objectives of the proposed in the exercises defined for the subject, the suitability of the interaction rate during the dialog. The sets of points that they mention to be improved include the correction of system errors and a better clarification of the set of actions expected by the platform at each time.

6. CONCLUSION

The development of social networks and virtual worlds brings a wide set of opportunities that can be exploited for education purposes, as they provide an enormous range of possibilities for evaluating new learning scenarios given that users inside this world can explore, meet other residents, socialize, participate in individual and group activities, and create and trade virtual property and services with one another, or travel throughout the world.

In this chapter, we have proposed a methodology to develop embodied conversational agents that are able to interact as conversational metabots in virtual worlds, thus complementing the state-of-the-art approaches, which are usually based solely on visual information. A practical implementation of an automatic avatar that provides academic information has been integrated and evaluated in an academic application in Second Life.

As a future work, we intend to study the differences between the student models generated in this chapter and the ones that could be obtained from real interactions in the classroom. This way, we plan to study the similarities and differences in the behavior of the students when influenced by the image of their avatar compared to their usual conversational behavior. Additionally, we want to carry out a more detailed study on the effect of emotional behavior of metabots by integrating an emotion recognizer in the system to improve the communication between the system and the bots and avoid negative emotions that can influence the learning process such as frustration.

REFERENCES

Andrade, A., Bagri, A., Zaw, K., Roos, B. A., & Ruiz, J. G. (2010). Avatar-mediated training in the delivery of bad news in a virtual world. *Journal of Palliative Medicine, 13*(12), 1–14. doi:10.1089/jpm.2010.0108

Andreas, K., Tsiatsos, T., Terzidou, T., & Pomportsis, A. (2010). Fostering collaborative learning in second life: Metaphors and affordances. *Computers & Education*, *55*(2), 603–615. doi:10.1016/j.compedu.2010.02.021

Anthamatten, P., & Ziegler, S. S. (2006). Teaching geography with 3-D visualization technology. *The Journal of Geography*, *105*(6), 231–237. doi:10.1080/00221340608978692

Arroyo, A., Serradilla, F., & Calvo, O. (2009). Multimodal agents in second life and the new agents of virtual 3D environments. In *Proceedings of the 3rd International Work-Conference on the Interplay Between Natural and Artificial Computation (IWINAC 2009)*, (pp. 506–516). IWINAC.

Bailenson, J. N., Yee, N., Blascovich, J., Beall, A. C., Lundblad, N., & Jin, M. (2008). The use of immersive virtual reality in the learning sciences: Digital transformations of teachers, students, and social context. *Journal of the Learning Sciences*, *17*(1), 102–141. doi:10.1080/10508400701793141

Bailly, G., & Raidt, F. E. (2010). Gaze, conversational agents and face-to-face communication. *Speech Communication*, *52*(6), 598–612. doi:10.1016/j.specom.2010.02.015

Bakas, C., & Mikropoulos, T. (2003). Design of virtual environments for the comprehension of planetary phenomena based on students' ideas. *International Journal of Science Education*, *25*(8), 949–967. doi:10.1080/09500690305027

Barab, S., Sadler, T., Heiselt, C., Hickey, D., & Zuiker, S. (2007). Relating narrative, inquiry, and inscriptions: Supporting consequential play. *Journal of Science Education and Technology*, *16*(1), 59–82. doi:10.1007/s10956-006-9033-3

Benotti, L., Estrella, P., & Areces, C. (2010). Dialogue systems for virtual worlds. In *Proceedings of NAACLT HLT 2010 Young Investigators Workshop on Computational Approaches to Languages of the Americas*, (pp. 132-140). NAACLT.

Beskow, J., Edlund, J., Granström, B., Gustafson, J., Skantze, G., & Tobiasson, H. (2009). The MonAMI reminder: A spoken dialogue system for face-to-face interaction. In *Proceedings of Interspeech* (pp. 296–299). Interspeech.

Beveridge, M., & Fox, J. (2006). Automatic generation of spoken dialogue from medical plans and ontologies. *Biomedical Informatics*, *39*(5), 482–499. doi:10.1016/j.jbi.2005.12.008

Callejas, Z., & López-Cózar, R. (2005). Implementing modular dialogue systems: A case study. In *Proceedings of Applied Spoken Language Interaction in Distributed Environments (ASIDE 2005)*. Aalborg, Denmark: ASIDE.

Callejas, Z., & López-Cózar, R. (2008). Relations between de-facto criteria in the evaluation of a spoken dialogue system. *Speech Communication*, *50*(8-9), 646–665. doi:10.1016/j.specom.2008.04.004

Cassell, J., Bickmore, T., Billinghurst, M., Campbell, L., Chang, K., Vilhálmsson, H., & Yan, H. (1999). Embodiment in conversational interfaces: Rea. In *Proceedings of Computer-Human Interaction* (pp. 520–527). ACM Press.

Cavazza, M., de la Cámara, R. S., & Turunen, M. (2010). How was your day? A companion ECA. In *Proceedings of AAMAS 2010 Conference*, (pp. 1629–1630). AAMAS.

Chi, M., De Leeuw, N., Chiu, M., & Lavancher, C. (1994). Eliciting self-explanations improves understanding. *Cognitive Science*, *18*, 439–477.

Cole, R., & Zue, V. (1997). *Survey of the state of the art in human language technology*. Cambridge, UK: Cambridge University Press.

Ducheneaut, N., Wen, M. H., Yee, N., & Wadley, G. (2009). Body and mind: A study of avatar personalization in three virtual worlds. In *Proceedings of the 27th International Conference on Human Factors in Computing System (CHI 2009)*, (pp. 1151-1160). Boston, MA: ACM Press.

Ellison, K., & Matthews, C. (2010). Virtual history: A socially networked pedagogy of enlightenment. *Educational Research, 52*(3), 297–307. doi:10.1080/00131881.2010.504065

Engwall, O., Wik, P., Beskow, J., & Gransröm, G. (2004). Design strategies for a virtual language tutor. In *Proceedings of ICSLP*, (pp. 1693-1696). ICSLP.

Evens, M., Brandle, S., Chang, R., Freedman, R., Glass, M., & Lee, Y. … Rovick, A. A. (2001). Circsimtutor: An intelligent tutoring system using natural language dialogue. In *Proceedings of Midwest AI and Cognitive Science Conference*. IEEE.

Forbes-Riley, K., & Litman, D. (2011). Designing and evaluating a wizarded uncertainty-adaptive spoken dialogue tutoring system. *Computer Speech & Language, 25*(1), 105–126. doi:10.1016/j.csl.2009.12.002

Fryer, L., & Carpenter, R. (2006). Bots as language learning tools. *Language Learning & Technology, 10*(3), 8–14.

Gibbon, D., Mertins, I., & Moore, R. (2000). *Handbook of multimodal and spoken dialogue systems: Resources, terminology and product evaluation*. Dordrecht, The Netherlands: Kluwer Academic Publishers. doi:10.1007/978-1-4615-4501-9

Girvan, C., & Savage, T. (2010). Identifying an appropriate pedagogy for virtual worlds: A communal constructivism case study. *Computers & Education, 55*(1), 342–349. doi:10.1016/j.compedu.2010.01.020

Graesser, A. C., VanLehn, K., Rose, C., Jordan, P., & Harter, D. (2001). Intelligent tutoring systems with conversational dialogue. *AI Magazine, 22*, 39–51.

Griol, D., Hurtado, L., Segarra, E., & Sanchis, E. (2008). A statistical approach to spoken dialog systems design and evaluation. *Speech Communication, 50*(8–9), 666–682. doi:10.1016/j.specom.2008.04.001

Griol, D., Rojo, E., Callejas, Z., & López-Cózar, R. (2010). Development of an academic assistant in second life. In *Proceedings of 10th Spanish Symposium on Information and Communication Technologies for Education*, (pp. 81-84). IEEE.

Hausmann, R., & Chi, M. (2002). Can a computer interface support self-explanation? *International Journal of Cognitive Technology, 7*(1).

Helal, A., Moore, S. E., & Ramachandran, B. (2001). Drishti: An integrated navigation system for visually impaired and disables. In *Proceedings of 5th International Conference on Wearable Computers*, (pp. 149-156). IEEE.

Hofs, D., Theune, M., & Op den Akker, R. (2010). Natural interaction with a virtual guide in a virtual environment. *Journal on Multimodal User Interfaces, 3*, 141–153. doi:10.1007/s12193-009-0024-6

Huang, C., Xu, P., & Zhang, X. Zhao, S., Huang, T., & Xu, B. (1999). LODESTAR: A Mandarin spoken dialogue system for travel information retrieval. In *Proceedings of Eurospeech*, (pp. 1159-1162). Eurospeech.

Ibrahim, A., & Johansson, P. (2002). Multimodal dialogue systems for interactive TV applications. In *Proceedings of 4th IEEE International Conference on Multimodal Interfaces*, (pp. 117-122). IEEE Press.

Jarmon, L., Traphagan, T., Mayrath, M., & Trivedi, A. (2009). Virtual world teaching, experiential learning, and assessment: An interdisciplinary communication course in Second Life. *Computers & Education, 53*(1), 169–182. doi:10.1016/j.compedu.2009.01.010

Johnson, W. L., & Valente, A. (2008). Tactical language and culture training systems: Using artificial intelligence to teach foreign languages and cultures. In *Proceedings of IAAI*, (pp. 1632-1639). IAAI.

Kanematsu, H., Fukumura, Y., Barry, D. M., Sohn, S. Y., & Taguchi, R. (2010). Multilingual discussion in metaverse among students from the USA, Korea, and Japan. *Lecture Notes in Computer Science, 6279*, 200–209. doi:10.1007/978-3-642-15384-6_22

Kerly, A., Ellis, R., & Bull, S. (2008). Conversational agents in e-learning. [AI.]. *Proceedings of AI, 2008*, 169–182.

Lee, E. A.-L., Wong, K. W., & Fung, C. C. (2010). How does desktop virtual reality enhance learning outcomes? A structural equation modeling approach. *Computers & Education, 55*(4), 1424–1442. doi:10.1016/j.compedu.2010.06.006

Limniou, M., Roberts, D., & Papadopoulos, N. (2008). Full immersive virtual environment CAVETM in chemistry education. *Computers & Education, 51*(2), 584–593. doi:10.1016/j.compedu.2007.06.014

Litman, D., & Silliman, S. (2004). ITSPOKE: An intelligent tutoring spoken dialogue system. In *Proceedings of the Human Language Technology Conference of the North American Chapter of the Association for Computational Linguistics (HLT/NAACL)*. NAACL.

López-Cózar, R., & Araki, M. (2005). *Spoken, multilingual and multimodal dialogue systems: Development and assessment*. Hoboken, NJ: Wiley.

Lucia, A. D., Francese, R., Passero, I., & Tortora, G. (2009). Development and evaluation of a virtual campus on second life: The case of secondmi. *Computers & Education, 52*(1), 220–233. doi:10.1016/j.compedu.2008.08.001

Mairesse, F., Gasic, M., Jurcicek, F., Keizer, S., Thomson, B., Yu, K., & Young, S. (2009). Spoken language understanding from unaligned data using discriminative classification models. In *Proceedings of ICASSP*, (pp. 4749-4752). ICASSP.

Maragoudakis, M. (2007). MeteoBayes: Effective plan recognition in a weather dialogue system. *IEEE Intelligent Systems, 22*(1), 66–77. doi:10.1109/MIS.2007.14

Martins, F., Parda, J. P., Franqueira, L., Arez, P., & Mamede, N. J. (2008). Starting to cook a tutoring dialogue system. In *Proceedings of Spoken Language Technology Workshop*, (pp. 145-148). NAACL.

McTear, M. F. (2004). *Spoken dialogue technology: Toward the conversational user interface*. Berlin, Germany: Springer.

Mikropoulos, T. A., & Natsis, A. (2011). Educational virtual environments: A ten-year review of empirical research (1999-2009). *Computers & Education, 56*(3), 769–780. doi:10.1016/j.compedu.2010.10.020

Nielsen. (2009). *Global faces and networked places: A Nielsen report on social networking's new global footprint*. Nielsen.

Paek, T., & Horvitz, E. (2004). Optimizing automated call routing by integrating spoken dialogue models with queuing models. In *Proceedings of HLT-NAACL*, (pp. 41-48). NAACL.

Park, H. (2010). The effect of activities in virtual worlds as a communication environment to understand each other. *Journal of Cyber Therapy and Rehabilitation, 3*(1), 71–82.

Perry, S. J., & Bulatov, I. (2010). The influence of new tools in virtual learning environments on the teaching and learning process in chemical engineering. *Chemical Engineering Transactions, 21*, 1051–1056.

Petrakou, A. (2010). Interacting through avatars: Virtual worlds as a context for online education. *Computers & Education, 54*(4), 1020–1027. doi:10.1016/j.compedu.2009.10.007

Pon-Barry, H., Schultz, K., Bratt, E. O., Clark, B., & Peters, S. (2006). Responding to student uncertainty in spoken tutorial dialogue systems. *International Journal of Artificial Intelligence in Education*, *16*, 171–194.

Rabiner, L. R., & Juang, B. H. (1993). *Fundamentals of speech recognition*. Upper Saddle River, NJ: Prentice-Hall.

Raux, A., Langner, B., Blac, A. W., & Eskenazi, M. (2003). Let's go: Improving spoken dialog systems for the elderly and non-natives. In *Proceedings of Interspeech* (pp. 753–756). Interspeech.

Roussou, M., Oliver, M., & Slater, M. (2006). The virtual playground: an educational virtual reality environment for evaluating interactivity and conceptual learning. *Virtual Reality (Waltham Cross)*, *10*, 227–240. doi:10.1007/s10055-006-0035-5

Seneff, S. (2002). Response planning and generation in the mercury flight reservation system. *Computer Speech & Language*, *16*(3-4), 283–312. doi:10.1016/S0885-2308(02)00011-6

Stent, A., Dowding, J., Gawron, J. M., Bratt, E., & Moore, R. (1999). The CommandTalk spoken dialogue system. In *Proceedings of 37th Annual Meeting of the ACL*, (pp. 183-190). ACL.

Strothotte, T., Fritz, S., Michel, R., Raab, A., Petrie, H., & Johnson, V. (1996). Development of dialogue systems for a mobility aid for blind people: Initial design and usability testing. In *Proceedings of 2nd Annual ACM Conference on Assistive Technologies*, (pp. 139-144). ACM Press.

Traum, D., & Larsson, S. (2003). *Current and new directions in discourse and dialogue: The information state approach to dialogue management*. Dordrecht, The Netherlands: Kluwer Academic Publishers.

Utama, R. J., Syrdal, A. K., & Conkie, A. (2006). Six approaches to limited domain concatenative speech synthesis. In *Proceedings of Interspeech* (pp. 2058–2061). Interspeech.

Vaquero, C., Saz, O., Lleida, E., Marcos, J., & Canalís, C. (2012). Vocaliza: An application for computer-aided speech therapy in Spanish language. In *Proceedings of IV Jornadas en Tecnología del Habla*, (pp. 321–326). Academic Press.

Wang, Y., Wang, W., & Huang, C. (2007). Enhanced semantic question answering system for e-learning environment. In *Proceedings of AINAW 2007 Conference*, (pp. 1023–1028). AINAW.

Winn, W., Stahr, F., Sarason, C., Fruland, R., Oppenheimer, P., & Lee, Y.-L. (2006). Learning oceanography from a computer simulation compared with direct experience at sea. *Journal of Research in Science Teaching*, *43*(1), 25–42. doi:10.1002/tea.20097

Wrzesien, M., & Raya, M. A. (2010). Learning in serious virtual worlds: Evaluation of learning effectiveness and appeal to students in the e-junior project. *Computers & Education*, *55*(1), 178–187. doi:10.1016/j.compedu.2010.01.003

Yee, N., & Bailenson, J. (2009). The difference between being and seeing: The relative contribution of self-perception and priming to behavioral changes via digital self-representation. *Media Psychology*, *12*(2), 195–209. doi:10.1080/15213260902849943

ADDITIONAL READING

Annetta, L. A., Folta, E., & Klesath, M. (2010). *V-learning: Distance education in the 21st century through 3D virtual learning environments*. Berlin, Germany: Springer.

Molka-Danielsen, J. (2009). *Learning and teaching in the virtual world of Second Life*. Trondheim, Norway: Tapir Academic Press.

Peachey, A., Gillen, J., Livingstone, D., & Smith-Robbins, S. (Eds.). (2010). *Researching learning in virtual worlds*. Berlin, Germany: Springer. doi:10.1007/978-1-84996-047-2

Savin-Baden, M. (2010). *A practical guide to using Second Life in higher education*. London, UK: Open University Press.

Wankel, C., & Kingsley, J. (2009). *Higher education in virtual worlds: Teaching and learning in Second Life*. Dublin, Ireland: Emeral Group Publishing Limited.

KEY TERMS AND DEFINITIONS

Immersive Virtual World/Environment: A virtual world/environment that surrounds the user and during the interaction is perceived more intensively than the real one. Usually immersive virtual worlds require to use special hardware to reproduce the movements and position of the users in the virtual world (e.g. virtual reality helmet), or to physically envelop the user such in the case of virtual reality CAVEs.

Manipulability: We refer as manipulability the ability to interact with the system from a first-hand perspective, being able to modify, control or alter the elements of the virtual world and receive an appropriate response.

Metaverse: Our collective online-shared space, created by the convergence of virtually enhanced physical reality and physically persistent virtual space, including the sum of all virtual worlds, augmented reality, and the Internet.

OpenSimulator: Open source multi-platform, multi-user 3D simulator that uses the same standard as Second Life to communicate with their users, and emulates virtual environments independently from the world of Second Life, using its own infrastructure.

Second Life: Second Life (SL) is a three dimensional virtual world developed by Linden Lab in 2003 and accessible via the Internet.

Sloodle: Simulation Linked Object Oriented Dynamic Learning Environment. Open source project which integrates Second Life with the Moodle (Modular Object-Oriented Dynamic Learning Environment) learning-management system.

Virtual World/Environment: Synthetic environment which resembles real world or can be perceived as a real world by their users.

ENDNOTES

1. http://opensimulator.org/wiki/Main_Page
2. http://www.osgrid.org
3. http://openlifegrid.com/
4. http://www.wonderlandblog.com
5. http://www.opencroquet.org/index.php/Main_Page
6. http://www.opencobalt.org/
7. http://site.3rdrockgrid.com
8. http://www.newworldgrid.com/lang/en-us
9. http://www.association-virtus.org
10. http://www.talentraspel.com/grid_open_neuland.html
11. http://www.talentraspel.com/grid_wilder_westen.html
12. http://virtyou.com/en/
13. http://www.youralternativelife.com/
14. http://www.hypergridbusiness.com
15. http://www.pitt.edu/~rimac/
16. http://www.w3.org/TR/voicexml21

Chapter 14
Immersive Virtual Worlds for (E-) Learning:
Towards an Interdisciplinary Research Agenda

Matthias Rehm
Aalborg University, Denmark

Ulla Konnerup
Aalborg University, Denmark

ABSTRACT

Virtual worlds are becoming more popular and important for the information society, allowing people to meet "face-to-face" and at the same time be distributed across different places. This offers numerous possibilities of revolutionizing the way learning is realized over long distances and at a given location. However, current uses of environments like Second Life make it very clear that there is a lack of interaction, and the learning concepts that are tailored to these kinds of collaborative environments result more or less in the replication of "always the same," but this time in a virtual world. An example is a typical lecture that is now available as an in-world podcast. This chapter examines current state-of-the-art approaches of learning in and with virtual worlds in relation to the features of such environments and then proposes a research agenda tailored to making the learning experience truly interactive, collaborative, multi modal, and situation- and context-aware.

INTRODUCTION

With the advent of Second Life, there has been an increased interest in utilizing virtual worlds for learning objectives. In addition, there are good reasons for this endeavor as such environments offer "face-to-face" communication and at the same time allow the participants to be spatially distributed. However, looking at learning experiences in such virtual worlds reveals that there is a lack of learning concepts that make use of the distinguishing features of virtual worlds and ex-

DOI: 10.4018/978-1-4666-2670-6.ch014

ploit the chances offered by these environments. The first part of this chapter examines what virtual worlds have to offer for learning purposes and analyzes the features of virtual worlds that add value to the learning experience and the learning outcome. The second part then ambitiously aims at establishing an interdisciplinary research agenda by focusing on three aspects that could make a difference for learning purposes: (1) the integration of autonomous agents as tutors and peers, (2) the seamless integration of users with special needs, and (3) the integration of real and virtual worlds.

VIRTUAL COMMUNITIES OF PRACTICE: A SOCIO-CONSTRUCTIVISTIC VIEW ON LEARNING

Two main development strands can currently be distinguished when reviewing work on learning in virtual worlds. The first one is centered on the virtual world itself. In such approaches, learning is targeted at mastering the art of controlling the virtual world itself, creating objects, and scripting simple actions. The second concept is to transfer real life teaching events into virtual world events, e.g. by providing lectures on demand or giving online lectures or seminars, which is nothing more than an elaborate video conference; often not based on didactic arguments, but with an aim to save time and cost. There are very few concepts that truly embrace the possibilities virtual worlds can offer. The TECH museum[1] is such an example, where the traditional concept of a museum has been enriched with the ideas of collaborative and social interactions, allowing the layman to participate in the curatory process and propose as well as develop exhibits, which interactively demonstrate technical principles.

Our approach to learning in immersive virtual worlds is based on socio-constructivistic conceptions that learning and knowledge are culturally and historically interdependent. We are strongly influenced by Lave and Wenger's ideas about learning as participation in social context (Lave & Wenger, 1991; Wenger, 2000). They describe learning as situated in communities of practice, where learning extends beyond the pedagogical structuring context and involving the social world. According to Lave and Wenger (1991), social interaction is the critical feature for this function and they describe learning as a process where the learner becomes involved in a community of practice, representing beliefs and behaviors, the learner has to acquire. Situated learning theory descended from Vygotsky's social development theory (1978), where he claims that social interaction plays a fundamental role in the development of cognition.

Besides considering learning as a means of developing practice, learning can also be viewed as a means of development and change of identities (Wenger, 2000). It has important implications for learning, identity, and self esteem to be part of a community, both with peers and with family and friends. One of the characteristics of a community of practice is mutual engagement and participation (Wenger, 2000). A focal point of a community is a common goal. Each participant comes with his own repertoire and his own history to be distributed. In a virtual community of practice, people have the opportunity to share experiences, meanings, and repertoire, and thus create a common culture.

Through avatar mediation, immersive virtual worlds open up for bodily immersion and interaction, affording users the semantics of place, including deixis, indexical language, and body orientation. Compared to many other technologies, the characteristics of multi-user virtual environments are the presence of avatars, a shared space, and shared activities. Avatars can communicate via text, voice, or symbols. The multimodality conveys not just language symbols, but also information about the interlocutors themselves. Schroeder (2002) noted that in the context of virtual environments, media richness is often called 'co-presence' and that the feeling of "being there" make users feel they are together in the same (virtual) space. With a focus on the community as the agent of situated learning the users will be enrolled in what Dourish (2001) define as embodied interaction: "Embodied interaction is the creation, manipulation, and sharing of meaning through engaged interaction with artefacts" (p. 126).

The features of environments like Second Life establish such immersive virtual worlds as ideal candidates for realizing innovative learning experiences. We already stressed the importance of embodiment and its feeling of presence that has been shown to create positive effects for the learning task (Lane, et al., 2010). By allowing a large number of users to be part of the environment at the same time, the potential of collaborative learning is stressed. We will show below that this also opens up new concepts of peer-based learning making use of intelligent agent technologies.

Apart from these social features of immersive virtual worlds, a number of technical features allow for innovative interaction and learning concepts. As each user generally connects to the virtual world with her own device, it becomes possible to realize a distinction between public interactions and views of the world and private ones with the chance of tailoring information in a user-centered manner and making it available to a select group of users. Moreover, by integrating contextual information like location or time (both virtual and real), information can also be tailored to the given context and situation of the user. Additionally, the integration of arbitrary computational models is possible, for instance a weather simulation where parameters can be manipulated by the user to get a grasp on the mechanics behind such phenomena and resulting in different weather conditions in the virtual world to showcase the effects of these parameters.

To sum up, immersive virtual world offer the features of embodiment, presence, collaboration,

user-centeredness, context-awareness, cross-real interactions, and simulations to enhance the learning experience.

One problem for really convincing learning concepts is the distribution of the necessary knowledge over various disciplines. Apart from the technical expertise, for instance to develop interactive presentations or to integrate non-standard interface devices, knowledge about learning concepts, about motivational aspects and collaboration, about creating curricula, and suitable content, and even about brain functions and plasticity have to be put together, making the development of learning concepts for virtual worlds a truly interdisciplinary endeavor.

AN INTERDISCIPLINARY RESEARCH AGENDA

In this section, we argue that learning in virtual worlds can be truly interactive, collaborative, multimodal, and situation- and context-aware. As mentioned before, technical requirements have to be met by pedagogical requirements, taking up concepts from intelligent tutoring systems and ambient intelligence. To this end, we define three main research areas, which are motivated with three sample scenarios and will be discussed in relation to existing concepts and research challenges that will have to be tackled.

Integrating Autonomous Virtual Agents

Imagine two Danish pensioners planning to stay in the south of France for the winter. On the purpose of freshen up their French they enter a language learning area of Second Life. As has convincingly been shown, collaborative learning can enhance motivation and learning success. In order to realize this learning concept and at the same time ensure the quality of the learning outcome, the real users are supported in their endeavor by virtual intelligent peers. Language learning in virtual worlds can be extended to nonverbal behavior as well, allowing the learner, for instance, to practice typical gestural behavior or proxemics in an experience-based way. This scenario draws on work on intelligent tutoring systems and enhances this notion significantly with the introduction of virtual intelligent peers that serve as co-learners and at the same time are able to monitor and steer the learning process if necessary. By the introduction of this concept it exemplifies the feature of collaborative learning. Contextual factors can be regarded by tailoring the behavior, knowledge and learning concept to the target user, for instance children, high school students, elderly and digital immigrants. Additionally, it emphasizes the need of integrating non-standard input components for multi modal interaction, for instance, for gesture and speech recognition.

General Introduction to Virtual Agents

A number of different notions exist to describe embodied interaction partners in interactive systems like games or virtual worlds ranging from virtual and/or autonomous agents or characters to the more specific notion of embodied conversational agents. Central aspect of such agent systems is the use of multiple input and output channels in order to realize a communicative experience for the user that resembles as far as possible his natural communicative behavior. Most of the time, these agents also follow their own agenda, i.e. they have their own task and goals and thus represent autonomous and dynamic interaction partners for the user. The agent's body presents a rich repertoire of output channels allowing making use of facial expressions (e.g. for affective feedback), gestures (e.g. pointing out relevant objects), speech (e.g. for verbal content), or body posture (e.g. for affective feedback). In contrast to standard game characters, animations are not pre-rendered and

then just re-played, but the nonverbal behavior of the agents is dynamically planned and realized at runtime making it possible to react adequately to the user interaction.

In the area of learning, we can broadly distinguish between four agent categories that play distinct roles in learning environments: (1) tutor agents, (2) teachable agents, (3) role-play agents, and (4) peer agents. In addition, all these types of agents can be learning themselves, i.e. can be adaptive to the context or the user. In the following, we shortly introduce the first three types by reviewing some representative systems before we delve into a detailed analysis of the concept of peer agents. Afterwards, we formulate the research challenges of integrating autonomous agents into virtual world learning environments.

Tutor Agents

The standard version of agent usage in learning scenarios is to employ the agent in the role of an intelligent tutor, which is able to instruct the user, give feedback on the user's performance, and motivate them in the learning process.

Bertrand et al. (2010) present a recent version of such a system that is used to train hand hygiene procedures for health care workers. The tutor agent poses as the expert in the domain and explains the procedures in an introductory presentation. Then the trainees are presented with different scenarios where they have to rate if the depicted agents follow the procedures or not. Afterwards they get feedback by the tutor agent on their assessment of the different situations. This is the classic version of a tutor agent, focusing on providing information, and then evaluating the user in exercises.

D'Mello et al. (2010) model a dialogical computer tutor based on an analysis of sessions with expert tutors. Those sessions showed that experts do not only present the material in a lecturing style but rather create an interactive session by triggering questions and feedback from the learner. An evaluation of their system shows that such an interactive style in a tutor agent is beneficial compared with a simple presentation of the material.

A different aspect is investigated by Kumar et al. (2010), who examine the dialogue strategies of tutor agents and show that when moving from dyadic to multiparty interactions taking into account socio-emotional factors of the relations between interlocutors becomes increasingly important. This aspect of social group dynamics is highlighted below in the discussion of virtual peers.

Teachable Agents

The second variety of agents reverses the roles and puts the user in the position of the teacher. The general idea of this learning by teaching approach is that the learner is forced to make his mental models of the subject area explicit and represent them in a way that they can be used by the agent system as a knowledge base. By applying the agent then to a given problem, the learner gets feedback about flaws in his representation of the domain.

A classic approach in this respect is the work on Betty's Brain (e.g. Biswas, et al., 2005), which embraces a visual approach of representing the learners domain knowledge. The learner creates a conceptual structure of this knowledge by defining nodes and relations between them. This structure is then used as the knowledge representation of the agent, who can now employ qualitative reasoning mechanism on the representation. To test their grasp of the domain knowledge, the learners can then query the agent about the conceptual map and thus get feedback on its correctness.

Mehlmann et al. (2010) present an approach where the learner expresses his domain knowledge in a similar manner in the form of ontologies, which can be used for qualitative reasoning about this knowledge. The advantage is that this ontological representation can be used directly as a representation format for the teachable agents. What distinguishes their work from the classic

approach is the use of multiple interacting agents that communicate about this model and thus deliver feedback to the user by using his domain model as a reference point and without the user having to actively engage in a dialogue about his knowledge. They can e.g. engage in a quiz with a moderator agent. Their answers are then derived from the representation and thus deliver feedback to the user about the correctness of his conceptual domain model.

Role Play Agents

Agents also offer possibilities for experience-based learning encounters by realizing interactive role-plays. Isbister (2004) argues that virtual agents are the ideal cast for these types of learning approaches because of the following features. Agents have the advantage of not getting tired by repetitive exercises and of being able of replicating specific behaviors without deviation if necessary (repeatability). Although agents allow experiencing nonverbal behavior, there is no danger of social embarrassment when the user tries out different interactions, which might fail (emotional distance). Agents can also easily exaggerate specific behaviors, even in a way that would not be possible for humans, to clarify a certain aspect of this behavior (intensity). One and the same agent can be used to exemplify and contrast different behaviors making it easy to compare different settings (generalization). In addition, of course the agent enables personal feedback if the learner's behavior has been tracked (dynamic and personal feedback).

Zoll et al. (2006) give an overview of the Fear-Not system, which is employed in primary schools to educate children about strategies against bullying. To this end, a multi agent approach is realized, where different agents are assigned different roles like the bully, the victim or the helper. The user is assigned the role of a consultant of the victim and gives advice on how to behave the next time the victim encounters the bully. Thus, the user can try out different strategies like "hit back" or "talk to a friend" in a safe way. Sapouna et al. (2010) present details of a longitudinal evaluation study with the system that shows that role-plays with empathic characters can be employed successfully for learning.

Johnson and Valente (2008) present the tactical language training system, which is used to train the language skills of soldiers for ex-patriate missions. The system utilizes role-plays with virtual agents that do not only allow training the language skills but at the same time employing these skills in the context of the pending mission.

Peer Agents

The above-mentioned types of agents have become widely applicable in learning environments although they have not yet been standardized in a way to make them available for open virtual worlds. Those environments feature interactions in form of avatars, which makes it possible for autonomous agents to be not noticed as such and thus open up the chance of a new variety of agent systems that come in the shape of virtual peers, which collaborate with the user in the learning endeavor.

The key idea is the simulation of a community of learners, with the user in the role of one of the learners, establishing relations and interacting with the agents to collaboratively solve a given task. Collaborating in learning situations has been shown to be superior compared to individual study approaches, for instance according to Johnson, Johnson, and Skon (1979), students performed better in post-tests and according to Wood et al. (1995) they acquired more knowledge facts when studying together with others. John-Steiner (1996) argues that social interaction during the learning process is a key ingredient for the cognitive development of the learner. McInerney and Van Etten (2000) additionally collect evidence for a positive impact on the motivation of the learner. Based on such findings, Marsella, Johnson, and

LaBore (2003) suggest that computer-based learning should (and could) be designed to afford such social contexts. The theoretical basis for this approach is situated learning theory, which poses that learning is a function of the activity, context, and culture it takes place in. Whereas there is abundant research on the role of agents as tutors in intelligent learning environments, the idea of considering agents as "peers" or "classmates" of the learner has only recently been taken up as a research challenge. Agents do not have to learn themselves in this case. Although they are "peers" or "classmates" of the user, they otherwise have some of the knowledge that is needed to solve the task. Thus, they can be seen as a model of distributed knowledge representation meaning that different agents can contribute differently to the solution of the task. Sklar and Davies (2005) describe a first approach where they model a whole classroom in a multiagent system including the roles of teacher and pupil in order to simulate the human learning process. In their approach, they acknowledge that learning is a social task, but fail to integrate this aspect in their model apart from a superficial emotional model. Moreover, they are interested in the general mechanics of intelligent learning systems, stressing an approach that relies on a central control component for structuring the learning process. Despite these shortcomings, Sklar and Davies present a useful analysis of the general components of an intelligent learning system: representation of domain knowledge, model of student knowledge, teacher behavior model, student behavior model, and assessment metrics.

Is it reasonable to expect an effect from interactions with such a virtual "peer" or "classmate"? Kim et al. (2006) give a positive answer to this question. They examined if and in what way such a peer advances a learner's positive affect and motivation to learn beyond his current level. Dimensions they examined include competence (high vs. low, positive effect [higher self-efficacy]), interaction initiation (proactive vs. responsive, no effect), multimodal (facial expression, voice, background color), emotion expression (positive, negative, neutral, no direct effect, tendency for higher interest when positive emotions present), gender (male vs. female, higher interest in task when working with male character), empathic reaction (to user's affective state given by one of six emoticons) (yes vs. no, significant effect for self-efficacy with yes-condition). Thus, they showed that the use of a virtual peer indeed contributed to students' self-efficacy and interest in solving the task. The dimension competence can be interpreted as a distinction between a tutor and a peer condition clearly giving evidence that modeling a virtual peer has positive effects for the task. Their use of emotions is completely out of context and does not make sense in the way they present it. Thus, the absence of an effect is not surprising. Instead of scripting the behavior, the agent needs to react emotionally to the performance of the user, i.e. taking the context into account. In the empathic reaction condition this was remedied a little bit by taking the user's self-report about his emotional state into account. Even with this crude form of contextual information, the effect of an affective reaction of the agent becomes apparent. A similar study was presented by Ju et al. (2005), who examined the effect of co-learning agents on learners behavior focusing on the two dimensions performance (high vs. low) and support (supporting vs. competitive). Learners performed significantly better with high performance agent and with supporting agents. The co-learner's performance provides a benchmark of how well a learner should do. Combining the results from both studies, we see that there always has to be a trade-off between motivating the learner by increasing his self-efficacy (Kim, et al., 2006, low competence condition) and by encouraging him to try harder (Ju, et al., 2005, high performance condition). Maldonado and colleagues (2005) present similar results focusing on the emotional involvement of the user. In their study, they show that cooperative co-learners facilitate the learning success of the user and additionally have an effect on the perception of the virtual character, which is perceived as more intelligent and credible. They mention explicitly culture and personality as relevant dimensions that might influence the effectiveness of the co-learner paradigm. Wang, Chignell, and Ishizuka (2006) give an account on how the use of more than one agent can serve as a motivational instrument for the learning task. Although their approach still focuses on the teaching role of the agents, it could be shown that the distribution of knowledge and interaction strategies on more than one interaction partner can be beneficial for the learner. They also introduce eye tracking as method for assessing the effect of the agent team by analyzing the user's attention.

All of the above approaches emphasize the importance of learning as a social and emotional activity but fail to address these aspects of the collaborative learning process by relying for instance on rather simplified ideas of emotional interactions. With the Gamble system (e.g. Rehm, 2008), we have shown that users are very responsive to emotional interactions in multiparty settings. In the CUBE-G project (e.g. Rehm, et al., 2009), we additionally showed that users are well aware of dissonant behaviors for instance when the agent's gestural behavior does not match the user's cultural patterns of gestural behavior. In Rehm and Endrass (2009), the focus is on the social emotional aspects of the learning process, modeling the agents as autonomous entities and the learning outcome as an emergent (by-)product of this interaction building up on a behavior toolbox for social group dynamics in multi agent systems.

Recently, some systems have been introduced that embrace the idea of virtual peers as learning companions. Kersey et al. (2010) present the KSC-Pal, which realizes a model of peer learning. They could show that the peer agent allows shifts in learner initiative and is able to activate the learner. Woolf et al. (2010) focus on the use of affective peers and were able to increase the motivation for learning in previously low achieving students.

Research Challenges

Integrating autonomous agents in any of the above-mentioned roles into open virtual worlds poses interesting research challenges on different levels. Here, we are going to highlight the two aspects of collaboration and context.

A pertinent feature of open virtual worlds is the strong focus on collaboration and interactions with often more than one interlocutor. Such multiparty interaction can be described on a social level by processes of group dynamics, which always kick in when more than two people interact. These processes are emergent social patterns based on a number of social parameters like liking or trust taking the social and emotional relationship between interlocutors into account (e.g. Shaw, 1971). So far, only first steps have been taken to incorporate models of social group dynamics into interactive agent systems and most of them focus on the agents themselves (Prada, Ma, & Nunes, 2010; Guye-Vuillème & Thalmann, 2001). Using this work as the starting point, it becomes indispensable to develop mechanisms that take the social and emotional relationship between user(s) and agent(s) into account, encompassing their respective personalities, emotions, goals, and motivations. Thus, such a model of social group dynamics will no longer be restricted to the agents but encompass all interlocutors, artificial and human alike. We have presented a first approach in this direction (Rehm & Endrass, 2009), when we investigated if the model applied to a group of agents can reliably predict the user's impression of the interaction.

Realizing peer agents also creates a need for a new didactic approach to learning in immersive worlds. The general advantages of peer learning have already been discussed above, but with peer agents it becomes possible to (pro-)actively exploit these advantages. This opens up a plethora of unsolved challenges. First and foremost, a sound didactic concept has to be established that leads the implementation of peer agents. This includes defining dramatic roles that should be impersonated by different agents as well as defining successful behavior patterns maybe indexed by (affective) user states and/or contextual cues. So far, agents in learning scenarios like the ones described above were restricted to very precise domains and a limited number of interlocutors. It remains to be shown how these approaches can scale up in open virtual worlds and how the inherent emerging complexity of interactions can be handled, where agents independently plan their next moves.

This brings us again to the notion of context and context-awareness. With the focus on collaboration, peer learning, and emergent aspects of social group dynamics, different types of context come into play. On the one hand, the users (and the other agents) present rich and highly variable contextual information, e.g. in terms of their prior knowledge or their learning characteristics (learning type). The work by Hayashi, Bourdeau, and Mizoguchi (2008) could be used as a starting point. They have shown how this kind of information can be represented by an ontology and then utilized this ontology in an interactive system to tailor a learning unit to a given user. On the other hand, introducing peer agents we create what we could term affective or relational context, which is dependent, e.g. on the interlocutors personality, on the (subjectively perceived) status of the different group members, or on the interpersonal relation to other interlocutors (in terms of liking/disliking, trust, familiarity, etc.). To uncover this type of context, it is indispensable to integrate methods of social signal processing (Vinciarelli, Pantic, & Bourlard, 2009), which means interpreting observable parameters like gestural activity, gaze, and facial expressions in terms of their impact on the social interaction/relation of the interlocutors.

Integrating Users with Special Needs

Imagine a group of persons with aphasia[2] after brain injury. They all suffer from different kinds of communication difficulties and are offered a rehabilitation course in an immersive virtual world. The learning environment is designed as a collaborative, media-rich online community where individuals interact and perform with a wide variety of tasks facilitated and supported by multi modal technologies adapted to their special communicative difficulties and abilities. The rehabilitation course is not only a teacher to student course, but is based on social interaction and communication activities due to the community-centred perspective. This scenario will argue new pedagogical possibilities and methods for participants suffering from aphasia and how the virtual environment supports re-development of language skills, communicative competence, accessibility to, and participation in discussion forays and society. Emphasis is on the avatar-mediated actions and an assumption that the embodiment will affect the brain re-establishing process positively and promote cognitive and communicative functions. Finally, we will reflect on the importance of multimodality and embodied interactions for communicative rehabilitation.

For the last 2 decades ICT facilitated speech therapy has been under discussion among speech therapists. A dominant view on learning within the discipline has put human-human interaction in focus, which some therapists had difficulties to reconcile with the use of technology, as they saw a risk that it would create an additional disturbing element in the communication between people who had communication difficulties (Konnerup & Schmidt, 2006). This has resulted in some resistance to technology. Nevertheless, when it has been used, there has been more focus on the technological options to improve speech and language production than on the communicative, participatory, and opinion-making dimension (Petheram, 2004). Research and practice within the field of computer mediated communicative and cognitive rehabilitation of adults with brain injuries have primarily focused on Web 1.0 (transmission, sending, receiving, and reading) (Wertz, 1992; Magnusson, 2000; Fredens, 2004) and an incipient use of Web 2.0 (Konnerup & Schmidt, 2006). New social media offer great opportunities for this group of participants who potentially are marginalized in the communication and learning society. Research indicates, that interacting and participation in media-rich Web 2.0-based communities of practice strengthen cognition, communication, acting competency, and, in the broader sense, personal and social mastering (Konnerup & Schmidt, 2006).

In the following, we will argue that 3D virtual learning environments offer new opportunities in the rehabilitation of people suffering from aphasia in relation to rehabilitation of language, social relations and in relation to people restoring themselves and their identity after a brain injury.

Importance of Language for Cognition and Thinking

Language is perceived functionalistic as a means of contact, communication, learning, and recognition, and can be characterized as a bringing-into-speech of a person and thus a part of identity and learning. To understand the constraints and opportunities affecting learning after a brain injury we will describe the significance of language in cognition and thinking and how we can incorporate the latest brain research to think in new virtual rehabilitation possibilities.

Language has many manifestations and expresses itself as spoken language, written language, body language, and imagery. Language is not a goal in itself, but a means of contact, communication, and learning. In order to define the concept of language, it is necessary to include both the linguistic and the psychological dimension. This makes it possible to describe language both as a linguistic structure and as an act with specific purposes from the use by people who act and perceive in certain situations (Nicolaisen & Vejleskov, 1996, p. 12). Linguistic processes are extremely complex and involve several areas of the brain at once. One can roughly distinguish between expressive and impressive speech activity. Expressive speech is brought to execution by means of inner speech, recoded based on an intention in verbal form into speech and expression and thus becoming narrative speech. Impressive speech, language comprehension, is contingent on an ability to link a variety of elements, namely: an acoustic perception, the separation of phonics, comprehension of the meaning behind the heard, an ability to keep the word in memory, and finally, the ability to command the elements and the structure of the speech and mould them to a logical scheme (Nicolaisen & Vejleskov, 1996, p. 268). Language can be characterized as an articulation of a person and as a part of our whole identity.

Besides being a means of communication, language plays an important role in cognition. Vygotsky (1971) was concerned with the relationship between language and thinking and considered language as an important role in social interaction. Language is fundamental to perception, memory, and thinking and thus becomes a tool of intellectual activity. It also has a regulatory function of importance for the planning and the control of behaviour (Vygotsky, 1971). The acquisition of language is closely related to experience and act as a game, rehearsal and practice. Language and thinking are inextricably linked; throughout life, it controls our knowledge and experience of the world. The relationship between thought and word is a living process: "The idea is born with the word. A word without thought is a dead thing, and a thought that is not embodied in words, shado" (Vygotsky, 1971). A loss of language has far- reaching consequences for the possibility to communicate, learn and maintain identity and social interactions.

Talking about learning in a rehabilitation process after a brain injury, it is relevant to include cognitive learning in order to gain insight into how each aphasia sufferer can restore strategies for learning. Discussing learning in relation to rehabilitation of language, a cognitive understand-ing of learning focuses on language production, while a social constructivist understanding of learning focuses on language function and social interaction.

Renegotiation of Identity

Identity is created through communication in social communities, and is something that must be maintained and sustained all your life, retold through language with narratives and images. Memory is a cognitive function related to many different areas of the brain, and many people suffering from aphasia will have memory difficulties of any nature. This affects identity. The autobiographical memory is organized as a narrative story (Fredens in: Konnerup & Schmidt, 2006). It can be difficult for people with aphasia and thus with limited communication skills and memory difficulties continuing to tell a story. Shadden and Agan (2003) stress that the greatest loss for individuals with aphasia may be the reduction in the fluidity and flexibility with which communication allows navigation of the complex challenges of life's social actions and interactions.

Identity is created through the practices one engages in, regardless of the degree of participation (Wenger, 2000). Through dialogue and meaningful debate in a virtual environment, both synchronously and asynchronously, where participants can mutually identify with peers, the identity of the practice is shaped. Wenger uses the term legitimate peripheral participation on the process through which newcomers become part of a community of practice (Lave & Wenger, 1991). It includes activities, identities, artefacts, and communities of knowledge and practice. Participation is seen not as something you can "turn on and off," but as something that becomes incorporated into our whole life as a constituent part of our identity (Wenger, 2000). Focus is on the reciprocal relationships between veterans and newcomers in communities of practice, where learning and development purposes as meaningful negotiation between the actors. Newcomers might have a more peripheral participation role, where lack of written and verbal skills might hamper the verbal interactions, but in an immersive virtual world, you are visible through the presence of your avatar. Through shared experiences, a shared repertoire with other participants, creating a common culture, narratives, profiles, creation of avatars, chats and any kind of interactions contribute to strengthen the individual's perception of their own identity and gives visibility to the other participants.

Brain Research

The brain consists of a complex network of nerve cells that are connected by nerves. Recent brain research has shown that, if they are stimulated, nerve cells can proliferate throughout life, damaged nerve cells can form new offshoots on the basis of stem cells and that nerve cells can divide (Bjarkam, 2004; Goldberg, 2005; Fredens, 2004). It has also been shown that some brain cells, called mirror neurons, respond actively to other people's actions in the same way as if they themselves had performed the action, which means that the brain is activated through the notions of actions (Rizzolatti, 2008). If the nervous system is challenged and stimulated and senses and emotions are affected, the plasticity of the brain makes it able to learn throughout life—even after a brain injury. The brain develops by being challenged, and context and feedback play a crucial role for the opportunity to learn (Bjarkam, 2004; Fredens, 2004; Goldberg, 2005; Konnerup & Schmidt, 2006). With the development of new biotechnological registration options, it is now possible to see both brain structures, to study brain activity and to gain an insight into electrical and chemical processes. The understanding of brain processes, damage localization, and the knowledge of which areas of the brain play together is accordingly extended. The functional imaging of the brain shows that language is not related to limited ar-

eas, but is "distributed throughout the neocortex" (Goldberg, 2005). Language can be described as an emergent size, "made possible when the brain's neural circuits have reached a certain degree of complexity" (Goldberg, 2005, p. 106). In Goldberg's understanding, language is not only shaped from specifics of neural organization, but to a high degree by socio-cultural factors (Goldberg, 2005). Today several brain researchers within both the clinical and the biotechnological field have a shared understanding of a dynamic brain. The flexibility of the brain is maintained longer than we thought before. Rehabilitation is not just about restructuring the functional systems, but also about challenges, activities and recreating of oneself. The knowledge about a brain injury, its anatomical localization, and causing disturbance you can achieve through testing and brain scans has to be translated into educational practice. A brain injury, impact, and development must be understood as an interaction between the biological damage and the psychological and social aspects.

Social Interaction and Self-Construction

Like Fredens (2006) and Shadden, Hagstrom, and Koski (2008), we have the assumption that the creation of the self is created in communication with others through narratives and life stories. Thus, based on these fundamental considerations on the relationship between language, mental activity, and self-creation it must be assumed that getting aphasia will affect the sufferers self-understanding and have implications for identity and perhaps lead to psychological problems. Language difficulties make it hard to communicate with the surroundings, limit the opportunity to test ideas, tell one's life story, and consequently weaken the ability to express opinion and hamper the ability to continuously create the self. Persons with language difficulties are likely to experience a change in the way other people relate and react to them; one is seen as someone with a different identity (Vestberg, 2002). Social relationships can be difficult to maintain because communication is difficult and it becomes difficult to interact. Thus, the greatest loss for people suffering from aphasia may be the reduction in the fluidity and flexibility with which communication allows navigation of the complex challenges of life's social actions and interactions (Shadden & Agan, 2004). People with aphasia may experience not to be themselves any more (Shadden, Hagstrom, & Koski, 2008).

Loss of communication competences has crucial implications for social life and identity, thinking, cognition, and learning. If it is not possible to find alternatives and compensation strategies for participation and meaningful debate, it is likely that the intellectual level will gradually decrease. "It is often said that a person's language is at the level of his intelligence. It is probably largely correct. But the opposite also applies: Your intelligence is on par with your language" (Goldberg, 2005, p. 109). This tells us about how intrusive a language disorder might be for a person's ability to evolve and continue to be oneself.

Rehabilitation in 3D Immersive Virtual Worlds: Embodied Learning and Community-Based Actions

We have previously stressed that we have a socio-cultural view on learning. Related to the target group, individuals suffering from aphasia, our hypothesis is that rehabilitation in a community-based immersive virtual worlds could offer an environment for participation, storytelling, and re-creation of the self.

Virtual worlds exhibit a unique set of characteristics from a socio-cultural learning point of view. As early as in 1994, Hedberg and Alexander pointed out that a very important feature in virtual worlds is the "transparent interface with which the user directly controls the objects in the context of the virtual world" (p. 215). Hedberg and Alexander mention three aspects of virtual worlds

that contribute to this transparency and through which such environments have "the potential to offer a superior learning experience" (p. 218): increased 'immersion,' increased 'fidelity,' and a higher level of 'active learner participation.'

Related to the target group, these aspects are of particular interest since many have an injured neural pathway in the brain and as a result physical and cognitive-communicative difficulties. Based on an assumption that the involvement of body and nonverbal activities will affect the brain, we expect as a result a process of re-establishing and positively promoting cognitive and communicative functions. Immersive virtual worlds provide the opportunity for using multiple sensory stimuli, and for the promotion and development of the nerves in the brain. Moreover, experiences and actions on a conceptual level might stimulate nerves as well.

Our hypothesis is that participation and interaction in immersive virtual worlds develop, socialize, and train cognition, action, and communication skills of people with brain injuries. We also claim that such worlds offer special opportunities to facilitate learning and (re)develop communicative competence in an active interaction with the media, other participants, and professionals and thus develop skills and strategies that enable them to re-create their self and maintain themselves as knowing and informed human beings. Such an environment, which offer possibilities for interactions among multiple agents and multimodal perceptions and communication, opens up a new kind of aphasia-pedagogy

Research Challenges

The socio-cultural approach to learning implies that learning in new learning environments like 3D virtual worlds always will lead to a change of practice at various levels such as changes of the available tools and the methods existing within a given context. The virtual learning environment may also result in a change of the conceptual perceptions and in that relation lead to a transformation and alteration of context and the pedagogical plans. In that aspect, virtual worlds function as an opportunity for reflection over the already established practices with the purpose of a more radical development of new practices.

One hypothesis is that social interactions by the mirror neurons in the brain might facilitate regeneration of the nerve lanes, a study integrated across many areas in neurophysiology, psychology, neurology, linguistics, speech-language pathology, and learning. Rizzolatti and Craighero (2004) stress in their research that the human mirror-neuron system might explain the human capacity to learn by imitation and the relationship between the mirror-neuron system and language. It is interesting to investigate if the mirror neurons are activated if you imagine actions through avatar mediated actions and observe if mirrored activities in immersive virtual worlds have the same effect on the brain activity as mirrored activities in the real world. Related to that it would be relevant to include the work of Frith (2004, 2007) about neuroscience of social interactions and the social brain.

As mentioned, Shadden had been researching in recreating the self and the identity after a brain injury. She claims it is very important to participate in social relations. Thus, a promising challenge is to research whether it is possible to negotiate the self through verbal and non-verbal activities and social interactions in virtual worlds and if tailored social interactions in virtual worlds will have any impact on the nerves in the brain and in the end lead to a rebuilding of the communicative competencies.

To take full advantage of the multimodality in immersive virtual worlds, there is a need of a reformulation of the speech pedagogical practices. A cross-disciplinary research agenda is needed to rethink the area of the speech and language field where participation in social communities, narratives, self-reflection, and self-presentation must be emphasized and designed in a virtual learning and communication environments.

Integrating the Real and the Virtual

Imagine a scenario where an arts class teacher prepares a visit to the local arts museum. In order to do so, she visits the virtual representation of this museum and prepares a treasure hunt through the current exhibition with a number of exercises for her pupils. She leaves hints and information at the virtual representation of the exhibits in the museum. On the day of the visit, the pupils are able to access this information with their mobiles at the real exhibits and also to leave their answers and/or messages at the objects. To prepare the debriefing session, the teacher visits the virtual representation again and collects the answers and messages. This scenario clearly draws from ideas of pervasive interactions in ambient intelligence and exemplifies some of the above-mentioned features. It allows context specific access to information depending on the location of the user. This information can be multi modal ranging from simple text over audio and video to interactive presentations, for instance a wireframe model of an architectural exhibit. It can further collaboration between pupils for instance by providing different information for different pupils, enforcing them to collaborate in solving the tasks.

General Introduction

There are two main features in this scenario that allow for new and innovative learning experiences. First, there is the mutual influence between the real and the virtual world, and second, there is the integration of a social reality apart from the physical reality that is virtualized. Facer et al. (2004) present an intriguing first approach for a cross reality learning environment with the Savannah project. Pupils assume the roles of lions and explore the virtual environment of a pack of lions by moving physically around a sports field, where events are triggered by their previous actions and their current location. In a feedback session, this exploration can be replayed in the virtual world to discuss key events and reactions. Although there is a mutual influence between the virtual and the real, this is not exactly what we mean by cross-reality interactions. In case of the Savannah project, the real world is used as a large board in a board game that makes it necessary to move around in the world to trigger events in the game. The real world itself and its rich representations are of no interest for the interaction, i.e. with the right mapping to in-game coordinates the game could equally take place in a shopping mall or anywhere else. An essential feature we are interested in is making use of the real world itself and combining interactions there with what is happening in a virtual physical or social world. Hansen and Bouvin (2009) present the HyCon framework for context aware mobile learning that heavily focuses instead on the real world as a context provider for the learning endeavor. In their application scenarios, pupils explore a city and get additional information, which is triggered by different context information, e.g. their location. Again, a mutual influence between the real and the virtual is evident in this approach but it has similar shortcomings in regard to our idea of cross-reality interaction as the Savannah project by emphasizing the interaction in one of the two realities without putting much effort in the other reality.

An integration of the real and the virtual is not a new concept. Milgram and Kishino (1994) analyzed the combination of the real and the virtual in what they termed the virtuality continuum, where they distinguished between interactions in the real world, interactions in the virtual world, as well as mixed reality interactions that are divided into the two options of augmented reality and augmented virtuality.

The inherent characteristics of immersive worlds in combination with current trends in pervasive and ubiquitous computing make it necessary to revise and extend their ideas about the mixed reality continuum in two ways:

1. **Social world:** The last years have seen a virtualization of a completely different aspect of reality, namely the social or relational reality. Thus, analyzing how the real and virtual world can be integrated is not limited anymore to physical aspects. People spend time in virtual social networks that may or may not be congruent with their real social relations and where real world actions (e.g. traveling, taking pictures) directly influence the virtual interactions (e.g. in the form of comments or "liking" statements).

2. **Mutual influence between real and virtual world:** Both standard mixed reality interactions (augmented reality and virtuality) are aimed at creating a single reality that co-exists at the same time/place. However, immersive virtual worlds like Second Life or World of Warcraft are persistent just like the real world and thus employing augmented reality/virtuality techniques are just temporal portals between the two realities. Thus, the question is if and how the real or the virtual are affected by what is going on in the other realities.

Figure 1 gives our take on the virtuality continuum. To take the above additions into account, first of all the real and virtual respectively encompass not only the physical but also the social world. Real+ denotes a direct influence of interactions in the real on the social or physical virtual reality. The example in Figure 1 gives an impression from a recent project with a local art museum, where the user can purchase pieces of art for his own virtual gallery, which is part of a social network game. Virtual+ denotes an influence the other way around, i.e. what happens in the virtual world affects the social or physical reality. In the example, the user acts on the virtual environment, which changes the state of the program running on his real mobile phone, in this case a program to control features of a smart home environment (Leichtenstern, André, & Rehm, 2010). The augmented reality example shows an application allowing placing virtual organs in a real skeleton (Wiendl, et al., 2007). The augmented virtuality example gives an impression of a digital story-telling system, where the user assumes the role of one of the characters and is integrated in the virtual environment as a live video feat (Cavazza, et al., 2003). Parallel Interaction denotes a mutual influence between real and virtual that takes place at the same time here presented with another example from a recent project, where a virtual world is utilized for managing and retrieving indigenous knowledge in the form of video recordings[3]. This comes closest to our understanding of cross reality interactions. In this case, the virtual as well as the real world persist independent from each other, but at the same time, what happens in either might influence the other. If, e.g., a new narrative

is recorded in the real world it will be linked to a given place or person in the virtual world and made available for retrieval there. On the other hand, interactions like feedback to or sharing of the videos in the virtual world can trigger new narratives or a reorganization of the knowledge in the real world.

Research Challenges

Integrating real and virtual worlds poses interesting research challenges on different levels. Apart from the physical real world, recent years saw the virtualization of the social world as well. People nowadays have virtual social networks that only partly overlap with their real social networks and which let them not only meet people that share similar ideas and values but also let them assume different role compared to their real social networks (Jensen, 2007). To link the virtualized social relations and the users different social identities back to the real world is a largely unexplored challenge.

In terms of interaction, context awareness is one of the main ingredients to integrate the

Figure 1. Milgram reloaded: in addition to the physical real and virtual world, the social real and virtual worlds are affected by mixed reality interactions

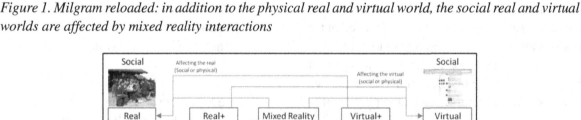

real and the virtual. To be able to react to users and event in the real world, it is indispensable to acquire knowledge about the current situation of the user taking information from all kind of different sensors into account like location (e.g. GPS), activity (e.g. acceleration), or weather (e.g. Internet service). Currently, such interactions are mostly enabled making use of mobile devices like smartphones. This also introduces technical challenges as operating platforms greatly differ and change rapidly. Examples include Symbian, Android, I-OS, RIM-BB OS to name only those with the largest market share. As these platforms typically vary in the way they address sensors, i.e. in the way contextual information can be processed, to develop applications bridging the real and the virtual becomes a tedious technical business.

CONCLUSION

This chapter focused on a socio-constructivist approach to learning and presented scenarios how such an approach can be beneficial in immersive virtual environments. To this end, we presented three different learning scenarios that focus on different aspects of learning and features of immersive environments thereby emphasizing that new learning concepts can only be developed as an interdisciplinary endeavor due to the inherent technical and social complexity of immersive virtual worlds.

The three scenarios—virtual peers, users with special needs, and cross reality interactions—are showcases of the potential of virtual worlds and in analyzing these potentials and the research challenges for realizing such scenarios we hope to pave the way for an interdisciplinary research agenda that embraces the potential for virtual worlds for learning.

REFERENCES

Bertrand, J., Babu, S. V., Polgreen, P., & Segre, A. (2010). Virtual agents based simulation for training healthcare workers in hand hygiene procedures. In Allbeck, J. (Eds.), *Intelligent Virtual Agents (IVA)* (pp. 125–131). Berlin, Germany: Springer. doi:10.1007/978-3-642-15892-6_13

Biswas, G., Leelawong, K., Schwartz, D., & Vye, N. (2005). Learning by teaching: A new agent paradigm for educational software. *Applied Artificial Intelligence*, *19*, 363–392. doi:10.1080/08839510590910200

Bjarkam, C. R. (2004). *Neuroanatomi*. Munksgaard, Germany: København.

Cavazza, M., Martin, O., Charles, F., Mead, S. J., & Marichal, X. (2003). Users Acting in mixed reality interactive storytelling. In Balet, O., Subsol, G., & Torguet, P. (Eds.), *Virtual Storytelling* (pp. 189–197). Berlin, Germany: Springer. doi:10.1007/978-3-540-40014-1_24

D'Mello, S., Hays, P., Williams, C., Cade, W., Brown, J., & Olney, A. (2010). Collaborative lecturing by human and computer tutors. In Aleven, V., Kay, J., & Mostow, J. (Eds.), *Intelligent Tutoring Systems (ITS)* (pp. 178–187). Berlin, Germany: Springer. doi:10.1007/978-3-642-13437-1_18

Dourish, P. (2001). *Where the action is: The foundations of embodied interaction*. Cambridge, MA: MIT Press.

Facer, K., Joiner, R., Stanton, D., Reid, J., Hull, R., & Kirk, D. (2004). Savannah: Mobile gaming and learning? *Journal of Computer Assisted Learning*, *20*, 399–409. doi:10.1111/j.1365-2729.2004.00105.x

Fredens, K. (2004). *Mennesket i hjernen – En grundbog i neuropædagogik*. Århus, Denmark: Systime Academic.

Frith, C. (2007). *Making up the mind: How the brain creates our mental world.* Oxford, UK: Blackwell Publishing.

Goldberg, E. (2005). *The wisdom paradox: How your mind can grow stronger as your brain grows older.* New York, NY: Gotham Books.

Guye-Vuillème, A., & Thalmann, D. (2001). A high level architecture for believable social agents. *Virtual Reality Journal, 5,* 95–106. doi:10.1007/BF01424340

Hansen, F. A., & Bouvin, N. O. (2009). Mobile learning in context – Context-aware hypermedia in the wild. *International Journal of Interactive Mobile Technologies, 3*(1), 3–21.

Hayashi, Y., Bourdeau, J., & Mizoguchi, R. (2008). Structurization of learning/instructional design knowledge for theory-aware authoring systems. In Woolf, B. P., Aïmeur, E., Nkambou, R., & Lajoie, S. (Eds.), *Intelligent Tutoring Systems* (pp. 573–582). Berlin, Germany: Springer. doi:10.1007/978-3-540-69132-7_60

Hedberg, J., & Alexander, S. (1994). Virtual reality in education: Defining researchable issues. *Educational Media International, 31*(4), 214–220. doi:10.1080/0952398940310402

Isbister, K. (2004). Building bridges through the unspoken: Embodied agents to facilitate intercultural communication. In Payr, S., & Trappl, R. (Eds.), *Agent Culture: Human-Agent Interaction in a Multicultural World* (pp. 233–244). London, UK: Lawrence Erlbaum Associates.

Jensen, S. S. (2007). Acts of learning with avatars in a virtual world. In Mayer, I., & Mastik, H. (Eds.), *Organizing and Learning through Gaming and Simulation* (pp. 159–166). Delft, The Netherlands: Eburon.

John-Steiner, V. (1996). Sociocultural approaches to learning and development: A Vygotskian framework. *Educational Psychologist, 31,* 191–206.

Johnson, D., Johnson, R., & Skon, L. (1979). Student achievement on different types of tasks under cooperative, competitive, and individualistic conditions. *Contemporary Educational Psychology, 4,* 99–106. doi:10.1016/0361-476X(79)90063-8

Johnson, W. L., & Valente, A. (2008). Tactical language and culture training systems: Using artificial intelligence to teach foreign languages and cultures. In *Proceedings of IAAI 2008.* IAAI.

Ju, W., Nickel, S., Eng, K., & Nass, C. (2005). Influence of colearner agent behavior on learner performance and attitudes. In *Proceedings of CHI,* (pp. 1509-1512). ACM.

Kersey, C., Di Eugenio, B., Jordan, P., & Katz, S. (2010). KSC-PaL: A peer learning agent. In Aleven, V., Kay, J., & Mostow, J. (Eds.), *Intelligent Tutoring Systems (ITS), Part II* (pp. 72–81). Berlin, Germany: Springer. doi:10.1007/978-3-642-13437-1_8

Kim, Y., Hamilton, E. R., Zheng, J., & Baylor, A. L. (2006). Scaffolding learner motivation through a virtual peer. In *Proceedings of ICLS,* (pp. 335-341). ICLS.

Konnerup, U., & Schmidt. (2006). *Det virtuelle miljø – En mulighed for nye læreprocesser i rehabiliteringen af afasiramte.* (Masters Thesis). Aalborg Universitet. Aalborg, Denmark.

Kumar, R., Ai, H., Beuth, J. L., & Rosé, C. P. (2010). Socially capable conversational tutors can be effective in collaborative learning situations. In Aleven, V., Kay, J., & Mostow, J. (Eds.), *Intelligent Tutoring Systems (ITS), Part I* (pp. 156–164). Berlin, Germany: Springer. doi:10.1007/978-3-642-13388-6_20

Lave, J., & Wenger, E. (1991). *Situated learning: Legitimate peripheral participation.* Cambridge, UK: Cambridge University Press. doi:10.1017/CBO9780511815355

Leichtenstern, K., André, E., & Rehm, M. (2010). using hybrid simulations for early user evaluations of pervasive interactions. In *Proceedings of NordiCHI*, (pp. 315-324). ACM Press.

Magnusson, M. (2000). *Language in life – Life in language*. Karlstad, Sweden: Karlstad University Studies.

Maldonado, H., Lee, J.-E. R., Brave, S., Nass, C., Nakajima, H., & Yamada, R. … Morishima, Y. (2005). We learn better together: Enhancing elearning with emotional characters. In *Proceedings of Computer Support for Collaborative Learning: Learning 2005 – The Next 10 Years!* (pp. 408-417). CSCL.

Marsella, S., Johnson, W. L., & LaBore, C. M. (2003). Interactive pedagogical drama for health interventions. In *Proceedings of the 11th International Conference on Artificial Intelligence in Education (AIED)*. AIED.

McInerney, S. M., & Van Etten, S. (Eds.). (2000). *Research on sociocultural influences on motivation and learning*. Greenwich, CT: Information Age Publishing.

Mehlmann, G., Haering, M., Buehling, R., Wissner, M., & André, E. (2010). Multiple agents roles in an adaptive virtual classroom environment. In Allbeck, J. (Eds.), *Intelligent Virtual Agents (IVA)* (pp. 250–256). Berlin, Germany: Springer. doi:10.1007/978-3-642-15892-6_26

Milgram, P., & Kishino, F. (1994). A taxonomy of mixed reality visual displays. *IEICE Transactions on Information and Systems*, *77*, 1321–1329.

Nicolaisen, K., & Vejleskov, H. (1996). *Dysfatiske småbørn*. Berlin, Germany: Danmarks Lærerhøjskole.

Petheram, B. (2004). Computers and aphasia: A mean to delivery and a delivery of means. *Aphasiology*, *18*(3), 187–191. doi:10.1080/02687030444000020

Prada, R., Ma, S., & Nunes, M. A. (2010). Personality in social group dynamics. In *Proceedings of the International Conference on Computational Science and Engineering*, (pp. 607-612). IEEE.

Rehm, M. (2008). She is just stupid – Analyzing user-agent interactions in emotional game situations. *Interacting with Computers*, *20*(3), 311–325. doi:10.1016/j.intcom.2008.02.005

Rehm, M., & Endrass, B. (2009). Rapid prototyping of social group dynamics in multiagent systems. *AI & Society*, *24*(1), 13–23. doi:10.1007/s00146-009-0191-8

Rehm, M., Nakano, Y., André, E., Nishida, T., Bee, N., & Endrass, B. (2009). From observation to simulation: Generating culture-specific behavior for interactive systems. *AI & Society*, *24*(3), 267–280. doi:10.1007/s00146-009-0216-3

Rizzolatti, G. (2008). *Mirrors in the brain*. Oxford, UK: Oxford University Press.

Rizzolatti, G., & Craighero, L. (2004). The mirror neuron system. *Annual Review of Neuroscience*, *27*, 169–192. doi:10.1146/annurev.neuro.27.070203.144230

Schroeder, R. (2002). Copresence and interaction in virtual environments: An overview of the range of issues. [Presence.]. *Proceedings of Presence*, *2002*, 274–295.

Shadden, B., & Agan, J. P. (2004). Renegotiation of identity: The social context of aphasia support groups. *The Social Construction of Identity: The Clinical Challenge*, *24*(3), 174.

Shadden, B. B., Hagstrom, F., & Koski, P. (2008). *Neurogenic communication disorders: Life stories and the narrative self*. San Diego, CA: Plural Publishing.

Shaw, M. (1971). *Group dynamics – The psychology of small group behavior*. New York, NY: McGraw Hill Inc.

Sklar, E., & Davies, M. (2005). Multiagent simulation of learning environments. In *Proceedings of the 4ᵗʰ International Conference on Autonomous Agents and Multiagent Systems (AAMAS),* (pp. 953-959). ACM Press.

Vestberg, P. (2002). Hjerneskade og personlighed. *Kognition & Pædagogik, 43.*

Vinciarelli, A., Pantic, M., & Bourlard, H. (2009). Social signal processing: Survey of an emerging domain. *Image and Vision Computing Journal, 27*(12), 1743–1759. doi:10.1016/j.imavis.2008.11.007

Vygotsky, L. S. (1978). *Mind in society.* Cambridge, MA: Harvard University Press.

Vygotsky, L. S. (1986). *Thought and language.* Cambridge, MA: MIT Press.

Wang, H., Chignell, M., & Ishizuka, M. (2006). Are two talking heads better than one? When should use more than one agent in e-learning? In *Proceedings of IUT.* IUT.

Wenger, E. (2000). *Communities of practice: Learning, meaning, and identity.* Cambridge, UK: Cambridge University Press.

Wertz, R. T. (1992). Potential of television and telephonic technology for appraising and diagnosing neurogenic communication disorders in remote settings. *Aphasiology, 6.*

Wiendl, V., Dorfmüller-Ulhaas, K., Schulz, N., & André, E. (2007). Integrating a virtual agent into the real world: The virtual anatomy assistant ritchie. In *Proceedings of Intelligent Virtual Agents (IVA)* (pp. 211–224). Berlin, Germany: Springer. doi:10.1007/978-3-540-74997-4_20

Wood, E., Willoughby, T., Reille, S., Elliot, S., & DuCharme, M. (1995). Evaluating students' acquisition of factual material when studying independently or with a partner. *The British Journal of Educational Psychology, 65,* 237–247. doi:10.1111/j.2044-8279.1995.tb01145.x

Woolf, B. P., Arroyo, I., Muldner, K., Burleson, W., Cooper, D. G., Dolan, R., & Christopherson, R. M. (2010). The effect of motivational learning companions on low achieving students and students with disabilities. In Aleven, V., Kay, J., & Mostow, J. (Eds.), *Intelligent Tutoring Systems (ITS), Part I* (pp. 327–337). Berlin, Germany: Springer. doi:10.1007/978-3-642-13388-6_37

Zoll, C., Enz, S., Schaub, H., Aylett, R., & Paiva, A. (2006). Fighting bullying with the help of autonomous agents in a virtual school environment. In *Proceedings of the 7th International Conference on Cognitive Modeling (ICCM).* ICCM.

ENDNOTES

1. http://www.thetech.org/techvirtual/
2. Aphasia is an impairment of the speech-language function as a result of a brain injury. Aphasia influences a person's ability to produce and understand speech and language. In addition, the ability to read, write, spell, and calculate is affected.
3. http://e-hci.org/a4ikm

Chapter 15
Digital Structures and the Future of Online Leadership

Moses Wolfenstein
University of Wisconsin – Extension, USA

ABSTRACT

This chapter discusses findings from a study that looked at organizational leadership in the massively multiplayer online game World of Warcraft® in an attempt to inform the future of leadership in schools and other online and blended learning organizations. After offering a general orientation to the game world and the original study, this chapter delineates the ways in which studying virtual worlds of this sort can and cannot inform theory and practice of instructional leadership. It then examines the organizational leadership and learning cycle that emerged in the original study. Finally, it considers implications from the research for instructional and organizational leadership in a data rich environment.

INTRODUCTION

The ongoing advancement of online and blended learning, particularly in secondary and higher education institutions, has resulted in a growing consensus that both practitioners and researchers in the arena of education need new models for looking at professional practices at school and classroom levels (Collins & Halverson, 2009). In particular, the geographically distributed and digitally mediated nature of online learning has highlighted the ways in which traditional models of classroom and school leadership need to be revised in the face of a changing field (NSF Task Force on Cyberlearning, 2008). The research described in this chapter[1] was undertaken in an attempt to advance an understanding of some of the issues that may be presented by these infrastructural changes through looking at the nature of organizational leadership practices around one type of learning organization (Senge, 2006) in a contemporary immersive online environment.

The learning organizations in question are known as raiding guilds. Groups of this sort range

DOI: 10.4018/978-1-4666-2670-6.ch015

in size from a dozen to a few hundred in size, and are found in certain types of Massively Multiplayer Online games (MMOs). MMOs are game worlds that allow thousands, or even hundreds of thousands of people to play online together at the same time in a persistent virtual world[2]. While some of these games are structured to allow all of the players of the game to literally play in the same virtual world, in most instances a game's developers will host numerous copies of the world, such that the total number of players of the game far exceeds the portion occupying a single version of the online space. This is the case with *World of Warcraft*®[3] by Blizzard Entertainment™, the largest MMO in terms of playership, and the most profitable game in the history of the genre.

World of Warcraft, known to players of the game as *WoW*, was the virtual world that this research focused on. A video game, and especially a game with the word war in the title, might seem like an odd place to look to when considering the future of instructional leadership. However, there are a number of features of raiding guilds as organizations, including the manner in which they are situated within a larger affinity space (Gee, 2004), that make them particularly promising for looking at how an online learning organization can function, and what the shape of leadership practices within such organizations can look like. Perhaps even more significantly, organizations like *WoW* raiding guilds exist in extremely data rich environments as a result of the digital structures through which the game functions. By considering the interplay between these structures and the human agents within a space like *WoW*, it is possible to gain some perspective on how ubiquitous access to data might affect member participation and leadership practices in developing online learning organizations.

Following the provision of some necessary background for understanding the findings from this work and an explanation of the methods utilized in the study, this chapter will proceed by delineating those ways in which *WoW* raid-

ing guilds provide a useful point of reference for looking at the present and future of education and instructional leadership, and those ways in which leadership in *WoW* is highly context dependent and less useful outside of the domain of online gaming. The next section will offer an overview of the core model of leadership and learning practices in *World of Warcraft* that emerged through the study. Finally, this chapter will look specifically at what the implications of this research are for instructional leadership in increasingly data rich ecologies.

BACKGROUND AND METHODS

Before considering research that provided a precedent for the study presented here or looking at the specific approach taken in this work, some readers will likely benefit from a basic introduction to *World of Warcraft* in order to understand the context in which this study took place. Within the game "genre"[4] of MMOs, massively multiplayer online *role-playing* games like *WoW* are a sub-genre in which core game mechanics are drawn from the much older genre of role-playing games. Players in these virtual worlds create fantasy characters for themselves (often referred to as player avatars), take on quests from various pre-programmed "non-player" characters in the game, create in-game goods which can be used or traded to other players, fight virtual monsters by themselves and in groups of various sizes, and receive virtual rewards for doing so in the form of in-game currency or virtual items that their characters can use. You may gather from this description that *WoW* is based in a fantasy setting populated by creatures like elves and trolls, and filled with items like magic swords and potions. While not all MMOs (or for that matter all role-playing games) take place in this sort of fantasy setting, it's an extremely common type of world for games of this sort. Graphically speaking, *WoW* is a 3D game with a stylized cartoonish look, and players usually view the world from a third person perspective where they can see their own avatars.

After peeling back the fantasy setting of *WoW*, one finds several core elements that define the actual player activities in and around the game. Beneath the shiny graphical exterior is a complex game simulation model structured around a variety of characteristics assigned by the designers to player avatars, the virtual creatures they regularly encounter, and the various virtual goods (i.e. armor, magic potions, etc.) they find or create. This rich statistical system is utilized to determine the outcomes of everything from a player's chance of catching a certain type of virtual fish, to their ability to successfully block an attack from a monster or another player (the latter if they are engaged in competitive play against each other).

In addition to the computational simulation that makes *WoW* tick, the game world is also deeply dependent on a sort of social simulation space that the players develop on top of the game. These emergent spaces are in large part the result of game design that rewards players for working together in larger groups. In *WoW*, the most difficult content requires intense player collaboration, and many in-game groups called guilds form for the purpose of attempting to complete these intense game play challenges (Williams, et al., 2006; Nardi, 2010). This activity, known as raiding, requires groups of 10, 25, or 40 players in order to engage in it. Players in a raid group enter into separate spaces in the game called instances where they can attempt the toughest encounters in the game without interference from any of the thousands of other players who might be online in the larger game world. The goal of defeating the "boss" monsters in these instances is the primary defining objective for raiding guilds. When victorious, players are not only provided with the satisfaction of working together to overcome a complex challenge, they are also rewarded with a handful of powerful virtual items which can be used to enhance their avatars both visually and functionally. Ultimately the designed cycle of

play, including the reward system put in place by the developers, is reinforced by a rich network of interactions between individuals and groups of players who reside both in and outside of various formal communities around *WoW*.

To support player interaction, MMOs have a built in chat feature which functions like an instant messaging service, only with the capacity to field a large number of individual and group conversations within the same interface. Additionally, players engaged in raiding generally use third party VoIP (Voice over Internet Protocol) software to converse and plan. While these tools are key for the activity of raiding, MMOs like *WoW* are also inherently social spaces that players come to not only for the activity of gaming itself, but also to hang out and converse about a huge variety of topics (Williams, et al., 2006; Steinkuehler & Williams, 2006; Nardi & Harris, 2006). The emergent social simulation space is then defined by the negotiation of individual and group objectives adopted by players, and based on a mesh of the designed goals created by the game developers, the emergent goals adopted by the players within the bounds of the game as a designed space, and the social dynamics that drive less game oriented community building (Steinkuehler, 2006).

In addition to the computational and social simulations that structure the space in which players interact in *WoW*, a larger player community is an essential feature for any successful MMO. James Paul Gee (2005) has referred to loosely organized groups of this sort as affinity spaces in part as a way of distinguishing them from more formally structured tightly coupled communities. Gee's definition for an affinity space is complex and involves 10 distinct features, several of which are particularly useful in approaching the study of leadership in an MMO. Most crucially, people in an affinity space relate to each other primarily in terms of their common interest in a shared endeavor as opposed to other aspects of their identities (e.g. gender, ethnicity, etc.). In some respects, this basic point of departure guides the rest of the rules that are formed within affinity spaces. Indeed as a correlate of the fact that members of an affinity space are primarily connected by their common interest, knowledge about the relevant domain becomes the primary force structuring leadership and learning in such a space. Additionally, knowledge in affinity spaces is decentralized such that it is distributed across people and artifacts in the system. That is to say that no individual, group, or resource contains all of the relevant knowledge about the domain of practice, and as a result a new entrant into the space is potentially capable of being as valuable a contributor as a long time participant.

One other essential feature of affinity spaces in the context of the research presented here is the idea that leadership in affinity spaces is "porous," in that boundaries between leaders and followers are vague. Leaders in affinity spaces operate not as directors of activities but as resources for the group (Gee, 2004). In the case of *WoW* as with many other video games, the affinity space surrounding the game connects individuals and groups through a complex network of knowledge sharing realized across a variety of online portals and inter-connected communities. Some of these hubs are sponsored by the game's developer. Many others are supported through the efforts of passionate players. In addition, a handful function as independent businesses gaining revenue by hosting online advertisements. This mixture of different resources serves to diversify the way in which a given player or guild can approach learning in and around the game, and ultimately learning about the game is the essential activity which characterizes participation in a raiding guild.

While the general nature of *WoW* as an MMO is essential for understanding this work, there are a few specific features of the game that are also necessary to acknowledge in framing this study. First, *WoW* represents the single most successful game of its type with estimates of total playership hovering around 12 million worldwide (Blizzard, 2010), and prior measurements indicating that it

controls 62.2% percent of the total MMO market (Woodcock, 2007). Although Blizzard Entertainment has never released demographic data around the game's playership, it is possible to field a reasonable guess about the characteristics of the playership as anecdotal evidence would seem to support the notion that *WoW* players like those of other MMOs are fairly diverse in terms of both age and gender (Williams, Yee, & Kaplan, 2008). More anecdotal reports indicate that MMOs like *WoW* are not only played by solitary individuals who meet through the online space, but that it is also played by couples and families as a bonding activity (Yee, 2006). *WoW* has even been used as a curricular tool in after school and classroom settings (Johnson, Smith, Levine, & Hayward, 2010; WoW in School, 2011). Finally, *WoW* has been running since late 2004, but over the course of that time, the game has changed substantially as the designers have altered and retuned basic game mechanics. Primarily this has been done with the release of new game content referred to as expansions. Each expansion has included both new game content, and a reconfiguration or tuning of core game mechanics. *WoW* has received three expansions since its original release. At the time, this research was undertaken only the first two expansions, The Burning Crusade® and Wrath of the Lich King®, had been released.

In general, over the last 10 years research on video games and learning has gone from being a fringe area to a significant element in the landscape of both educational research and practice (Squire, 2011). Work related to the topic of MMOs has had a particularly strong showing over the course of that time, beginning with research from scholars like Steinkuehler (2006) and Barab (Barab, et al., 2007), and manifesting more recently with game based learning initiatives like the WoW in Schools Project and Quest2Learn (Quest to Learn, 2011). The topic of leadership in games like *WoW* has also received some prior attention from the academic community as well. For instance, in a 2006 article for *Wired* magazine, Thomas and

Brown made the claim that a Massively Multiplayer Online Games like *WoW* can serve as "a total immersion course in leadership" (Brown & Thomas, 2006). Additionally, the private sector has taken an interest in how MMOs and other virtual worlds can potentially offer opportunities for leadership learning (IBM, 2005; Reeves & Malone, 2007). At the same time, there has been an explosion more generally in academic studies of MMOs more generally. This general interest has highlighted the potential of looking at games to learn about the future of online leadership. It also served as an impetus for this study, which sought to specifically unpack actual leadership practices in *WoW* as prior work had generally only approached this topic at a surface level.

Methodologically this study was carried out by interviewing leaders from guilds that regularly participated in the activity of raiding. Given the inductive nature of the research, theoretical sampling (Strauss & Corbin, 1990) was utilized to develop a broad based model of leadership practices in *WoW* raiding guilds. The sample was developed starting with a focus on successful raiding guild leaders, and then built outwards to more casual guilds in order to capture a broad array of leadership practices. The study adopted a distributed leadership model (Spillane, Halverson, & Diamond, 2004). The theory of distributed leadership comes out of the theory of distributed cognition (Hutchins, 1996), which takes an ecological view of practice, looking to see how people and artifacts work together within a system to realize specific tasks. As such the interview protocol for the study was structured around the contexts in which different tasks of guild leadership are practiced, so as to capture some sense of both what leadership in game entails, and who and what the various individuals and artifacts are in guilds that help to realize leadership practices.

14 interviews were conducted with leaders from 11 unique guilds between Fall of 2009 and Spring of 2010. The interviews were coded using open coding to capture emergent themes, as well

as using Bolman and Deal's Four Frames model (2003) for studying organizations. This latter model, which consists of the Structural, Human Resource, Political, and Symbolic frames, was used because it is a common model that has been utilized previously in school leadership research (Deal & Peterson, 1999; Bolman & Deal, 2002). As a result, in the process of data analysis and interpretation it was possible to gain a general sense of areas of isomorphism between school and guild leadership. Member checks (Lincoln & Guba, 1985) and data analysis with members of a community of games and learning researchers were utilized to enhance the trustworthiness (Golafshani, 2003) of the findings. However, it should be recognized that this study sought to establish a general framework and some key trends around leadership practices in an MMO, but that the findings discussed in this chapter have not been tested against a large random sample of guild leaders, and as such, the findings presented here illustrate emergent trends, but are not fully generalizable.

LIMITATIONS ON READING BETWEEN DOMAINS OF PRACTICE

While prior claims that MMOs provide viable platforms for leadership learning (Brown & Thomas, 2006; Reeves & Malone, 2007) served as a major impetus for the research presented in this chapter, one useful outcome of this work was the provision of a clearer sense of how leadership in an online game can and cannot inform leadership practice more generally. It is worth recognizing at the outset that there are significant differences between schools and MMO guilds as domains for practicing leadership. While some of these differences are due to the playful nature of the activities carried out in online games, others are more specifically tied to features of educational institutions as domains of practice that distinguish them from leadership in almost any other context.

In this section, we will consider first the ways in which leadership in *WoW* can potentially inform school leadership (only some of which will receive more extensive attention in this chapter), and then those ways in which it cannot.

One core feature of guilds that has drawn the attention from researchers in sectors outside of education lies in the fact that they are geographically dispersed organizations that operate collaboratively online. In this most general sense, there are certainly lessons to be learned for educational organizations that operate online, due to the fact that MMO raiding guilds represent relatively advanced online organizations that need to engage in a continuous learning cycle while contending with many of the same basic conditions of practice as any online organization. While online learning goes back at least as far as the MMO genre (as both rely on similar levels of computing technology), unlike schools guilds have assembled their organizational structures and mechanisms for negotiating the challenges inherent to being geographically distributed without obvious recourse to pre-existing norms for organizational behavior. That is to say, online schools have tended to work by adopting or adapting theories and practices developed around both brick and mortar settings and prior standards for distance learning (Anderson, 2008).

By contrast, guild dynamics have developed from the ground up around challenges like the intrusion of individual interruptions into collaborative practice, or the difficulty of scheduling activities across time zones and various individual schedules. While players certainly have access to other individual experiences to inform mechanisms for handling these challenges, there were no common organizational norms for confronting these sorts of challenges prior to the development of MMOs. In this sense, guild leadership offers us the opportunity to see if there are effective mechanisms for negotiating these challenges for which educational institutions have a blind spot based on norms of practice.

In addition, MMO designers and players have created or adopted tools for communication that are native to the digital environment. As a result, guilds offer viable points of reference for looking at how different media for communication (e.g. IM, email, voice) influence the potential outcomes of leadership activities, and even the ways in which individual styles for communicative action can benefit from the use of a given tool. Over the course of this study, it became evident that factors like the circumstances in which a conflict takes place and leadership style are both relevant in informing how an individual leader chooses to confront a given challenge. However, it is also evident that different digital tools for communication have their own unique constraints and affordances quite apart from user preference. This latter topic has been explored in some respects through prior research (Shaffer & Clinton, 2006), but still deserves greater attention in looking at the future of online leadership, and guild leadership offers some insight into this topic as well.

This study has also helped to illuminate what a rich network of online learning organizations looks like. Other research into MMOs and the affinity groups that surround various digitally mediated groups has already greatly expanded our understanding of what learning in digitally mediated affinity spaces can look like (Steinkuehler, 2008; Jenkins, et al., 2006). However, this study has helped to clarify how learning organizations like guilds fit into a larger network of activity. In looking towards instructional leadership, this is particularly useful as professional educators are increasingly loosely networked through an array of online tools and services that in many ways already parallel the types of resources utilized by MMO players.

Finally, this research has helped to clarify what kinds of leadership practices are accessed through playing an MMO. While prior claims that there may be generic leadership practices that can be learned through guild leadership seemed generally viable (Reeves & Malone, 2007; Thomas &

Brown, 2009), this work has helped to clarify what the more generic leadership capacities are that players can potentially develop through leading in game. Through considering the shape of guild leadership practices, it has become evident that a general understanding of the challenges tied to the interpersonal dimensions of leadership can be cultivated through assuming a leadership role in game. Additionally, some of the basic complexities that attend organizational management surface through engaging in guild leadership. Most notably, guild leaders illustrate how leadership online is enacted through a blend of human and software agency. However, this research has also highlighted the way in which even fundamental management activities are highly dependent on the features of the specific domain of practice, and the nominal leader's understanding of that domain.

As a result of these domain specific requirements, there are crucial differences between MMO leadership and school leadership that fundamentally limit the ways in which looking at an online game can inform instructional leadership theory and practice. Most notably, this study provides little in the way of prescriptive findings that can directly guide the actual practice of leadership in current PK-20 institutions. Even in considering how leaders from this study responded to the conditions of leadership in a data rich environment, it is worth noting that the type of data which these leaders are responding to is fundamentally different from that which school leaders utilize.

Additionally, based on the data collected in this study it seems unlikely that a tool like *WoW* represents an easily scalable curricular intervention in K-16. While promising uses of *WoW* as a curricular tool have been realized at both the secondary (WoW in School, 2011) and higher education (McKnight, 2010) levels, the kind of game based expertise an instructor needs to effectively utilize a game of this sort as a curricular tool will serve as a hard limit for the time being on opportunities for implementing a game like *WoW* as a course "text."

This study has also made evident the limitations in suggesting that an environment like *World of Warcraft* can be used as a universal tool for providing future school leaders with leadership experience. Quite apart from the fact that *WoW* involves domain specific knowledge that won't transfer easily into the school context, in order for players to be capable of enacting leadership practices in game they need to have enough expertise in some aspect of the game for other players to recognize their leadership capacity. Even providing leadership around activities like in-game resource management or conflict resolution requires players to have a demonstrable understanding of the value of specific resources in game, or the aspects of the game that can enhance interpersonal conflict between players. As a result, while *WoW* might provide gamers or educators willing to devote a substantial amount of time to learning the game with an opportunity to develop a groundwork for leadership practice, game play itself is demanding enough that it would be extremely difficult to utilize it more broadly as a curricular component in an educational leadership program of study.

LEADERSHIP AND LEARNING CYCLES IN WORLD OF WARCRAFT

The research on which this chapter is based revealed nine core tasks of raiding guild leadership in *World of Warcraft*, as well as a large array of sub and micro tasks tied to these essential activities. In this section, we will consider how the entire assemblage of practices hangs together, with an eye towards understanding how a few specific tasks can be useful in examining the future of instructional leadership in both physical and online settings. Due to limitations of space in this chapter, not all tasks will be treated on in detail[5]. Additionally, in this chapter more attention will be given to the cycle of raid leadership tasks, as it is through an understanding of the activity of raiding that one can best make sense of the data rich environment that in-game leaders effectively navigate in guiding their organizations.

Figure 1 provides an illustration of the nine leadership tasks evidenced in the study as well as their constituent sub-tasks and micro tasks. In general, sub-tasks and micro tasks were the most easily identifiable elements in the data, while the nine tasks represent meaningful ways of clustering these various activities together. The terms utilized in the diagram have been shortened in order to provide space for the sub and micro tasks and to some extent as a way to visually represent how some tasks tend to cluster based on who carries them out, or when they are tended to. The complete task names are as follows:

- In-Game Preparation for Collaborative Play
- Live Facilitation and Coordination of Players
- Post-Gaming Cool Down and Reflection
- Game Related Research and Raid Planning
- Advanced Preparation of In-Game Resources
- Player Leadership and Membership Cultivation
- Guild Politics and Executive Management
- Software and Sociopolitical Artifact Creation
- Network Technology and In-Game Maintenance

As evidenced in Figure 1, the tasks were classified in a two by two matrix as part of the data analysis process. The first binary used to divide the tasks is the split between "Raid Leadership" and "Guild Management" (the left and right halves of the figure respectively). In general, the difference between these two types of tasks involves the manner in which raid leadership tasks tend to be highly game specific, and integral to the actual activity of raiding. Guild management tasks tend to be more generic in nature, and enacting them ensures a broader kind of support for the guild

as an organization. The arrows on the left hand side of Figure 1 are there to indicate that the raid leadership tasks can also collectively serve to represent the organizational learning cycle that *WoW* guilds engage in.

The second division utilized for task analysis in the study was between synchronous activities that require live interaction between players (on the top), and more asynchronous activities that various players can carry out in their own time, or in many instances outside of the game (on the bottom). This division operates differently in considering raid leadership tasks and guild management tasks. In the case of the former, synchronous literally indicates tasks that take place with a large group of players in the game around scheduled raid times, while asynchronous raid leadership tasks do not involve working with an entire raid group simultaneously and are more removed in time from the actual activity of raiding. For guild management tasks, synchronous tasks are those that require live interaction between players, while asynchronous tasks are generally carried out without players being co-present in some way. It is worth emphasizing that to a great extent both of these divisions serve to support analysis, but in actuality many of the sub-tasks and micro-tasks that constitute the nine primary tasks are less easily defined as being truly synchronous and asynchronous, or guild management and raid leadership focused in nature.

As noted previously, the cycle of raid leadership tasks can be understood as a representation of the continuous learning process that *WoW* raiding guilds engage in over the course of their existence. While the cycle is continuous, it can be approached conceptually by starting with the task of In-Game Preparation for Collaborative Play. In one sense, this preparation task can be thought about in terms of the process of getting the right avatars together in the same location in game, and ensuring that those avatars are fully prepared to begin raiding. In another sense, it can be thought of as the process of coordinating 10 to

Figure 1. The nine tasks of raiding guild leadership

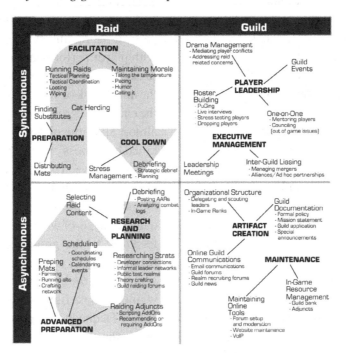

40 players, each likely behind a different hardware and software set up, usually playing in different physical locations, and if playing on an American server, quite likely in three different time zones.

It is perhaps due to the attendant complexity of all of these aspects of preparation that one of the sub-tasks most guild leaders in the study emphasized as being onerous was "Cat Herding." While this phrase is not unique to *WoW*, it is commonly used by guild leaders to indicate the activity of pulling together all of the players in the guild who have made a prior commitment to (or are otherwise interested in) raiding, and getting them ready to go. By contrast, the sub-task of Finding Substitutes might mean finding players in the guild who hadn't signed up to play that night in advance, or in some contexts it might mean going outside of the guild at the last minute to find trustworthy players in another guild who can fill in for a specific role. One essential feature of the game that informs both of these sub-tasks is that in creating a new character, players commit to specializing their avatar to perform one or

two of a variety of different roles in game, and in fact a variety of different specialized abilities are required in order for a raiding group to be successful. As a consequence, these preparation activities are driven by the need to have a properly balanced group, with enough people filling in all of the necessary roles.

The manner in which in-game roles are tied to coded features of the game environment, in combination with the repeating nature of a task like In-game Preparation for Collaborative Play, emphasizes a fundamental difference between leadership in an MMO like *WoW*, and leadership in other contexts. By looking at the connection between player roles and features of the game design, we begin to get a sense of how games can provide constrained spaces where the dimensions of leadership practice are necessarily narrowed because the simulation space itself creates a streamlined, better ordered problem space than most organizational contexts provide (Halverson, 2005). Equally, the repeating nature of an activity like Cat Herding emphasizes how the social simulations that exist on top of the digital systems of a game like *WoW* are not generic spaces for learning leadership. Rather the organizational structures and objectives of guilds are deeply informed by the game design that structures activities.

Moving on, the task that truly rests at the heart of raiding is Live Facilitation and Coordination of Players. The act of facilitation bears less of a resemblance to the work carried out by a school principal, and more resemblance to the work carried out by an athletic coach, or in some respects even a classroom teacher (Wolfenstein & Dikkers, 2009). The two sub-tasks that constitute facilitation, Running Raids and Maintaining Morale, represent the necessary technical and interpersonal work that leaders engage in. While a more detailed description of these aspects of raiding can be found in a number of other scholarly works (Nardi, 2010; Chen, 2010) including the full dissertation on which this article is based (Wolfenstein, 2010), for the present purpose it's enough to know that running raids involves keeping a group of players focused for anywhere from one hour to four, often in the face of repeated failures. The nominal leaders in the raid setting (usually referred to as raid leaders) might consistently be the same individual within a guild, or the role may be passed around depending on the organization. Additionally, this individual may or may not be the same person as the official head of the guild (usually referred to as the guild master). Regardless, raid leadership is a deeply distributed activity, with the raid leader usually relying on a handful of people who have been delegated to tend to certain concerns (i.e. directing different types of players in the group, explaining possible strategies, etc.). In addition, the requirements of raiding are such that in more competitive guilds all members of a raid need to self-manage at an extremely high level.

Despite the fundamental differences between classroom teaching and raiding as the core functions of schools and guilds respectively, there is one type of activity that takes place during both raid facilitation and Post-Gaming Cool-Down and

Reflection that is worth particular attention in looking at instructional leadership. Both of these parts of the raiding cycle include an engagement with player performance data, and opportunities to engage in formative feedback. During the raid, the micro-task of Wiping is literally the process of the entire raid group losing a battle in which all or almost all of the player's avatars are temporarily killed by a "boss" monster. In the relatively brief window between one defeat and the next attempt, either the nominal leadership team or various members of the larger group will engage in a quick analysis of what happened, provide general feedback to the group, or tailored suggestions for individuals, and the players will adjust their approach to the encounter as required. Losing or winning a boss fight is the ultimate form of summative feedback, as it provides a direct indication of whether or not the group was collectively competent enough to survive the encounter. However, guild leaders in the study recognized that despite the binary nature of this game based feedback, both victories and defeats could be more nuanced experiences. Some leaders emphasized how in both situations there were often still opportunities for further learning and that only once the guild had an instance "on farm"[6] were opportunities for learning generally exhausted.

In thinking about educational leadership online, the feedback processes in *WoW* generally provide a useful point of departure. To begin with, the general nature of this cycle resembles almost any generic cycle for continuous improvement, especially if the organization is concerned with performance, rather than production based outcomes. In a generic version of this cycle, an opportunity for evaluation occurs which is followed by a review of the performance. Further analysis is performed to set priorities for the next performance cycle. If deemed necessary modifications are made based on prior analysis and/or changes in organizational priorities. Finally, relevant agents (be they human or artifact) in the organization undergo some form of preparation for the next performance, in which a new measurement will be taken. This generic model could be utilized to describe everything from software support services to financial management, but it is also evident when looking at schools in an evaluation driven learning ecology.

In fact, Halverson's model of Data Driven Instructional Systems (DDIS) echoes this same basic structure. The DDIS model begins with Data Acquisition, followed by Data Reflection. The products of Data Reflection are utilized for Program Alignment (opportunities to check whether the instructional program is aligned with the evaluation mechanisms), and Program Design. Finally, Formative Feedback is utilized to implement changes to actual practice, and Test Preparation takes place prior to the next opportunity for Data Acquisition (Halverson, Grigg, Prichett, & Thomas, 2007). Like Halverson's DDIS model, the raiding guild leadership and learning cycle is specifically structured to describe an iterative process utilized by a learning organization. While the scale of the two cycles differs drastically, the general shape of the two processes is more or less consistent with the generic cycle described above.

It is noteworthy that within the learning cycle raiding guilds employee, data driven feedback plays a role not only in the "offline" task of Game Related Research and Raid Planning, but also throughout the tasks of Facilitation and Cool Down. Due to its computationally driven nature, *WoW* generates metrics for every action a player takes through their avatar. While video games have long had features that provide powerful performance feedback through a point system of some sort (Gee, 2003), the player community around *World of Warcraft* has developed a variety of adjunct software tools (Steinkuehler & Duncan, 2009) including tools to capture, report, and analyze a huge range of player performance data. Modifications made by players through the use of software AddOns can capture and display performance data during a raid. However, players can also enter a command into the game at the end of

an encounter to receive a file with a performance log for the entire group. These combat log files are then commonly analyzed using an online resource outside of the game that can generate a variety of data representations.

While one guild in this study utilized combat logs on the fly in the process of managing a wipe, many guilds integrate data analysis into the sub-tasks of In-Game and Web-Based Debriefing. In Figure 1, those two sub-tasks have been intentionally placed in a cluster with Leadership Meetings and Organizational Structure due to the fact that these tasks often overlapped in the actual practices of guilds in the study, and can be carried out via both synchronous and asynchronous player interaction. In considering the data from this study, the debriefing process commonly began with conversation by voice and/or text chat among the leadership team in guilds with a steeper hierarchy, or among a broader swath of raiding members in guilds with a flatter organizational structure. It was then often continued via further synchronous conversation, individual analysis of the combat logs, or asynchronously through online forums or email communications. Ultimately, this process was often concluded with one member summarizing the results via electronic communication (i.e. blog post, Web forum, email, etc.) so that raiding players who were not actively involved in the debriefing could be brought up to speed.

The task of Game Related Research and Raid Planning also contains a cycle of raiding leadership tasks in the form of its constituent sub-tasks. However, unlike the larger raiding cycle that generally takes place over the course of a few days or a week, the raiding guild research and planning cycle is generally carried out along a much longer time frame. Starting from the point that Blizzard releases new content, the raiding guilds in the sample engaged in a process of researching strategies, raiding, and debriefing, and selecting raid content and scheduling. It's noteworthy that this process begins with the sub-task of Researching Strats, as this points to the fact that for all guilds there are opportunities to learn about new content before they engage with it as a group.

However, those learning opportunities are also stratified such that not all guilds have or take the opportunity to access the same resources. As a result, the rest of the raiding guild research and planning cycle differs vastly between different guilds playing at different levels of intensity. While the average guild might start by researching content about the game written on various *WoW* related wikis and blogs, an extremely competitive guild will likely field several players into Public Test Realms (PTRs) made available by Blizzard while new content is in beta testing[7]. In other words, a relatively small portion of guilds generally engage in the most rigorous learning cycles possible around the game, while a much larger population absorbs (re)mediated knowledge about strategies and tactics that are effective in approaching various challenges. At the same time, at least one less competitive guild in the sample paid little attention to the existing strategies, preferring to try each new encounter without a proven strategy, and then iteratively devise possible solutions and test them on their own.

For all guilds, the sub-task of Researching Strats leads to selecting specific content to try, and setting a schedule for moving forward. Much of the time a guild's schedule will be set at the release of new content and only shifted occasionally (i.e. raiding twice a week on Mondays and Wednesdays), but other guilds utilize a more flexible approach to scheduling so that additional attempts at a new challenge can be undertaken, or to advance their progression through the new content at a faster rate. There is generally a fairly linear progression of actual content selection due to the fact that Blizzard usually develops instances in a series gauged by difficulty. However, a number of factors including a guild's mission, the possible provision of comparably difficult but distinct content by Blizzard, and changes in the membership of a guild can factor into the content selection process.

In looking towards educational contexts, the key thing to note about the preparation processes that guilds engage with is the manner in which players in guilds at different levels of capacity have access to a range of different resources to support their play and learning. Schools are of course fundamentally different in that unlike players in an MMO, students are expected to display individual mastery in content areas. However, outside of the realm of summative evaluation, schools working with the power of digital media could potentially borrow from MMOs to provide students with a network of resources to more effectively differentiate instruction than any single teacher could ever do in the classroom (Collins & Halverson, 2009).

The task of Advanced Preparation of In-Game Resources and Game Interface provides less useful material for considering instructional leadership than many of the other elements in the raiding leadership cycle as much of the activity that characterizes this task is enacted by players engaging with core game mechanics in the game world. However, there are a few features of Advanced Preparation that are noteworthy in considering instructional leadership. To begin with, the sub-task of Preparing Mats is one of the most deeply distributed leadership activities in the game. In more serious guilds in the sample, this activity was generally carried out in some measure by all of the raiding players in various groupings and individually. Notably, while all of the constituent micro-tasks of Preparing Mats are enacted through game play, they are to a great extent defined in terms of a grind that players recognize as a fundamentally boring and repetitive activity (Dibbell, 2006). They engage this grind not because they find it fun per se, but through some combination of feeling a need to serve their guild qua community and/or experiencing a flow state[8] through engaging in the grind (Ducheneaut, Yee, Nickel, & Moore, 2006). In looking to instructional leadership, both the deeply distributed nature of this task, and the manner in which game mechanics serve to make an otherwise dull activity deeply engrossing serve as worthwhile areas for further consideration in considering what the future of online learning might look like.

In looking at the future of online education, the sub-task of Raiding Adjuncts is also worthy of brief consideration. In most current institutional online learning settings, students have very limited control over their interface with the online space. Apart from relatively simple mechanisms for authoring content, students may at best be able to alter the position of some elements within their interface to a Learning or Content Management System (LMS/CMS), and instructors have little more control. The use of software AddOns in a game like *WoW* represents an extension of a set of norms around user interface that differ drastically from those that define the standard eLearning environment. While the basic game interface is already highly configurable to match the needs and preferences of different players, AddOns represent both the assumption that an advanced user might require a deeper level of control over interface than the developers provide, and the assumption of ability within the player community to effectively develop and distribute adjunct software tools. In other words, in many ways the infrastructure of *WoW* as a digital environment has been designed to support and enhance the capacities players bring with them into the system. By contrast, most eLearning enterprise software development has been driven by assumptions of the need to limit both student and teacher control within the system for reasons tied to both network safety and run time stability. Nevertheless, online learning systems are becoming richer and developing a more sophisticated data layer, and some developers like Instructure™ have begun to create more adaptable configurable systems so that learners and teachers can modify their UI to represent the teaching and learning assets they need (Instructure, 2011).

While the tasks of raid leadership form a coherent cycle comparable to cycles executed in other domains of practice, the four tasks of guild management represent generic leadership capacities enacted within the context of an MMO. Player Leadership and Membership Cultivation, and Guild Politics and Executive Management represent the specialized forms of leadership practice required to field interpersonal and political issues within guilds as organizations. In addition, many of their affiliated sub and micro tasks are game specific versions of traditional management and human resource practices. Similarly, Software and Sociopolitical Artifact Creation and Adaptation, and Network Technology and In-Game Maintenance represent specialized variations of the leadership work that takes place in other domains through the creation and maintenance of various technical and social, professional, and organizational artifacts (i.e. mission and vision documents, specialized software tools, curricular materials, etc.).

In the instance of the guild management tasks, it is primarily the software mediated (and specifically game based) nature of them that distinguishes them from generic leadership practices in any other domain of practice. MMOs like *WoW* have a tremendous effect on the nature of even these basic practices, and as a result, there are ways in which the unique realization of these standard practices is worth brief consideration. In particular, given recent conversations around the use of gamification (Schell, 2010) in a wide variety of contexts including education (Deeper, 2011), it is worth considering briefly how *WoW* has already "gamified" fundamental practices of organizational leadership.

To begin with, the game like aspect of leadership in *WoW* has less to do with the application of surface features of games, as the term gamification is commonly used, and more to do with what Malaby (2009) has referred to as "play as a disposition." That is to say, it isn't necessarily the technical features of *WoW* as a game that make the gamified practices of guild leadership interesting, so much as it is the ways in which the context of

WoW as a game makes it possible for players to approach leadership practices playfully.

For example, within guilds as game based organizations, traditional leadership tasks like employee training and team management becomes aspects of a task like Player Leadership and Membership Cultivation. Ultimately, all of the activities that constitute Player Leadership are carried out in, or at least deeply informed by, the highly contingent game world. This very contingency seems to reframe the nature of these classic leadership activities. For instance, there are different character classes in the game that can fulfill the same basic role within the context of raiding. Depending on modifications made to the game by the developers, some will be more effective than others will in that same role. A guild leader may accordingly attempt to recruit players with an advanced avatar in the right class in order to build the group's capacity. However, the developers may decide several months down the line to rework the system reducing the effectiveness of that type of character in that role and enhancing it in some other way. These game based contingencies have nothing to do with the other features of players, and are completely outside of the control of the leadership.

This same sort of contingency is of course evident in other domains of practice (i.e. credentialing requirements can change, markets can shift, etc.), but in *WoW* it is endemic as the game world is shot through with both features that intentionally create contingency (i.e. randomly generated creatures and items in the game world), and structures to which it is inherent (e.g. playing a game on a distributed network of computers). As a result the contingent nature of the space is also a persistent condition for leadership that shapes not only broader decisions like when to raid and what types of players to seek out, but informs almost every aspect of leadership in game.

All of this goes into supporting a second feature of playfulness Malaby highlights, namely the manner in which play as a disposition lends itself towards improvisation. While the core objectives of *WoW* raiding guilds (successfully defeating boss monsters) is in part a matter of a group learning a series of routine behaviors, good leadership (and player performance more generally) is multifaceted, and requires the ability to adapt. For example, because there is no well-defined contractual model for how leadership in *WoW* is realized, leaders have to handle standard tasks like the creation of a leadership team in novel ways. While some leadership teams are assembled simply through prior networks, several of the guilds in the study went through various processes of delegating formal leaders or constructing models for decision making that were more broadly distributed. These solutions to the classic leadership problem of delegation were arrived at in large part because these leaders had no script for a correct way to handle these issues.

Ultimately, all leadership tasks in *WoW* are informed by the unique way in which *WoW* as a playful environment, is nonetheless not entirely a low stakes affair. In fact, players in *WoW* consider the stakes involved in raiding as an activity to be fairly intense, as this game (and not just gaming in general) is for many of them their leisure activity of choice. As a result, guild leadership tasks in *WoW* are attended by challenges made more substantial than one might anticipate for a game-based setting. It is for this reason that the tasks of raid leadership are consistently driven by a real engagement with individual and organizational learning. While the game based context might limit the utility of such spaces as environments for preparing education professionals or approaching instructional leadership topics like curricular development, MMOs nevertheless offer us several avenues for considering what organizational leadership in a primarily online or otherwise computationally driven learning organization looks like. This is particularly true with regard to the role that data can play in leadership for learning.

LEADERSHIP IN AN INCREASINGLY DATA RICH ENVIRONMENT

As instructional leadership in schools becomes an increasingly data driven enterprise (Halverson, Grigg, Prichett, & Thomas, 2007), raiding guild leadership provides us with a perspective on what it means to engage in effective leadership in a data-rich environment. Even the most casual raiding guild leaders in *World of Warcraft* depend on effective use of real-time data generated in game. As explained in the previous section, guilds engaged in more serious raiding harness much of this performance data for later analysis. In addition, players within the community utilize game data to test theories about how to improve individual and group performance (Steinkuehler & Duncan, 2009), and to create both static and interactive artifacts for evaluating individual and guild-level performance across the larger player community.

In fact, the data immersive nature of leadership in *WoW* as a domain of practice is one of the key features that sets it apart from leadership in many other domains including schools. When we look at the tasks of raiding guild leadership, we see the prominence of data as a tool that informs decision making in everything from Running Raids, to Researching Strats, to Roster Building. In addition, unlike in schools, leadership in *WoW* involves both the analysis of static data after opportunities for evaluation have arisen, as well as the use of dynamic data that is generated and analyzed on the fly.

However, with current trends in education policy and technology development, schools (and especially schools utilizing blended or online approaches) are becoming increasingly data rich environments for learning and leadership. In looking to the near future of instructional leadership, leaders in *WoW* help us see how: 1) Making data available to all members creates more opportunities for meaningful interaction with it, 2) Data that

can be captured during practice can be utilized in situ to inform practice meaningfully, 3) Good data driven leadership means understanding the limitations of what can be measured, and 4) Leaders need to know when to encourage their members to focus on tools that provide quantitative measurements and when to de-prioritize them.

First let us consider how the availability of data in organizations like guilds creates opportunities for interaction focused on practices, and how the nature of that data as both a living and static record can provide opportunities for formative and summative feedback. Due to the fact that game play in *WoW* (as in any digital game) is realized through player interaction with a quantitatively driven simulation space, every player action in game is rendered as a piece of data that is in theory retrievable. While there are a huge number of actions players might take that are inconsequential for leadership in the game, the capacity to retrieve and analyze vast swaths of data related to the activity of raiding is hugely important. As we saw when looking at leadership across the raiding cycle, both guild leaders and other players can choose to harness the various types of quantitative data available to them on the fly and after the fact.

One immediate consequence of the availability of player performance data in raiding is the manner in which leadership can become more deeply distributed. The use of software AddOns makes it possible for players to monitor their own performance as well as that of their fellow guild members. One example of this is a common form of AddOn known as a Damage Meter. Software adjuncts of this sort allow players to get in the moment updates of how much damage every character in the raid is delivering to a boss or other monster over the course of a fight. While the information conveyed through Damage Meters represents only one aspect of player performance (there are many actions different types of players must perform apart from delivering damage for a raid to be successful), the availability of this data means that any player whose job it is to deliver damage, and who is interested in improving their play has the capacity to not only evaluate their performance after the raid is completed, but even to monitor it in the midst of an encounter and respond accordingly.

In *WoW* the nature of the simulation space guarantees that all players have access to performance data as it is generated, and have the ability to use the AddOns or out of game tools of their choosing to analyze it. In schools both the collection and dissemination of data generally proceeds along different lines. Certain types of data collection like standardized test data, attendance data, and data tied to student discipline is centralized in schools, maintained through data warehousing systems, and can be made available to education professionals as needed to inform practice and advance conversations between educators. However, more immediately useful classroom level student performance data has traditionally been collected by individual teachers using idiosyncratic low-tech tools (Halverson, Grigg, Prichett, & Thomas, 2007). While certain highly prescriptive learning products like Direct Instruction do provide teachers with the capacity to collect data about student performance, and a common language for discussing this data in relation to their own teaching practices (Halverson & Smith, 2009), these tools come with their own limitations with regard to long-term learning.

Crucially new tools are being developed that provide educators with the capacity to both collect formative student data using more adaptable higher tech solutions, and develop a common language of assessment for advancing their own teaching practices (Rhodes & Halverson, 2009). These sorts of tools provide the opportunity for school and classroom uses of data to come into greater parity with the sorts of sophisticated data practices leaders and players engage with in *WoW*. They can potentially provide teachers with the op-

portunity to engage in classroom level (teacher) leadership in a manner that is directly informed by meaningful living data about student performance much as raid leaders (and players) consult with performance data in the process of raiding. For school level leaders, these artifacts can be utilized to advance the use of a common language in their organizations for discussing teaching and learning outside of instructional time much as guild leaders might consult player performance data through the use of combat logs.

In both instances, the technology for the collection of data needs to be uniform, while tools for the analysis of data benefit from customization. Much as each player has the capacity to choose from a variety of AddOns and log analysis tools that offer different perspectives on the same data set, teachers can benefit from flexible data analysis tools that provide them with a variety of data representations to fit their individual contexts. So long as data collection is grounded in a unified format and given a consistent terminology for discussing performance, customization affords individuals the opportunity to use data at the level with which they are comfortable while establishing a common vocabulary for discussing evidence of teaching and learning across classrooms.

While school leaders can look to the data rich nature of an environment like *WoW* as a model for ramping up the intensity and variability of data usage in their organizations, the manner in which guild leaders in the study discussed the limitations of data is equally important in looking at school leadership practices. Guild leaders in the sample emphasized both the manner in which quantitative data serves to capture only some aspects of player and raid performance, and the way in which they had to intervene at times to ensure that players were focused on the numbers only when they provided a useful means for improving performance. For one guild leader in the study, this meant only turning to combat logs when the raid was getting hung up on a specific encounter rather than utilizing them as a regular part of the debriefing process. For another leader of a serious raiding guild it meant both knowing which players in his guild to talk to in order to gain an adequate understanding of what specific player-generated statistics might mean, and maintaining a narrative perspective on raiding during the debriefing process as well so as to have some means of assessing those aspects of individual and group performance that were not evident in the combat logs.

In general, successful guild leaders in the study displayed both an understanding of the limitations of quantitative data, and an awareness of how player usage of data analysis tools can require management as well. Damage Meter AddOns are a useful touchstone for not only seeing how individual players in *WoW* can take up data for motivation and self evaluation, but also for seeing how leaders can cue into both appropriate and inappropriate uses of the information these tools provide. While some guild leaders in the study emphasized how a tool like Damage Meters can generate healthy competition between guild mates, others emphasized how the data represented by these tools can also function as a distracter for players by de-emphasizing other essential aspects of game play. One guild leader noted that the utility of these tools was contingent based on the structure of each individual encounter, and that his job in the raiding context was to pay careful attention to the nature of the encounter and the behaviors of his players, and then to direct them as the need arose to either lean heavily on the data during an encounter, or ignore it entirely until the fight was finished.

In looking to school leadership this second set of lessons from the data rich context of *WoW* is equally important. We've already seen numerous instances in which standardized test data has been taken as more than just a proxy for student learning (and teacher performance), coming to represent an ends in itself. Allegations of cheating against educators in the Atlanta area in 2010

(Lohr, 2010) serve as just one reminder of the unfortunate consequences that can come from focusing too much on quantitative representations as an actual objective. With the development of new tools educators gain the capacity to take more frequent and finer grained measurements of student performance in the service of classroom level leadership, and while the issues tied to an exclusive focus on quantitative data in this context may not be as morally dubious, they still have the capacity to become problematic.

As schools become increasingly data rich environments, school leaders will need to develop a more nuanced understanding of when and how quantitative measures should be used. Like effective guild leaders with raiding, both teachers and principals will need to maintain sensitivity to the actual activity of teaching and learning so as to understand not only what student and teacher generated data can tell them, but also what it fails to convey. Equally, they will need to know when to guide their faculty and colleagues (and in the near future quite probably students) towards a focus on quantitative measurements, and when to ignore those measurements to focus on other aspects of the teaching and learning process.

Finally, it is worth emphasizing again that there are fundamental differences between performance data in schools and in a game like *WoW*. An obvious difference lies in the fact that data in the school context represents learning that is meant to prepare students for performance in another context, be it further education or the work place. By contrast, data in game is used only for judging player capacity and guild success within that self same context. This difference is essential, although it may be diminished in time with the development of new curricula and new pedagogical tools including games and game like learning systems (Klopfer, Osterweil, & Salen, 2009).

For our considerations, a more crucial difference between the two domains of practice lies in the distance between the data and the object of measurement in each context. In *WoW* there is a one to one correspondence between player performance and the measurements it yields. For guild leaders looking at the performance of members in a raid, the quantitative data rendered in a combat log might not tell the whole story, but each number is a direct representation of player actions during combat. For school leaders, even newer more fine-grained measurements of teacher performance leverage student data as a proxy for teacher activity. While teachers as classroom leaders can look to student data in a similar manner to how a raid leader looks at player data, principals looking at aggregated classroom data are looking at something more closely akin to guild rankings that employ player gear across a guild as a proxy for evaluating the performance of the whole group[9]. While further investigations of player leaders using game based data can certainly serve to inform school and classroom leadership, a keen attention to the nature of the quantitative tools and what they measure will always be essential in framing how in-game leadership practices around data can inform present and future leadership practices for teaching and learning in schools.

Finally, many guild leaders in the study emphasized the manner in which game mechanics and other structural features of an MMO, including assessment opportunities in game, can heighten the need for strong interpersonal leadership. These descriptions serve as reminders for the ways in which the already significant interpersonal demands of school leadership (Harris & Chapman, 2002) might become intensified through the use of both game-like structures and virtual worlds, as school systems embrace digital tools for learning and evaluation. As with any artifact a school adopts, it will behoove school leaders to pay careful attention to both the technical and personal affordances and constraints that accompany powerful data driven tools.

CONCLUSION

In general, the study discussed in this chapter has confirmed the idea that games like *WoW* work as simulations that provide unique opportunities for both researching and learning leadership. Leaders in these worlds must be capable of basic management of a complex online organization (Brown & Thomas, 2006; Reeves & Malone, 2007). At the same time, the specialized knowledge they need in order to be effective leaders in game is grounded in understanding the game itself. While not addressed in this chapter directly, in some respects the findings from this research also raise questions about claims like those made by Thomas and Brown five years ago. *World of Warcraft* as a simulation space has evolved over time to meet the aims of Blizzard as an entertainment software developer. In tuning the software over time, some of the changes Blizzard has made to the game have had consequences for the digital structures that inform the imperatives of leadership in game. Many players argue that those changes have actually reduced some of the complexity attending in-game activities and objectives, and in fact this is a topic worthy of further research.

At the same time, changes to one game certainly cannot be taken to indicate that leadership learning in MMOs is no longer viable, nor even that *WoW* can no longer provide opportunities for players to develop some leadership capacity. It does however point us towards a better understanding of how leadership-learning opportunities in games and other virtual worlds are deeply defined by the structures of these synthetic worlds (Malaby, 2006). At its best, leadership in *WoW* can in fact help us see how a learning organization (Senge, 2006) operating in a digital game can utilize the affordances provided by an affinity space (Gee, 2004) to engage in powerful iterative learning cycles. Raiding guilds as communities of practice

(Lave & Wenger, 1991) avail themselves of both the rich performance measurements provided by the game itself and the software adjuncts developed by the player community. At the same time, education practitioners and researchers would do well to remember that MMOs like *WoW* represent just one kind of possible virtual world, and that lessons gleaned through understanding the structures of these game worlds represent only one frontier in the future of digitally mediated learning.

REFERENCES

Anderson, T. A. (2008). Towards a theory of online learning. In Anderson, T. A. (Ed.), *The Theory and Practice of Online Learning* (2nd ed.). Edmonton, Canada: Athabasca University.

Barab, S. A., Zuiker, S., Warren, S., Hickey, D., Ingram-Goble, A., & Kwon, E.-J. (2007). Situationally embodied curriculum: Relating formalisms and contexts. *Science Education, 91*(5), 750–782. doi:10.1002/sce.20217

Blizzard Entertainment. (2010). *World of Warcraft ® subscriber base reaches 12 million world-wide.* Retrieved from http://us.blizzard.com/en-us/company/press/pressreleases.html?101007

Blizzard Entertainment. (2011). *World of Warcraft ®: Catalcysm™ one month sales top 4.7 million.* Retrieved from http://us.blizzard.com/en-us/company/press/pressreleases.html?110110

Bolman, L. G., & Deal, T. E. (2002). *Reframing the path to school leadership: A guide for teachers and principals.* Thousand Oaks, CA: Corwin Press.

Bolman, L. G., & Deal, T. E. (2003). *Reframing organizations: Artistry, choice, and leadership.* San Francisco, CA: Jossey-Bass.

Brown, J. S., & Thomas, D. (2006). You play World of Warcraft, you're hired!, *Wired. 14*(4).

Chen, M. (2010). *Leet noobs: Expertise and collaboration in a World of Warcraft player group as distributed sociomaterial practice.* (Doctoral Dissertation). University of Washington. Seattle, WA.

Collins, A., & Halverson, R. (2009). *Rethinking education in the age of technology: The digital revolution and schooling in America.* New York, NY: Teachers College Press.

Deal, T. E., & Peterson, K. (1999). *Shaping school culture: The heart of leadership.* San Francisco, CA: Jossey-Bass.

Deeper, G. (2011). Predictions for e-learning in 2011. *eLearn Magazine.* Retrieved from http://www.elearnmag.org/subpage.cfm?searchterm=learning+reflection&article=148-1&section=articles

Dibbell, J. (2006). *Play money: Or how I quit my day job and struck it rich in virtual loot farming.* New York, NY: Basic Books.

Duchenaut, N., Yee, N., Nickel, E., & Moore, R. J. (2006). Building an MMO with mass appeal: A look at gameplay in World of Warcraft. *Games and Culture, 1*(4), 281–317. doi:10.1177/1555412006292613

Gee, J. P. (2003). *What video games have to teach us about learning and literacy.* New York, NY: Palgrave/Macmillan. doi:10.1145/950566.950595

Gee, J. P. (2004). *Situated language and learning: A critique of traditional schooling.* New York, NY: Routledge.

Gee, J. P. (2005). Semiotic social spaces and affinity spaces: From the age of mythology to today's schools. In Barton, D., & Tusting, K. (Eds.), *Beyond 395 Communities of Practice: Language, Power, and Social Context.* New York, NY: Cambridge University Press. doi:10.1017/CBO9780511610554.012

Golafshani, N. (2003). Understanding reliability and validity in qualitative research. *Qualitative Report*, *8*(4), 597–607.

Guba, E. G., & Lincoln, Y. S. (1994). Competing paradigms in qualitative research. In Denzin, N. K. (Ed.), *Handbook of Qualitative Research*. Thousand Oaks, CA: Sage Publications.

Halverson, R. (2005). What can K-12 leaders learn from video games and gaming?. *Innovate, 1*(6).

Halverson, R., & Clifford, M. (2006). Evaluation in the wild: A distributed cognition perspective on teacher assessment. *Educational Administration Quarterly*, *42*(4), 578–619. doi:10.1177/0013161X05285986

Halverson, R., Grigg, J., Prichett, R., & Thomas, C. (2007). The new instructional leadership: Creating data-driven instructional systems in schools. *Journal of School Leadership*, *17*(2), 159–194.

Halverson, R., & Smith, A. (2009). How new technologies have (and have not) changed teaching and learning in schools. *Journal of Computing in Teacher Education*, *26*(2), 49–54.

Harris, A., & Chapman, C. (2002). *Effective leadership in schools facing challenging circumstances*. Nottingham, UK: NCSL.

Hutchins, E. (1996). *Cognition in the wild*. Cambridge, MA: MIT Press.

IBM. (2005). *Virtual worlds real leaders: Online games put the future of business leadership in display*. Palo Alto, CA: Seriosity Inc.

Instructure. (2011). *Instructure canvas*. Retrieved from http://www.instructure.com

Jenkins, H., Clinton, K., Purushotma, R., Robinson, A. J., Weigel, M., John, D., et al. (2006). *Confronting the challenges of participatory culture: Media education for the 21st century*. Retrieved from http://dmlcentral.net/sites/dmlcentral/files/resource_files/Confronting_the_Challenges.pdf

Johnson, L., Smith, R., Levine, A., & Haywood, K. (2010). *The 2010 horizon report: K-12 edition*. Austin, TX: The New Media Consortium.

Klopfer, E., Osterweil, S., & Salen, K. (2009). *Moving learning games forward: Obstacles, opportunities, and openness*. Cambridge, MA: The Education Arcade.

Lave, J., & Wenger, E. (1991). *Situated learning: Legitimate peripheral participation*. Cambridge, UK: Cambridge University Press. doi:10.1017/CBO9780511815355

Lincoln, E. G., & Guba, Y. S. (1985). Competing paradigms in qualitative research. In Denzin, N., & Lincoln, Y. (Eds.), *The SAGE Handbook of Qualitative Research* (pp. 163–194). Thousand Oaks, CA: SAGE Publications.

Lohr, K. (2010, October 12). Cheating investigation focuses on Atlanta schools. *National Public Radio*. Retrieved from http://www.npr.org/templates/story/story.php?storyId=130335370

Malaby, T. M. (2006). Parlaying value: Capital in and beyond virtual worlds. *Games and Culture*, *1*(2), 141–162. doi:10.1177/1555412006286688

Malaby, T. M. (2009). *Anthropology and play: The contours of playful experience*. Retrieved from http://ssrn.com/abstract=1315542

McKnight, J. C. (2010). *The devils made me do it: An experiment in teaching collaborative governance in World of Warcraft*. Paper presented at the Games+Learning+Society Conference 6.0. Madison, WI.

Nardi, B. A. (2010). *My life as a night elf priest: An anthropological account of World of Warcraft*. Ann Arbor, MI: The University of Michigan Press.

Nardi, B. A., & Harris, J. (2006). *Strangers and friends: Collaborative play in World of Warcraft*. Retrieved from http://portal.acm.org/citation.cfm?id=1180875.1180898

NSF Task Force on Cyberlearning. (2008). *Fostering learning the networked world*. Washington, DC: National Science Foundation.

Quest to Learn. (2011). *Quest to learn school website*. Retrieved from http://q2l.org/

Reeves, B., & Malone, T. (2007). *Leadership in games and at work: Implications for the enterprise of massively multiplayer online role-playing games. Report Prepared for IBM*. New York, NY: IBM.

Rhodes, S., & Halverson, R. (2009). *KidGrid*. Paper presented at the Games+Learning+Society 5.0 conference. Madison, WI.

Schell, J. (2010) *Design outside the box*. Paper presented at the 9ᵗʰ Annual Design Innovate Communicate Entertain (D.I.C.E.) Summit. Las Vegas, NV.

Senge, P. (2006). *The fifth discipline: The art & practice of the learning organization*. New York, NY: Doubleday. doi:10.1002/pfi.4170300510

Shaffer, D. W., & Clinton, K. A. (2006). Tool-forthoughts: Reexamining thinking in the digital age. *Mind, Culture, and Activity, 13*(4), 283–300. doi:10.1207/s15327884mca1304_2

Spillane, J. P., Halverson, R., & Diamond, J. (2004). Towards a theory of school leadership practice: Implications of a distributed perspective. *Journal of Curriculum Studies, 36*(1), 3–34. doi:10.1080/0022027032000106726

Squire, K. D. (2011). *Video games and learning: Teaching and participatory culture in the digital age*. New York, NY: Teachers College Press.

Steinkuehler, C., & Duncan, S. (2009). Informal scientific reasoning in online virtual worlds. *Journal of Science Education and Technology, 17*(6), 530–543. doi:10.1007/s10956-008-9120-8

Steinkuehler, C. A. (2006). The mangle of play. *Games and Culture, 1*(3), 1–14. doi:10.1177/1555412006290440

Steinkuehler, C. A. (2008). Cognition and literacy in massively multiplayer online games. In Coiro, J., Knobel, M., Lankshear, C., & Leu, D. (Eds.), *Handbook of Research on New Literacies* (pp. 611–634). Mahwah, NJ: Erlbaum.

Steinkuehler, C. A., & Williams, D. (2006). Where everybody knows your (screen) name: Online games as third places. *Journal of Computer-Mediated Communication, 11*(4). doi:10.1111/j.1083-6101.2006.00300.x

Strauss, A. L., & Corbin, J. (1990). *Basics of qualitative research: Grounded theory procedures and techniques*. Thousand Oaks, CA: Sage Publications.

Thomas, D., & Brown, J. S. (2009). Why virtual worlds can matter. *International Journal of Media and Learning, 1*(1).

Williams, D., Ducheneaut, N., Xiong, L., Zhang, Y., Yee, N., & Nickell, E. (2006). From tree house to barracks: The social life of guilds in World of Warcraft. *Games and Culture, 1*(4), 338–361. doi:10.1177/1555412006292616

Williams, D., Yee, N., & Kaplan, S. E. (2008). Who plays, how much, and why? Debunking the stereotypical gamer profile. *Journal of Computer-Mediated Communication, 13*, 993–1018. doi:10.1111/j.1083-6101.2008.00428.x

Wolfenstein, M. (2010). *Leadership at play: How leadership in digital games can inform the future of instructional leadership*. (Doctoral Dissertation). University of Wisconsin–Madison. Madison, WI.

Wolfenstein, M., & Dikkers, S. (2009). *My raid leader, my teacher: What we can learn about schools from guild leadership*. Paper presented at the American Education Research Association Conference. San Diego, CA.

Woodcock, B. (2008). *MMOG chart*. Retrieved from http://www.mmogchart.com/

WoW in School. (2011). *The World of Warcraft in school wiki*. Retrieved from http://wowinschool. pbworks.com/

Yee, N. (2005). *The Daedalus gateway*. Retrieved from http://www.nickyee.com/daedalus

Yee, N. (2006). The demographics, motivations and derived experiences of users of massively-multiuser online graphical environments. *Presence (Cambridge, Mass.)*, *15*, 309–329. doi:10.1162/ pres.15.3.309

Yee, N., Ducheneaut, & Moore. (2006). Building a MMO with mass appeal: A look at gameplay in World of Warcraft. *Games and Culture*, *1*(4), 1–38.

KEY TERMS AND DEFINITIONS

Affinity Space: The term affinity space was developed by James Paul Gee in response to Lave and Wenger's concept of community of practice. Gee offers the concept of affinity space as a way of handling issues around boundaries, participation, and membership that arise through use of the term community. One key property of an affinity space is the manner in which individuals within such a space relate to each other primarily in terms of their interest in a shared endeavor or practice.

Distributed Leadership: Distributed leadership is a theory developed by Jim Spillane and others based on of the concept of distributed cognition first put forth by Edwin Hutchins. Distributed leadership is a descriptive theory that can be used to characterize the manner and degree to which leadership is distributed throughout the people and artifacts within an organization. Since it is not prescriptive in nature, distributed leadership is not useful in defining how leadership should be distributed within a given organization.

Game Mechanics: Game mechanics are the core design elements designers deploy in making a digital or analog game. A core mechanic in the game chess would be the rule set governing the motion of individual pieces on the board. A core mechanic in the arcade classic PacMan™ would be the ability for the titular character to earn points by eating dots.

Gamification: Gamification generally refers to deploying game mechanics (i.e. scoring systems, "badges," leader boards, etc.) in non-game systems with the intention of creating a more game like experience for end users. In more theoretical contexts, gamification can also refer to any alterations to an existing system that can make it more game like. Such augmentations could be driven by the introduction of game mechanics, or by the development of a narrative or behavioral wrapper that causes end users to approach the experience in a more playful manner.

Massively Multiplayer Online Game (MMO): The MMO genre refers to online games that are capable of allowing thousands or even hundreds of thousands of players to engage in online play in the same virtual world simultaneously. There are a wide range of different sub-genres of MMO based in large part on other pre-existing video game genres. In addition, while many such games carry a fantasy theme like *World of Warcraft*, the settings for these virtual worlds vary as well.

Raiding Guild: A raiding guild is an organization that exists in certain types of MMOs which is primarily focused around the activity of large-scale cooperative play within the game. For example, in the MMO *World of Warcraft*, raiding guilds organize around the objective of completing challenging "dungeons" in the game that require live coordination of 10 to 25 players simultaneously. Raiding guilds are sometimes contrasted with social guilds, which may engage in the activity of raiding, but exist primarily for the purpose of socializing around a shared activity.

ENDNOTES

1. The content in this chapter is based on the author's 2010 dissertation research *Leadership at Play: How Leadership in Digital Games can inform the Future of Instructional Leadership* (Wolfenstein, 2010).

2. The number of players a single game can support online in a game world is significantly larger than the number who can gather for simultaneous interaction with each other in the same virtual location. This is a result of the fact that extreme concentrations of players in small areas create greater computational demands on both individual players' computers, and the server on which a copy of a game is running.

3. According to Blizzard Entertainment, as of October 2010 *World of Warcraft* had in excess of 12 million players worldwide. The company subsequently reported that following its December release, the third expansion to the game called Cataclysm™ sold more than 4.7 million copies in its first month setting a record for monthly PC-game sales.

4. The term genre in games designates the core mechanics or form of player interaction rather than narrative or thematic content. For instance, *World of Warcraft* is classified in full as a MMORPG (Massively Multiplayer Online Roleplaying Game). This means that it features massive scale player interaction as described in the text, and utilizes the mechanics of the role-playing game genre. In video games, these mechanics generally revolve around the distribution of points to different character attributes, random systems for determining certain types of encounters in game, and leveled system through which characters progress becoming more powerful through the acquisition of "experience points" and in-game items.

5. A complete explanation of the leadership tasks along with examples of supporting evidence from the research can be found in chapters 5 and 6 of the author's dissertation.

6. The term "on farm" is used to indicate that a guild has complete mastery over a specific instance. This allows the organization to take less experienced players with less powerful avatars into the dungeon to "farm" the boss monsters for better gear that can increase the abilities of less powerful player avatars.

7. Game companies, like most software developers, usually develop and test alpha and beta versions of their software prior to a "gold" release. MMO developers will often run a version of their virtual world during these testing phases and invite selected players in to test out the new content prior to release. In the case of *WoW*, servers on which these tests are conducted are referred to as Public Test Realms.

8. If you are unfamiliar with the concept of flow, it is a widely used term in video game studies developed by Csikszentmihaly (1990). While the conceptual model behind flow is quite complex, at its core a flow state is one in which the individual is completely occupied with the experience in which they are engaged creating a type of positive feedback loop.

9. Because virtual items in *World of Warcraft* are standardized along an underlying model that maps to the difficulty of the in-game content, guild member possession of certain virtual items can be utilized as a proxy for rating the advancement of a guild in the game. While Blizzard does not provide a ranking of guilds, several player-supported sites scan the public database of player avatars Blizzard does provide, and use this information to create guild rankings.

Compilation of References

Agami, A. (2003). Using internet resources in teaching financial reporting and analysis of multinational enterprises. In Russow, L. C. (Ed.), *Digital Technology in Teaching International Business* (pp. 115–131). Binghamton, NY: International Business Press. doi:10.1300/J066v14n02_08

Aldrich, C. (2009). Virtual worlds, simulaltions, and games for education: A unifying view. *Innovate, 5*(5). Retrieved January 11, 2011 from http://www.innovateonline.info/pdf/vol5_issue5/Virtual_Worlds,_Simulations,_and_Games_for_Education-__A_Unifying_View.pdf

Alice. (2007). *Website.* Retrieved August 15, 2007, from http://www.alice.org

Anderson, L. W., & Krathwohl, D. R. (Eds.). (2001). *A taxonomy for learning, teaching and assessing: A revision of Bloom's taxonomy of educational objectives: Complete edition.* New York, NY: Longman.

Anderson, T. (2002). Revealing the hidden curriculum of e-learning. In Glass, G., & Vrasidas, C. (Eds.), *Distance Education and Distributed Learning* (pp. 113–115). New York, NY: Information Age.

Anderson, T. A. (2008). Towards a theory of online learning. In Anderson, T. A. (Ed.), *The Theory and Practice of Online Learning* (2nd ed.). Edmonton, Canada: Athabasca University.

Andrade, A., Bagri, A., Zaw, K., Roos, B. A., & Ruiz, J. G. (2010). Avatar-mediated training in the delivery of bad news in a virtual world. *Journal of Palliative Medicine, 13*(12), 1–14. doi:10.1089/jpm.2010.0108

Andreas, K., Tsiatsos, T., Terzidou, T., & Pomportsis, A. (2010). Fostering collaborative learning in second life: Metaphors and affordances. *Computers & Education, 55*(2), 603–615. doi:10.1016/j.compedu.2010.02.021

Angeli, C. (2004). The effects of case-based learning on early childhood pre-service teachers' beliefs about the pedagogical uses of ICT. *Journal of Educational Media, 29*(2), 139–151. doi:10.1080/1358165042000253302

Angrosino, M. V. (Ed.). (2007). *Doing cultural anthropology: Projects in ethnographic data collection.* Long Grove, IL: Waveland Press Inc.

Anthamatten, P., & Ziegler, S. S. (2006). Teaching geography with 3-D visualization technology. *The Journal of Geography, 105*(6), 231–237. doi:10.1080/00221340608978692

Antonova, A., & Martinov, M. (2010). Educational and business applications of serious games and virtual worlds. In *Proceedings of SAI Conference.* Sofia, Bulgaria: SAI.

Antonova, A., & Todorova, K. (2010). Serious games and virtual worlds for high-level learning experiences. In *Proceedings of S3T Conference,* (pp. 250-255). S3T.

Apple, M. W. (2004). *Ideology and curriculum.* New York, NY: RoutledgeFalmer.

Arnheim, R. (1970). *Visual thinking.* London, UK: Faber.

Arroyo, A., Serradilla, F., & Calvo, O. (2009). Multimodal agents in second life and the new agents of virtual 3D environments. In *Proceedings of the 3rd International Work-Conference on the Interplay Between Natural and Artificial Computation (IWINAC 2009),* (pp. 506–516). IWINAC.

Aukstakalnis, S. (1991). *Silicon mirage: The art and science of virtual reality*. Berkeley, CA: Peachpit Press.

Bagley, E., & Shaffer, D. W. (2009). When people get in the way: Promoting civic thinking through epistemic game play. *International Journal of Gaming and Computer-Mediated Simulations, 1*(1). doi:10.4018/jgcms.2009010103

Bailenson, J. N., Yee, N., Blascovich, J., Beall, A. C., Lundblad, N., & Jin, M. (2008). The use of immersive virtual reality in the learning sciences: Digital transformations of teachers, students, and social context. *Journal of the Learning Sciences, 17*(1), 102–141. doi:10.1080/10508400701793141

Bailly, G., & Raidt, F. E. (2010). Gaze, conversational agents and face-to-face communication. *Speech Communication, 52*(6), 598–612. doi:10.1016/j.specom.2010.02.015

Bainbridge, W. S. (2007). The scientific research potential of virtual worlds. *Science, 317*(5837), 472–476. doi:10.1126/science.1146930

Bakas, C., & Mikropoulos, T. (2003). Design of virtual environments for the comprehension of planetary phenomena based on students' ideas. *International Journal of Science Education, 25*(8), 949–967. doi:10.1080/09500690305027

Bandura, A. (1977). *Social learning theory*. Englewood Cliffs, NJ: Prentice-Hall.

Bandura, A. (1997). *Self-efficacy: The exercise of control*. New York, NY: W. H. Freeman and Company.

Barab, S. A., Dodge, T., Ingram-Goble, A., Volk, C., Peppler, K., & Pettyjohn, P. (2009). Pedagogical dramas and transformational play: Narratively-rich games for education. In Lurgel, I. A., Zagalo, N., & Petta, P. (Eds.), *Interactive Storytelling* (pp. 332–335). Heidelberg, Germany: Springer. doi:10.1007/978-3-642-10643-9_42

Barab, S. A., Hay, K. E., Barnett, M., & Keating, T. (2000). Virtual solar system project: Building understanding through model building. *Journal of Research in Science Teaching, 38*, 70–102. doi:10.1002/1098-2736(200101)38:1<70::AID-TEA5>3.0.CO;2-L

Barab, S. A., Hay, K. E., Barnett, M., & Squire, K. (2001). Constructing virtual worlds: Tracing the historical development of learner practices. *Cognition and Instruction, 19*(1), 47–94. doi:10.1207/S1532690XCI1901_2

Barab, S. A., Hay, K. E., & Duffy, T. M. (1998). Grounded constructions and how technology can help. *TechTrends, 43*(2), 15–23. doi:10.1007/BF02818171

Barab, S. A., Thomas, M., Dodge, T., Carteaux, R., & Tuzun, H. (2005). Making learning fun: Quest Atlantis, a game without guns. *Educational Technology Research and Development, 53*(1), 86–107. doi:10.1007/BF02504859

Barab, S. A., Zuiker, S., Warren, S., Hickey, D., Ingram-Goble, A., & Kwon, E.-J. (2007). Situationally embodied curriculum: Relating formalisms and contexts. *Science Education, 91*(5), 750–782. doi:10.1002/sce.20217

Barab, S., Sadler, T., Heiselt, C., Hickey, D., & Zuiker, S. (2007). Relating narrative, inquiry, and inscriptions: Supporting consequential play. *Journal of Science Education and Technology, 16*(1), 59–82. doi:10.1007/s10956-006-9033-3

Barry, A. (1997). *Visual intelligence: Perception, image, and manipulation in visual communication*. Albany, NY: State University of New York Press.

Barry, A. M. (1994). Perceptual aesthetics and visual language. In *Visual Literacy: A Spectrum of Visual Learning*. New York, NY: Tech Publishing.

Barth, H., La Mont, K., Lipton, J., Dehaene, S., Kanwisher, N., & Spelke, E. (2006). Non-symbolic arithmetic in adults and young children. *Cognition, 98*(3), 199–222. doi:10.1016/j.cognition.2004.09.011

Bateson, G. (1979). *Mind and nature: A necessary unity*. New York, NY: Dutton.

Baumard, P. (1999). *Tacit knowledge in organizations*. London, UK: Sage.

Beatty, K., & Nunan, D. (2004). Computer-mediated collaborative learning. *System, 32*, 165–183. doi:10.1016/j.system.2003.11.006

Becerra-Fernandez, I., & Stevenson, J. M. (2001). Knowledge management systems & solutions for the school principal as chief learning officer. *Education*, *121*, 508–519.

Bell, M. (2008). Toward a definition of virtual worlds. *Journal of Virtual Worlds Research*, *1*(1).

Benbunan-Fich, R., & Stoever, W. A. (2003). Using information technology to promote multi-cultural case teaching: A pedagogical framework. In Russow, L. C. (Ed.), *Digital Technology in Teaching International Business* (pp. 13–27). Binghamton, NY: International Business Press.

Bennet, A., & Bennet, D. (2004). *Organizational survival in the new world*. Burlington, UK: Elsevier.

Benotti, L., Estrella, P., & Areces, C. (2010). Dialogue systems for virtual worlds. In *Proceedings of NAACLT HLT 2010 Young Investigators Workshop on Computational Approaches to Languages of the Americas*, (pp. 132-140). NAACLT.

Berger, J. (1977). *Ways of seeing*. New York, NY: Penguin.

Bernard, H. R. (2011). *Research methods in anthropology: Qualitative and quantitative approaches*. Lanham, MD: AltaMira Press.

Bertrand, J., Babu, S. V., Polgreen, P., & Segre, A. (2010). Virtual agents based simulation for training healthcare workers in hand hygiene procedures. In Allbeck, J. (Eds.), *Intelligent Virtual Agents (IVA)* (pp. 125–131). Berlin, Germany: Springer. doi:10.1007/978-3-642-15892-6_13

Beskow, J., Edlund, J., Granström, B., Gustafson, J., Skantze, G., & Tobiasson, H. (2009). The MonAMI reminder: A spoken dialogue system for face-to-face interaction. In *Proceedings of Interspeech* (pp. 296–299). Interspeech.

Beveridge, M., & Fox, J. (2006). Automatic generation of spoken dialogue from medical plans and ontologies. *Biomedical Informatics*, *39*(5), 482–499. doi:10.1016/j.jbi.2005.12.008

Biswas, G., Leelawong, K., Schwartz, D., & Vye, N. (2005). Learning by teaching: A new agent paradigm for educational software. *Applied Artificial Intelligence*, *19*, 363–392. doi:10.1080/08839510590910200

Bittarello, M. (2008). Another time, another space: Virtual worlds, myths and imagination. *Journal of Virtual Worlds Research*, *1*(1).

Bjarkam, C. R. (2004). *Neuroanatomi*. Munksgaard, Germany: København.

Blizzard Entertainment. (2010). *World of Warcraft ® subscriber base reaches 12 million world-wide*. Retrieved from http://us.blizzard.com/en-us/company/press/press-releases.html?101007

Blizzard Entertainment. (2011). *World of Warcraft ®: Catalcysm™ one month sales top 4.7 million*. Retrieved from http://us.blizzard.com/en-us/company/press/press-releases.html?110110

Blizzard. (2010). *World of Warcraft*. Retrieved from http://us.blizzard.com/en-us/company/

Bloom, B. S., & Krathwohl, D. R. (1956). *Taxonomy of educational objectives: The classification of educational goals, by a committee of college and university examiners: Handbook 1: Cognitive domain*. New York, NY: Longmans.

Boellstorff, T. (2008). *Coming of age in second life: An anthropologist explores the virtually human*. Princeton, NJ: Princeton University Press.

Bogdan, R. C., & Biklen, S. K. (2007). *Qualitative research for education: An introduction to theory and methods* (5th ed.). Boston, MA: Pearson/Allyn and Bacon.

Bolman, L. G., & Deal, T. E. (2002). *Reframing the path to school leadership: A guide for teachers and principals*. Thousand Oaks, CA: Corwin Press.

Bolman, L. G., & Deal, T. E. (2003). *Reframing organizations: Artistry, choice, and leadership*. San Francisco, CA: Jossey-Bass.

Bonk, C. J., Kim, K. J., & Zeng, T. (2006). Future directions of blended learning in higher education and workplace learning settings. In Bonk, C. J., & Graham, C. R. (Eds.), *Handbook of Blended Learning: Global Perspectives, Local Designs* (pp. 550–567). San Francisco, CA: Pfeiffer Publishing.

Boon, S., & Sinclair, C. (2009). A world I don't inhabit: Disquiet and identity in Second Life and Facebook. *Educational Media International*, *46*(2), 99–110. doi:10.1080/09523980902933565

Boud, D., Keogh, R., & Walker, D. (1985). *Reflection: Turning experience into learning*. London, UK: Routledge.

Bowers, C., Smith, P. A., Cannon-Bowers, J., & Nicholson, D. (2008). Using virtual world to assist distributed teams. In Zemliansky, P., & St. Amant, K. (Eds.), *Handbook of Research on Virtual Workspaces and the New Nature of Business Practices*. Hershey, PA: IGI Global. doi:10.4018/978-1-59904-893-2.ch029

Brenner, J. (2012). *Pew internet: Mobile*. Retrieved from http://pewinternet.org/Commentary/2012/February/Pew-Internet-Mobile.aspx

Bronack, S., Riedl, R., Tashner, J., & Greene, M. (2006). Learning in the zone: A social constructivist framework for distance education in a 3D virtual world. In *Proceedings of Society for Information Technology and Teacher Education International Conference 2006*, (pp. 268-275). IEEE.

Brophy, J. (1999). Toward a model of the value aspects of motivation in education: Developing appreciation for particular learning domains and activities. *Educational Psychologist*, *34*, 75–85. doi:10.1207/s15326985ep3402_1

Brown, J. S., & Thomas, D. (2006). You play World of Warcraft, you're hired!, *Wired*. *14*(4).

Brown, J. S., Collins, A., & Duguid, P. (1989). Situated cognition and the culture of learning. *Educational Researcher*, *18*(1), 32–42.

Brown, P., & Levinson, S. C. (1987). *Politeness: Some universals in language use*. Cambridge, UK: Cambridge University Press.

Bruffee, K. A. (1999). *Collaborative learning: Higher education, interdependence, and the authority of knowledge* (2nd ed.). Baltimore, MD: Johns Hopkins University Press. doi:10.2307/358879

Burbules, N. (2006). Rethinking the virtual. In Weiss, J. (Ed.), *The International Handbook of Virtual Learning Environments* (pp. 37–58). New York, NY: Springer. doi:10.1007/978-1-4020-3803-7_1

Burnett, R. (2004). *How images think*. Cambridge, MA: The MIT Press.

Burton, B., & Chin, J. (2007). *Inclusion of game concepts in introductory programming courses*. Paper presented at Illinois Online Conference. Chicago, IL.

Burton, B., & Martin, B. N. (2010). Learning in virtual environments: Collaboration and knowledge spirals. *Journal of Educational Computing Research*, *43*(2), 259–273. doi:10.2190/EC.43.2.f

Callejas, Z., & López-Cózar, R. (2005). Implementing modular dialogue systems: A case study. In *Proceedings of Applied Spoken Language Interaction in Distributed Environments (ASIDE 2005)*. Aalborg, Denmark: ASIDE.

Callejas, Z., & López-Cózar, R. (2008). Relations between de-facto criteria in the evaluation of a spoken dialogue system. *Speech Communication*, *50*(8-9), 646–665. doi:10.1016/j.specom.2008.04.004

Campbell, C. (2009). Learning in a different life: Preservice education students using an online virtual world. *Journal of Virtual Worlds Research*, *2*(1).

Carpenter, S. (2009). Virtual worlds as educational experience: Living and learning in interesting times. *Journal of Virtual Worlds Research*, *2*(1).

Cassell, J., Bickmore, T., Billinghurst, M., Campbell, L., Chang, K., Vilhálmsson, H., & Yan, H. (1999). Embodiment in conversational interfaces: Rea. In *Proceedings of Computer-Human Interaction* (pp. 520–527). ACM Press.

Castronova, E. (2007). *Exodus to the virtual world: How online fun is changing reality*. New York, NY: Palgrave Macmillan.

Cavazza, M., de la Cámara, R. S., & Turunen, M. (2010). How was your day? A companion ECA. In *Proceedings of AAMAS 2010 Conference*, (pp. 1629–1630). AAMAS.

Cavazza, M., Martin, O., Charles, F., Mead, S. J., & Marichal, X. (2003). Users Acting in mixed reality interactive storytelling. In Balet, O., Subsol, G., & Torguet, P. (Eds.), *Virtual Storytelling* (pp. 189–197). Berlin, Germany: Springer. doi:10.1007/978-3-540-40014-1_24

Cennamo, K., & Kalk, D. (2005). *Real world instructional design*. Belmont, CA: Thomson Wadsworth.

Chandler, D. (2008). *Visual perception*. Retrieved November 2008, from http://www.aber.ac.uk/media/Modules/MC10220/lectures.html

Chapman, P. (2010). More professors are using Twitter – But mostly not for teaching. *The Chronicle of Higher Education*. Retrieved from http://chronicle.com/blogs/wiredcampus/more-professors-are-using-twitter-but-mostly-not-for-teaching/27354

Cheal, C. (2007). Second life: Hype or hyperlearning? *Horizon, 15*(4), 204–210. doi:10.1108/10748120710836228

Chen, B. (2010, June 18). Analyst: iPhone sales to surpass 100 million by 2011. *Gadget Lab*. Retrieved from http://www.wired.com/gadgetlab/2010/06/analyst-iphone-sales-to-surpass-100-million-by-2011/

Chen, M. (2010). *Leet noobs: Expertise and collaboration in a World of Warcraft player group as distributed sociomaterial practice*. (Doctoral Dissertation). University of Washington. Seattle, WA.

Chiang, O. (2010). *How playing video games can boost your career*. Retrieved August 20, 2011 from http://www.forbes.com/2010/07/19/career-leadership-strategy-technology-videogames.html

Chickering, A. W., & Gamson, Z. F. (1987). Seven principles for good practice in undergraduate education. *The American Association for Higher Education Bulletin*. Retrieved from http://www.uis.edu/liberalstudies/students/documents/sevenprinciples.pdf

Chi, M., De Leeuw, N., Chiu, M., & Lavancher, C. (1994). Eliciting self-explanations improves understanding. *Cognitive Science, 18*, 439–477.

Choo, C. W. (1998). *Information management for the intelligent organization: The art of scanning the environment*. Medford, NJ: Information Today.

Christensen, C. M. (1997). *The innovator's dilemma: When new technologies cause great firms to fail*. Boston, MA: Harvard Business School Press.

Cole, R., & Zue, V. (1997). *Survey of the state of the art in human language technology*. Cambridge, UK: Cambridge University Press.

Collins, A., & Halverson, R. (2009). *Rethinking education in the age of technology: The digital revolution and schooling in America*. New York, NY: Teachers College Press.

Conceicao, S. C. O. (2006). Faculty lived experiences in the online environment. *American Association for Adult and Continuing Education, 57*(1), 26–45. doi:10.1177/1059601106292247

Corno, L., & Mandinach, E. B. (1983). The role of cognition engagement in classroom learning and motivation. *Educational Psychologist, 18*(2), 88–108. doi:10.1080/00461528309529266

Craig, E. (2007). *Meta-perspectives on the metaverse: A blogsphere debate on the significance of second life*. Paper presented at ED-MEDIA World Conference on Educational Multimedia, Hypermedia & Telecommunications. Vancouver, Canada.

Csíkszentmihályi, M. (1990). *Flow: The psychology of optimal experience*. New York, NY: Harper and Row.

Cupach, W. R., & Metts, S. (1994). *Facework*. Thousand Oaks, CA: Sage.

D'Mello, S., Hays, P., Williams, C., Cade, W., Brown, J., & Olney, A. (2010). Collaborative lecturing by human and computer tutors. In Aleven, V., Kay, J., & Mostow, J. (Eds.), *Intelligent Tutoring Systems (ITS)* (pp. 178–187). Berlin, Germany: Springer. doi:10.1007/978-3-642-13437-1_18

Dake, D. M. (1999). A natural visual mind: The art and science of visual literacy. *Journal of Visual Literacy, 27*(1), 7–28.

Dalgarno, B. (2002). The potential of 3D virtual learning environments: a constructivist analysis. *E-Journal of Instructional Science and Technology, 5*(2). Retrieved November 24, 2010, from http://www.usq.edu.au/electpub/e-jist/docs/Vol5_No2/dalgarno_frame.html

Dalgarno, B., & Lee, M. (2010). What are the learning affordances of 3-D virtual environments? *British Journal of Educational Technology, 41*(1), 10–32. doi:10.1111/j.1467-8535.2009.01038.x

Darts, D. (2004). Visual culture jam: Art, pedagogy, and creative resistance. *Studies in Art Education, 45*(4), 313–327.

Davenport, M. (2003). Using simulations to ground intercultural inquiry in the art classroom. *Art Education, 56*(5), 13–18.

Davenport, T. H., & Prusak, L. (1998). *Working knowledge: How organizations manage what they know*. Boston, MA: Harvard Business School Press.

Davis, N., Preston, C., & Sahin, I. (2009). Training teachers to use new technologies impacts multiple ecologies: Evidence from a national initiative. *British Journal of Educational Technology, 40*(5), 861–878. doi:10.1111/j.1467-8535.2008.00875.x

de Winter, J., Winterbottom, M., & Wilson, E. (2010). Developing a user guide to integrating new technologies in science teaching and learning: teachers' and pupils' perceptions of their affordances. *Technology, Pedagogy and Education, 19*(2), 261–267. doi:10.1080/1475939X.2010.491237

Deal, T. E., & Peterson, K. (1999). *Shaping school culture: The heart of leadership*. San Francisco, CA: Jossey-Bass.

Dede, C., Clarke, J., Ketelhut, D., Nelson, B., & Bowman, C. (2005). *Fostering motivation, learning, and transfer in multi-user virtual environments*. Paper presented at the American Educational Research Association Conference. Montreal, Canada.

Dede, C., Ketelhut, D. J., & Reuss, K. (2003). *Motivation, usability, and learning outcomes in a prototype museum-based multi-use virtual environment*. Paper presented at the Fifth International Conference of the Learning Sciences. New York, NY.

Dede, C., Nelson, B., Ketelhut, D. J., Clarke, J., & Bowman, C. (2004). Design-based research strategies for studying situated learning in a multi-user virtual environment. In *Proceedings of the Sixth International Conference on the Learning Sciences,* (pp. 158-165). Mahwah, NJ: Lawrence Erlbaum. Retrieved May 20, 2010, from http://muve.gse.harvard.edu/muvees2003/documents/dedeICLS04.pdf

Dede, C. (1997). Rethinking: How to invest in technology. *Educational Leadership, 55*(3), 12–16.

Dede, C. (2005). Planning for neomillinnial learning styles. *EDUCAUSE Quarterly, 1*, 7–12.

Deeper, G. (2011). Predictions for e-learning in 2011. *eLearn Magazine*. Retrieved from http://www.elearnmag.org/subpage.cfm?searchterm=learning+reflection&article=148-1&section=articles

Dehaene, S. (1997). *The number sense*. Oxford, UK: Oxford University Press.

Dehaene, S., & Cohen, L. (1999). Language and elementary arithmetic: Dissociations between operations. *Mathematical Cognition, 1*, 83–120.

DeMaria, R. (2007). *Reset: Changing the way we look at video games*. San Francisco, CA: Berret-Koehler Publishers.

Dewey, J. (1934). *Art as experience*. New York, NY: Penguin.

Dewey, J. (1938). *Education and experience*. New York, NY: Macmillan.

Diablo III Auction House Overview. (2011). *Website*. Retrieved August 20, 2011 from http://us.blizzard.com/en-us/company/events/diablo3-announcement/index.html#auction:auction-summary

Dibbell, J. (2006). *Play money: Or how I quit my day job and struck it rich in virtual loot farming*. New York, NY: Basic Books.

Dickey, M. (2005). Brave new (interactive) worlds: A review of the design affordances and constraints of two 3D virtual worlds as interactive learning environments. *Interactive Learning Environments, 13*(1), 121–137. doi:10.1080/10494820500173714

Dickey, M. D. (2003). Teaching in 3D: Pedagogical affordances and constraints of 3D virtual worlds for synchronous distance learning. *Distance Education, 24*(1), 105. doi:10.1080/01587910303047

Dickey, M. J. (2005). Three-dimensional virtual worlds and distance learning: Two case studies of active worlds as a medium for distance education. *British Journal of Educational Technology, 36*(3), 439–451. doi:10.1111/j.1467-8535.2005.00477.x

Dick, W., & Carey, L. (1978). *The systematic design of instruction*. Glenview, IL: Scott Foresman.

Dick, W., Carey, L., & Carey, J. O. (2001). *The systematic design of instruction* (5th ed.). New York, NY: Longman.

Didactic. (2010). *Oxford english dictionary.* Retrieved May 31, 2010, from http://dictionary.oed.com/

Diertle, E., & Clarke, J. (2008). Multi-user environment for teaching and learning. In Pagani, M. (Ed.), *Encylopedia of Multimedia Technology and Networking.* Hershey, PA: IGI Global.

DiPaola, S., & Collins, D. (2003). A social metaphor-based 3D virtual environment. In *Proceedings of the Educators Program from the 30th Annual Conference on Computer Graphics and Interactive Techniques, Quicktakes,* (pp. 1-2). Quicktakes.

DiPaola, S., Dorosh, D., & Brandt, G. (2008). *Ratava's line: Emergent learning and design using collaborative virtual worlds.* Unpublished manuscript. Retrieved March 1, 2008 from http://ivizlab.sfu.ca/research/colabdesign/dipaolaF1.pdf

Dodge, B. (2007). *What is a WebQuest?* Retrieved from http://webquest.org/index.php

Dodge, T., Barab, S. A., Stuckey, B., Warren, S., Heiselt, C., & Stein, R. (2008). Children's sense of self: Learning and meaning in the digital age. *Journal of Interactive Learning Research, 19*(2), 225–249.

Dorsey, L. T., Goodrum, D. A., & Schwen, T. M. (1997). Rapid collaborative prototyping as an instructional development paradigm. In Bills, C. R., & Romiszowski, A. J. (Eds.), *Instructional Development Paradigms.* Englewood Cliffs, NJ: Educational Technology.

Douglas, Y., & Hargadon, A. (2000). The pleasure principle: Immersion, engagement, flow. In *Proceedings from ACM Hypertext 2000* (pp. 153–160). New York, NY: ACM Press. doi:10.1145/336296.336354

Dourish, P. (2001). *Where the action is: The foundations of embodied interaction.* Cambridge, MA: MIT Press.

Dreher, C., Reiners, T., Dreher, N., & Dreher, H. (2009). Virtual worlds as a context suited for information systems education: Discussion of pedagogical experience and curriculum design with reference to second life. *Journal of Information Systems Education, 20*(2), 211–224.

Duchenaut, N., Yee, N., Nickel, E., & Moore, R. J. (2006). Building an MMO with mass appeal: A look at gameplay in World of Warcraft. *Games and Culture, 1*(4), 281–317. doi:10.1177/1555412006292613

Ducheneaut, N., Wen, M. H., Yee, N., & Wadley, G. (2009). Body and mind: A study of avatar personalization in three virtual worlds. In *Proceedings of the 27th International Conference on Human Factors in Computing System (CHI 2009),* (pp. 1151-1160). Boston, MA: ACM Press.

Duncum, P. (1999). A case for an art education of everyday aesthetic experiences. *Studies in Art Education, 40*(4), 295–311. doi:10.2307/1320551

Dweck, C. S., & Leggett, E. L. (1988). A social-cognitive approach to motivation and personality. *Psychological Review, 95,* 256–273. doi:10.1037/0033-295X.95.2.256

Eccles (Parsons). J. S., Adler, T. F., Futterman, R., Goff, S. B., Kaczala, C. M., Meece, J. L., & Midgley, C. (1983). Expectancies, values, and academic behaviors. In J. T. Spence (Ed.), *Achievement and Achievement Motivation,* (pp. 75-146). San Francisco, CA: W. H. Freeman.

Eccles, J. S. (1993). School and family effects on the ontogeny of children's interests, self-perceptions, and activity choice. In J. Jacobs (Ed.), *Nebraska Symposium on Motivation, 1992: Developmental Perspectives on Motivation,* (pp. 145-208). Lincoln, NE: University of Nebraska Press.

Eccles, J. S. (1987). Gender roles and women's achievement-related decisions. *Psychology of Women Quarterly, 11,* 135–172. doi:10.1111/j.1471-6402.1987.tb00781.x

Eccles, J., Wigfield, A., Flanagan, C., Miller, C., Reuman, D., & Yee, D. (1989). Self-concepts, domain values, and self-esteem: Relations and changes at early adolescence. *Journal of Personality, 57,* 283–310. doi:10.1111/j.1467-6494.1989.tb00484.x

Eco, U. (1990). *Travels in hyper reality.* Fort Washington, PA: Harvest Books.

Edelson, D. C., Gordin, D. N., & Pea, R. D. (1999). Addressing the challenges of inquiry-based learning through technology and curriculum design. *Journal of the Learning Sciences, 8*(3/4), 391–450.

Eisner, E. W. (2000). Those who ignore the past...: 12 'easy' lessons for the next millennium. *Journal of Curriculum Studies, 32*(2), 343–357. doi:10.1080/002202700182808

Elliott, J., & Bruckman, A. (2002). Design of a 3D interactive math learning environment. In *Proceedings of the Conference on Designing Interactive Systems: Processes, Practices, Methods, and Techniques,* (vol. 1, pp. 64-74). IEEE.

Ellison, K., & Matthews, C. (2010). Virtual history: A socially networked pedagogy of enlightenment. *Educational Research, 52*(3), 297–307. doi:10.1080/0013188 1.2010.504065

Engwall, O., Wik, P., Beskow, J., & Gransröm, G. (2004). Design strategies for a virtual language tutor. In *Proceedings of ICSLP*, (pp. 1693-1696). ICSLP.

ESA. (2010). *Industry facts.* Retrieved January 14, 2011 from http://www.theesa.com/facts/index.asp

Evens, M., Brandle, S., Chang, R., Freedman, R., Glass, M., & Lee, Y. ... Rovick, A. A. (2001). Circsimtutor: An intelligent tutoring system using natural language dialogue. In *Proceedings of Midwest AI and Cognitive Science Conference.* IEEE.

Ewins, R. (2005). Who are you? Weblogs and academic identity. *E-learning, 2*(4), 368–377. doi:10.2304/elea.2005.2.4.368

Facer, K., Joiner, R., Stanton, D., Reid, J., Hull, R., & Kirk, D. (2004). Savannah: Mobile gaming and learning? *Journal of Computer Assisted Learning, 20,* 399–409. doi:10.1111/j.1365-2729.2004.00105.x

Faculty Focus. (2010). *Twitter in higher education 2010: Usage habits and trends of today's college faculty.* Madison, WI: Faculty Focus.

Falk, J. (2004). The director's cut: Toward an improved understanding of learning from museums. *Science Education, 88*(1), 83–96. doi:10.1002/sce.20014

Ferdig, R. E. (2007). Preface: Learning and teaching with electronic games. *Journal of Educational Multimedia and Hypermedia, 16*(3), 217–223.

Ferster, C. B., & Skinner, B. F. (1957). *Schedules of reinforcement.* New York, NY: Appleton-Century-Crofts. doi:10.1037/10627-000

Fields, D. A., & Kafai, Y. B. (2009). A connective ethnography of peer knowledge sharing and diffusion in a tween virtual world. *International Journal of Computer-Supported Collaborative Learning, 4*(1), 47–68. doi:10.1007/s11412-008-9057-1

Finnegan, R. (2002). *Communicating: The multiple modes of human interconnection.* New York, NY: Routledge.

FitzGerald, S. (2007). *Virtual worlds - What are they and why do educators need to pay attention to them?* Paper presented at E-learning Networks June Online Event Retrieved July 13, 2007, from http://seanfitz.wikispaces.com/virtualworldsenetworks07

Flavin, M. (2012). Enabling disruptive technologies for higher education learning and teaching. In *Proceedings of ECEL.* ECEL.

Flores, F., Lopez, A., Gallegos, L., & Barojas, J. (2000). Transforming science and learning concepts of physics teachers. *International Journal of Science Education, 22*(2), 197–208. doi:10.1080/095006900289958

Flynn, E. A. (1988). Composing as a woman. *College Composition and Communication, 39*(4), 423–435. doi:10.2307/357697

Forbes-Riley, K., & Litman, D. (2011). Designing and evaluating a wizarded uncertainty-adaptive spoken dialogue tutoring system. *Computer Speech & Language, 25*(1), 105–126. doi:10.1016/j.csl.2009.12.002

Fosnot, C. T. (1996). Constructivism: A psychological theory of learning. In Fosnot, C. T. (Ed.), *Constructivism: Theory, Perspectives, and Practice* (pp. 8–33). New York, NY: Teachers College Press.

Franklin, T., & Peng, L.-W. (2009). Mobile math: Math educators and students engage in mobile learning. *Journal of Computing in Higher Education, 20,* 69–80. doi:10.1007/s12528-008-9005-0

Frechette, J. D. (2002). *Developing media literacy in cyberspace pedagogy and critical learning for the twenty-first-century classroom.* Westport, CT: Praeger.

Fredens, K. (2004). *Mennesket i hjernen – En grundbog i neuropædagogik.* Århus, Denmark: Systime Academic.

Freedman, K. (2003). *Teaching visual culture.* New York, NY: Teachers College Press.

Freedman, K., & Wood, J. (1999). Reconsidering critical response: Student judgments of purpose, interpretation, and relationships in visual culture. *Studies in Art Education, 40*(2), 128–142. doi:10.2307/1320337

Frith, C. (2007). *Making up the mind: How the brain creates our mental world.* Oxford, UK: Blackwell Publishing.

Fryer, L., & Carpenter, R. (2006). Bots as language learning tools. *Language Learning & Technology, 10*(3), 8–14.

Gair, M., & Mullins, G. (2001). Hiding in plain sight. In Margolis, E. (Ed.), *The Hidden Curriculum in Higher Education.* London, UK: Routledge.

Gange, R. M., & Briggs, L. J. (1974). *Principles of instructional design.* New York, NY: Holt, Rinehart & Winston.

Garage Games. (2012). *Website.* Retrieved January 5, 2006, from http://www.garagegames.com

Gee, J. P. (2005). Good video games and good learning. *Phi Kappa Phi Forum, 85*(2), 33 - 37.

Gee, J. P. (1996). *Social linguistics and literacies ideology in discoures.* New York, NY: RoutledgeFalmer.

Gee, J. P. (2003). Turning games into learning machines. *Game Developer, 10*(9), 56.

Gee, J. P. (2003). *What videogames have to teach us about learning and literacy.* New York, NY: Palgrave Macmillan.

Gee, J. P. (2004). *Situated language and learning: A critique of traditional schooling.* New York, NY: Routledge.

Gee, J. P. (2005). Semiotic social spaces and affinity spaces: From the age of mythology to today's schools. In Barton, D., & Tusting, K. (Eds.), *Beyond 395 Communities of Practice: Language, Power, and Social Context.* New York, NY: Cambridge University Press. doi:10.1017/CBO9780511610554.012

Gee, J. P. (2007). *What video games have to teach us about learning and literacy.* New York, NY: Palgrave Macmillan. doi:10.1145/950566.950595

Gee, J. P., & Shaffer, D. W. (2010). Looking where the light is bad: Video games and the future of assessment. *EDge, 6*(1), 1–19.

Ge, X., & Land, S. M. (2004). A conceptual framework for scaffolding ill-structured problem-solving processes using question prompts and peer interactions. *Educational Technology Research and Development, 52*(2), 5–22. doi:10.1007/BF02504836

Gibbon, D., Mertins, I., & Moore, R. (2000). *Handbook of multimodal and spoken dialogue systems: Resources, terminology and product evaluation.* Dordrecht, The Netherlands: Kluwer Academic Publishers. doi:10.1007/978-1-4615-4501-9

Gilllies, R. M. (2003). Structuring cooperative group work in classrooms. *International Journal of Educational Research, 39*, 35–49. doi:10.1016/S0883-0355(03)00072-7

Girvan, C., & Savage, T. (2010). Identifying an appropriate pedagogy for virtual worlds: A communal constructivism case study. *Computers & Education, 55*(1), 342–349. doi:10.1016/j.compedu.2010.01.020

Goffman, E. (Ed.). (1967). *Interaction ritual: Essays on face-to-face behavior.* Garden City, NY: Anchor Books.

Golafshani, N. (2003). Understanding reliability and validity in qualitative research. *Qualitative Report, 8*(4), 597–607.

Goldberg, E. (2005). *The wisdom paradox: How your mind can grow stronger as your brain grows older.* New York, NY: Gotham Books.

Goldstein, J. (2001). *Does playing violent video games cause aggressive behaviour.* Retrieved from http://culturalpolicy.uchicago.edu/papers/2001-video-games/goldstein.html

Goldsworthy, R. C., Barab, S. A., & Goldsworthy, E. L. (2000). The STAR project: Enhancing adolescents' social understanding through video-based, multimedia scenarios. *Journal of Special Education Technology, 15*(2), 13–26.

Graesser, A. C., VanLehn, K., Rose, C., Jordan, P., & Harter, D. (2001). Intelligent tutoring systems with conversational dialogue. *AI Magazine, 22*, 39–51.

Graves, L. (2008, January 10). A second life for higher ed: A virtual world offers new opportunities for teaching. *US News and World Report Online.* Retrieved October 2, 2008 from http://www.usnews.com/articles/education/e-learning/2008/01/10/a-second-life-for-higher-ed.html

Greeno, J. G., & van de Sande, C. (2005). *A situative perspective on conceptual growth*. Paper presented at the Annual Meeting of the American Educational Research Association. Montreal, Canada.

Green, T., & Bailey, B. (2010). Academic uses of facebook: Endless possibilities or endless perils? *TechTrends*, *54*(3), 20–22. doi:10.1007/s11528-010-0398-z

Gregory, S., Lee, M., Ellis, A., Gregory, B., Wood, D., Hillier, M., et al. (2010). *Australian higher education institutions transforming the future of teaching and learning through virtual worlds*. Paper presented at the Curriculum, Technology & Transformation for an Unknown Future, ASCILITE 2010. New York, NY.

Griol, D., Rojo, E., Callejas, Z., & López-Cózar, R. (2010). Development of an academic assistant in second life. In *Proceedings of 10th Spanish Symposium on Information and Communication Technologies for Education*, (pp. 81-84). IEEE.

Griol, D., Hurtado, L., Segarra, E., & Sanchis, E. (2008). A statistical approach to spoken dialog systems design and evaluation. *Speech Communication*, *50*(8–9), 666–682. doi:10.1016/j.specom.2008.04.001

Groom, D., Dewart, H., Esgate, A., Gurney, K., Kemp, R., & Towell, N. (1999). *An introduction to cognitive psychology*. Hove, UK: Psychology Press.

Gros, B. (2003). The impact of digital games in education. *First Monday*, *8*(7).

Grossman, L. (2010, December 15). Person of the year 2010: Mark Zuckerberg. *Time*. Retrieved from http://www.time.com/time/specials/packages/article/0,28804,2036683_2037183,00.html

Grubb, A., & Hines, M. (2000). Tearing down barriers and building communities: pedagogical strategies for web-based environment. In Cole, R. (Ed.), *Issues in Web-Based Pedagogy* (pp. 365–380). Westport, CT: Greenwood Press.

Grunwald Associates LLC. (2010). *PBS annual survey report*. Retrieved from http://www.grunwald.com/reports/

Guba, E. G., & Lincoln, Y. S. (1994). Competing paradigms in qualitative research. In Denzin, N. K. (Ed.), *Handbook of Qualitative Research*. Thousand Oaks, CA: Sage Publications.

Gunawardena, C. N., & Zittle, F. J. (1997). Social presence as a predictor of satisfaction within a computer-mediated conferencing environment. *American Journal of Distance Education*, *11*(3), 8–26. doi:10.1080/08923649709526970

Guye-Vuillème, A., & Thalmann, D. (2001). A high level architecture for believable social agents. *Virtual Reality Journal*, *5*, 95–106. doi:10.1007/BF01424340

Hall, E. T., & Hall, M. R. (1989). *Understanding cultural differences*. Yarmouth, ME: Intercultural Press, Inc.

Halverson, R. (2005). What can K-12 leaders learn from video games and gaming?. *Innovate, 1*(6).

Halverson, R., & Clifford, M. (2006). Evaluation in the wild: A distributed cognition perspective on teacher assessment. *Educational Administration Quarterly*, *42*(4), 578–619. doi:10.1177/0013161X05285986

Halverson, R., Grigg, J., Prichett, R., & Thomas, C. (2007). The new instructional leadership: Creating data-driven instructional systems in schools. *Journal of School Leadership*, *17*(2), 159–194.

Halverson, R., & Smith, A. (2009). How new technologies have (and have not) changed teaching and learning in schools. *Journal of Computing in Teacher Education*, *26*(2), 49–54.

Hannula, M. M., Räsänen, P., & Lehtinen, E. (2007). Development of counting skills: Role of spontaneous focusing on numerosity and subitizing-based enumeration. *Mathematical Thinking and Learning*, *9*(1), 51–57.

Hansen, F. A., & Bouvin, N. O. (2009). Mobile learning in context – Context-aware hypermedia in the wild. *International Journal of Interactive Mobile Technologies*, *3*(1), 3–21.

Hara, N., Bonk, C. J., & Angeli, C. (2002). Content analysis of online discussion in an applied educational psychology course. *Instructional Science*, *28*, 115–152. doi:10.1023/A:1003764722829

Harasim, L. (2006). A history of e-learning: Shift happened. In Weiss, J. (Ed.), *The International Handbook of Virtual Learning Environments* (pp. 59–94). Dordrecht, The Netherlands: Springer. doi:10.1007/978-1-4020-3803-7_2

Harris, A., & Chapman, C. (2002). *Effective leadership in schools facing challenging circumstances.* Nottingham, UK: NCSL.

Harris, J. H. (1998). *Hamlet on the holodeck: The future of narrative in cyberspace.* Cambridge, MA: The MIT Press.

Harrow, A. (1972). *A taxonomy of psychomotor domains: A guide for developing behavioral objectives.* New York, NY: David McKay.

Hartmann, T., & Klimmt, C. (2006). Gender and computer games: Exploring females' dislikes. *Journal of Computer-Mediated Communication, 11*(4), 910-931. Retrieved January 14, 2011 from http://jcmc.indiana.edu/vol11/issue4/hartmann.html

Hausmann, R., & Chi, M. (2002). Can a computer interface support self-explanation? *International Journal of Cognitive Technology, 7*(1).

Hayashi, Y., Bourdeau, J., & Mizoguchi, R. (2008). Structurization of learning/instructional design knowledge for theory-aware authoring systems. In Woolf, B. P., Aïmeur, E., Nkambou, R., & Lajoie, S. (Eds.), *Intelligent Tutoring Systems* (pp. 573–582). Berlin, Germany: Springer. doi:10.1007/978-3-540-69132-7_60

Haynes, S. N., Richard, D. C., & Kubany, E. S. (1995). Content validity in psychological assessment: A functional approach to concepts and methods. *Psychological Assessment, 7*(3), 238-247. Retrieved May 7, 2006, from http://www.personal.kent.edu/~dfresco/CRM_Readings/Haynes_1995.pdf

Hedberg, J., & Alexander, S. (1994). Virtual reality in education: Defining researchable issues. *Educational Media International, 31*(4), 214–220. doi:10.1080/0952398940310402

Heeter, C. (1992). Being there: The subjective experience of presence. *Presence (Cambridge, Mass.), 1*(2), 262–271.

Helal, A., Moore, S. E., & Ramachandran, B. (2001). Drishti: An integrated navigation system for visually impaired and disables. In *Proceedings of 5th International Conference on Wearable Computers*, (pp. 149-156). IEEE.

Hennessy, S., Ruthven, K., & Brindley, S. (2005). Teacher perspectives on integrating ICT into subject teaching: commitment, constraints, caution, and change. *Journal of Curriculum Studies, 37*(2), 155–192. doi:10.1080/0022027032000276961

Henri, F. (1992). Computer conferencing and content analysis. In Kaye, A. R. (Ed.), *Collaborative Learning Through Computer Conferencing: The Najaden Papers* (pp. 116–136). Berlin, Germany: Springer-Verlag. doi:10.1007/978-3-642-77684-7_8

Henriques, L. (2002). Preparing tomorrow's science teachers to use technology: An example from the field. *Contemporary Issues in Technology & Teacher Education, 2*(1).

Herrera, D. R., & Margitay-Becht, A. (2008). Fun is learning: A case study of gaming as education in virtual worlds. In Nygaard, C., & Holtham, C. (Eds.), *Understanding Learning-Centered Higher Education* (pp. 95–110). Copenhagen, Denmark: Copenhagen Business School Press.

Herrera, D. R., & Margitay-Becht, A. (2010). Cyberdiasporas: The affects of migration to virtual worlds. In DePretto, L., Macri, G., & Wong, C. (Eds.), *Diasporas: Revisiting and Discovering* (pp. 287–298). Oxfordshire, UK: Inter-Disciplinary Press.

Herrera, D. R., & Margitay-Becht, A. (2010). Do-it-yourself learning: Case studies of gaming as education in virtual worlds. In Riha, D. (Ed.), *Videogame Cultures and the Future of Interactive Entertainment* (pp. 33–42). Oxfordshire, UK: Inter-Disciplinary Press.

Herrington, J., Reeves, T. C., Oliver, R., & Woo, Y. (2004). Designing authentic activities in web-based courses. *Journal of Computing in Higher Education, 16*(1), 3–29. doi:10.1007/BF02960280

Hewitt, A., & Forte, A. (2006). Crossing boundaries: Identity management and student/faculty relationships on the Facebook. In *Proceedings of the ACM 2006 Conference on Computer Supported Cooperative Work*. Banff, Canada. Retrieved from http://wwwstatic.cc.gatech.edu/~aforte/HewittForteCSCWPoster2006.pdf

Hew, K., & Cheung, W. (2010). Use of three-dimensional (3-D) immersive virtual worlds in K-12 and higher education settings: A review of the research. *British Journal of Educational Technology*, *41*(1), 33–55. doi:10.1111/j.1467-8535.2008.00900.x

Hisnanick, J. J. (2002). Knowledge emergence: Social, technical, and evolutionary dimensions of knowledge creation. *Journal of Economic Issues*, *36*, 819–821.

Hoffmann, M. (2007). Learning from people, things, and signs. *Studies in Philosophy and Education*, *26*(3), 185–204. doi:10.1007/s11217-007-9027-5

Hofs, D., Theune, M., & Op den Akker, R. (2010). Natural interaction with a virtual guide in a virtual environment. *Journal on Multimodal User Interfaces*, *3*, 141–153. doi:10.1007/s12193-009-0024-6

Holmes, R., & Beaumont, L. (2010). Teaching mathematics in a virtual world. In Frenburg, U., & Reiniger, R. (Eds.), *VWBPE 2010 Presentation*. EdTech Island, NY: Second Life.

Howell, S. C., & Kemp, C. R. (2010). Assessing preschool number sense: Skills demonstrated by children prior to school entry. *Educational Psychology*, *30*(4), 411–429. doi:10.1080/01443411003695410

Howell, S., & Kemp, C. (2005). Defining early number sense: A participatory Australian study. *Educational Psychology*, *25*(5), 555–571. doi:10.1080/01443410500046838

Howell, S., & Kemp, C. (2009). A participatory approach to the identification of measures of number sense in children prior to school entry. *International Journal of Early Years Education*, *17*(1), 47–65. doi:10.1080/09669760802699902

Huang, C., Xu, P., & Zhang, X. Zhao, S., Huang, T., & Xu, B. (1999). LODESTAR: A Mandarin spoken dialogue system for travel information retrieval. In *Proceedings of Eurospeech*, (pp. 1159-1162). Eurospeech.

Hudson, K., & Degast-Kennedy, K. (2009). Canadian border simulation at Loyalist College. *Journal of Virtual Worlds Research, 2*(1). Retrieved July 1, 2009 from https://journals.tdl.org/jvwr/article/view/374/449

Hutchins, E. (1996). *Cognition in the wild*. Cambridge, MA: MIT Press.

IBM. (2005). *Virtual worlds real leaders: Online games put the future of business leadership in display*. Palo Alto, CA: Seriosity Inc.

Ibrahim, A., & Johansson, P. (2002). Multimodal dialogue systems for interactive TV applications. In *Proceedings of 4th IEEE International Conference on Multimodal Interfaces*, (pp. 117-122). IEEE Press.

Instructure. (2011). *Instructure canvas*. Retrieved from http://www.instructure.com

Isbister, K. (2004). Building bridges through the unspoken: Embodied agents to facilitate intercultural communication. In Payr, S., & Trappl, R. (Eds.), *Agent Culture: Human-Agent Interaction in a Multicultural World* (pp. 233–244). London, UK: Lawrence Erlbaum Associates.

Jacobson, M. J., June Lee, B. K., Hong Lim, S., & Hua Low, S. (2008). *An intelligent agent augmented multiuser virtual environment for learning science inquiry: Preliminary research findings*. Paper presented at the 2008 American Educational Association Conference. New York, NY.

Jacobson, M. J., Kim, B., Miao, C.-H., Shen, Z., & Chavez, M. (2009). Design perspectives for learning in virtual worlds. In Jacobson, M. J., & Reimann, P. (Eds.), *Designs for Learning Environments of the Future: International Perspectives from the Learning Sciences*. New York, NY: Springer. doi:10.1007/978-0-387-88279-6_5

Jamieson, H. (2007). *Visual communication: More than meets the eye*. Chicago, IL: University of Chicago Press.

Jarmon, L., Traphagan, T., Mayrath, M., & Trivedi, A. (2009). Virtual world teaching, experiential learning, and assessment: An interdisciplinary communication course in Second Life. *Computers & Education*, *53*(1), 169–182. doi:10.1016/j.compedu.2009.01.010

Jenkins, H., Clinton, K., Purushotma, R., Robison, A. J., & Weigel, M. (2006). *Confronting the challenges of participatory culture: Media education for the 21st century*. Chicago, IL: The MacArthur Foundation. Retrieved December 30, 2008 from http://www.digitallearning.macfound.org/atf/cf/%7BE45C7E0-A3E0-4B89-AC9C-E807E1B0AE4E%7D/JENKINS_WHITE_PAPER.PDF

Jensen, S. S. (2007). Acts of learning with avatars in a virtual world. In Mayer, I., & Mastik, H. (Eds.), *Organizing and Learning through Gaming and Simulation* (pp. 159–166). Delft, The Netherlands: Eburon.

Jeong, H., & Chi, M. T. H. (2007). Knowledge convergence and collaborative learning. *Instructional Science*, *35*, 287–315. doi:10.1007/s11251-006-9008-z

Johnson, L., Levine, A., Smith, R., Smythe, T., & Stone, S. (2009). *Horizon report: 2009 Australia - New Zealand edition*. Austin, TX: Horizon Report.

Johnson, W. L., & Valente, A. (2008). Tactical language and culture training systems: Using artificial intelligence to teach foreign languages and cultures. In *Proceedings of IAAI*, (pp. 1632-1639). IAAI.

Johnson, D. W., & Johnson, R. T. (1985). The internal dynamics of cooperative learning groups. In Slavin, R., Shlomo, S., Spencer, K., Hertz-Lazarowitz, R., Webb, C., & Schmuck, R. (Eds.), *Learning to Cooperate, Cooperating to Learn* (pp. 103–124). New York, NY: Plenum.

Johnson, D., Johnson, R., & Skon, L. (1979). Student achievement on different types of tasks under cooperative, competitive, and individualistic conditions. *Contemporary Educational Psychology*, *4*, 99–106. doi:10.1016/0361-476X(79)90063-8

Johnson, L., Smith, R., Levine, A., & Haywood, K. (2010). *The 2010 horizon report: K-12 edition*. Austin, TX: The New Media Consortium.

John-Steiner, V. (1996). Sociocultural approaches to learning and development: A Vygotskian framework. *Educational Psychologist*, *31*, 191–206.

Jones, P. C., & Merritt, Q. (1999). The TALESSI project: Promoting active learning for interdisciplinary, values awareness and critical thinking in environmental higher education. *Journal of Geography in Higher Education*, *23*(3), 335–348. doi:10.1080/03098269985281

Jossey-Bass, I. (2008). *The Jossey-Bass reader on the brain and learning*. San Francisco, CA: Jossey-Bass.

Ju, W., Nickel, S., Eng, K., & Nass, C. (2005). Influence of colearner agent behavior on learner performance and attitudes. In *Proceedings of CHI*, (pp. 1509-1512). ACM.

Jukes, I., McCain, T., & Crockett, L. (2011). Education and the role of the educator in the future. *Phi Delta Kappan*, *92*(4), 15–21.

Kafai, Y. B., & Ching, C. C. (2001). Affordances of collaborative software design planning for elementary students' science talk. *Journal of the Learning Sciences*, *10*(3), 323–363. doi:10.1207/S15327809JLS1003_4

Kameda, N. (2004). Englishes in cross-cultural business communication. In Puffer, S. M. (Ed.), *International Management: Insights from Fiction and Practice* (pp. 67–75). Armonk, NY: M.E. Sharpe.

Kanematsu, H., Fukumura, Y., Barry, D. M., Sohn, S. Y., & Taguchi, R. (2010). Multilingual discussion in metaverse among students from the USA, Korea, and Japan. *Lecture Notes in Computer Science*, *6279*, 200–209. doi:10.1007/978-3-642-15384-6_22

Kang, I. (1998). The use of computer-mediated communication: Electronic collaboration and interactivity. In Bonk, C. J., & King, K. S. (Eds.), *Electronic Collaborators: Learner-Centered Technologies for Literacy, Apprenticeship, and Discourse* (pp. 315–337). Mahwah, NJ: Erlbaum.

Kaufman, E. L., Lord, M. W., Reese, T. W., & Volkman, J. (1949). The discrimination of visual number. *The American Journal of Psychology*, *62*(4), 27. doi:10.2307/1418556

Keegan, V. (2008, October 2). We'll all be citizens of virtual worlds. *Guardian*. Retrieved October 5, 2008 from http://www.guardian.co.uk/technology/2008/oct/02/virtual.worlds

Keller, J. M. (1983). Motivational design of instruction. In Reigeluth, C. M. (Ed.), *Instructional-Design Theories and Models: An Overview of Their Current Status*. Hillsdale, NJ: Lawrence Erlbaum Associates.

Keller, J. M. (1987). Development and use of the ARCS model of motivational design. *Journal of Instructional Development*, *10*(3), 2–10. doi:10.1007/BF02905780

Keller, J. M. (1987). Strategies for stimulating the motivation to learn. *Performance & Instruction*, *26*(8), 1–7. doi:10.1002/pfi.4160260802

Keller, J. M. (1999). Motivation in cyber learning environments. *Educational Technology International, 1*(1), 7–30.

Kellner, D. (2006). Technological transformation, multiple literacies, and the re-visioning of education. In Weiss, J., Nolan, J., Hunsinger, J., & Trifonas, P. (Eds.), *The International Handbook of Virtual Learning Environments*. Dordrecht, The Netherlands: Springer. doi:10.1007/978-1-4020-3803-7_9

Kellogg, R. T. (1995). *Cognitive psychology*. Thousand Oaks, CA: SAGE.

Kemp, J. E. (1971). *Instructional design: A plan for unit and course development*. Belmont, CA: Fearon.

Kerfoot, K. (2003). Learning organizations need teachers: The leader's challenge. *Nursing Economics, 21*, 148–151.

Kerly, A., Ellis, R., & Bull, S. (2008). Conversational agents in e-learning. [AI.]. *Proceedings of AI, 2008*, 169–182.

Kersey, C., Di Eugenio, B., Jordan, P., & Katz, S. (2010). KSC-PaL: A peer learning agent. In Aleven, V., Kay, J., & Mostow, J. (Eds.), *Intelligent Tutoring Systems (ITS), Part II* (pp. 72–81). Berlin, Germany: Springer. doi:10.1007/978-3-642-13437-1_8

Ketelhut, D. J., Dede, C., Clarke, J., & Nelson, B. (2006). *A multi-user virtual environment for building higher order inquiry skills in science*. Paper presented at the American Educational Research Association. Retrieved 22/07/2008, from http://muve.gse.harvard.edu/rivercity-project/research-publications.htm

Ketelhut, D., Nelson, B., Clarke, J., & Dede, C. (2010). A multi-user virtual environment for building and assessing higher order inquiry skills in science. *British Journal of Educational Technology, 41*(1), 56–68. doi:10.1111/j.1467-8535.2009.01036.x

Kim, B. (2001). Social constructivism. In M. Orey (Ed.), *Emerging Perspectives on Learning, Teaching, and Technology*. Retrieved from http://www.coe.uga.edu/epltt/SocialConstructivism.htm

Kim, Y., Hamilton, E. R., Zheng, J., & Baylor, A. L. (2006). Scaffolding learner motivation through a virtual peer. In *Proceedings of ICLS*, (pp. 335-341). ICLS.

Kirner, T. G., Kirner, C., Kawamoto, A. L., Cantao, J., Pinto, A., & Wazlawick, R. S. (2001). Development of a collaborative virtual environment for educational applications. In *Proceedings of the Sixth International Conference on 3D Web Technology*, (pp. 61-68). IEEE.

Kirriemuir, J., & McFarlane, A. (2003). *Literature review in games and learning*. Retrieved August 10, 2006, from http://www.futurelab.org.uk/research/lit_reviews.htm#lr08

Kirriemuir. (2008). *Measuring the impact of SL for educational purposes*. New York, NY: Eduserv Foundation.

Klopfer, E., Osterweil, S., & Salen, K. (2009). *Moving learning games forward: Obstacles, opportunities, and openness*. Cambridge, MA: The Education Arcade.

Kolb, D. A. (1984). *Experiential learning: Experience as the source of learning and development*. Englewood Cliffs, NJ: Prentice-Hall.

Kolb, D. A., Rubin, I. M., & McIntyre, J. M. (1994). *Organizational psychology: An experiential approach to organizational behavior* (4th ed.). London, UK: Prentice Hall.

Kolek, E., & Saunders, D. (2008). Online disclosure: An empirical examination of undergraduate Facebook profiles. *National Association of Student Personnel Administrators Journal, 45*(1), 1–25.

Konnerup, U., & Schmidt. (2006). *Det virtuelle miljø – En mulighed for nye læreprocesser i rehabiliteringen af afasiramte*. (Masters Thesis). Aalborg Universitet. Aalborg, Denmark.

Koopman, B. L. (2011). From Socrates to wikis using online forums to deepen discussions. *Phi Delta Kappan, 92*(4), 24–27.

Kozma, R. (2003). The material features of multiple representations and their cognitive and social affordances for science understanding. *Learning and Instruction, 13*, 205–226. doi:10.1016/S0959-4752(02)00021-X

Kramarski, B. (2004). Making sense of graphs: Does metacognitive instruction make a difference on students' mathematical conceptions and alternative conceptions? *Learning and Instruction, 14*, 593–619. doi:10.1016/j.learninstruc.2004.09.003

Kumar, R., Ai, H., Beuth, J. L., & Rosé, C. P. (2010). Socially capable conversational tutors can be effective in collaborative learning situations. In Aleven, V., Kay, J., & Mostow, J. (Eds.), *Intelligent Tutoring Systems (ITS), Part I* (pp. 156–164). Berlin, Germany: Springer. doi:10.1007/978-3-642-13388-6_20

Kun, A., & Weiner, B. (1973). Necessary versus sufficient causal schemata for success and failure. *Journal of Research in Personality*, 7, 197–207. doi:10.1016/0092-6566(73)90036-6

Kutner, L., & Olson, C. (2011). *Grand theft childhood: The surprising truth about violent video games and what parents can do*. New York, NY: Simon & Schuster.

Kzero Worldwide. (2010). *Virtual world registered accounts Q3 2010*. Retrieved from http://www.kzero.co.uk/blog/?p=4448

la Velle, L., Wishart, J., McFarlane, A., Brawn, R., & John, P. (2007). Teaching and learning with ICT within the subject culture of secondary school science. *Research in Science & Technological Education*, 25(3), 339–349. doi:10.1080/02635140701535158

Lamb, G. M. (2006). Real learning in a virtual world. *The Christian Science Monitor*. Retrieved from http://www.csmonitor.com/2006/1005/p13s02-legn.html

Lamb, A., & Johnson, L. (2009). The potential, the pitfalls, and the promise of multi-user virtual environments: Getting a second life. *Teacher Librarian*, 36(4), 68–78.

Lane, H. W., Maznevski, M., Deetz, J., & DiStefano, J. (2009). *International management behavior: Leading with a global mindset*. Hoboken, NJ: Wiley.

Lave, J., & Wenger, E. (1991). *Situated learning: Legitimate peripheral participation*. Cambridge, UK: Cambridge University Press. doi:10.1017/CBO9780511815355

Lee, D. (1997). Factors influencing the success of computer skills learning among in-service teachers. *British Journal of Educational Technology*, 28(2), 139–141. doi:10.1111/1467-8535.00018

Lee, E. A.-L., Wong, K. W., & Fung, C. C. (2010). How does desktop virtual reality enhance learning outcomes? A structural equation modeling approach. *Computers & Education*, 55(4), 1424–1442. doi:10.1016/j.compedu.2010.06.006

Lee, P. (2009). Using second life to teach operations management. *Journal of Virtual Worlds Research*, 2(1).

Leichtenstern, K., André, E., & Rehm, M. (2010). using hybrid simulations for early user evaluations of pervasive interactions. In *Proceedings of NordiCHI*, (pp. 315-324). ACM Press.

Li, D., & Lim, C. P. (2007). Scaffolding online historical inquiry tasks: A case study of two secondary school classrooms. *Computers & Education*, 50, 1394–1410. doi:10.1016/j.compedu.2006.12.013

Lim, C. P., & Chai, C. S. (2004). An activity-theoretical approach to research of IlT integration in Singapore schools: Orienting activities and learner autonomy. *Computers & Education*, 43(3), 215–236. doi:10.1016/j.compedu.2003.10.005

Lim, C. P., Nonis, D., & Hedberg, J. (2006). Gaming in a 3D multiuser virtual environment: Engaging students in science lessons. *British Journal of Educational Technology*, 37(2), 211–231. doi:10.1111/j.1467-8535.2006.00531.x

Lim, K. (2009). The six learnings of second life. *Journal of Virtual Worlds Research*, 2(1).

Limniou, M., Roberts, D., & Papadopoulos, N. (2008). Full immersive virtual environment CAVETM in chemistry education. *Computers & Education*, 51(2), 584–593. doi:10.1016/j.compedu.2007.06.014

Lincoln, E. G., & Guba, Y. S. (1985). Competing paradigms in qualitative research. In Denzin, N., & Lincoln, Y. (Eds.), *The SAGE Handbook of Qualitative Research* (pp. 163–194). Thousand Oaks, CA: SAGE Publications.

Linden Lab. (2007). *Website*. Retrieved May 2, 2007, from http://lindenlab.com/

Linden Research, Inc. (2007). *Second life*. Retrieved October 5, 2007, from www.secondlife.com

Litman, D., & Silliman, S. (2004). ITSPOKE: An intelligent tutoring spoken dialogue system. In *Proceedings of the Human Language Technology Conference of the North American Chapter of the Association for Computational Linguistics (HLT/NAACL)*. NAACL.

Lohr, K. (2010, October 12). Cheating investigation focuses on Atlanta schools. *National Public Radio*. Retrieved from http://www.npr.org/templates/story/story.php?storyId=130335370

López-Cózar, R., & Araki, M. (2005). *Spoken, multilingual and multimodal dialogue systems: Development and assessment.* Hoboken, NJ: Wiley.

Lucia, A. D., Francese, R., Passero, I., & Tortora, G. (2009). Development and evaluation of a virtual campus on second life: The case of secondmi. *Computers & Education, 52*(1), 220–233. doi:10.1016/j.compedu.2008.08.001

Magnusson, M. (2000). *Language in life – Life in language.* Karlstad, Sweden: Karlstad University Studies.

Mairesse, F., Gasic, M., Jurcicek, F., Keizer, S., Thomson, B., Yu, K., & Young, S. (2009). Spoken language understanding from unaligned data using discriminative classification models. In *Proceedings of ICASSP*, (pp. 4749-4752). ICASSP.

Malaby, T. M. (2009). *Anthropology and play: The contours of playful experience.* Retrieved from http://ssrn.com/abstract=1315542

Malaby, T. M. (2006). Parlaying value: Capital in and beyond virtual worlds. *Games and Culture, 1*(2), 141–162. doi:10.1177/1555412006286688

Maldonado, H., Lee, J.-E. R., Brave, S., Nass, C., Nakajima, H., & Yamada, R. … Morishima, Y. (2005). We learn better together: Enhancing elearning with emotional characters. In *Proceedings of Computer Support for Collaborative Learning: Learning 2005 – The Next 10 Years!* (pp. 408-417). CSCL.

Maloney, J., & Simon, S. (2006). Mapping children's discussions of evidence in science to assess collaboration and argumentation. *International Journal of Science Education, 28*(15), 1817–1841. doi:10.1080/09500690600855419

Manlove, S., Lazonder, A. W., & de Jong, T. (2005). Regulative support for collaborative scientific inquiry learning. *Journal of Computer Assisted Learning, 22,* 87–98. doi:10.1111/j.1365-2729.2006.00162.x

Mannecke, B., McNeil, D., Ganis, M., Roche, E., Bray, D., Konsynski, T. A., & Lester, J. (2008). Second life and other virtual worlds: A roadmap for research. *CAIS, 22,* 371-388.

Maragoudakis, M. (2007). MeteoBayes: Effective plan recognition in a weather dialogue system. *IEEE Intelligent Systems, 22*(1), 66–77. doi:10.1109/MIS.2007.14

Márquez, G. G. (2004). One of these days. In Puffer, S. M. (Ed.), *International Management: Insights from Fiction and Practice* (pp. 173–174). Armonk, NY: M.E. Sharpe.

Marsella, S., Johnson, W. L., & LaBore, C. M. (2003). Interactive pedagogical drama for health interventions. In *Proceedings of the 11th International Conference on Artificial Intelligence in Education (AIED).* AIED.

Marshall, C. M. (2007). Cultural identity, creative processes, and imagination: Creating cultural connections through art making. *Journal of Cultural Research in Art Education, 25,* 1–12.

Marshall, J. (2004). Articulate images: Bringing the pictures of science and natural history into the art curriculum. *Studies in Art Education, 45*(2), 135–152.

Marshall, J. A. (2004). Construction of meaning: Urban elementary students' interpretation of geometric puzzles. *The Journal of Mathematical Behavior, 23*(2), 169–182. doi:10.1016/j.jmathb.2004.03.002

Martins, F., Parda, J. P., Franqueira, L., Arez, P., & Mamede, N. J. (2008). Starting to cook a tutoring dialogue system. In *Proceedings of Spoken Language Technology Workshop*, (pp. 145-148). NAACL.

Masalela, R. K. (2005). Electronic literacies in virtual classrooms: Is this a one size fits all? Visual literacy and development an African experience. In *Proceedings of IVLA.* IVLA.

Mason, H., & Moutahir, M. (2006). Multidisciplinary experiential education in second life: A global approach. In *Proceedings of the Second Life Education Workshop at the Second Life Community Convention*, (pp. 30-34). San Francisco, CA: Second Life Community.

Mazer, J. P., Murphy, R. E., & Simonds, C. J. (2007). I'll see you on "facebook": The effects of computer-mediated teacher self-disclosure on student motivation, affective learning, and classroom climate. *Communication Education, 56*(1), 1–17. doi:10.1080/03634520601009710

McBrien, J. L., Jones, P., & Cheng, R. (2009). Virtual spaces: Employing a synchronous online classroom to facilitate student engagement in online learning. *International Review of Research in Open and Distance Learning, 10*(3), 5–10.

McClenney, K. M. (2007). Research update: The community college survey of student engagement. *Community College Review, 35*(2), 137–146. doi:10.1177/0091552107306583

McFee, J. K., & Degge, R. M. (1977). *Art, culture, and environment: A catalyst for teaching.* Belmont, CA: Wadsworth.

McKerlich, R., & Anderson, T. (2007). Community of inquiry and learning in immersive environments. *Journal of Asynchronous Learning Networks, 11*(4).

McKnight, J. C. (2010). *The devils made me do it: An experiment in teaching collaborative governance in World of Warcraft.* Paper presented at the Games+Learning+Society Conference 6.0. Madison, WI.

McInerney, S. M., & Van Etten, S. (Eds.). (2000). *Research on sociocultural influences on motivation and learning.* Greenwich, CT: Information Age Publishing.

McMahan, A. (2003). Immersion, engagement, and presence: A method for analyzing 3-D video games. In Wolf, M. J. P., & Perron, B. (Eds.), *The Video Game Theory Reader* (pp. 25–46). New York, NY: Routledge.

McMahon, M. (1997). *Social constructivism and the world wide web - A paradigm for learning.* Paper presented at the ASCILITE Conference. Perth, Australia.

McMillin, D. C. (2007). *International media studies.* Oxford, UK: Blackwell.

McTear, M. F. (2004). *Spoken dialogue technology: Toward the conversational user interface.* Berlin, Germany: Springer.

Mehlmann, G., Haering, M., Buehling, R., Wissner, M., & André, E. (2010). Multiple agents roles in an adaptive virtual classroom environment. In Allbeck, J. (Eds.), *Intelligent Virtual Agents (IVA)* (pp. 250–256). Berlin, Germany: Springer. doi:10.1007/978-3-642-15892-6_26

Merriam, S. B. (1998). *Qualitative research and case study applications in education.* San Francisco, CA: Jossey-Bass.

Merriam, S. B. (2002). *Qualitative research in practice: Examples for discussion and analysis.* San Francisco, CA: Jossey-Bass.

Messinger, P., Stroulia, E., & Lyons, K. (2008). A typology of virtual worlds. *Journal of Virtual Worlds Research, 1*(1).

Metiri Group. (2000). *Twenty-first century skills.* Retrieved from http://ncrel.engauge.org

Metros, S. (1999). Making connections: A model for on-line interaction. *Leonardo, 32*(4), 281–291. doi:10.1162/002409499553433

Meyers, E. (2009). Tip of the iceberg: Meaning, identity, and literacy in preteen virtual worlds. *Journal of Education for Library and Information Science, 50*(4), 226–236.

Mikropoulos, T. A., & Natsis, A. (2011). Educational virtual environments: A ten-year review of empirical research (1999-2009). *Computers & Education, 56*(3), 769–780. doi:10.1016/j.compedu.2010.10.020

Milgram, P., & Kishino, F. (1994). A taxonomy of mixed reality visual displays. *IEICE Transactions on Information and Systems, 77,* 1321–1329.

Miller, H. B., & Burton, J. K. (1994). Images and imagery theory. In Moore, D. M., & Dwyer, F. M. (Eds.), *Visual Literacy: A Spectrum of Visual Learning* (pp. 65–83). Englewood Cliffs, NJ: Educational Technology Publications.

Miller, V. V. (2003). Teaching business strategy for an emerging economy: An internet-based simulation. In Russow, L. C. (Ed.), *Digital Technology in Teaching International Business* (pp. 99–114). Binghamton, NY: International Business Press.

Mirzoeff, N. (1999). *An introduction to visual culture.* New York, NY: Routledge.

Mishra, P., & Koehler, M. (2006). Technological pedagogical content knowledge. *Teachers College Record, 108*(6), 1017–1054. doi:10.1111/j.1467-9620.2006.00684.x

Misirlaki, S., & Paraskeva, F. (2011). Massively multiplayer online games as activity systems: The relationship between motivation, performance and community. In *Proceedings of ECGBL.* Athens, Greece.

Moeller, K., Neuburger, S., Kaufmann, L., Landerl, K., & Nuerk, H. C. (2009). Basic number processing deficits in developmental dyscalculia: Evidence from eye tracking. *Cognitive Development, 24*(4), 371–386. doi:10.1016/j.cogdev.2009.09.007

Moore, A., Masterson, J. T., Christophel, D. M., & Shea, K. A. (1996). College teacher immediacy and student ratings of instruction. *Communication Education*, *45*, 29–39. doi:10.1080/03634529609379030

Moos, D. C., & Marroquin, E. (2010). Multimedia, hypermedia, and hypertext: Motivation considered and reconsidered. *Computers in Human Behavior*, *26*, 265–276. doi:10.1016/j.chb.2009.11.004

Morand, D. A., & Ocker, R. J. (2003). Politeness theory and computer-mediated communication: A sociolinguistic approach to analyzing relational messages. In *Proceedings of the 36ᵗʰ Hawaii International Conference on System Sciences*. IEEE Press. Retrieved June 1, 2007, from http://ieeexplore.ieee.org/xpl/freeabs_all.jsp?arnumber=1173660

Morgan, J., & Welton, P. (1992). *See what I mean: An introduction to visual communication*. Oxford, UK: Oxford University Press.

Multimedia Development Corporation. (2005). *Smart school roadmap 2005-2020*. New York, NY: Multimedia Development Corporation.

Myles, B. (2004). *The hidden curriculum: Practical solutions for understanding unstated rules in social situations*. Shawnee Mission, KS: Autism Asperger Publishing.

Nardi, B. A., & Harris, J. (2006). *Strangers and friends: Collaborative play in World of Warcraft*. Retrieved from http://portal.acm.org/citation.cfm?id=1180875.1180898

Nardi, B. A. (2010). *My life as a night elf priest: An anthropological account of World of Warcraft*. Ann Arbor, MI: The University of Michigan Press.

NCTM. (2006). *Curriculum focal points for prekindergarten through grade 8 mathematics*. Reston, VA: National Council of Teachers of Mathematics.

Neulight, N., Kafai, Y. B., Kao, L., Foley, B., & Galas, C. (2007). Children's participation in a virtual epidemic in the science classroom: Making connections to natural infectious diseases. *Journal of Science Education and Technology*, *16*(1), 47–58. doi:10.1007/s10956-006-9029-z

New Media Consortium and EDUCAUSE Learning Initiative. (2007). *The horizon report*. Retrieved March 20, 2007, from http://www.nmc.org/pdf/2007_Horizon_Report.pdf

Newmann, F. (1996). *Authentic achievement: Restructuring schools for intellectual quality*. San Francisco, CA: Jossey-Bass.

Nicholls, J. (1978). The development of concepts of effort and ability, perception of own attainment, and the understanding that difficult tasks require more ability. *Child Development*, *49*, 800–814. doi:10.2307/1128250

Nickerson, S. D., & Whitacre, I. (2010). A local instruction theory for the development of number sense. *Mathematical Thinking and Learning*, *12*(3), 227–252. doi:10.1080/10986061003689618

Nicolaisen, K., & Vejleskov, H. (1996). *Dysfatiske småbørn*. Berlin, Germany: Danmarks Lærerhøjskole.

Nielsen. (2009). *Global faces and networked places: A Nielsen report on social networking's new global footprint*. Nielsen.

Nonaka, I. (1991, November/December). The knowledge-creating company. *Harvard Business Review*, 96–104.

Nonaka, I., & Takeuchi, H. (1995). *The knowledge-creating company: How Japanese companies create the dynamics of innovation*. Oxford, UK: The Oxford University Press. doi:10.1016/0024-6301(96)81509-3

Novak, K. (2008). RezEd: The hub for learning in virtual worlds. *Social Presence Effects Group*. Retrieved on January 13, 2009 from http://www.rezed.org/forum/topics/2047896:Topic:6518?groupUrl=socialpresenceinvirtualworlds&id=2047896%3ATopic%3A6518&groupId=2047896%3AGroup%3A6392&page=6#comments

NSF Task Force on Cyberlearning. (2008). *Fostering learning the networked world*. Washington, DC: National Science Foundation.

O'Driscoll, T. (2007). *Learning in three dimensions: Experiencing the sensibilities and imagining the possibilities*. Retrieved November 13, 2010, from http://www.youtube.com/watch?v=O2jY4UkPbAc&feature=player_embedded#!

OECD. (2005). *The definition and selection of key competencies*. New York, NY: OECD.

Oetzel, J. G., Ting-Toomey, S., Masumoto, T., Yukochi, Y., Pan, X., Takai, J., & Wilcox, R. (2001). Face and facework in conflict: A cross-cultural comparison of China, Germany, Japan, and the United States. *Communication Monographs*, *68*, 235–258. doi:10.1080/03637750128061

Owyang, J. (2010, January 19). A collection of social networking stats for 2010. *Web Strategy*. Retrieved from http://www.web-strategist.com/blog/2010/01/19/a-collection-of-social-network-stats-for-2010/

Paek, T., & Horvitz, E. (2004). Optimizing automated call routing by integrating spoken dialogue models with queuing models. In *Proceedings of HLT-NAACL*, (pp. 41-48). NAACL.

Park, H. (2010). The effect of activities in virtual worlds as a communication environment to understand each other. *Journal of Cyber Therapy and Rehabilitation*, *3*(1), 71–82.

Parliament, E. U. (2007). *Key competences for life-long learning: A European framework*. Geneva, Switzerland: European Union.

Partnership for 21st Century Skills. (2008). *21st century skills, education & competitiveness, resource and policy guide*. Partnership for 21st Century Skills.

Patton, M. Q. (1997). *Utilization-focused evaluation*. Thousand Oaks, CA: Sage Publications, Inc.

Perry, S. J., & Bulatov, I. (2010). The influence of new tools in virtual learning environments on the teaching and learning process in chemical engineering. *Chemical Engineering Transactions*, *21*, 1051–1056.

Petheram, B. (2004). Computers and aphasia: A mean to delivery and a delivery of means. *Aphasiology*, *18*(3), 187–191. doi:10.1080/02687030444000020

Petrakou, A. (2010). Interacting through avatars: Virtual worlds as a context for online education. *Computers & Education*, *54*(4), 1020–1027. doi:10.1016/j.compedu.2009.10.007

Pettersson, R. (1993). *Visual information*. Englewood Cliffs, NJ: Educational Technology Publications.

Pettey, C. (2007, April 24). Gartner says 80 percent of active internet users will have a 'second life' in the virtual world by the end of 2011. *Gartner.com*. Retrieved October 2, 2008 from http://gartner.com/it/page.jsp?id=503861

Piaget, J. (1985). *The equilibration of cognitive structures: The central problem of intellectual development*. Chicago, IL: University of Chicago Press.

Pinar, W. F., Reynolds, W. M., Slattery, P., & Taubman, P. M. (2002). *Understanding curriculum: An introduction to the study of historical and contemporary curriculum discourses*. New York, NY: Peter Lang.

Pink, D. (2006). *A whole new world*. New York, NY: Berkley.

Pon-Barry, H., Schultz, K., Bratt, E. O., Clark, B., & Peters, S. (2006). Responding to student uncertainty in spoken tutorial dialogue systems. *International Journal of Artificial Intelligence in Education*, *16*, 171–194.

Popper, K. (1999). *All life is problem-solving*. London, UK: Routledge.

Prada, R., Ma, S., & Nunes, M. A. (2010). Personality in social group dynamics. In *Proceedings of the International Conference on Computational Science and Engineering*, (pp. 607-612). IEEE.

Prensky, M. (2001). *Digital natives, digital immigrants*. Retrieved from http://www.marcprensky.com/writing/prensky%20%20digital%20natives,%20digital%20immigrants%20-%20part1.pdf

Prensky, M. (2005). Engage me or enrage me: What today's learners demand. *EDUCAUSE Review*, 60-64. Retrieved January 3, 2009 from http://net.educause.edu/ir/library/pdf/erm0553.pdf

Prensky, M. (2006). *Don't bother me, mom, I'm learning! How computer and video games are preparing your kids for 21st century success and how you can help!* St. Paul, MN: Paragon House.

President's Council of Advisors on Science and Technology. (2010). *Report to the president: Prepare and inspire: K-12 education in science, technology, engineering, and math (STEM) for America's future*. Washington, DC: Office of Science and Technology Policy.

Puffer, S. M. (Ed.). (2004). *International management: Insights from fiction and practice.* Armonk, NY: M.E. Sharpe.

Punnett, B. J. (2010). *Experiencing international business and management: Exercises, projects, and cases.* Armonk, NY: M.E. Sharpe.

Putz, T. (2012). The project mobile game based learning. In *Proceedings of ECEL*. ECEL.

Quest to Learn. (2011). *Quest to learn school website.* Retrieved from http://q2l.org/

Rabiner, L. R., & Juang, B. H. (1993). *Fundamentals of speech recognition.* Upper Saddle River, NJ: Prentice-Hall.

Raux, A., Langner, B., Blac, A. W., & Eskenazi, M. (2003). Let's go: Improving spoken dialog systems for the elderly and non-natives. In *Proceedings of Interspeech* (pp. 753–756). Interspeech.

Read, J., MacFarlane, S., & Casey, C. (2002). Endurability, engagement and expectations: Measuring children's fun. In *Proceedings of the International Workshop on Interaction Design and Children,* (pp. 189-198). Eindhoven, The Netherlands: Shaker Publishing.

Reeves, B., & Malone, T. (2007). *Leadership in games and at work: Implications for the enterprise of massively multiplayer online role-playing games. Report Prepared for IBM.* New York, NY: IBM.

Reeves, T. C., Herrington, J., & Oliver, R. (2005). Design research: A socially responsible approach to instructional technology research in higher education. *Journal of Computing in Higher Education, 16*(2), 97–116. doi:10.1007/BF02961476

Rehm, M. (2008). She is just stupid – Analyzing user-agent interactions in emotional game situations. *Interacting with Computers, 20*(3), 311–325. doi:10.1016/j.intcom.2008.02.005

Rehm, M., & Endrass, B. (2009). Rapid prototyping of social group dynamics in multiagent systems. *AI & Society, 24*(1), 13–23. doi:10.1007/s00146-009-0191-8

Rehm, M., Nakano, Y., André, E., Nishida, T., Bee, N., & Endrass, B. (2009). From observation to simulation: Generating culture-specific behavior for interactive systems. *AI & Society, 24*(3), 267–280. doi:10.1007/s00146-009-0216-3

Reid, A., Houchen-Clagett, D., & Browning, J. B. (2010). *Integration of microblogging in post secondary courses.* Manuscript submitted for publication (copy on file with author). Unpublished.

Rhodes, S., & Halverson, R. (2009). *KidGrid.* Paper presented at the Games+Learning+Society 5.0 conference. Madison, WI.

Richardson, J., & Swan, K. (2003). Examining social presence in online courses in relation to students' perceived learning and satisfaction. *Journal of Asynchronous Learning Networks, 7*(1), 68–88.

Rieber, L. P. (1996). Seriously considering play: Designing interactive learning environments based on the blending of microworlds, simulations, and games. *Educational Technology Research and Development, 44*(2), 43–58. doi:10.1007/BF02300540

Rizzolatti, G. (2008). *Mirrors in the brain.* Oxford, UK: Oxford University Press.

Rizzolatti, G., & Craighero, L. (2004). The mirror neuron system. *Annual Review of Neuroscience, 27,* 169–192. doi:10.1146/annurev.neuro.27.070203.144230

Robben, C. G. M., & Sluka, J. A. (2012). *Ethnographic fieldwork: An anthropological reader.* Malden, MA: Blackwell Publishing.

Roblyer, M. D., & Doering, A. H. (2010). *Integrating educational technology into teaching.* Upper Saddle River, NJ: Pearson Educatiion Inc.

Robson, C. (2002). *Real world research: A resource for social scientists and practitioner-research.* Malden, MA: Blackwell.

Rogoff, I. (2005). Studying visual culture. In Mirzoeff, N. (Ed.), *The Visual Culture Reader* (pp. 24–36). New York, NY: Routledge.

Roschelle, J. (1992). Learning by collaborating: Convergent conceptual change. *Journal of the Learning Sciences, 2*(3), 235–276. doi:10.1207/s15327809jls0203_1

Rosenman, M. A., Smith, G., Maher, M. L., Ding, L., & Marchant, D. (2007). Multidisciplinary collaborative design in virtual environments. *Automation in Construction, 16*(1), 37–44. doi:10.1016/j.autcon.2005.10.007

Rouselle, L., & Noël, M.-P. (2008). The development of automatic numerosity processes in preschoolers: Evidence for numerosity-perceptual interference. *Developmental Psychology, 44*(2), 544–560. doi:10.1037/0012-1649.44.2.544

Roussou, M., Oliver, M., & Slater, M. (2006). The virtual playground: an educational virtual reality environment for evaluating interactivity and conceptual learning. *Virtual Reality (Waltham Cross), 10*, 227–240. doi:10.1007/s10055-006-0035-5

Rubin, H. J., & Rubin, I. S. (2005). *Qualitative interviewing: The art of hearing data* (2nd ed.). Thousand Oaks, CA: SAGE Publications.

Russow, L. C. (Ed.). (2003). *Digital technology in teaching international business*. Binghamton, NY: International Business Press.

Salzman, M. C., Dede, C., Loftin, R. B., & Chen, J. (1999). The design and evaluation of virtual reality-based learning environments. *Presence*. Retrieved August 12, 2009, from http://www.virtual.gmu.edu/ss_pdf/presence.pdf

Savicki, V., & Kelley, M. (2000). Computer mediated communication: Gender and group composition. *Cyberpsychology & Behavior, 3*(5), 817–826. doi:10.1089/10949310050191791

Schallert, D. L., Reed, J. H., Kim, M., Beth, A. D., Chen, Y., Yang, M., & Chang, Y. (2004). *Online learning or learning on the line: Do students learn anything of value in sa CMD?* Paper presented at the meeting of the National Reading Conference. San Antonio, TX.

Schallert, D. L., Chiang, Y., Park, Y., Jordan, M. E., Lee, H., & Cheng, A. (2009). Being polite while fulfilling different discourse functions in online classroom discussions. *Computers & Education, 53*, 713–725. doi:10.1016/j.compedu.2009.04.009

Schallert, D. L., & Martin, D. B. (2003). A psychological analysis of what teachers and students do in the language arts classroom. In Flood, J., Lapp, D., Squire, J. R., & Jensen, J. M. (Eds.), *Handbook of Research on Teaching the English Language Arts* (pp. 31–45). Mahwah, NJ: Lawrence Erlbaum Associates.

Schell, J. (2010) *Design outside the box*. Paper presented at the 9th Annual Design Innovate Communicate Entertain (D.I.C.E.) Summit. Las Vegas, NV.

Schiffrin, D. (1994). *Approaches to discourses*. Malden, MA: Blackwell Publishing.

Schliemann, A. D., Carraher, D. W., Brizuela, B. M., & Jones, W. (1998). *Solving algebra problems before algebra instruction*. Paper presented at the Second Early Algebra Meeting. New York, NY.

Schroeder, R. (2002). Copresence and interaction in virtual environments: An overview of the range of issues. [Presence.]. *Proceedings of Presence, 2002*, 274–295.

Schroeder, R. (2008). Defining virtual worlds and virtual environments. *Journal of Virtual Worlds Research, 1*(1).

Selfe, C. L., & Hawisher, G. E. (Eds.). (2007). *Gaming lives in the twenty-first century: Literate connections*. New York, NY: Palgrave Macmillan. doi:10.1057/9780230601765

Seneff, S. (2002). Response planning and generation in the mercury flight reservation system. *Computer Speech & Language, 16*(3-4), 283–312. doi:10.1016/S0885-2308(02)00011-6

Senge, P. (2006). *The fifth discipline: The art & practice of the learning organization*. New York, NY: Doubleday. doi:10.1002/pfi.4170300510

Senge, P. M. (1990). *The fifth discipline: The art and practice of the learning organization*. New York, NY: Doubleday/Currency. doi:10.1002/pfi.4170300510

Shadden, B. B., Hagstrom, F., & Koski, P. (2008). *Neurogenic communication disorders: Life stories and the narrative self*. San Diego, CA: Plural Publishing.

Shadden, B., & Agan, J. P. (2004). Renegotiation of identity: The social context of aphasia support groups. *The Social Construction of Identity: The Clinical Challenge, 24*(3), 174.

Shaffer, D. W. (2006). *How computer games help children learn*. New York, NY: Palgrave Macmillan. doi:10.1057/9780230601994

Shaffer, D. W. (2008). Education in the digital age. *Digital Kompetanse, 1*(3), 37–50.

Shaffer, D. W., & Clinton, K. A. (2006). Toolforthoughts: Reexamining thinking in the digital age. *Mind, Culture, and Activity, 13*(4), 283–300. doi:10.1207/s15327884mca1304_2

Shaffer, D. W., & Gee, J. P. (Eds.). (2007). *Epistemic games as education for innovation.* Leicester, UK: British Journal of Educational Psychology.

Shaw, M. (1971). *Group dynamics – The psychology of small group behavior.* New York, NY: McGraw Hill Inc.

Short, J., Williams, E., & Christie, B. (1976). *The social psychology of telecommunications.* London, UK: John Wiley and Sons.

Simmons, P. E., Emory, A., Carter, T., Coker, T., Finnegan, B., & Crockett, D. (1999). Beginning teachers: Beliefs and classroom actions. *Journal of Research in Science Teaching, 36*(8), 930–954. doi:10.1002/(SICI)1098-2736(199910)36:8<930::AID-TEA3>3.0.CO;2-N

Singhanayok, C., & Hooper, S. (1998). The effects of cooperative learning and learner control on students' achievement, option selections, and attitudes. *Educational Technology Research and Development, 46*(2), 17–32. doi:10.1007/BF02299787

Siorenta, A., & Jimoyiannis, A. (2008). Physics instruction in secondary schools: An investigation of teachers' beliefs towards physics laboratory and ICT. *Research in Science & Technological Education, 26*(2), 185–202. doi:10.1080/02635140802037328

Sivan, Y. (2009). *Overview: State of virtual worlds standards in 2009.* Retrieved from http://journals.tdl.org/jvwr/article/view/671/539

Skinner, B. F. (1938). *The behavior of organisms.* Upper Saddle River, NJ: Prentice Hall.

Skinner, E. A., Wellborn, J. G., & Connell, J. P. (1990). What it takes to do well in school and whether I've got it: A process model of perceived control and children's engagement in school. *Journal of Educational Psychology, 82*, 22–32. doi:10.1037/0022-0663.82.1.22

Sklar, E., & Davies, M. (2005). Multiagent simulation of learning environments. In *Proceedings of the 4ᵗʰ International Conference on Autonomous Agents and Multiagent Systems (AAMAS),* (pp. 953-959). ACM Press.

Slavin, R. E. (1996). Research for the future: Research on cooperative learning and achievement: What we know, what we need to know. *Contemporary Educational Psychology, 21*, 43–69. doi:10.1006/ceps.1996.0004

Smith, M., & Berge, Z. (2009). Social learning theory in second life. *MERLOT Journal of Online Learning and Teaching, 5*(2).

Snyder, B. R. (1971). *The hidden curriculum.* New York, NY: Alfred A. Knopf.

Soukup, C. (2004). Multimedia performance in a computer-mediated community: Communication as a virtual drama. *Journal of Computer-Mediated Communication, 9*(4). Retrieved July 24, 2007, from http://jcmc.indiana.edu/vol9/issue4/soukup.html

Soukup, C. (2007). Mastering the game: Gender and the entelechial motivational system of video games. *Women's. Studies in Communications, 30*, 157–179.

Spillane, J. P., Halverson, R., & Diamond, J. (2004). Towards a theory of school leadership practice: Implications of a distributed perspective. *Journal of Curriculum Studies, 36*(1), 3–34. doi:10.1080/0022027032000106726

Squire, K. D. (2004). *Replaying history: Learning world history through playing "Civilization III".* (Unpublished Ph.D. Thesis). Indiana University. Indianapolis, IN.

Squire, K. D. (2005). Changing the game: What happens when video games enter the classroom?. *Innovate: Journal of Online Education, 1*(6).

Squire, K. D., Barnett, M., Grant, J. M., & Higginbottom, T. (2004). *Electromagentism supercharged! Learning physics with digital simulation games.* Paper presented at the International Conference of the Learning Sciences. Santa Monica, CA.

Squire, K. (2007, September-October). Games, learning, and society: Building a field. *Educational Technology*, 51–54.

Squire, K. D. (2006). From content to context: Videogames as designed experience. *Educational Researcher, 35*(8), 19–29. doi:10.3102/0013189X035008019

Squire, K. D. (2011). *Video games and learning: Teaching and participatory culture in the digital age.* New York, NY: Teachers College Press.

Stacey, R. D. (2001). *Complex responsive processes in organizations: Learning and knowledge creation.* New York, NY: Routledge.

Steen, L. A. (1997). *Why numbers count: Quantitative literacy for tomorrow's America.* New York, NY: College Entrance Examination Board. doi:10.1177/019263659808260020

Steinkuehler, C. A. (2004). Learning in massively multiplayer online games. In Y. B. Kafai, W. A. Sandoval, N. Enyedy, A. S. Nixon, & F. Herrera (Eds.), *Proceedings of the Sixth International Conference of the Learning Sciences,* (pp. 521–528). Mahwah, NJ: Erlbaum.

Steinkuehler, C. A. (2006). Massively multiplayer online videogaming as participation in a discourse. *Mind, Culture, and Activity, 13*(1), 38–52. doi:10.1207/s15327884mca1301_4

Steinkuehler, C. A. (2006). The mangle of play. *Games and Culture, 1*(3), 1–14. doi:10.1177/1555412006290440

Steinkuehler, C. A. (2008). Cognition and literacy in massively multiplayer online games. In Coiro, J., Knobel, M., Lankshear, C., & Leu, D. (Eds.), *Handbook of Research on New Literacies* (pp. 611–634). Mahwah, NJ: Erlbaum.

Steinkuehler, C. A., & Williams, D. (2006). Where everybody knows your (screen) name: Online games as third places. *Journal of Computer-Mediated Communication, 11*(4). doi:10.1111/j.1083-6101.2006.00300.x

Steinkuehler, C., & Duncan, S. (2009). Informal scientific reasoning in online virtual worlds. *Journal of Science Education and Technology, 17*(6), 530–543. doi:10.1007/s10956-008-9120-8

Stent, A., Dowding, J., Gawron, J. M., Bratt, E., & Moore, R. (1999). The CommandTalk spoken dialogue system. In *Proceedings of 37th Annual Meeting of the ACL,* (pp. 183-190). ACL.

Stephen, J. (2007). Virtually sacred: The performance of asynchronous cyber-rituals in online spaces. *Journal of Computer-Mediated Communication, 12*(3), 1103–1121. doi:10.1111/j.1083-6101.2007.00365.x

Stern, R. C., & Robinson, R. S. (1994). Perception and its role in communication and learning. In Dwyer, F. M., & Moore, D. M. (Eds.), *Visual Literacy: A Plectrum of Visual Learning.* Englewood Cliffs, NJ: Educational Technology Publications.

Strauss, A. L., & Corbin, J. (1990). *Basics of qualitative research: Grounded theory procedures and techniques.* Thousand Oaks, CA: Sage Publications.

Strothotte, T., Fritz, S., Michel, R., Raab, A., Petrie, H., & Johnson, V. (1996). Development of dialogue systems for a mobility aid for blind people: Initial design and usability testing. In *Proceedings of 2nd Annual ACM Conference on Assistive Technologies,* (pp. 139-144). ACM Press.

Sturken, M., & Cartwright, L. (2004). *Practices of looking: An introduction to visual culture.* Oxford, UK: Oxford University Press.

Suthers, D. D., & Hundhausen, C., D. (2003). An experimental study of the effects of representational guidance on collaborative learning processes. *Journal of the Learning Sciences, 12*(2), 183–218. doi:10.1207/S15327809JLS1202_2

Sweeney, B. (2008). Mathematics in a virtual world: How the immersive environment of second life can facilitate the learning of mathematics and other subjects. *ReLive 08: Researching learning in virtual environments.* Retrieved November, 2008, from http://www.open.ac.uk/relive08/documents/ReLIVE08_conference_proceedings_Lo.pdf

Takayoshi, P. (2007). Gender matters: Literacy, learning, and gaming in one American family. In Selfe, C. L., & Hawisher, G. E. (Eds.), *Gaming Lives in the Twenty-First Century: Literate Connections* (pp. 229–249). New York, NY: Palgrave Macmillan.

Tal, R. T. (2001). Incorporating field trips as science learning environment enrichment: An interpretive study. *Learning Environments Research, 4,* 25–49. doi:10.1023/A:1011454625413

Tavin, K. M. (2003). Wrestling with angels, searching for ghosts: Toward a critical pedagogy of visual culture. *Studies in Art Education, 44*(3), 197–213.

Taylor, P. G. (2000). Madonna and hypertext: Liberatory Learning in art education. *Studies in Art Education, 41*(4), 376–389. doi:10.2307/1320680

Thomas, D. C. (2002). *Essentials of international management.* Thousand Oaks, CA: Sage Publications, Inc.

Thomas, D., & Brown, J. S. (2009). Why virtual worlds can matter. *International Journal of Media and Learning, 1*(1).

Thomas, M. K., Barab, S. A., & Tuzun, H. (2009). Developing critical implementations of technology-rich innovations: A cross-case of the implementation of quest Atlantis. *Journal of Educational Computing Research, 41*(2), 125–153. doi:10.2190/EC.41.2.a

Thomas, R. M., & Brubaker, D. L. (2000). *Theses and dissertations: A guide to planning, research, and writing.* Westport, CT: Bergin & Garvey.

Thompson, A., & Mishra, P. (2008). Breaking news: TPCK becomes TPACK! *Journal of Computing in Teacher Education, 24*(2). Retrieved October 29, 2010 at http://punya.educ.msu.edu/publications/journal_articles/jcteeditorial-24-2-038.pdf

Ting-Toomey, S., & Kurogi, A. (1998). Facework competence in intercultural conflict: An updated face negotiation theory. *International Journal of Intercultural Relations, 22*, 187–225. doi:10.1016/S0147-1767(98)00004-2

Tiwana, A. (1999). *The knowledge management toolkit.* Upper Saddle River, NJ: Prentice Hall.

Traum, D., & Larsson, S. (2003). *Current and new directions in discourse and dialogue: The information state approach to dialogue management.* Dordrecht, The Netherlands: Kluwer Academic Publishers.

Tsiatsos, T., Andreas, K., & Pomportsis, A. (2010). Evaluation framework for collaborative educational virtual environments. *Journal of Educational Technology & Society, 13*(2), 65–77.

Twining, P. (2009). Exploring the educational potential of virtual worlds--Some reflections from the SPP. *British Journal of Educational Technology, 40*(3), 496. doi:10.1111/j.1467-8535.2009.00963.x

Tzelgov, J., & Ganor-Stern, D. (2005). *Automaticity in processing ordinal information.* New York, NY: Psychology Press.

Urhahne, D., Schanze, S., Bell, T., Mansfield, A., & Holmes, J. (2010). Role of the teacher in computer-supported collaborative inquiry learning. *International Journal of Science Education, 32*(2), 221–243. doi:10.1080/09500690802516967

Utama, R. J., Syrdal, A. K., & Conkie, A. (2006). Six approaches to limited domain concatenative speech synthesis. In *Proceedings of Interspeech* (pp. 2058–2061). Interspeech.

Vaquero, C., Saz, O., Lleida, E., Marcos, J., & Canalís, C. (2012). Vocaliza: An application for computer-aided speech therapy in Spanish language. In *Proceedings of IV Jornadas en Tecnología del Habla*, (pp. 321–326). Academic Press.

Vestberg, P. (2002). Hjerneskade og personlighed. *Kognition & Pædagogik, 43.*

Vinciarelli, A., Pantic, M., & Bourlard, H. (2009). Social signal processing: Survey of an emerging domain. *Image and Vision Computing Journal, 27*(12), 1743–1759. doi:10.1016/j.imavis.2008.11.007

Von Krogh, G., Ichijo, K., & Nonaka, I. (2000). *Enabling knowledge creation: How to unlock the mystery of tacit knowledge and release the power of innovation.* Oxford, UK: Oxford University Press.

Vygotsky, L. (1978). *Mind in society: The development of higher psychological processes.* Cambridge, MA: Harvard University Press.

Vygotsky, L. S. (1986). *Thought and language.* Cambridge, MA: MIT Press.

Wagner, C. (2008). Learning experience with virtual worlds. *Journal of Information Systems Education, 19*(3), 263–266.

Wagner, C., & Rachael, K. F. (2009). Action learning with second life - A pilot study. *Journal of Information Systems Education, 20*(2), 249–258.

Wagner, D., & Davis, B. (2010). Feeling number: Grounding number sense in a sense of quantity. *Educational Studies in Mathematics, 74*(1), 39–51. doi:10.1007/s10649-009-9226-9

Walker, V. (2009). 3D virtual learning in counselor education: Using second life in counselor skill development. *Journal of Virtual Worlds Research, 2*(1).

Walsh, S. L., Gregory, E., Lake, Y., & Gunawardena, C. N. (2003). Self-construal, facework, and conflict styles among cultures in online learning environments. *Educational Technology Research and Development, 51*(4), 113–122. doi:10.1007/BF02504548

Walther, J. (1996). Computer-mediated communication: Impersonal, interpersonal, and hyperpersonal interaction. *Communication Research, 23*(1), 3–43. doi:10.1177/009365096023001001

Walther, J. B., Van Der Heide, B., Kim, S., Westerman, D., & Tong, S. T. (2008). The role of friends' appearance and behavior on evaluations of individuals' Facebook profiles: Are we known by the company we keep? *Human Communication Research, 34*, 28–49. doi:10.1111/j.1468-2958.2007.00312.x

Wang, H., Chignell, M., & Ishizuka, M. (2006). Are two talking heads better than one? When should use more than one agent in e-learning? In *Proceedings of IUT*. IUT.

Wang, Y., Wang, W., & Huang, C. (2007). Enhanced semantic question answering system for e-learning environment. In *Proceedings of AINAW 2007 Conference*, (pp. 1023–1028). AINAW.

Wang, F., & Hannafin, M. J. (2005). Design-based research and technology-enhanced learning environments. *Educational Technology Research and Development, 53*(4), 5–23. doi:10.1007/BF02504682

Wang, X. C., Hinn, D. M., & Kanfer, A. G. (2001). Potential of computer-supported collaborative learning for learners with different learning styles. *Journal of Research on Technology in Education, 34*(1), 75–85.

Wang, Y., & Braman, J. (2009). Extending the classroom through second life. *Journal of Information Systems Education, 20*(2), 235–247.

Warburton, S. (2009). Second life in higher education: Assessing the potential for and the barriers to deploying virtual worlds in learning and teaching. *British Journal of Educational Technology, 40*(3), 414–426. doi:10.1111/j.1467-8535.2009.00952.x

Waterworth, J., & Waterworth, E. (1999). Education as exploration: Being, going and changing the world. In *Proceeding of Didactics of Informatics and Mathematics in Education* (pp. 42–55). IEEE.

Watson, S., Smith, Z., & Driver, J. (2006). Alcohol, sex and illegal activities: An analysis of selected Facebook central photos in fifty states. *Online Submission*. Retrieved from EBSCOhost.

Watson, W. R., Mong, C. J., & Harris, C. A. (2011). A case study of the in-class use of a video game for teaching high school history. *Computers & Education, 56*, 466–474. doi:10.1016/j.compedu.2010.09.007

Webb, M. E. (2005). Affordances of ICT in science learning: implications for an integrated pedagogy. *International Journal of Science Education, 27*(6), 705–735. doi:10.1080/09500690500038520

Webb, M., & Cox, M. (2004). A review of pedagogy related to information and communications technology. *Technology, Pedagogy and Education, 13*(3), 235–286. doi:10.1080/14759390400200183

Weber, A., Rufer-Bach, K., & Platel, R. (2008). *Creating your world: The official guide to advanced content creation for second life*. Indianapolis, IN: Wiley Publishing, Inc.

Weiner, B. (1986). *An attributional theory of motivation and emotion*. New York, NY: Springer-Verlag. doi:10.1007/978-1-4612-4948-1

Weiss, J. (2006). Introduction: Virtual learning and learning virtually. In Weiss, J., Nolan, J., Hunsinger, J., & Trifonas, P. (Eds.), *The International Handbook of Virtual Learning Environments*. Dordrecht, The Netherlands: Springer. doi:10.1007/978-1-4020-3803-7

Wells, G. (2001). The case for dialogic inquiry. In Wells, G. (Ed.), *Action, Talk, and Text: Learning and Teaching through Inquiry* (p. 184). New York, NY: Teachers College Press.

Wenger, E. (2000). *Communities of practice: Learning, meaning, and identity*. Cambridge, UK: Cambridge University Press.

Wertsch, J. V. (1991). *Voices of the mind: A sociocultural approach to mediated action*. Cambridge, MA: Harvard University Press.

Wertz, R. T. (1992). Potential of television and telephonic technology for appraising and diagnosing neurogenic communication disorders in remote settings. *Aphasiology, 6*.

Wiendl, V., Dorfmüller-Ulhaas, K., Schulz, N., & André, E. (2007). Integrating a virtual agent into the real world: The virtual anatomy assistant ritchie. In *Proceedings of Intelligent Virtual Agents (IVA)* (pp. 211–224). Berlin, Germany: Springer. doi:10.1007/978-3-540-74997-4_20

Wigfield, A. (1994). Expectancy-value theory of achievement motivation: A developmental perspective. *Educational Psychology Review*, 6, 49–78. doi:10.1007/BF02209024

Wigfield, A., & Eccles, J. (1992). The development of achievement task values: A theoretical analysis. *Developmental Review*, 12, 265–310. doi:10.1016/0273-2297(92)90011-P

Wigfield, A., & Eccles, J. S. (2000). Expectancy-value theory of motivation. *Contemporary Educational Psychology*, 25, 68–81. doi:10.1006/ceps.1999.1015

Wiggins, G., & McTighe, J. (2005). *Understanding by design* (2nd ed.). Upper Saddle River, NJ: Prentice Hall.

Wiig, E., & Wiig, K. (1999). *Conceptual learning considerations*. Retrieved from http://www.krii.com/downloads/conceptual_learning.pdf

Williams, D., Ducheneaut, N., Xiong, L., Zhang, Y., Yee, N., & Nickell, E. (2006). From tree house to barracks: The social life of guilds in World of Warcraft. *Games and Culture*, 1(4), 338–361. doi:10.1177/1555412006292616

Williams, D., Yee, N., & Kaplan, S. E. (2008). Who plays, how much, and why? Debunking the stereotypical gamer profile. *Journal of Computer-Mediated Communication*, 13, 993–1018. doi:10.1111/j.1083-6101.2008.00428.x

Williams, R. (2006). Theorizing visual intelligence: Practices, development, and methodologies for visual communication. In Hope, D. S. (Ed.), *Visual Communication: Perception, Rhetoric, and Technology* (pp. 32–42). Cresskill, NJ: Hampton Press.

Winn, W., Stahr, F., Sarason, C., Fruland, R., Oppenheimer, P., & Lee, Y.-L. (2006). Learning oceanography from a computer simulation compared with direct experience at sea. *Journal of Research in Science Teaching*, 43(1), 25–42. doi:10.1002/tea.20097

Winterton, J., Delamare, F., & Stringfellow, E. (2005). *Typology of knowledge skills and competences*. Research report. CEDEFOP project

Wlodkowski, R. J. (1985). *Enhancing adult motivation to learn*. San Francisco, CA: Jossey-Bass.

Wlodkowski, R. J. (1989). Instructional design and learner motivation. In Johnson, K. A., & Foe, L. J. (Eds.), *Instructional Design: New Alternatives for Effective Education and Training* (pp. 47–60). New York, NY: Macmillan.

Wolfenstein, M. (2010). *Leadership at play: How leadership in digital games can inform the future of instructional leadership*. (Doctoral Dissertation). University of Wisconsin – Madison. Madison, WI.

Wolfenstein, M., & Dikkers, S. (2009). *My raid leader, my teacher: What we can learn about schools from guild leadership*. Paper presented at the American Education Research Association Conference. San Diego, CA.

Woodcock, B. (2008). *MMOG chart*. Retrieved from http://www.mmogchart.com/

Wood, E., Willoughby, T., Reille, S., Elliot, S., & DuCharme, M. (1995). Evaluating students' acquisition of factual material when studying independently or with a partner. *The British Journal of Educational Psychology*, 65, 237–247. doi:10.1111/j.2044-8279.1995.tb01145.x

Woolf, B. P., Arroyo, I., Muldner, K., Burleson, W., Cooper, D. G., Dolan, R., & Christopherson, R. M. (2010). The effect of motivational learning companions on low achieving students and students with disabilities. In Aleven, V., Kay, J., & Mostow, J. (Eds.), *Intelligent Tutoring Systems (ITS), Part I* (pp. 327–337). Berlin, Germany: Springer. doi:10.1007/978-3-642-13388-6_37

WoW in School. (2011). *The World of Warcraft in school wiki*. Retrieved from http://wowinschool.pbworks.com/

Wren, D. J. (1999). School culture: Exploring the hidden curriculum. *Adolescence*, 34(135), 593–596.

Wrzesien, M., & Raya, M. A. (2010). Learning in serious virtual worlds: Evaluation of learning effectiveness and appeal to students in the e-junior project. *Computers & Education*, 55(1), 178–187. doi:10.1016/j.compedu.2010.01.003

Wulff, S., Hanor, J., & Bulik, R. J. (2000). The roles and interrelationships of presence, reflection, and self-directed learning in effective world wide web-based pedagogy. In Cole, R. (Ed.), *Issues in Web-Based Pedagogy* (pp. 143–160). Westport, CT: Greenwood Press.

Yang, M., Chen, Y., Kim, M., Chang, Y., Cheng, A., & Park, Y. ... Jordan, M. (2006). Facilitating or limiting? The role of politeness in how students participate in an online classroom discussion. *Yearbook of the National Reading Conference, 55*, 341-356.

Yang, D.-C., & Li, M.-N. F. (2008). An investigation of 3rd-grade Taiwanese students' performance in number sense. *Educational Studies, 34*(5), 443–455. doi:10.1080/03055690802288494

Yang, D.-C., Reys, R., & Reys, B. (2009). Number sense strategies used by pre-service teachers in Taiwan. *International Journal of Science and Mathematics Education, 7*(2), 383–403. doi:10.1007/s10763-007-9124-5

Yee, N. (2005). *The Daedalus gateway*. Retrieved from http://www.nickyee.com/daedalus

Yee, N. (2006). The demographics, motivations and derived experiences of users of massively-multiuser online graphical environments. *Presence (Cambridge, Mass.), 15*, 309–329. doi:10.1162/pres.15.3.309

Yee, N., Ducheneaut, & Moore. (2006). Building a MMO with mass appeal: A look at gameplay in World of Warcraft. *Games and Culture, 1*(4), 1–38.

Yee, N., & Bailenson, J. (2009). The difference between being and seeing: The relative contribution of self-perception and priming to behavioral changes via digital self-representation. *Media Psychology, 12*(2), 195–209. doi:10.1080/15213260902849943

Yin, R. K. (1989). *Case study research: Design and methods*. Newbury Park, CA: Sage Publications.

Zacharia, Z. (2003). Beliefs, attitudes, and intentions of science teachers regarding the educational use of computer simulations and inquiry-based experiments in physics. *Journal of Research in Science Teaching, 40*(8), 792–823. doi:10.1002/tea.10112

Zickuhr, K. (2010)... *Generations (San Francisco, Calif.), 2010*, Retrieved from http://pewinternet.org/Reports/2010/Generations-2010.aspx

Zoll, C., Enz, S., Schaub, H., Aylett, R., & Paiva, A. (2006). Fighting bullying with the help of autonomous agents in a virtual school environment. In *Proceedings of the 7th International Conference on Cognitive Modeling (ICCM)*. ICCM.

About the Contributors

Steven D'Agustino holds a Doctorate from Fordham University in Educational Leadership, Administration, and Policy. He is the Director of Online Learning for the School of Professional and Continuing Studies and the Director of Fordham University's Center for Professional Development. Dr. D'Agustino researches in the area of instructional improvement through the integration of technology and has been awarded a number of grants to provide access to technology to historically underserved populations. He teaches a variety of courses in Fordham University's Gabelli School of Business and has taught in the doctoral program at the Graduate School of Education. Dr. D'Agustino has designed and implemented a number of Web-based ethics surveys and training programs and is a consultant to accounting firms and regulatory agencies in the areas of Ethics and Communication. He is the editor of *Adaptation, Resistance, and Access to Instructional Technologies: Assessing Future Trends in Education,* published in 2010 by IGI Global. His most recent publication is "Toward a Course Conversion Model for Distance Learning: A Review of Best Practices" in the *Journal of International Education in Business*, 2012.

* * *

Albena Antonova is a Lecturer at Sofia University, Faculty of Economics and Business Administration. She works on number of projects in the field of knowledge management, serious games, business and management education, e-learning and TEL models and methods, e-Business, technology entrepreneurship, innovation management, and living labs. Her research interests include knowledge management, serious games, knowledge management systems, innovation processes, technology entrepreneurship, knowledge sharing, knowledge transfer, and others.

Brian Burton is Asst. Professor of Digital Entertainment and Information Technology at Abilene Christian University. Dr. Brian Burton teaches Mobile Application Development for Apple iOS and Android OS devices and game development courses. He is the author of *Beginning Mobile App Development with Corona*, a textbook on cross-platform mobile application development, and a series of forthcoming books on game development for mobile devices. Dr. Burton regularly speaks internationally on game development, mobile app development, and online learning in virtual environments. Additional information on Dr. Burton's projects, books, research, as well as tutorials on mobile application development and game development can be found on his website at http://www.BurtonsMediaGroup.com.

Zoraida Callejas is Assistant Professor in the Department of Languages and Computer Systems at the Technical School of Computer Science and Telecommunications of the University of Granada (Spain). She completed a PhD in Computer Science at University of Granada in 2008 and has been a Visiting Researcher in University of Ulster (Belfast, UK), Technical University of Liberec (Liberec, Czech Republic), University of Trento (Trento, Italy), and Technical University of Berlin (Berlin, Germany). Her research activities have been mostly related to speech technologies and in particular to the investigation of dialogue systems. Her results have been published in several international journals and conferences. She has participated in numerous research projects, and is a member of several research associations focused on speech processing and human-computer interaction.

Jason A. Chen is an assistant professor of educational psychology at the College of William and Mary. His research interests center around students' beliefs about the malleability of their intellectual capacities (implicit theories of ability), the nature of knowledge and knowing (epistemic beliefs), and beliefs about one's capabilities to learn or perform tasks (self-efficacy). Most recently, he has researched the motivational affordances of innovative technologies among adolescents.

Yueh-Hui Vanessa Chiang is a recent graduate of the Instructional Technology program at the University of Texas at Austin. She currently works as an instructional technology specialist in distance learning programs. Her research interests include the discourse in online text-based and virtual world collaborative learning environments.

Beth Davies-Stofka received her Ph.D. in 2003 from the University of Toronto. She is currently Department Chair of Literature, Journalism, and Developmental Studies at Colorado Community Colleges Online, and is a member of the Adjunct Faculty in the Master of Arts in Liberal Studies program at Excelsior College. She has taught exclusively online since 2004, and is a founding member of the Center for EduPunx.

Chris Dede is the Timothy E. Wirth Professor in Learning Technologies at Harvard Graduate School of Education. His current research focuses on three areas: emerging technologies for learning and assessment, leadership in educational technology implementation, and effective policy for educational technology utilization. His research in emerging technologies includes funded projects on Multi-User Virtual Environments, augmented realities, sociosemantic networking, distance education, and Web 2.0 tools. His research on leadership focuses on issues of scaling up innovations from local to widespread use, and his work in policy centers on state and national level educational improvement strategies.

Ramón López-Cózar Delgado is Professor at the Faculty of Computer Science and Telecommunications of the University of Granada (Spain). His main research interests in the last 15 years include spoken and multimodal dialogue systems, focusing on speech processing and dialogue management. He has coordinated several research projects, has published a number of journal and conference papers, and has been invited speaker at several scientific events addressing these topics. In 2005, he published the book *Spoken, Multilingual, and Multimodal Dialogue Systems: Development and Assessment* (Wiley). Recently, he co-edited the book *Human-Centric Interfaces for Ambient Intelligence* (Elsevier Academic Press, 2010), in which he coordinated the section concerning speech processing and dialogue management. He is a member of ISCA (International Speech Communication Association), FoLLI (Association for Logic, Language, and Information), AIPO (Spanish Society on Human-Computer Interaction), and SEPLN (Spanish Society on Natural Language Processing).

David Griol obtained his Ph.D. degree in Computer Science from the Technical University of València (Spain) in 2007. He also has a B.S. in Telecommunication Science from this university. He is currently Professor at the Department of Computer Science in the Carlos III University of Madrid (Spain). He has participated in several European and Spanish projects related to natural language processing and dialogue systems. His research activities are mostly related to the development of statistical methodologies for the design of spoken dialogue systems. His research interests include dialogue management/optimization/simulation, corpus-based methodologies, user modeling, adaptation, and evaluation of spoken dialogue systems and machine learning approaches. Before starting his Ph.D. study, he worked as a Network Engineer in Motorola. He is a member of ISCA (International Speech Communication Association), IEEE (Institute of Electrical and Electronics Engineers), and AEPIA (Spanish Association of Artificial Intelligence).

Hsiao-Cheng (Sandrine) Han is an Assistant Professor in Faculty of Education, the Department of Curriculum and Pedagogy. In her research, she combines the fields of technology, visual culture, visual communication, semiotics, education, and cognitive psychology. Her research focuses on the visual culture in the virtual world of Second Life. In 2007, she founded the International Art Education Association (InAEA) in the Second Life and on the Web (http://www.inaea.org). She currently leads the association's monthly meetings in Second Life. She is also a practicing artist. She uses her art as a communication tool to explore ideas about culture and representation. Her interests include oil painting, Chinese painting, Chinese calligraphy, multi-media and virtual world 3D construction, and modeling.

Dana R. Herrera is currently a tenured Associate Professor of Anthropology at Saint Mary's College of California. She received her Masters and Doctorate degrees from the University of California at Davis. Dr. Herrera teaches courses in Cultural Anthropology, Biological Anthropology, as well as St. Mary's College Collegiate Seminar "great books" courses. She has conducted research studies in the Philippines, United States, and Hungary. Her current scholarly interests include the intersection between virtual environments and pedagogy, Filipino immigration, and the life histories of people who are the first in their family to attend college.

Raja Maznah Raja Hussain is a Professor in the Department of Curriculum and Instructional Technology at the University of Malaya. Holding a PhD from Indiana University, her areas of expertise are instructional technology, instructional design, academic staff development, and many more. She has contributed to a number of academic publications.

Shannon Kennedy-Clark is an ICT Pedagogy Officer on the Australian Teaching Teachers for the Future Project at the University of Sydney. Her research interests lie in game-based learning, discourse analysis, and pre-service teacher training. Shannon is a Lecturer in ICT in Education and Academic Communication at the University of Technology. She is in the final stages of her PhD on the use of games in computer-supported inquiry learning. Shannon managed the Education Development Unit and worked as a Learning Adviser at the Learning Centre at the University of New South Wales. Shannon lectured at Takushoku University in Tokyo for three years, and before that, she worked as a teacher.

Mimma Sayuti Mat Khalid is an educator attached to Educational Technology Department of Institute of Teachers' Education Malay Language Campus in Malaysia. Her 18 years of teaching experience includes Teaching of English as a Second Language for secondary schools and Technology in Education, for which she served as one of the National Master Trainer under Ministry of Education. She was awarded the State Excellent Teacher Award in 2006 and National Teacher-in-ICT Award (runner-up) in 2007. Her interests are in instructional design and Web-based 3D virtual worlds in education. She is currently a PhD candidate researching and creating 3D virtual learning spaces.

Ulla Konnerup is a Teaching Associate Professor at the Department for Communication at Aalborg University. Her primary research interests are within the field of adults with communication difficulties as a result of a brain injury, community-centered rehabilitation and communication, and learning in Web 2.0 environments and in 3D immersive virtual worlds. She is a former speech therapist with experiences with people suffering from aphasia and developing net-based aphasia pedagogy, where participation in social communities, narrativity, self-reflection, and self-presentation are emphasized. From August 2009-2014 she is doing a PhD under the programme Human-Centered Communication and Informatics with the working title: *Cognitive Fitness in Immersive Virtual Worlds: Developing a Learning Design for People with Aphasia*. The objective is to study how interaction in a 3D virtual cognitive fitness centre might contribute to reconstruction of the communication competency among people with aphasia caused by a brain injury.

Chris Luchs is the Associate Dean of Career and Technical Education at CCCOnline.org. He earned his Master's of Business Administration from the University of Nebraska – Lincoln. He is currently the Co-Investigator for the World of Warcraft in Business pilot project that is part of the Colorado Community College System (CCCS) Immersive and Games-Based Learning Challenged Program. This project looks at utilizing World of Warcraft as a business simulator. For the past two years, Chris has also served as the Executive at Large for the Virtual Worlds Best Practice in Education Conference, which routinely draws over 2,000 educators each year.

Barbara Martin is a Professor of Educational Leadership at University of Central Missouri. Her current teaching courses are Instructional Leadership and School Improvements, Administration of K-12 Curriculum, Cooperative Doctoral Classes, and Dissertation Supervisor. She has collaborated on many seminars, conferences, and presentations.

András Margitay-Becht is currently a Faculty Member in the School of Economics and Business Administration at Saint Mary's College of California. Holding Master's degrees in Finance, Stochastic Methods, and Computer Science and a Doctorate in Economics and Business Administration, he focuses on agent-based simulation of economic development and the international financial aiding process. Dr. Margitay-Becht's primary research is on incorporating sociological, anthropological, and political effects into economic simulations, while his alternate research examines virtual simulations and its influence on education and corporate management.

Kristen B. Miller earned her Doctorate in English, focusing in Rhetoric and Composition, from Auburn University in 2010, and is an Assistant Professor at Tuskegee University in Tuskegee, Alabama. In addition to video games, her research interests are rhetorical theory, composition pedagogy, film, popular culture, and the horror genre.

Kae Novak is an Instructional Designer for Student Engagement and Assessment for Online Learning at Front Range Community College. She earned her Master of Educational Technology at Boise State University. She is currently the Principal Investigator for Games Based Learning MOOC project http://gamesmooc.shivtr.com/, which is part of the Colorado Community College System (CCCS) Immersive and Games-Based Learning Challenged Program. She is the instructional designer on two additional projects in that program, Teaching Business with WoW (World of Warcraft) and Project Outbreak. Kae is the chair elect for International Society for Technology in Education (ISTE) SIG - Virtual Environments and on the Steering Committee for the Mobile Learning SIG. She has been the Program Chair for the Virtual Worlds Best Practice in Education Conference for the last two years and is currently working G.A.M.E. http://g.a.m.e.shivtr.com/ on Webinar series of educators who have been utilizing games in their classrooms.

Daniel Cooper Patterson has a BSEE and MSEE from the University of Missouri. He has an additional 40+ post master graduate hours in education and virtual world technologies from Texas State University, Avila University, University of Washington, and Boise State University. He utilized his knowledge for twenty years in Silicon Valley, CA; Phoenix, AZ; and Austin, TX, solving computer architectural problems. These problems ranged from chip development to digital animation, from asset depreciation to data warehousing, from nuclear bomb simulations to medical instrumentation. His customers included Amdahl, Apple Computer, Cisco Systems, Disney, DreamWorks, Hewlett-Packard, Intel, IBM, Lawrence Livermore Labs, Motorola, Nvidia, Sandia Labs, Siemens, U-Haul International, Warner Bros., and scores more.

Kate Prudchenko is pursuing a PhD in Education: Instructional Design and Technology at Old Dominion University. She holds a BA in Mathematics from University of Southern California and an MA equivalency in Applied Mathematics from California State University Long Beach. Her dissertation research is focused on the effects of asynchronous feedback on ill-structured problem-solving skills and creativity in a distance-learning environment. She resides in Los Angeles with her husband and their dog.

Matthias Rehm is Associated Professor for Media Technology at Aalborg University, where he works on Cultural Aspects of HCI, Social Robotics, and Mobile Interaction. Prior to that, he has worked at Augsburg University at the lab for multimedia concepts and applications, where he has been leading several international projects in the area of multimodal interactive systems. His research interests include embodied conversational agents, cultural aspects of human computer interaction, modeling of social behavior, as well as multimodal user interfaces. Matthias Rehm has published over 50 papers in the area of human-centered computing.

Alan Reid resides in Wilmington, North Carolina, with his wife, daughter, and two ocean-loving dogs. In addition to pursuing a PhD in Instructional Design and Technology, Alan holds a Master of Arts in Teaching from the University of North Carolina – Wilmington and a B.A. in English from The Ohio State University. As the Lead Instructor for Developmental English at Brunswick Community College, he has developed the asynchronous online course: Reading Comprehension and Strategies. Additionally, he serves as the Vice-President of Faculty Senate for Brunswick Community College and as Secretary for Old Dominion University's Graduate Student Organization in Instructional Design and Technology.

Rebecca Reiniger graduated from Purdue University in Indiana with a Math and German BA. She received her Master's in Secondary Education at George Fox University in 2011. While at Purdue, she studied abroad at the University of Hamburg, Germany. After college, she taught high school Math and German in LaGrange, Indiana. Rebecca moved to Oregon and worked at Albertina Kerr in Developmental Difficulties Job Training. She then taught several years at Central Catholic High School in Portland before moving to St. Helens. There, she tutored in Math and German, which included the design of programs to fit individual and special needs students.

Anna-Marie Robertson has earned a BS in Secondary Education with an emphasis in Mathematics and Business Education from Idaho State University. She holds the Masters of Educational Technology from Boise State University and an Online Teaching Endorsement. Prior to becoming a teacher in 1996, she worked for over 20 years as a paraprofessional in an accounting firm. It was not until her children became teenagers that she realized she wanted to teach. She tried substitute teaching and found her passion in life. From 1996–2005, she was the Math, Careers, and Technology Instructor at an alternative school she helped open in her home district. In 2000, she shifted her focus to Online Education and became one of Idaho's first Online Math Instructors and Educational Technologists. In 2008, she expanded her horizons into international education communities. She is currently the Educational Technologist/Instructional Design Consultant for Dream Realizations.

Diane L. Schallert is a Professor of Educational Psychology at the University of Texas at Austin, where she teaches graduate courses in learning, psycholinguistics, comprehension, and writing. Her research interests are on the interface of language and learning and on how emotion and motivation participate in this interaction.

Kate Thompson is the Postdoctoral Research Associate at the University of Sydney. Her research interests include learning sciences and research on teaching and learning. In addition to contributing book chapters and journal articles to a variety of publications, she also acts as the Senior Research Associate, ARCL: Learning the Complexity of Scientific Knowledge about Climate Change with Computer Modelling and Visualization Technologies, CoCo Research Centre 2010-2011, and the Postdoctoral Research Associate, ARC Laureate Fellowship Learning, Technology, and Design: Architectures for Productive Networked Learning, CoCo Research Centre 2011-present.

Moses Wolfenstein, before beginning work at the Academic Co-Lab in September of 2010, he was a Doctoral student at the University of Wisconsin – Madison, where he completed his dissertation on the topic of how leadership in massively multiplayer online games can inform research on and practice of instructional leadership. In other words, he looked at guild leadership in *World of Warcraft* and discussed the implications of those leadership practices for current and future practices of school leadership. This rather unlikely topic was the result of having an official academic home at UW in the Department of Educational Leadership and Policy Analysis while also working as an active member in the Games+Learning+Society Research Group.

Nick Zap is a PhD candidate in Educational Psychology at Simon Fraser University. His research over the past decade has included e-learning, simulation, educational gaming, cognitive development, and problem solving. As an innovator in the field of e-learning, his work has been recognized with numerous international awards including the WebCT/Blackboard Exemplary Course Project, the ED-MEDIA Outstanding Paper Award, and several invited speaking and keynote presentations.

Index

U

ubiquitous computing 204, 251
user support 25-26
utility value 47

V

value chain 186, 189, 192
video games 21, 36, 38, 40, 48-49, 68, 106-113,
    116-121, 146, 159, 190-191, 260, 267, 275-
    277, 279
    gender differences 111
virtuality continuum 251
Virtual Reality (VR) 2
Virtual Singapura 17, 19-22, 24-30, 33, 40-41
virtual teaming 2
Virtual Worlds (VW) 78-79, 194, 196

visual representation 2, 89, 121, 206
VoiceXML 229, 231, 237
VoIP (Voice over Internet Protocol) 259

W

Web comics 150-153
WebQuest 131, 145
Whyville 18-19, 24, 32, 41, 81, 126
wikis 14, 131, 162-163, 220, 268
World of Warcraft 12, 18, 61, 125, 178-180, 183,
    186, 188-189, 251, 257-258, 263, 267, 271,
    274-279

Z

Zone of Proximal Development (ZPD) 43, 48